Hitchcock and Art: Fatal Coincidences

The Montreal Museum of Fine Arts
Jean-Noël Desmarais Pavilion
November 16, 2000, to March 18, 2001

Chief Exhibition Curators
Guy Cogeval
Dominique Païni

Curator and General Co-ordinator
Nathalie Bondil-Poupard

THE MONTREAL MUSEUM OF FINE ARTS
Guy Cogeval, Director
Paul Lavallée, Director of Administration
Danielle Sauvage, Director of Communications

P.O. Box 3000, Station "H"
Montreal, Quebec
H3G 2T9
www.mmfa.qc.ca

Cover:
James Stewart in *Vertigo*, 1958
London, The Cinema Museum
© 1958 Universal City Studios, Inc.
All rights reserved
Courtesy of Universal Studios Licensing, Inc.

Alberto Martini, Self-Portrait (detail), 1929
Galerie Elstir, Paris

HITCHCOCK AND ART

FATAL COINCIDENCES

Edited by
Dominique Païni
Guy Cogeval

**THE MONTREAL MUSEUM
OF FINE ARTS**
Jean-Noël Desmarais Pavillon

Mazzotta

Lenders to the Exhibition

We gratefully acknowledge the generosity of the institutions and individuals whose loans have made this exhibition possible.

AUSTRIA
Linz
Oberösterreichisches Landesmuseum
Sankt Pölten
Stadtmuseum
Vienna
Collection Dietmar Siegert
Münchner Stadtmuseum
Museum Villa Stuck
Wiesbaden
Graphische Sammlung
Albertina

BELGIUM
Brussels
Bibliothèque Royale de Belgique
Cinémathèque Royale de Belgique
Ministère de la Communauté française
Musée d'Ixelles
Musées Royaux des Beaux-Arts de Belgique
Ostend
Deforche-Tricot collection
Museum voor Schone Kunsten

CANADA
Montreal
Cinémathèque québécoise
Holly King collection
McGill University Libraries, Rare Books and Special Collections Division
The Montreal Museum of Fine Arts
Collection Tugault-Lafleur, L'Affiche Vivante
Ottawa
National Gallery of Canada

Regina
Mackenzie Art Gallery, University of Regina
Toronto
Art Gallery of Ontario
Thomas H. Bjarnason collection
Eldon Garnet collection
Vancouver
Vancouver Art Gallery
Vancouver Museum

FRANCE
Orléans
Musée des beaux-arts d'Orléans
Paris
Association française pour la diffusion du Patrimoine photographique
BIFI (Bibliothèque du Film)
Cinémathèque française, Musée du Cinéma
Alain Fleischer collection
Galerie Adrien Maeght, Paule and Adrien Maeght collection
Galerie Alain Blondel
Marin Karmitz collection
Lobster Films
Magnum Photos Paris
Musée National Auguste Rodin
Musée National d'Art Moderne, Centre Georges Pompidou
Musée Picasso
Saint-Tropez
Musée de l'Annonciade

GERMANY
Berlin
Bauhaus-Archiv
Museum für Gestaltung
Cologne
Museum Ludwig
Wallraf-Richartz-Museum
Hamburg
Herbert List Estate
Munich
Münchner Stadtmuseum
Museum Villa Stuck
Dietmar Siegert collection

Wiesbaden
Frank Brabant collection

ITALY
Milan
Fondazione Antonio Mazzotta
Galleria Milano
Saronno
Tischer collection

THE NETHERLANDS
Amsterdam
Rijksmuseum
Stedelijk Museum

SPAIN
Figueres
Gala–Salvador Dalí Foundation
Madrid
Museo Thyssen-Bornemisza

SWITZERLAND
Basel
Fondation Beyeler
Geneva
Cabinet des estampes du Musée d'Art et d'Histoire
Lugano-Castagnola
Fondazione Thyssen-Bornemisza

UNITED KINGDOM
Bath
The Royal Photographic Society
London
British Film Institute, National Film & Television Archive
The Cinema Museum
Mary Evans Picture Library
Bridget Riley collection
Royal Academy of Arts
Tate Gallery
Vestry House Museum
Manchester
The Whitworth Art Gallery, University of Manchester
Plymouth
City Museum and Art Gallery, Alfred A. de Pass Collection

York
National Railway Museum,
The National Museum
of Science and Industry

UNITED STATES
Austin
Harry Ransom Humanities
Research Center, The
University of Texas at Austin
Berkeley
University of California,
Berkeley Art Museum
Beverly Hills
Academy of Motion Picture
Arts and Sciences, Center
for Motion Picture Study
Boston
Museum of Fine Arts,
Boston
Buffalo
Albright-Knox Art Gallery
Cleveland
The Cleveland Museum of Art
Dallas
Dallas Museum of Art
Houston
The Menil Collection
Los Angeles
Robert Morton collection
New Orleans
The Historic New Orleans
Collection
New York
Alexander and Bonin Gallery
Bonni Benrubi Gallery
Isabelle del Frate collection
Fashion Institute of Technology,
Gladys Marcus Library
The Hearn Family Trust
Luhring Augustine Gallery Inc.
Metro Pictures
The Metropolitan Museum
of Art
The Museum of Modern Art
Wildenstein & Co.
Ian Woodner
family collection
Oberlin
Allen Memorial Art Museum,
Oberlin College
Philadelphia
Free Library of Philadelphia,
Rare Book Department

Rochester
Memorial Art Gallery,
University of Rochester
Santa Monica
Baldessari Studios
Studio City
Mark H. Wolff collection
Washington
National Gallery of Art

We are also grateful to the
following individuals, galleries
and organizations for
their co-operation:

Bern'Art, Brussels
Galerie Elstir, Paris
Diana Kunkel
Ministère de la Culture,
France
Museo Teatro Dalí
Peter Nahum at The Leicester
Galleries, London
Antoine and Colette Salomon
Taylor and Faust

and those lenders
who prefer to
remain anonymous.

Acknowledgements

The curators of the exhibition
thank the following people
for their kind co-operation:

Cristina Agostinelli
Carolyn Alexander
Darsie Alexander
Mr. and Mrs.Gaetano
Anderloni
Debra R. Armstrong-Morgan
Eduardo Arroyo
Maureen Attrill
Lucile Audouy
Daina Augaitis
Roland Augustine
Jacques Aumont
Jacques Ayroles
Christine Bader
Colin Bailey
Joseph Baillio
John Baldessari
Simon Beaudry
Sylvain Bellenger
Luc Bellier
Bernard Benoliel
Alain Bergala
Ernst Beyeler
Lorena Biffi
James Bigwood
Jo-Anne Birnie Danzker
Dr. Reinhold Bißelbeck
Thomas H. Bjarnason
Alain Blondel
Alf Bogusky
Pierre Bonhomme
Frank Brabant
Marie-Ève Breton-Bélanger
Serge Bromberg
Lisa Calden
Michael Caldwell
Mathias Chivot
Andrée-Anne Clermont
Pierre Cockshow
Anne Coco
Jeanne Collins
Mary Corliss
Victoria Coxon
Gregory Crewdson
Dr. Götz Czymmek
Stéphane Dabrowsky
Malcolm Daniel

Giovanni Danzi
Patrice Dartevelle
Robert Daudelin
Suzan Davidson
Kate Davis
Sarah Dawbarn
Marianne de Fleury
Mme Deforche-Tricot
Eric De Gelaen
Béatrice de Loppinot
Philippe de Montebello
Isabelle del Frate
Claire Denis
Eliane de Wilde
Nicole d'Huart
Frédéric Doat
Willie Doherty
Jean-Paul Dorchain
Catherine Dufayet
Dominique Dupuis-Labbé
Greg Evans
Leland H. Faust
Alain Fleischer
Anne Fleming
Michael Friend
Rudi H. Fuchs
Eldon Garnet
David Gaucher
Stephen Gong
Ronald Grant
Pierre Gras
Charles and Angella Hack
Tom Heman
Stephane Heuer
Donald Hogan
Grant Holcomb
Norbert Hostyn
Renée Hudon
Martin Humphries
Debbie Ireland
Jennifer Jones
Paul and Ellen Josefowitz
Samuel Josefowitz
Marin Karmitz
Claudine Kaufmann
Holly King
J.P. Filedt Kok
Steven B. Kravitz
Bill Krohn
Kristine Krueger
André Labarthe

Geert Lambert
Barry Lane
John R. Lane
William Lang
Nicole Laurin
Brigitte Leal
Jean-Jacques Lebel
June and Robert Leibowits
Janet Leigh
Antoinette Le Normand-
Romain
Blandine Lepage
Tomàs Llorens
Glenn Lowry
Lawrence Luhring
Rodolphe Lussiana
Michelle Maccarone
Laurence Madeline
Adrien, Paule and Yoyo
Maeght
John Magill
Dr. Ekkehard Mai
Elvira Maluquer
Karen Marks
Rainer Mason
Georges Mathysen-Gerst
Emeline Max
Gabriele and Bianca Mazzotta
Elizabeth McMahon
Linda Mehr
Cäsar Menz
Ian Millman
Eric Moinet
Jean-Paul Monery
Robert Morton
Sandy Naime
Constance Naubert-Riser
Patricia Hitchcock O'Connell
Gisèle Ollinger-Zinque
Didier Ottinger
Tony Oursler
Alexandra Partow
Sharon F. Patton
Luigi Pellegrini
Domenico Pertocoli
Walter Pils
Antoni Pixtot
Ulrich Pohlmann
Earl A. Powell
Hélène Prélot
Thomas Pulle

Gérard Régnier
Katharine Lee Reid
Raffaella Resch
Ned Rifkin
Bridget Riley
Pam Roberts
Malcolm Rogers
Alberto Romanzi
Norman Rosenthal
Cora Rosevear
Catherine Rouvière
Fatima Sarsari
Jean Louis Schefer
Max Scheler
Klaus Albrecht Schröder
Douglas G. Schultz
Andrew Scott
Aurora Scotti
Joan Seidl
Sir Nicholas Serota
George T.M. Shackelford
Sally Shafto
Cindy Sherman
Alan Shestack
Dietmar Siegert
Alistair Smith
Werner Spies
Donald Spoto
Mary Anne Stevens
Alain Tarica
Michael Parke Taylor
Matthew Teitelbaum
Pierre Théberge
Dodge Thomson
Dall'Armellina Denis Dialma
   Vedova Tischer
Yannis Triantafyllou
Xavier Tricot
Bruno Trombetti
Marc Tugault
S. Van Heusden

Massimo Vecchia
Marc Vernet
Marie-Paule Vial
Gaëlle Vidalie
Jacques Villain
Mark Vivian
Leslie Wearb Hirsch
John Weber
Evelyn Weiss
Betsy Wieseman
Agnès Wildenstein
Daniel Wildenstein
Michael Henry Wilson
Steve Wilson
Mark H. Wolff

We gratefully acknowledge
the co-operation of
Carlton International,
Buena Vista International,
Paramount Pictures,
STUDIOCANAL,
the Saul Bass Estate,
20th Century Fox Film Corp.,
Universal Studios,
Warner Bros. and, particularly,
the Alfred J. Hitchcock Estate.

The curators wish to thank Stéphane Aquin, who was responsible for choosing the contemporary works, Maryse Ménard,
who carried out research and compiled documentation on the
works in the exhibition, and Julia Tanski, who was in charge of
cinema-relatcd documents.

The curators are extremely grateful to the staff of The Montreal
Museum of Fine Arts, without whose collaboration in a variety of
capacities the exhibition could not have taken place.

Raymond Voinquel, *Alfred Hitchcock during shooting of* Topaz, 1969

*"He who seeks to write his dream
has to be infinitely awakened."
(Paul Valéry)*

Ten years have passed since Dominique Païni and I first entertained the notion of dedicating a "fine arts" exhibition to Alfred Hitchcock. The Montreal Museum of Fine Arts once again showed its enterprising spirit and stepped forward to provide an optimal setting in which to stage this exhibition. For the project has always been faced with a subtle paradox. Hitchcock is one of the world's best-known cultural figures and, over time, has earned an excellent reputation in academic circles. This was not always the case, however: in the 1950s, the young French critics who would later epitomize the *Nouvelle Vague* – Truffaut, Chabrol, Godard – stood alone in their bold assertion that Hitchcock was a true master, steadily crafting a body of work, in the true artistic sense. Like that of other artists, the Hitchcockian oeuvre is rich in religious and philosophical themes – not to mention "noble" obsessions with form. To mount an exhibition tracing parallels between Hitchcock's creative development and the artistic and philosophical trends spanning the entire breadth of the century just past was a *beau risque* indeed; in fact, we often wondered whether we were not attempting the impossible. On the one hand, I suspect that many art historians and museum experts – with their hermetically sealed specializations and rampant "attribution-itis" – are not yet ready to accept the idea that filmmakers such as Eisenstein, Mizoguchi, Lang . . . and Hitchcock created visual universes with as much coherence, *mutatis mutandis,* as those of Miró, Picasso and Matisse. For instance, critics long considered cross-media artists like Jean Cocteau or Salvador Dalí to be "impure." And on the other hand, film critics will sometimes object (although far less nowadays) to exegeses of Hitchcock's work that are not based on Hitchcock himself or on film history and technique, *stricto sensu.* The project we are unveiling is at once exuberant and risky, provocative and open, mysterious and popular, in that it draws tangible relations between important features of Hitchcock's world and the different ways in which painters, sculptors, photographers and illustrators – from the Victorian era to the present – have responded to the same cultural stimuli, in their respective creative languages. I hope that readers of this catalogue will discover these endlessly fascinating themes with each turn of the page. In addition, I hope that visitors to the exhibition itself will, at the very least, discover Alfred Hitchcock anew, but above all, have fun and, perhaps most importantly, leave with a feeling of happiness – because it is impossible to deny that, during the three years it has taken to bring this project into being, our goal has been to create a joyful experience. I believe the enthusiasm of all who participated pervades every line of the catalogue and every room of the museum. For this I should first like to thank Dominique Païni, my faithful accomplice in this long-meditated and long-awaited achievement (there are others in the making...). I also thank Nathalie Bondil-Poupard and her stalwart team, who coordinated the exhibition with aplomb; Stéphane Aquin, who selected the contemporary works; the Publications Department, which under the supervision of Francine Lavoie and in collaboration with Edizioni Mazzotta performed the daunting task of assembling the astonishing variety of texts and images in the catalogue into a coherent whole; Danielle Sauvage and her able communications staff, who are in charge of presenting this extravagant project to the public; and finally, Paul Lavallée, who personally assured the support of the Administration Department. Congratulations are due as well to Michel Poulette, Christiane Lebrun-Michaud and Guy Lalande, who designed the exhibition and worked together with Paul Tellier's teams... and to the personnel in all the Museum's departments, who showed an exceptional degree of enthusiasm. I extend thanks to the institutions that supported and financed the exhibition: Investors Group, the presenting sponsor, the Ministère des Affaires municipales et de la Métropole du Québec, and the Ministère de la Culture et des Communications du Québec. The support of Métro, the promotional support of Tourisme Montréal and *La Presse,* and the organizational assistance of the British Council are much appreciated, as is the ongoing support of the Department of Canadian Heritage (Museums Assistance Program) and of the Montreal Urban Community Arts Council. I should like to conclude on a personal note: my heartfelt thanks go to my former literature professor Jacques Guérif, who was the first to give me a taste for *cinéma d'auteur,* and who taught me to see the intimate connections between film and the other visual arts. His guidance was not in vain.

Guy Cogeval
Director
The Montreal Museum of Fine Arts

The images of Alfred Hitchcock have become synonymous with the most chilling and creative visions of the 20th century. His very name conjures up a sense of mystery, an air of unpredictability and the uneasy feeling that the inner reaches of your mind are about to be explored and challenged.

Through the course of his life, Hitchcock earned the title Master of Suspense, which in the world of cinema is akin to a royal knighthood. His ubiquitous profile has become a trademark for terror, and his cryptic style has inspired countless filmmakers who have followed him.

This exhibition is a celebration of the artist's personal creative expression. But it is much more than that. It also delves into the symbolic and surreal works of art that inspired him and, importantly, works inspired by him.

Investors Group is proud to present this major new exhibition as part of our *Sharing Culture with Canadians* program. This is part of our ongoing commitment to contribute to the quality of life in the communities where we live and work. As a Canadian company, we believe very strongly in not only supporting Canadian artists and institutions, but also sharing the experience of artists from around the world who have made a lasting impression on our people and our culture.

We are very pleased to partner with The Montreal Museum of Fine Arts to bring you *Hitchcock and Art: Fatal Coincidences,* and hope that you will come away with a new appreciation for and a deeper understanding of the life, the inspiration and the work of a true Master.

H. Sanford (Sandy) Riley
President and Chief Executive Officer
Investors Group Inc.

Catalogue
Hitchcock and Art: Fatal Coincidences

Co-ordination in Montreal
The Montreal Museum of Fine Arts
Francine Lavoie
Nathalie Bondil-Poupard

Translation
Services d'édition Guy Connolly
Co-ordination: Guy Connolly
Michael Gilson
Diana Halfpenny
Vanessa Nicolai

Revision
Services d'édition Guy Connolly
Michael Gilson
Jonathan Kotcheff
The Montreal Museum of Fine Arts
Jo-Anne Hadley
Donald Pistolesi

Research and Documentation
The Montreal Museum of Fine Arts
Maryse Ménard
Julia Tanski
Sylvie Ouellet
Majella Beauregard
Danielle Sarault

Word Processing
Services d'édition Guy Connolly
Louiselle Gagnon
The Montreal Museum of Fine Arts
Marthe Lacroix
Micheline Poulin

Copyright
The Montreal Museum of Fine Arts
Linda-Anne D'Anjou
Marie-Claude Saia
Michael Henry Wilson

Photographic Services
The Montreal Museum of Fine Arts
Jeanne Frégault
Brian Merrett

ISBN 2-89192-243-3
Legal deposit – 4th quarter 2000
Bibliothèque nationale du Québec
National Library of Canada

© 2000 Edizioni Gabriele Mazzotta
Foro Buonaparte 52 - 20121 Milano
ISBN 88-202-1418-0
Printed in Italy

Contents

Portrait of Alfred Hitchcock

Associations, Constellations, Likenesses, Construction

Dominique Païni

Who would have dared imagine that the films of Alfred Hitchcock would one day "hang" from museum picture rails?

When the Hitchcockian oeuvre reached its most "metaphysical" point, with *Vertigo,* art lovers entertained a stubborn contempt for the filmmaker: he of the rotund, amorphous silhouette who, paradoxically, was a creature of the media; a clown cleverer than all the others; a mere jester whose "trademark" – suspense – made him automatically, irrevocably "impure."

Film buffs, for their part, have only recently been able to accept that the history of cinema is a valid field of study, one that bears comparisons with art history. That the cinema could also be considered, along with other visual arts, according to iconographic principles, and could therefore exert a representational power, had always been disclaimed. Film lovers remained jealously wary of a certain seriousmindedness that, in their eyes, was crystallized by museums housing examples of the "fine" arts. After all, being a film buff was supposed to mean belonging to a delectable counterculture – a clandestine culture established parallel to the official outlets for the dissemination of Knowledge.

Bringing the works of filmmakers into a museum setting (beyond simply holding retrospectives of their films), then, is not an everyday occurrence. The works of Luis Buñuel were the subject of an exhibition in 1995, some years after his death. Yasha David, the curator of that remarkable show, which was first presented in Bonn, aimed especially to clarify and "validate" the relationships that the director of *L'âge d'or* had maintained consistently, throughout his career, with Surrealism. The exhibition's raison d'être was easily justified in view of the filmmaker's origins and the references deliberately claimed by him.

But Alfred Hitchcock is precisely the one filmmaker who most specifically embodied *the* cinema, and only the cinema. His is one of the most legendary names among movie-goers – who as a group are not particularly concerned with remembering the names of the authors of the films they see. If a survey were held, though, the name Alfred Hitchcock would doubtless be the one most spontaneously recalled as representative of the cinema, and *The Birds* and *Psycho* cited as two of the most famous works in the entire history of film.

Devoting an exhibition to a filmmaker – let alone the most famous filmmaker of all – is a daunting, but legitimate, challenge. For three decades Hitchcock's work has fascinated ever-growing numbers of intellectuals. Philosophers, art historians and contemporary artists have all found new inspirations for their own works within a corpus whose apparent emphasis on spectacle no longer seemed in contradiction with learned, literary and pictorial culture. The films of Alfred Hitchcock, while remaining first and foremost popular entertainment (and, as such, beyond reproach), commanded attention because they stemmed from a broader view of cinema as encompassing other art forms as well as the mysteries of the human soul. It is this dual openness that grants the Hitchcockian oeuvre its romantic constancy and its Symbolist *style* – twin legacies of the 19th century *maintained* during the 20th.

Hitch's films amaze, mesmerize, and rivet our gaze – but no matter how great the terror or puzzlement, he always engages our intellect. Often, in fact, his films are truly and intensely thought provoking. In this way, from philosophy to psychoanalysis, from cinema to the contemporary visual arts of the latter part of this century, the Hitchcockian oeuvre has, through the consistency of his universe, imprinted itself in no small way on our ideas and dreams. "Perhaps there are ten thousand people who haven't forgotten Cezanne's apple, but there must be a billion spectators who will remember the lighter of the stranger on the train, and the reason why Alfred Hitchcock became the only *poète maudit* to meet with success was that he was the greatest creator of forms of the twentieth century, and it's forms that tell us finally what lies at the bottom of things; now, what is art if not that through which forms become style."[1]

This exhibition is intended neither as a demonstration nor a sequence of comparative proofs. It is meant as a *reading* – an *interpretation* based on three approaches that we have not attempted to differentiate either in the exhibition space or in the catalogue.

[1] Jean-Luc Godard, *Histoire(s) du cinéma,* trans. John Howe (Paris: Gallimard/Gaumont; New York: ECM New Series, 1998), p. 11.

Ingrid Bergman in Under Capricorn, 1949

Ford Madox Brown, *The Last of England,* 1855

The first of these approaches, the scholarly and documentary dimension, aims to foster an appreciation of Hitchcock's filmic oeuvre through source material culled from film archives around the world as well as private collections: production stills, scripts, original set designs and costume sketches, correspondence, posters, home movies and documentary films.

Secret Agent, 1936

The second approach – which cannot, obviously, be given full justice in this catalogue – focusses on showmanship and fantasy. It invites visitors to physically re-experience the internal atmosphere of the films, the better to grasp the ingenuity of their *mise en scène* as well as the ways in which the director manipulated viewers' perception and imagination. Hitchcock's scenographic art is evoked by the reconstruction of a number of sets, accompanied by clips from his films, which visitors will pass in front of in the same manner as actors performing against rear-projected settings – a technique for which Hitchcock had a particular fondness.

Objects signifying the films' identities give the exhibition a metonymical dimension: a rope *(Rope)*, a cigarette lighter *(Strangers on a Train)*, the mummified head of Norman Bates's mother *(Psycho)*, a glass of milk *(Suspicion)*, a bottle of Pommard wine filled with uranium *(Notorious)*, Carlotta Valdés's jewelled pendant *(Vertigo)*, and so on.

Charles Sheeler, *Winter Window*, 1941

The third approach, a more interpretational one, will point up the influences, inspirations, and legacies from the visual arts of centuries past that mark the Master's oeuvre. Hitchcock was an admirer of Georges Rouault, Milton Avery, Walter Sickert, Raoul Dufy, Maurice de Vlaminck, Paul Klee and Auguste Rodin, and owned a number of their works. Salvador Dalí collaborated on the dream sequence of *Spellbound,* and a special display is devoted to that partnership.

Hitchcock's films resonate with numerous iconographic themes descended from Symbolism and Surrealism. The Victorian vestiges of his early schooling in England are discernible as well, even in his last films (e.g., *Frenzy*). The director of *Rebecca* and *Vertigo,* who was a reader of Poe, Wilde and Chesterton, often cast portrait paintings in a central role, to mesmerizing and even terrifying effect, regardless of their artistic value. Indeed, painting – with its spatial trickery, troubling resemblances and mythological representations – left its imprint on the entire Hitchcockian oeuvre. From Pre-Raphaelite hairstyles to Symbolist

Eduardo Arroyo, *L'inconnu du Nord-Express de Alfred Hitchcock, Excerpts from the screenplay,* 1984

sphinxes, from Giorgio De Chirico's metaphysical cities to Edward Hopper's urban visions, the artworks selected for this exhibition will afford a better understanding of some of the cryptic visual references in Hitchcock's world.

In turn, Hitchcock has become an extraordinary "purveyor of images" to late-20th-century art. A great many contemporary visual artists have drawn on the filmmaker's motifs to create artistic offspring that would doubtless have astounded him. In the process, Hitchcock's works remain forever current. The Master's influence is also felt in 20th-century performing arts, as in the work of Bob Wilson and Robert Lepage.

In fact, Hitchcock is not so much exhibited here as "dreamt," through the *associations* that the sleep state encourages – or perhaps "authorizes" is the better term. We have attempted to "let go," in the manner favoured by Robert Bresson, who in his *Notes on the Cinematographer* gave the following advice: "Bring together things that have as yet never been brought together and did not seem predisposed to be so."[2]

We have placed our trust in intuitive *constellations* of images that stood out upon seeing the films again.

We have not shied away from *likenesses* – on the condition, however, that they *"cry out"* (to take up the call once issued by that prodigious manipulator of images, Georges Bataille).

Perhaps our true goal was to consider this exhibition as an exercise in *construction,* rather than interpretation, in the sense that Hubert Damisch has ascribed to Freud's objective: "Interpretation never deals only with elements or isolated traits, whereas construction takes on a linking function: linking of the pieces and fragments of the material that is being analysed; but also a linking of the two plays (the two monologues) being acted out on the two stages that are present. The construction in question reaches its objective when, from one scene and one monologue to the next, communication is established and something resembling a *truth* comes to light."[3]

[2] Robert Bresson, *Notes on the Cinematographer,* trans. J. Griffin, intro. J.M.G. Le Clézio (Los Angeles: Sun & Moon Press, 1997), p. 22.
[3] Hubert Damisch, *Un souvenir d'enfance par Piero Della Francesca* (Paris: Seuil, 1997), p. 173. (Free translation.)

Party scene in the boxer's apartment (The Ring), 1927

The boxer's delirium (The Ring), 1927

Carl Brisson and Ian Hunter in The Ring, 1927

What Brings You to the Museum, Mr. Hitchcock?

Guy Cogeval

For us, Alfred Hitchcock remains the inventor of a visual universe where windmills turn against the wind, where the shower is a dangerous place to be, and where respectable upper-class citizens are scum who have sold out to the Nazis. With him, we have learned that bottles of Pommard contain enriched uranium and that diamond bracelets are good for catching fish. He is an artist who, like Jean Cocteau, knows that one can drown in a mirror. A connoisseur of the social and historical realities of his time, yet attracted to the languidness of dreams, in each of his films he forcefully argues his conviction that substance is form's subconscious. And like all demiurgical creators, he distills his dreams into *memory*. By his choice of scripts and his systematic renewing of the themes that haunted him, Hitchcock emerges as a conveyor of myths from the 19th to the 20th century. The most popular film director of the modern era was, paradoxically, among those whose work provides us with subtle gateways to the visual arts of his time, deploying common threads that connect, for example, Symbolism to Surrealism – and Hitchcock was fully aware of this: "And surrealism? Wasn't it born as much from the work of Poe as from that of Lautréamont?"[1] Here he shows affinities with the Surrealists' patriarch, André Breton, who never concealed his passion for the art of the late 19th century: "My discovery of the Musée Gustave Moreau when I was sixteen forever conditioned the way I would love."[2] Initially, the Hitchcockian gaze taught us the importance of going beyond appearances to analyse the truth hidden behind the picture. And it behooves today's museums to make allowance for this pictorial shift, in particular the metamorphoses that result when pictures slip from the cinema into the visual arts.

Since its origins – this is a truism – cinema has had its affinities with painting, dance and opera. Even before Dalí's and Buñuel's perfect collaboration on *Un chien andalou* (1928), Louis Lumière had drawn from the same intimist well as Pierre Bonnard when he filmed *Le goûter de bébé* (1895);

[1] Sidney Gottlieb (ed.), *Hitchcock on Hitchcock: Selected Writings and Interviews* (Berkeley: University of California Press, 1995), p. 144.
[2] André Breton (1961), quoted in Gaëtan Picon, *Le surréalisme* (Geneva: Skira, 1976), p. 292. (Free translation.)

later, for his tracking shot amid the monumental Babylon set of *Intolerance* (1916), D.W. Griffith had in mind the academic, pseudo-antique paintings of Alma-Tadema, Rochegrosse and Gérôme. Sergei Eisenstein, who was an ingenious erotomaniac draftsman when it suited him, flirted with contemporary visual arts throughout his life – witness the purely mechanistic, constructivist imagery of *The Battleship Potemkin* (1925), or the copying of huge historical canvases in the style of Ilya Repin and Vassily Surikov for several scenes of *Ivan the Terrible* (1945). Does this mean that interest in the visual devices of painting is consubstantial with the filmmaker's gaze and the act of filming? It is not difficult to pick out, in Hitchcock's silent films, intentions parallel to those of the avant-gardists of the period, specifically Hans Richter and – why not? – Frantisek Kupka: in the scene in *The Ring* (1927) where the jazz band plays at the party in the boxer's apartment, the pianist's hands and the piano keys meld with the vibrations of the music in space, echoing – albeit probably unconsciously – an idea exploited by Kupka in such paintings as *The Piano Keys (or The Lake)* (1909). Later, during the final bout that is the film's bravura sequence, the hero (Carl Brisson) is knocked down by his opponent, and Hitchcock invents abstract, kaleidoscopic patterns of light – somewhere between Richter and Fernand Léger's *Ballet mécanique* (1924) – that assail the fighter as he loses consciousness. True to form, the director would employ this same type of purely graphic interlude for the nightmare scene in *Vertigo* (1958), inspired this time by a Pop Art aesthetic.

Albert Bloch, *Boxing Match*, 1912–1913

Hitchcock was extremely receptive to the provocative output of the Soviet and German schools of his time, and readily made use of rhythmically choreographed and expressed crowd movements, much in the same manner as King Vidor in Hollywood. The scene in the London Underground in *Rich and Strange* (1932), with employees robotically repeating the same gestures while the protagonist is completely out of synch with them, can be read as a humoristic take on Fritz Lang's *Metropolis* (1926). The scene in *Secret Agent* (1936) in which panic suddenly sweeps through the Swiss chocolate factory shows that Hitchcock knew his Pudovkin: when the general (Peter Lorre) sets off the false alarm, the workers suddenly rise up in rows and surge en masse into the hallways – unlike the two British spies, who flee down empty hallways. From the start, Hitchcock exhibited a penchant for masterfully composed images, stripped of anecdotal clutter and tending toward pure aesthetic beauty. Fortunately, the Hitchcockian approach is not literal; it is not about composing

*John Gielgud and Peter Lorre
on the run in the chocolate factory
(Secret Agent), 1936*

images as one would a painting – a method that can generate splendid results (Mizoguchi referencing Breughel in *Ugetsu* [1953] or Pasolini recreating Pontormo's *Deposition* in his sketch *La Ricotta* [1962]) but can also, on occasion, border on the most appalling pomposity (Godard's *Passion,* 1982). It would be more accurate to say that Hitchcock – and this is what is most striking in this exhibition – engages in a subtle, sometimes clandestine reactivation of Victorian, Decadent and Symbolist culture of the late 19th century, via a sort of ultimate, nostalgic, salvationist reflex, which is understandable for an auteur who was British and Catholic at the same time.

Far from being "inspired by" or copying, then, Hitchcock draws deeply from iconography, taking advantage of the manner in which painting orders reality frontally. In terms of cultural compatibility, one of the artists most akin to Hitchcock was perhaps Henry Fuseli, the Swiss-born Romantic painter celebrated for his inspired illustrations of the *Niebelungenlied* and Shakespeare, and who spent the major part of his artistic career in Great Britain. Both artists reveal a taste for the Gothic and the bizarre, tempered by a perverse sense of humour; and their shared appreciation of mannerist formal games belie a hyperesthesia of the libido. More profoundly, the painter of *The Nightmare* (1781) was ahead of his time in that he was a "purveyor of images," adapting elements of the styles of Michelangelo and Parmigianino to the more Northern sensibility of his audiences: his brush transformed the Damned of the Sistine Chapel into Macbeth or Kriemhilde. So, what of Fuseli – or of Blake?

This exhibition's chosen approach has been to start with a period close to Hitchcock – the end of the Victorian era (for, after all, the filmmaker's birth roughly coincided with the death of Edward Burne-Jones). Our interest led us to attempt to discover what artworks he owned and to collate all the comments he made about artists during his lifetime (some of them are quite handy). It soon became clear, however, that this endeavour should be more an exploration of Alfred Hitchcock's receptiveness to the myths and visual arts of his time. Visitors who come expecting a normative, inventory approach to this exhibition will be disappointed. Here, Dominique Païni and I have taken the liberty, and the risk, of overinterpreting, rather than the simple risk of documenting nomenclature. And risk is truly the word for it.

Notwithstanding this, it seemed to us more stimulating and more pertinent to proceed by equivalences of perceptibility, by parallel destinies – rather than a compendium of quotations or analyses of embedded images. It is hardly necessary to emphasize that Hitchcock's proclivity toward the language of painting permeated all of his films, not just those in which the script called for a painting to appear on camera. Incidentally, it bears mentioning that, in order to work on screen and to "stand out in relief" within an essentially cinematic vision, filmed works of art – canvases, most often – have to be cheesy.[3] The painterly features of the filmed work are exaggerated, kitschified, if you will, in order for them to be recognizable through the camera eye. The portrait of Carlotta Valdés in *Vertigo* (1957) and the huge portrait of Maxim de Winter's ancestor wearing the white dress in *Rebecca* (1939) are no exception to this rule. Our museums' reserves – including many in the English-speaking world – are overflowing with these types of academic, post-Romantic paintings, and even when Hitchcock had occasion to depict canvases of a more modern – say, expressionist – school, the camera captured a sort of uproarious pastiche of Soutine, as with the portrait painted by Bruno's mother in *Strangers on a Train* (1950); no wonder Bruno (Robert Walker) bursts out laughing.

An ardent music lover, Hitchcock was meticulous when it came to the scores for his films, not so much because he wanted to turn them into operas – as was certainly the case with Eisenstein, all grandiloquent poses and hieratic geometry – but rather to provide a rhythmic counterpoint to the visuals, and to mesh two parallel discourses. The filmmaker's most obvious borrowing from the realm of opera is perhaps his partiality for *dramatic continuity* and the idea of the *Gesamtkunstwerk* (total work of art) so emblematic of composers at the turn of the 19th and 20th centuries, whether of the generation of Verdi and Wagner or that of Puccini and Richard Strauss. Taking the paradox a step further, one might venture that Wagner's use of the uninterrupted melody, the art of transition, and *Durchkomposition* (dramatic ductility) finds an unexpected counterpart in several Hitchcock films – most notably *Rope* (1948), filmed (seemingly) in a single long take. This is what Hitchcock was expressing simply when he spoke of making a film with "no gaps or flaws."[4]

Far from being a creator of empty forms, Hitchcock set out to lay bare the psychology of his characters. He who valued so highly his image as a cool observer, who time and again nurtured his own legendary reputation as a cynical demiurge – just like Edgar Allan Poe picking apart, line by line, the

[3] See Dominique Païni's essay in the proceedings of the conference *Le portrait peint au cinéma* (Paris: Musée du Louvre, 1990).
[4] François Truffaut, with the collaboration of Helen G. Scott, *Hitchcock*, rev. ed. (New York: Simon & Schuster, 1984), p. 15.

composition of his *Raven*[5] – this same Hitchcock was capable of the most delicate and moving of discoveries. His characters discover that they have crystalline sensitivities; they metamorphose, become more human, as the plot thickens. Through the ordeals they experience, they are transformed into tragic heroes. If Hitchcock was the creator of a circumscribed universe, characterized by consistency and morality, this was due more to his sense of exposition and the psychological evolution he fashioned for his protagonists, rather than his propensity (for all its virtuoso skills) for creating atmospheres and designing settings that audiences could refer to and believe in. Here, as elsewhere – as we shall see later – a comparison with the universe of Fritz Lang is enlightening. In *House by the River* (1950) – to which the shower scene in *Psycho* (1960) pays a tribute of sorts – the German director presents us with two moral figures: two brothers who can only be adversaries once the murderous logic of the evil brother is engaged. There is something at once heraldic and titanic about their struggle; it is epic in its grandiose, declamatory style, and utterly desperate in its dénouement. In Hitchcock, even killers admit their weaknesses. In *Rope,* the two lovers (John Dall and Farley Granger), perpetrators of the perfect crime, of which they make a travesty through sacrifice, slip voluptuously into self-denunciation. Each has a burning desire, to a different degree, to reveal their crime bit by bit, caught as they are in the regressive spiral of their macabre Eros. Only rarely in Hitchcock's films is the "pleasure of the crime" – so emblematic of fin-de-siècle culture – presented thusly, as "a thing of beauty." The character of Uncle Charlie (Joseph Cotten) in *Shadow of a Doubt* (1942) is so deeply unsettling because, like a sort of reverse Don Juan, he flits from one killing to the next, finding neither rest nor happiness. A "twilight stalker" of merry (and rich) widows, he is definable only in terms of his catalogue of conquests, a morbid list that he cynically keeps up to date.

Unlike Fritz Lang's *Spionen* (1928), Hitchcock's spies are wracked with doubt, trembling, hesitating like Shakespearean villains, more in the manner of Claudius than Gloucester. Where Lang is overwhelmingly convinced that, in the cosmic struggle of Good versus Evil, Good is destined to lose because the gods are dead, Hitchcock answers with his conviction that his characters become gradually humanized, under the effect of the trials imposed by the divine *caritas*. Hitchcock knows that the eye of God is watching us. He knows that art will create order out of chaos.

Oscar Homolka in Sabotage, 1936

Fritz Lang, *Spies,* 1928

[5] See Edgar Allan Poe, "The Philosophy of Composition," *The Complete Works of Edgar Allan Poe* (New York: AMS Press, 1965).

The Hitchcockian universe, then, is partially circumscribed by the confrontation between Good and Evil. To take up another much-favoured reference point, the existence of Evil: Eisenstein cared not a whit about this, not so much because he had been won over by Marxist beliefs, whereby any moral or psychological reality is subordinated to the relations of production, but because he was mesmerized, tetanized by beauty – he would suspend it, immobile, and create a complementary stasis in the film's rhythm, in the manner of an opera composer slowing down a prima donna's declamatory rhythm the better to let her bask in a dramatic spotlight beam. In the midst of the feverish montage depicting the Bolshevik charge in *October* (1927) Eisenstein's camera lingers on the young girl whose hair falls between the two halves of the opening drawbridge. In *Potemkin,* it emphasizes the muscled back of the whipped sailor. In Eisenstein, though, the bad guys – the capitalists – disappear into the crowd; they are engulfed by the masses; they do not suffer – and at any rate this is not important. Only *Ivan the Terrible,* which, significantly, was Eisenstein's last work, dramatizes the pain and the pleasure provoked by execution; the scene in which the boyars are put to death, in Part II, is built around a montage of shots of the condemned men's necks, the executioner's sabre, and the Czar's gaze; then, when we understand that the heads are rolling, the camera follows Ivan in a downward "à la Hitchcock" tracking shot, as he calls for more executions. In the Hitchcockian view, on the other hand, compassion conquers all. If his philosophical foundations can be traced back to his Catholic upbringing, the visual ornaments of that frame of mind originate in the films of F.W. Murnau. It is fair to say that Hitchcock depicts situations similar to those in the films of Fritz Lang, but with a tender gaze, an iridescent, pearly light – in a word, a poetic approach – taken from Murnau. Sensitive to the morality of *The Last Laugh* (1924) and *Sunrise* (1927), Hitchcock also understands that miracles *do happen.*

When a Hitchcock hero, indicted by supreme contempt, accepts to bear the guilt of another, the director's camera ascends to superhuman altitudes to contemplate the loneliness of the fugitive from on high: Father Logan (Montgomery Clift) in *I Confess* (1952), thwarted by the Confessional Seal, is an unlucky cousin of Roger Thornhill in *North by Northwest* (1958) who, when he flees on foot from the United Nations, hands bloodied, is nothing but a tiny speck, dwarfed by the General Assembly Building – or, more precisely, an obviously fake re-creation thereof. As has so very often been pointed out, this theme of flight, to which Hitchcock continually returned – from *The Thirty-nine Steps* (1935) through *Young and Innocent* (1937) and *Saboteur* (1942), right up to *North by Northwest* – leads to a narrative in *ballad* form. The Hitchcockian hero is thus a rover, always escaping the police, society, himself or the "clutches of the past."

Images and situations derivative of Late Romanticism and the spirit of the Decadents are recurrent in the cinema of Alfred Hitchcock. He cleaved to Wilde's adage that "[a]ll art is at once surface and symbol. Those who go beneath the surface do so at their peril."[6] It is impossible not to acknowledge the Symbolist origins of the sequence in *Vertigo* in which Madeleine (Kim Novak) strews rose petals into the water beneath the Golden Gate Bridge before attempting to drown herself. Her uncontrollable attraction to the water and its gyratory rhythms stirs memories of Ophelia. In *Rebecca,* when Mrs. Danvers (Judith Anderson) terrorizes the new Mrs. de Winter (Joan Fontaine) by suggesting that Rebecca comes back to haunt her during the night, she murmurs: "Listen to the sea. […] It's easy, isn't it?", thereby linking the desire to drown with the celebration of death. Hitchcock himself analysed the menacing symbol of the exaggeratedly black smoke billowing from the train as Uncle Charlie arrives at the Santa Rosa station in *Shadow of a Doubt*[7]; the smoke is a harbinger of the evil that will soon haunt the small town, but that for now remains hidden by a seductive veil. The underrated original version of *The Man Who Knew Too Much* (1934) contains a scene straight out of a nightmare. The hero's young daughter has just been kidnapped by spies in St. Moritz: a quick, dizzying tracking shot begins with an extreme close-up of the badge pinned to her jacket; the camera then backs away to capture her look of horror as she struggles in the arms of her abductor; the shot ends with a wide view of the sleigh rushing away into the gloom of the forest, recalling Lénore carried off by a hellish horseman in Alexandre Dumas *père*'s *Les morts vont vite*. Here, the *Nachtschlittenfahrt* (or nighttime sleigh ride, so beloved of King Ludwig II of Bavaria) clearly has Romantic and Symbolist origins. And one cannot help but think of *Nosferatu* (1922), and the black sedan speeding off to its ghostly encounter in Murnau's forest.

Audiences recognized the complicities with late-19th-century culture in the haunted locales, burdened by the weight of the past, that Hitchcock was only too willing to depict: the estate of Manderley in *Rebecca,* the Bates motel in *Psycho* (ultimate avatar of the Grand Guignol inn where

[6] Oscar Wilde, *The Picture of Dorian Gray, The Complete Works of Oscar Wilde* (New York: Wm. H. Wise Company, 1927), Vol. 4, p. 6.
[7] Truffaut, p. 153–54.

hapless travellers are sliced and diced) or the windmill in *Foreign Correspondent* (1940), serving as an allegory of the wheels and cogs of Time. This osmosis with Late Romanticism was not only visual, however. As Truffaut emphasized, there was no one better than Hitchcock when it came to constructing a *motif of duality,* focussing our attention on what the script *does not say* by eschewing dialogue; he shows, via simple static shots and editing of exchanged glances, his characters' innermost thoughts: "Hitchcock is almost unique in being able to film directly, that is, without resorting to explanatory dialogue, such intimate emotions as suspicion, jealousy, desire, and envy. And herein lies a paradox: the director who, through the simplicity and the clarity of his work, is the most accessible to a universal audience is also the one who excels at filming the most complex and subtle relationships between human beings."[8] From this perspective, the filmmaker who once admitted that he was "never satisfied with the ordinary"[9] might be considered to be a disciple of Stéphane Mallarmé: "To name an object is to take away three-quarters of the enjoyment of the poem, which consists of the happiness of guessing bit by bit: to suggest it, that is the dream. It is the perfect use of this mystery that constitutes the symbol…"[10] Hitchcock hewed fully to the Maeterlinckian notion that we live *alongside* our real lives.

What's more, in commenting on his own style of theatre, Maurice Maeterlinck could easily have been describing the most well rounded and entrancing of the characters in Hitchcock's films – Alicia Huberman (Ingrid Bergman) in *Notorious* (1945), as moonlike as Madeleine (Kim Novak) in *Vertigo*: "For instance, in *La Princesse Maleine* it would have been easy to remove a number of dangeously naive passages, a few superfluous scenes, and most of the stupefaction and repetition that cause the characters to resemble half-deaf sleepwalkers continually being woken up from a dream. [...] Besides, this failure to hear and to answer promptly is largely due to their psychology and to their somewhat untamed worldview."[11] These sentences, meant to describe Maleine, Mélisande, Palomides and other frail creatures in the Belgian Symbolist writer's work, can be applied almost without transposition to Hitchcock's heroines, who often could pass for modern reincarnations of the women painted by Khnopff or Rossetti. And the analogy continues, in Maeterlinck's definition of the implicit meaning of his plays: "They contain the notion of the Christian God, melded with the Ancients' idea of fatality, buried in the unfathomable darkness of Nature, whence pleasure is taken in lurking and disconcerting, in casting a

[8] Truffaut, p. 18.
[9] Truffaut, p. 260.
[10] Stéphane Mallarmé, "Réponse à une enquête sur l'évolution littéraire (enquête de Jules Huret parue dans *L'Écho de Paris* du 3 mars au 5 juillet 1891)," *Oeuvres complètes* (Paris: Gallimard, Pléiade, 1944), p. 869.
[11] Maurice Maeterlinck, "Préface," *Théâtre complet* (Geneva: Slatkine, 1979), p. i–ii.

pall over the projects, the thoughts, the feelings and the humble felicity of men."[12] Hitchcock's affinities with the Late Romantics are also revealed in his tendency to willingly introduce dreamlike imagery into a fast-paced thriller narrative. A brutal scene near the beginning of *The Thirty-nine Steps* sparks the entire dramatic machinery of the film: a mysterious brunette (later revealed to have been working for British Intelligence) is murdered in the hero's flat. Hitchcock films the scene like a nightmare: he dwells on the quiet street outside as counterpoint, uses razor-sharp lighting on the surrounding architecture and lingers on the narratively insignificant detail of the wind blowing through the curtains, causing them to billow like mourning veils. All these elements lend a surrealist atmosphere to the proceedings, connecting the Gaston Leroux–esque scene with the aesthetics of Spilliaert, De Chirico or Jean Epstein. Indeed, the memory of Epstein's *The Fall of the House of Usher* (1927) left a lasting and haunting imprint on Hitchcock.

Judith Anderson in Rebecca, *1940*

Even more striking is the central scene in *Rebecca,* in which Mrs. Danvers (Judith Anderson), the housekeeper, surprises the new Mrs. de Winter in her predecessor's old bedroom. She shows the shy young woman the stifling luxury in which the deceased former bride lived, displaying Rebecca's furs, her silk lingerie, her ivory-handled hair-brushes. The entire film appears constructed around Joan Fontaine's intrusion into Rebecca's room: the whole narrative structure hinges on the scene, which appears as an empty magnetic pole. At this point, Franz Waxman's score becomes Debussy-esque, all open fifths and clarinet arpeggios, punctuated by notes played on the theremin and the shimmer of the harp. The episode could have come straight from the grotto scene in *Pelléas et Mélisande*; when Mrs. Danvers flings open the drapes covering the high Gothic window, one thinks of Pelléas's exclamation of amazement as a ray of moonlight illuminates the grotto: *"Oh! voici la clarté!"* Up to this point, we have been led to believe that the doors to the West Wing of Manderley hide some horrible secret. On the contrary: the unpleasant housekeeper is celebrating a rite of memory. Lost in her ecstasy, she twirls about in a *plus que lente,* necrophiliac waltz. The scene is unique in the history of cinema. Only Hitchcock could have indulged in such a whim: in terms of narrative economy, the scene is superfluous – it is absolute stasis, apparently gratuitous, akin to a favourite device of the ancient Greek bards, chanting their poems, lyre in hand, eyes rolling skyward. It is the rhapsodic moment in which Hitchcock knits together the

[12] Maeterlinck, p. iv.

scattered fragments of the storyline and lends the whole film a distinctly Romantic feel. In the end, it is Mrs. Danvers, not the "true" heroine, Joan Fontaine, who eroticizes the shimmering, rustling clothes that she voluptuously removes from the drawers.

Philip Hermogenes Calderon, *Whither?*, 1867

The theme of the secret beyond the door, the partner marked by the past, is hinted at in *Rebecca,* developed in *Suspicion* (1941), and finally comes to the fore in *Notorious*. Here we recognize variations on the Bluebeard theme, which had been resurrected by the Symbolists. Two operas helped to reinstate the timeless legend in the early part of the century: Paul Dukas' *Ariane et Barbe-Bleue* (1907), to a libretto by Maeterlinck, and especially Bartók's *Bluebeard's Castle* (1911), focussed more on the theme of the lovers' inability to communicate. In *Notorious,* Alicia uncovers the secret that her husband (Claude Rains) has locked behind a door by stealing the key (its brand name, UNICA, could not be more apt!) from him. The key – which in the film is a fetishized object that figures in one of the finest high-angle crane shots of all time – is central to the original Charles Perrault tale and both operas. Hitchcock here reveals his skill at re-creating legends founded on readable symbols, anchored in the collective unconscious. This is especially evident in the ease with which he uses the Bluebeard myth to develop a coherent discourse: beyond the espionage plot, the story is about the progressive disintegration of a couple. His sincere love and pride wounded, this Nazi version of Bluebeard has no choice but to attempt to discreetly eliminate his wife.

Notorious, 1946

At this point, it is crucial to emphasize the great debt that Hitchcockian cinema owes to the literature of Edgar Allan Poe, and its "hallucinatory logic." Hitchcock's greatest works can almost be considered Poe stories as retold by Oscar Wilde. The result of such a blend might have been unbearable, were it not for the sound moral content with which the filmmaker invested his mannerist constructions. On several occasions, he acknowledged his indebtedness to Poe – who, moreover, was among the authors who influenced Charles Baudelaire, Stéphane Mallarmé, Oscar Wilde, Claude Debussy, Odilon Redon and Alberto Martini. In other words, a key reference for the Symbolists. From Poe, Hitchcock learned the mastery of terror and the strangely attractive vortex that is vertigo: "We stand upon the brink of a precipice. We peer into the abyss – we grow sick and dizzy. Our first impulse is to shrink from the danger. Unaccountably we remain. By slow degrees our sickness and dizziness and horror become merged in a cloud of unnameable feeling."[13] There are many long-standing

Notorious, 1946

[13] Poe, "The Imp of the Perverse," p. 149.

connections between Poe's universe and the cinema. In addition to the 1927 Epstein film already mentioned, there was the spate of Poe-inspired Gothic films that emanated from Hollywood in the early 1930s, including Robert Florey's *The Murders in the Rue Morgue* (1932), Edgar G. Ulmer's *The Black Cat* (1934) and Louis Friedlander's *The Raven* (1935), which thrilled Depression-era audiences and showcased the priceless antics of Boris Karloff and Bela Lugosi. Though filled with dazzling ideas (especially the Florey film), most of these cinematic adaptations of Poe suffer from scripts that barely – and painfully so – provide enough material for more than an hour's running time, as they meander listlessly among such devices as shattered mirrors, Art Deco interiors worthy of Mallet-Stevens and torture chambers hidden behind swivelling bookshelves, with hints of sado-masochism and bestiality. For Poe cannot be *adapted* to the cinema, as seen even more disappointingly in Roger Corman's campy 1960s versions.

The influences of Poe on Hitchcock dwell in the characterization of place; in the subtle analysis of murderous impulses; and – this is the height of luxury – in the progressive deconstruction of the plot, simultaneous with its revelation. Illustration in its purest form. Driven by the "the imp of the perverse," the Hitchcockian psychopath views himself as a criminal aesthete. In the New York City loft behind which night falls inexorably, the two protagonists of *Rope* are overcome by a frenzy not unlike that in Poe's *The Tell-Tale Heart*: in this short story, the killer is driven hysterically to show the police the body he has buried under the floorboards, even though no one suspects him of anything: "In the enthusiasm of my confidence, I brought chairs into the room, and desired them *here* to rest from their fatigues, while I myself, in the wild audacity of my perfect triumph, placed my own seat upon the very spot beneath which reposed the corpse of the victim."[14] And in *Rear Window* (1953) it is not only in depicting Jeff (James Stewart) gazing at Lisa (Grace Kelly) that Hitchcock pays tribute to the Poe sensibility: the lesson of the film lies in the need for the artist/creator to literally "draw" his model to him from the other side of the observational medium, to contemplate her as an object of desire. Like the main character in Poe's *The Oval Portrait,* who "turned his eyes from the canvas rarely, even to regard the countenance of his wife,"[15] Jeff progressively draws toward him the substance – the life – of his beloved by delectably observing her through the camera lens.

[14] Poe, "The Tell-Tale Heart," p. 93.
[15] Poe, "The Oval Portrait," p. 248.

The way in which settings are constructed is of crucial importance in Hitchcock's films. The Master is widely recognized for his talent at conveying atmosphere – from the dog-days-of-August Manhattan heat wave in *Rear Window* to the Vermont fall foliage in *The Trouble with Harry* (1954). But there was more to it than mere picturesque effect. One must not forget his ever-ingenious introductions of monumental settings, which enabled him to exercise his grandiose obsession with the idea of falling. From the cathedral in *Foreign Correspondent* to the Statue of Liberty in *Saboteur* to Mount Rushmore in *North by Northwest,* his flamboyant mise en scène of the monumental allowed him to contrast the infinitely large with the infinitely small. Even more crucial is his ability to create settings inspired by the Gothic novel: the isolated house next to the beach in *Young and Innocent* and the deserted moors of *The Thirty-nine Steps* could pass for cleverly constructed backdrops. In the two "mother" films, *Rebecca* and *Vertigo,* the setting becomes an organic creation and attains the status of protagonist. As we have seen, Manderley functions as a psychological prison for the characters; still more subtle is the Hitchcockian gaze when he films San Francisco haunted by mist and the unceasing movement of the water – a city racked by generalized *Ophelization,*[16] so reminiscent (and with good reason) of the Symbolists' rendering of Bruges: Boileau and Narcejac's novel *D'entre les morts,* whose canvas Hitchcock borrowed for *Vertigo,* was a modern retelling of *Bruges-la-Morte* (1892) by the Belgian Symbolist author Georges Rodenbach.

Strictly speaking, Hitchcock was only rarely tempted by horror in his work leading up to *Psycho* and *The Birds* (1962). Rather, he relied on understatement, stupefied expectations, timid interrogations. Next to James Whale, Tod Browning or Jacques Tourneur, Hitchcock cannot really be considered to be one of the "pillars" of the horror film. Compare, for instance, Manderley to the castle in Victor Halperin's *White Zombie* (1932), which also rears up like ruins overlooking the sea – Böcklin lurks nearby. Hitchcock crafts the same type of setting but spares us the exsanguine, lobotomized woman playing the organ, and the zombie servants, with their impassive gestures. He would rather have us see that his characters are prisoners of themselves, and that their inner, obsessive fears are projected as horror.

And yet there are parallels with certain masterworks of the horror genre. The children's party falling under avian attack in *The Birds* is reminiscent of one in Jacques Tourneur's *Night of the Demon* (1957), in which the mad scientist Karswell similarly disrupts a Halloween party by conjuring

[16] The term is from Gaston Bachelard, *L'eau et les rêves* (Paris: José Corti, 1942), p. 121.

a fearsome windstorm. For *Saboteur,* Hitchcock would appear to have remembered the blind hermit of Whale's *Frankenstein* (1933), as well as the bearded lady, the dwarf and the conjoined twins of Tod Browning's *Freaks* (1932). In return, Joseph Mankiewicz, no doubt aware of the prestige of *Rebecca,* appropriated the secret-beyond-the-door theme when he made *Dragonwyck* in 1946: here, too, a young woman of humble birth (the sublime Gene Tierney) marries an aristocrat with a skeleton in his closet; the revelation of the manor as seen from the boat also echoes our first glimpse of Manderley. Better still: the aristocrat (Vincent Price) has little in common with Maxim de Winter (Laurence Olivier) but, on the other hand, is a counterpoint to the gentleman-farmer judge, at once a corrupt decadent and a criminal capable of generosity, played with inimitable humour by Charles Laughton in *Jamaica Inn* (1938). In fact, it was not until *Psycho,* in 1960, that Hitchcock openly played the horror-film card, alluding directly to *The Fall of the House of Usher* and the stifling fetishism of *Berenice.* It is hard to imagine Hitchcock giving us an umpteenth variation on the theme of Dracula, and yet, like the Transylvanian count, his most disturbing characters – Bruno Anthony, Mrs. Danvers, Norman Bates – are creatures of the night. Night falls quickly on the fairground in *Strangers on a Train,* allowing Bruno to strangle Miriam in convenient darkness at the end of the Tunnel of Love – to the audience's unavowable glee. The vestal virgin of Manderley always appears in silence: we never know whence she has come; she glides quietly rather than walking, in league with the shadows of the manor. Supremely sheathed in black, her face pallid, she is a cousin of Countess Aleska (Gloria Holden), the wretched vampire in Lambert Hillyer's *Dracula's Daughter* (1936), and another of the rare lesbian characters of prewar Hollywood cinema. In *Psycho,* as well, day turns to night without the slightest warning, for darkness befits crime, in the Bates Motel and elsewhere.

Here we see the importance of a very fin-de-siècle and very British concept: that of the night stalker. As a child, Hitchcock had been struck by the case of Dr. Crippen (in which a woman was murdered and her body found hacked to pieces, à la *Rear Window*), as well as by the many theatrical adaptations of the Jack the Ripper story. His first critical success, *The Lodger* (1926), was based on the legendary serial killer. *The Lodger* was almost exactly contemporary with Alban Berg's opera *Lulu,* which ends with the murder of the main female character by Jack the Ripper. In Germany of the 1920s, Jack the Ripper exemplified the archetypal *Lustmörder* (sex murderer) so beloved of

George Grosz, *John the Woman Slayer,* 1918

George Grosz; the scene in which the mob lynches the putative murderer in Hitchcock's film predated a similar one in Fritz Lang's *M.* by four years. *The Lodger* takes place mostly in the middle of the night, in that London fog that served the film versions of *Doctor Jekyll and Mister Hyde* (1931) and *The Picture of Dorian Gray* (1945) so well (in fact, its full title is *The Lodger: A Story of the London Fog*). It was probably during his 1924–25 visit to the UFA studios in Berlin that Hitchcock became aware of the significance of the Germanic city-as-Moloch: tentacular, illicit, dangerous – and, for all these reasons, fascinating. In *The Lodger,* however, he drifts with greater ease than his German colleagues into watercolour brushstrokes, with systematic swipes at the police and Cockney jokes.

Along with this portrait of the murderer as aesthete, we must not ignore the persistent Hitchcockian image of the artist as travelling player. At the turn of the century, *cafés concerts,* circuses and carnival stalls were locales of choice for painters such as Toulouse-Lautrec, Seurat, Sickert and Vuillard. All this was familiar to Hitchcock. An aficionado of lyric drama, he may also have been influenced by the Italian *verismo* opera *I Pagliacci* (1892), by Ruggero Leoncavallo – the epitome of the "play within the play," with its reliance on doubles and false pretences: Canio, the jealous, schizophrenic clown, no longer distinguishes between real life and the role he is playing, until the fateful moment when his wife is murdered and he regains the sole status of actor vis-à-vis the audience, blurting out *"La commedia è finita!"* as he brandishes his bloody knife before the horrified spectators. In his British films, Hitchcock retained this idea of the artist culprit who dies on stage – as Truffaut put it, "quite literally, the victim of his professional conscience."[17] This also happens to Mr. Memory in *The Thirty-nine Steps*: he takes his duties (to answer the audience's questions) to their logical conclusion; in doing so, he resembles Professor Echo (Lon Chaney) in Browning's *The Unholy Three* (1925), who was also devoured by a Doppelgänger, in this case his ventriloquist's dummy. Mr. Memory's death at the London Palladium, backstage, whence we see that a chorus line of showgirls has already replaced him onstage while he recites the memorized secret formula, is a truly operatic scene. Similarly, the dénouement of *Murder!* (1930) appears as one of the high points of Hitchcock's entire oeuvre. The homosexual murderer, about to be found out by the police, ends his days via a flamboyant circus act: dressed as a woman, covered in feathers and jewels, he performs on the trapeze to the disjointed din of a Nino

Thomas Theodor Heine, *Jealousy*, 1894

[17] Truffaut, p. 98.

Esme Percy in Murder!, 1930

Herbert Marshall in Murder!, 1930

Rota–style dancehall number that, after an inexorable rallentando, comes to a standstill. He then slips a noose around his neck and hangs himself in the air above the ring: the deceitful killer ascends to tragic-hero status by committing suicide dressed as the archetypal sad clown. Furthermore, in many of his films, Hitchcock deftly slips a certain number of dramatic, sometimes even operatic, effects into his almost detective novel–esque plot expositions. In the underrated *Jamaica Inn,* the action alternates between three (rather fake-looking) settings, with each scene relying on a narrative economy that is clearly reminiscent of opera: the inn, the inlet where the ships are dashed against the rocks, and the John Soane–style house where Judge Pengallon lives. The only foray outside this spatial triangle comes in a sort of fifth and concluding act, as the judge boards a ship in a bid to flee England, only to meet his death. To avoid the police's clutches, and in a completely improbable manner (but, here again, we find conventional Hitchcockian obsessions: the desire to fall and the intended theatrical effect) Pengallon throws himself from the ship's highest mast before the stunned crowd – another grandiose exit. With these Neronian excesses, he might well have declaimed, as Suetonius wrote of the Roman Emperor: "*Qualis artifex pereo!*" ("What a performer dies in me!"). The concluding sequence of *Rope* is a similar exercise in excessive theatricality: after a melodramatic pronouncement that would not have been out of place in Verdi or D'Annunzio ("You served food from his grave. And for that, you are going to die!") Rupert (James Stewart) fires a few shots into the street to attract the police, Phillip (Farley Granger) goes back to the piano, Brandon (John Dall) pours himself a drink, and we hear noises progressively rising up from the street until they become deafening.

If there is one opera composer, though, to whom Hitchcock continually referred (as did all the Symbolists) it is Richard Wagner. His music, occasionally, and more often his dramaturgy, are summoned in the films of the Master, for he was another who firmly believed in redemption through love, in the Catholic sense. It is while shaving and listening to the prelude to *Tristan und Isolde* on the radio that the hero of *Murder!* (Herbert Marshall) realizes that he has fallen in love with the young girl who has been accused of murder – possibly an homage, in the director's mind, to the recently released *Un chien andalou*. And of course, the "Tristan chord" is heard throughout *Vertigo,* in Bernard Herrmann's fine score, which was painstakingly overseen by Hitchcock himself. The obsessive manner in which he composes many master shots of his protagonists, by having the actors perform in front of rear-projection screens[18] (i.e., against a filmed backdrop on a soundstage instead of in a genuine exterior location), is an irresistible reminder of a Wagnerian invention, the *Verwandlung*. When *Parsifal* was first staged in 1882 – and for all subsequent productions for as long as Cosima Wagner sought to uphold the dogma – to avoid having to close the curtain when Gurnemanz sings the celebrated line *"Siehst du, mein Sohn. Zum Raum wird hier die Zeit!"* ("You see, my son. Time here becomes space!") the performers walked on a treadmill, so that they remained in the same spot on the stage, while the backdrop – a huge painted scroll – unfurled behind them, giving the impression of a shifting space. Wagner believed that with this technique he had achieved a complete dramatic and visual continuity, guaranteeing an illusion that nothing could disturb.

Judith Anderson in Rebecca, 1940

It is from a dramaturgic perspective, however, that the rapprochements between Wagner and Hitchcock are most unsettling. The filmmaker's insistence on remote sexuality, on unattainable blondes whose icy-cool exteriors belie a destructive fire, can be traced back not only to the women of Pre-Raphaelite paintings – especially when an Ingrid Bergman, Grace Kelly or Kim Novak is swathed in a costume by Edith Head – but, obviously, to the central character of Brünnhilde, lying on her rock surrounded by a ring of fire, to be awakened from her lethargic slumber by the intrepid warrior Siegfried. Moreover, Hitchcock shares with Wagner a taste for depicting incestuous relationships: an example is Uncle Charlie's fascination for his namesake niece (Teresa Wright) in *Shadow of a Doubt*. An even better example is the disturbing twinship, the superhuman, statuesque beauty of Maddalena Paradine (Alida Valli) and André Latour (Louis Jourdan) in *The Paradine Case* (1947): we never know the true nature of their relationship – was he the lover of the blind Colonel Paradine, whom he allowed to be killed? And in *Jamaica Inn,* Mary (Maureen O'Hara), who defies her family's wishes and frees the man she loves, riding on horseback through the storm and standing up to the thieves, is a sort of apprentice Valkyrie. Finally, the climactic scene of *Rebecca* is pure Wagner: to ensure that the truth is never revealed, Mrs. Danvers sets fire to Manderley and decides to burn herself up along with the former Mrs. de Winter's memories, calling to mind Brünnhilde's self-immolation on the pyre at Valhalla in the *Götterdämmerung*. Her suicide takes on the scope of a genocide. In the space of an instant, Hitchcock discovers the same devastating blast of absolute destruction, of permanent annihi-

The estate of Manderley in flames (Rebecca), 1940

[18] See Dominique Païni's essay,

Fritz Lang, *Das Nibelungen (II),* 1924

Franz von Stuck, *The Damnation of the Nibelungen,* about 1920

[19] Arthur Rimbaud, *Illuminations,* trans. Louise Varèse (New York: New Directions, 1957), p. 46.

lation – what the Germans call *Zusammenbruch* – that Fritz Lang had conveyed in the final scene of his own version of the *Nibelungen,* as flames sweep through the Burgunds' castle and engulf the last survivors.

Alfred Hitchcock ferried a number of themes that could be seen as vestiges of Late Romanticism into the late 20th century, reinvesting them with contemporary concerns. In *Strangers on a Train,* an updated version of the Faust myth and the pact with the Devil is played out. *The Paradine Case* and *Vertigo* lay bare the infernal machine – or rather the downward spiral – of conscience degraded by love, that old warhorse of the Decadents *(Weltuntergang).* And the "mark of the past" overhangs the Master's entire filmography. A wanderer with one foot in each century, he has taught us to connect the chains of Time. He has led us on a very special adventure through modern art, one that we more clearly understand now. He was the master of an art form marked by the triumph of ecstatic precision. He has also taught us to accept the reality of the world, without renouncing the pathetic fallacy. Hitchcock, too, could have given us these words, written by Arthur Rimbaud: "I have stretched ropes from steeple to steeple; garlands from window to window; golden chains from star to star, and I dance."[19]

Welcome to the museum, Mr. Hitchcock!

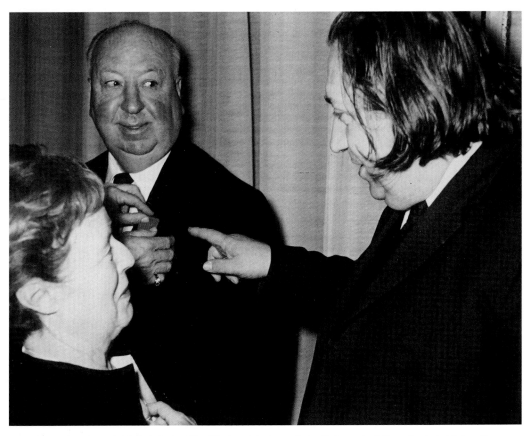

In the foyer of the Plaza-Athénée in Paris, Alfred Hitchcock is decorated with the rank of Chevalier de la Légion d'honneur by Henri Langlois, 1971

The Man Who Never Feared the Unknown

Henri Langlois

In the 1960s, Henri Langlois, founder of the Cinémathèque française and the man who presented Alfred Hitchcock with the Légion d'honneur on behalf of the French government, wrote the following lines in his "notebooks," which remain unpublished. Here, as always, Langlois was swept up by a characteristic lyricism born of enthusiasm, and so was not especially concerned with style. His words, though, have lost none of their resonance.

D.P.

Hitchcock is almost 40 perfect films, always astounding, always true to form, always unexpected.

He is a fountain of youth, who ensures that his work remains forever in the vanguard, always in step with new ideas.

His is a career that has never known failure – because of his humility, his refusal to wallow in disappointment. Because he has always known that in plying his trade he would find new raw materials to discover and appropriate.

He is a man who has never feared the unknown.

Of that, there is no more eloquent testimony than his first sound films, some of which are but pretexts for apprenticeship and self-affirmation, and point to the three major currents in his life's work.

He is a product of the end of the silent-film era, who learned ways of seeing and the joy of discovering how to fill the film frame – a man who understood and exploited the power of silence throughout his film career.

He is the discoverer of an aural canvas, a man who was not afraid, even in 1919, to tackle the challenges of speech and sound, who was alone among his countrymen in apprehending this new potential, and thus able to imbue the films he created at the time – from *Juno and the Paycock* to *Sabotage,* from *Number Seventeen* to *The Lady Vanishes* – with an extraordinary national character, through masterful use of accent, pronunciation and sound.

America would uproot him from his native soil – from London, its buses, its Cockneys, its myriad accents – and nudge him back to the realm of the abstract without stifling the tactile sense learned while making his first "talkies."

In Hollywood he would outdo himself, "slip the surly bonds of Earth," and attain the pure objectivity, the fluidity of line, the discipline inherent in the greatest art – along with that divine simplicity that makes him not only one of the most respected men of his industry, whose very name is a guarantee of success, but also one of the rare filmmakers who has never failed to attract the admiration of that most fickle and uncompromising of audiences: youth.

Yet if we analyse all that has been written by the critics – including those who, out of sheer laziness and advancing age, grow weary of fashion that refuses to fade, and find themselves forced, contrary to custom, to admire this man who cannot make an unsuccessful film – we quickly realize that, essentially, the Master of Suspense, the brilliant director, the skilled artisan, as some would have us believe, the formidable storyteller, despite all his glories and successes, remains misunderstood – because his reputation has not yet eclipsed his oeuvre, and because nobody dares guess what they would find if they were to unmask the King of Suspense, the Master of Mystery, the expert criminologist, the *bon vivant,* the lover of the good things in life who, it is said, likes to nap at the studio.

Because nobody dares intimate that, behind this diabolical mask that conceals him better than any other, lurks, quite simply, the Devil himself – the admirable countenance of Lucifer, clairvoyant, omniscient, fooled by nothing and no one, and whose humour remains intact.

That marvellous humour, which explains all of Hitchcock.

The intelligence, the mastery, the achievement, the wonderment of a life's work whose full breadth we cannot catch even a glimpse of, and which hides its own success from us.

An engineer of temporal rhythms, Hitchcock moulds the raw materials of cinema with a mastery and precision that equal absolute perfection.

In his hands, time, sight and sound are finely chiselled sculptures with a spellbinding power that has yet to be surpassed.

Hitchcock and the World of Dream
Donald Spoto

"Perhaps life is just that – a dream and a fear."
– Joseph Conrad

"At night you sleep your untroubled, ordinary little sleep, filled with peaceful, stupid dreams. And I brought you nightmares." With icy calm, those words are spoken by that attractive, well-dressed sociopath, Uncle Charlie (Joseph Cotten) in Alfred Hitchcock's *Shadow of a Doubt* (1943).

The director, whose centenary we marked in 1999, could have said the same words to us, for his films are nothing if not filmed dreams – a series of serenely coherent images, some of them suspenseful, all of them in the service of the great tradition of the romance. This is often a surprise to people, but when you stop to think about it, the Hitchcock canon is indeed a vast array of 53 romances: stories of love withheld, love denied, love derailed, love lost, love longed for, love regained. The espionage plot, the murderous impulse, the betrayal, the theft, the kidnapping, the flawed vision – all these are what he called MacGuffins, mere story pretexts to examine the real core, the deepest logic of the film. And in every case, this is some variation on the love story. This deserves a brief introductory comment.

Shadow of a Doubt (to stay with our example) is a love story; it even has a creepy sort of wedding scene between uncle and niece, as he places a ring on her finger and reminds her of their spiritual kinship. The film is a moral thriller in which a naïve young girl also named Charlie (Teresa Wright) learns about the mixed blood (that is, the dark impulse) she has inherited, the uneasy, common humanity that links her to her demented Uncle Charlie.

Psycho (1960) is a love story, too. The life of Norman Bates (Anthony Perkins) is destroyed by the illusion that a twisted, defensive love can cancel out the effects of a lunatic crime and keep alive a dead person. And the life of Marion Crane (Janet Leigh) is destroyed by the illusion that money will

Joseph Cotten's hands
(Shadow of a Doubt), 1943

finally solve her lover's financial problems and set them both free. A Hitchcock love story may be unlike any other love story you encounter in movies, but love stories they are.

Like all the Hitchcock masterworks, *Shadow of a Doubt* and *Psycho* have a dreamlike quality. Smooth Uncle Charlie – so polite, so handsome, so presentable, so *likeable* – is a serial killer. Norman Bates, that painfully shy young man who seems so suffocated by his mother, is a madman too. Appearances are, as usual in the Hitchcock filmography, no clear clues to reality.

It's the same in our dreams and nightmares. Love seems strange in dreams. There are sudden transitions from one place to another, the beloved refuses to act and react as we expect. The familiar place seems somehow different, and time slips and slides. Places bend, change shape. People enter our dreams, become other people, vanish, emerge again. Movies are like that. We are here, we're there, time is elastic.

No one knew this better than Alfred Hitchcock. He often compared his films to dreams: *North by Northwest* (1959), for example, he described as one long dream-fantasy of absurdity, a tale of what happens to a Madison Avenue businessman (Cary Grant) who loses virtually every security. The crop-dusting sequence is right from the world of dreamscape: look at that broad daylight pursuit of a man by a deadly biplane, with nowhere to hide but a cornfield. Is this nightmare or what? But *North by Northwest* is a love story. Our ultimate concern isn't for the darned microfilm (who cares?): it's about Cary Grant and Eva Marie Saint getting together despite her betrayal of him (an action typical of a Hitchcock blonde).

Similarly, think of the demented carousel in *Strangers on a Train* (1951), suddenly cranked up from normal to tornado-like speed, as Guy Haines (Farley Granger) and Bruno Anthony (Robert Walker) fight to the death beneath the hooves of painted wooden horses. Hitch knew what he was doing in transforming Patricia Highsmith's novel of a lethal gay courtship into a fight to the finish; he has turned it into a love story, with Freudian images strewn like confetti.

Even more hallucinatory is that great poem of his late career, *The Birds* (1963). The film is a series of dialogues between people, classic exchanges in which they discuss their fear of being abandoned – and after each dialogue, there's a bird attack. Nightmare imagery, all of it: those are such cute little sparrows!

Sometimes Hitchcock literally gives us his characters' dreams. For *Spellbound* (1945), he brought in artist Salvador Dalí for the sequence in which a masked man turns over huge, blank playing cards while enormous eyes stare from painted draperies; and at the next moment, another man, tiny and helpless, is overwhelmed as he flees from the shadow of an enormous pursuing bird.

And it's likely that few who saw it can ever forget the haunting nightmare sequence in *Vertigo* (1958), in which the breakdown of Scottie Ferguson (James Stewart) is precipitated by a dream in which guilt and love collide with longing for death, where he may be united with his beloved.

From here, there's a straight line to *Marnie* (1964), wherein a childhood trauma leads the title character (played by Tippi Hedren) to a restless and emotionally empty adulthood, which can be healed only by confronting a long-buried memory that has tried for years to surface in her dreams. The breakthrough comes in meeting the past as a hallucinatory kind of dream-remembrance, just as, throughout the story, the adult Marnie is troubled by bad dreams. This motif lasts right through to Hitchcock's last picture, *Family Plot,* whose action is catalysed by the haunted, guilt-ridden dreams of Julia Rainbird (Cathleen Nesbitt) in which her dead sister addresses her.

Not all the images are so eerie, threatening or upsetting as these examples, of course. Dreamy, romantic moments are even more numerous in Hitchcock than the terrifying kind. The final moments of *Notorious* (1946), for example, are straight from the conventions of the fairy tale – T.R. Devlin (Cary Grant, as Prince Not-So-Charming) snatches Alicia Huberman (Ingrid Bergman, as Snow Beige) from the jaws of death. But Hitch turns this into a classic, irresistible love scene, both tense and moving, as he encircles the lovers with his camera.

And what of the first kiss between Dr. Constance Petersen (Ingrid Bergman) and the false Anthony Edwardes (Gregory Peck) in *Spellbound* (1945), as all those hallucinatory doors suddenly open in a dream image behind them, indicating the undoing of repressions? It looks a little hokey today, but you don't laugh at Gainsborough simply because his technique preceded Picasso's.

While we're discussing romance: the kisses in Hitchcock's movies are justly famous. He liked to encircle the lovers with his camera, as if to embrace them, as if to rob us for just a moment of our sober, solidly objective viewpoint. The dream flashback in *I Confess,* when Ruth (Anne Baxter) kisses Michael (Montgomery Clift), is a good example, but probably the best of them all is in *Vertigo,* when at last Judy Barton (Kim Novak) has been transformed by Scottie (James Stewart) into the image of his dead beloved. Now there's a kiss between lovers that rivals any kiss in the history of movies.

* * *

One of the curious elements of dreams is how the dreamer seems invariably aware of observing, of watching a strange, diffident world that is in some senses set free from control: it has its own time-space continuum, and the familiar is turned just so, made surprisingly fresh and unfamiliar. This is not surprising, for filmmaking and film watching are themselves variants on the very nature of looking and the same sort of reordering of the familiar.

Directly related to this is that hoariest of genres, the spy story, for the business of watching is the spy's stock-in-trade. But Hitchcock's espionage thrillers *(The Man Who Knew Too Much, The Thirty-nine Steps, Secret Agent, The Lady Vanishes, Foreign Correspondent, Notorious, North by Northwest)* are, as I've suggested, mere pretexts for classical romances. It's in the *romance* that the theme of watching is italicized – just as in dreams. Think, in this regard, of the moments when the predator becomes the prey, moments linked with gazing, with the almost uncontrollable desire to see and to learn.

In *Rear Window,* the great moment of suspense occurs when Lars Thorwald (Raymond Burr) looks back across the courtyard to see Jeffries (James Stewart) watching him and us – what a frisson!

In *Vertigo,* Scottie watches and pursues Madeleine/Judy. This may be the ultimate film about watching and pursuit, about seeing as desire. We're not so far from Freud's fancily expressed idea of scoptophilia, the gazing impulse that, pathologically, becomes voyeurism (an idea Freud elaborates in an essay on Wilhelm Jensen's novella *Gradiva*).

This is the world of *Psycho,* of course: a twisted world from its opening shot. The camera seems to move through a partly open window – right over the sill and into a darkened room. It finds an empty chair nearby, moves over and, just like a spectator in a movie theatre, "sits" in the chair. The field of vision then tilts up, and we see a seminude couple (John Gavin and Janet Leigh, playing Sam Loomis and Marion Crane).

44

All the subsequent gazing in the picture – by us, by Marion, by the suspicious patrolman (Mort Mills), by Norman Bates (Anthony Perkins) – is revealed as partial and imperfect seeing, mere watching without real vision or perception. It's logical, therefore, that Arbogast (Martin Balsam), the private eye, is stabbed in the eye, and that Lila Crane (Vera Miles) hits a suspended bare light bulb, causing it to swing and cast shadows in the empty sockets of Mother Bates's skull. Like all the "seeing" in the film, the skull's "gaze" is an empty, dead stare that recalls the open stare of Marion's corpse. To make his point clear, Hitchcock photographed Norman spying on Marion as she disrobes for the fatal shower: Norman removes from the wall a painting of Susannah and the elders, the biblical story of a woman overtaken in her bath by voyeurs whose passions were aroused as they spied on her from a secret place. The artistic representation of voyeurism and sexual exploitation is thus replaced, in the world of *Psycho,* by the action itself.

James Stewart's nightmare (Vertigo), 1958

The brilliance of this, in Hitchcock's most nightmarish picture, is that the audience is supremely implicated. We not only watch Norman watching: the camera also swings around and the viewer stares *with* him. In a way, therefore, you can say that *Psycho* actualizes what *Rear Window* only observed, for in *Psycho* everyone gazes – especially in the last shot, when we gaze at the demented face gazing out at us. This is precisely the final image in Hitchcock's earlier TV drama *Lamb to the Slaughter,* when Mrs. Maloney (Barbara Bel Geddes) gazes, grinning in triumph, out at us.

* * *

The theme of moral (not merely physical) vision – the basis of our watching in dream (where we act) and nightmare (where we are passive) – is carried forward in Hitchcock's next picture, his poetic masterpiece *The Birds,* a film that was in a way necessitated by the bird picture *Psycho* (Perkins, who munches Kandy Korn like a hen, stuffs birds; the last bird he "stuffs" is a Crane from Phoenix, and so forth).

Remarkably often, characters in *The Birds* say "I see" or "You see." The words are like a refrain, punctuating every stanza of the visual poem – just as every sequence concludes with a character staring out into space. Mrs. Bates's empty eye sockets in *Psycho* become the triple jump cut to the pecked-out sockets of the dead farmer. A child's eyeglasses are shattered as she flees attacking birds.

All the images and words about seeing point forward to the main character's empty stare – wide and imperceptive – and just as the shower murder of *Psycho* is carried forward in the bird attack on Melanie Daniels (Tippi Hedren) in the attic, so Marion's dead "stare" becomes Melanie's open, unseeing, shocked gaze. Lashing out and beating at nothing with her arms, her gaze frantic with terror, Melanie is unknowingly striking at a man who tries to calm her. She becomes the horrifyingly literal fulfilment of Norman's remark in *Psycho*: "We scratch and claw, but only at the air, only at each other – and for all of it, we never budge an inch."

* * *

This brings us to the motif of punishment, which in nightmares has no logic at all – just as in Hitchcock's films.

Ordinarily, we are not shown the punishment of villains in Hitchcock's stories, but simply their capture. He has no interest in the application of the legal machinery to a situation. The capture, in fact, is usually tossed in as a concession to the censors – and often enough, it's handled humorously. Think of Tony Wendice (Ray Milland) offering a round of drinks at the fadeout of *Dial M for Murder,* or of Danielle Foussard (Brigitte Auber), blithely ignored after being unmasked as the robber at the end of *To Catch a Thief.* Arthur Adamson (William Devane) and Fran (Karen Black) hardly matter at the end of *Family Plot,* and the fate of killer Gavin Elster (Tom Helmore) is ignored in *Vertigo.* Even the horrors of *Frenzy* conclude not with a bang but a chuckle ("Why, Mr. Rusk! You're not wearing your tie!").

Gregory Peck and Ingrid Bergman in Spellbound, *1945*

With *Psycho,* as I've discussed elsewhere, there is a major shift in emphasis, for here the Furies drive mad the one guilty of matricide, Norman Bates (the Hitchcockian Orestes). But then those Furies abandon the vengeful insistence on the ancient law of blood for blood: the annihilation of personality is punishment enough.

The masterworks may well be those films in which Hitchcock enters the open country of freedom with his characters, quitting the question of desired pain for pain by eliciting compassion for the wrongdoer as well as the victim. It's uncomfortable for us to realize that Professor Jordan (Godfrey Tearle), the villain of *The Thirty-nine Steps,* is a devoted family man careful to protect his daughter from deadly knowledge; in this regard, he's a forerunner of Stephen Fisher (Herbert Marshall) with his daughter Carol (Laraine Day) in *Foreign Correspondent.* Likewise, Karl Verloc (Oscar Homolka) in *Sabotage* is a good family man (and a somewhat weak-willed saboteur). In *Notorious,* Alex Sebastian (Claude Rains) loves Alicia Huberman (Ingrid Bergman) more passionately than Devlin

Anthony Perkins in Psycho, 1960

(Cary Grant), and Mrs. Drayton (Brenda de Banzie) is a most disturbingly touching and devoted mother *manqué* in the remake of *The Man Who Knew Too Much.* Marnie's devotion to her mother may be the element that earns her a second chance: see how Hitchcock reverses the ending of the book.

* * *

I think it is this detachment from the machinery of punishment that is the means Hitchcock took – or better, the hope that he entertained – for the re-establishment of order of a higher kind than mere legality. Hitchcock, after all, placed little trust in the unfolding and disbursement of legal justice: we have only to recall the judges and all the detectives who are their surrogates in other films. Hitchcock arouses in us a curious kind of magnanimity – at least by implication – by placing the offender elsewhere for the appointment of judgment.

And so I think it is this striving for detachment – as much an element of dreams as is involvement – that ultimately explains the disturbing moral complexity of the Hitchcock filmography. It is precisely this detachment, this great haze of grey, this refusal to divide the world into sheep and goats before the final reckoning, the refusal to tear up the weeds. The great works may be great because they suggest that the most morally reprehensible attitude may be our own desire to see retribution meted out, to see punishment enacted – precisely the stance that would effectively further distance us from the villain with whom Hitchcock is so careful to link us spiritually.

* * *

In a sense, Hitchcock's films – poeticized dreams though they are – also reverse the chaos of the dream world. Carefully structured, they are (with one exception, *The Birds*) linear narratives with a beginning, a middle and an end. They resolve conflicts, they give finality to tension, and they order life. Having confronted the absurd and the chaotic, they open up for us a possibility of a return to the world of reason – hence the final image of *Psycho,* the dragging of the car from the slime – a powerful and therapeutic image of drawing up the shadow world into daylight. In this regard, Hitchcock's painstaking artistic method of filmmaking is in fact his meaning: the planning, the care, the symmetry – this was his way of taking a stand against chaos. The commitment to structure, not to disorder, was itself an ethos affirming the primacy of meaning in order.

* * *

But no one appreciated romantic fantasy more than Hitchcock did, and no one could show us more clearly how we can feel about that portion of human experience.

Dreamers and fantasists, lovers and killers crowd his films and leap out at us, astonishingly familiar cousins to our own hopes and fears. He never appealed to the processes of mere reason but rather to levels of feeling from which no one is exempt. He knew the fears and the longings first ("I'm afraid of everything," he once told me, "more afraid than anyone who sees my films"), which is why he could portray them so vividly to us.

The mummified Mrs. Bates (Psycho), 1960

Disturbingly often, romantic impulses have a dangerous undercurrent, and gestures of affection verge on the violent. The lovemaking of Roger Thornhill (Cary Grant) and Eve Kendall (Eva Marie Saint) aboard the train in *North by Northwest* is tinged with an uneasy dread as his hands encircle her neck and she asks, "How do I know you're not going to kill me, right here and now?"

"Shall I?" he counters.

"Please do," she purrs.

It's very much the same when the innocent man on the run from the police – Richard Blaney (Jon Finch) in *Frenzy* (1972) – places strangling hands around the neck of his girlfriend Babs Milligan (Anna Massey) and jokes that no, he's not the mad killer on the loose – but we know that his temper is as wild and murderous as the villain's. Just so: "She's the most precious thing in the world to me," says Uncle Charlie while he squeezes his niece's face so tightly she winces in pain.

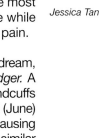

Jessica Tandy in The Birds, 1963

The complex of pleasure and pain, nightmare and dream, began in 1926, in Hitchcock's first British film, *The Lodger.* A detective (Malcolm Keen) boasts that after he's put handcuffs on the killer, he'll put a ring on the finger of his girlfriend (June) – and at once he playfully snaps the handcuffs on her, causing the poor woman to panic at the bondage. There's a similar attraction-repulsion business about romance (always linked to handcuffs) in *The Thirty-nine Steps* and *Saboteur* (1942), too, as blondes (Madeleine Carroll and Priscilla Lane) are unwillingly manacled to men (Robert Donat and Robert Cummings).

Hitchcock could also be prophetic in spinning his dream-tales. When he made *Sabotage* in 1936, people said the movie's plot of terrorists planting bombs in central London was a wild idea: now, alas, it's all too common. The kidnapping in *The Man Who Knew Too Much* (1934, revised and vastly improved in his 1956 remake) is no longer a fantastic fiction. And the lunatic serial killer of *Psycho* smiles grimly from our televisions at news time.

Leopoldine Konstantin and
Claude Rains in Notorious, 1946

The world of Hitchcock's dream-tales is opaque, full of surprise and treachery, thick with frustration and riddled with anxiety. But it is finally a world where men and women are usually offered a chastening, transforming experience. This is the classical structure of storytelling, of course – tales about the humanizing process, fables of conversion and redemption, whatever you call them. He takes us on tours, excursions to the frontiers of chaos, a world in which anything can happen and probably will. Unlike his inferiors, who too often gleefully concoct images of violence, decay and death, Hitchcock looks evil squarely in the face and calls it evil. Hitch shows us not how *all* life is, but how *some* of life is, and what all life is in constant danger of becoming. Fantasist and fabulist, the great Alfred Hitchcock remains disturbingly alive in his eternal dreams, those remarkable movies.

The Wandering Gaze:
Hitchcock's Use of *Transparencies*
Dominique Païni

Marlene Dietrich, 1942

Most contemporary dictionaries define *transparency* as the ability of a body or material to transmit light and allow the objects behind it to be seen clearly – and this is the meaning it is commonly given in everyday speech.

This is not the aspect I wish to examine here. Of course, the aforementioned property does play a vital role in the phenomenon known as film: the imprinting of contrasting shadows, colour and light on transparent celluloid, through which the light from the projector passes. Some conference aids used to draw diagrams on are called transparencies. During the 20th century a number of artists, such as Moholy-Nagy and Marcel Duchamp, to name the most representative, explored the concept of transparency through their choice of materials. Man Ray even entitled a number of his pieces *Les grands transparents* (The Mirror). Picabia's paintings, although themselves opaque, nevertheless portrayed transparency in a figurative way. Nor is it accidental that the last two artists mentioned should be featured in an exhibition dedicated to a director. After all, many directors used transparent materials extensively in their set designs: from Sternberg's and Hitchcock's veils half-covering Marlene's face (in *Dishonored* and *Stage Fright* respectively); to Tati's architectural structures in *Playtime*; or those used by Hitchcock in *North by Northwest* (the United Nations building, the copy of a Frank Lloyd Wright–designed house, etc.).

That is not, however, the kind of transparency I will evoke and discuss here. Rather, it is the cinematic special effect that uses the properties of transparency to create an illusion of space and distance. This technique is called *rear projection* (sometimes "back projection"), and can be defined as follows: "the projection of a film onto the rear of a translucent screen in front of which live action is being filmed."*

This kind of transparency makes it possible for an exterior scene to be projected as a background for live action filmed in the studio. The scene could be a landscape or

* Translator's note: Eventually, advances in special-effects cinematography resulted in these types of scenes being created by means of so-called *travelling matte* or *process* shots. Variations on both techniques can be seen in the films of Alfred Hitchcock, depending on their year of production. To avoid an ungainly alternation between the expressions *rear projection* and *process shot,* I have decided to use the term *transparency.* It is my hope that the translation of Mr. Païni's essay has been – dare I say – made more "transparent" as a result.

51

cityscape, an interior or the open sea, a moving or fixed stage setting. In the words of Pascal, infinity is "an idea of that which exists behind us."

This type of illusion allows a director the convenience of filming in the studio and eliminates the costs and technical arrangements associated with filming on location (transporting actors, technicians, equipment, etc.).

In order for this studio technique to produce the desired effect, the filming camera must be located exactly opposite the projecting apparatus, so that the projected, fake backdrop and the actors performing in front of it are combined as seamlessly as possible. Placing characters in a recognizable setting, imprinting forms on a surface is a pictorial preoccupation of very long standing.

How has cinema in general – and Hitchcock's films, which so frequently resorted to this device – responded to this preoccupation?

Before entering Hitchcock's world to find an answer to this question, I would like to go back in time briefly and provide an overview of the aesthetic reasons why Hitchcock was so attached to this illusory device. Anyone who watches his entire oeuvre, from the earliest films of his British period to the final Hollywood products, will be struck by the director's faithful adherence to this technique. The frequency and manner in which he uses it point to a significance that goes beyond mere technical convenience. In interviews with *Cahiers du cinéma* in the 1980s, Hitchcock's collaborators remarked on the director's near obsession with this outdated special effect. Robert Boyle, chief set designer for *The Birds* (and, earlier, for *Saboteur*, in 1942) commented at the time: "If he could have, he would have done everything in studio, without ever going outside."[1] Boyle's comment confirmed, perhaps unwittingly, the aesthetic preference revealed by Hitchcock's use of transparencies right up until his last films.

A Brief History of Transparencies

In the 19th century, transparencies were used by the performing arts in general, and Wagnerian opera in particular, as a means of creating illusions.

Wagnerian opera was a forum for experimenting with illusory devices that would later have a lasting impact on cinema, from Méliès to the German and Italian directors of the

The New Mitchell Background Projector

Rear projection technology, "The New Mitchell Background Projector"

[1] *Cahiers du cinéma*, no. 337, June 1982. (Free translation.)

The Ride of the Valkyries as staged in Paris, "La science au théâtre", La Nature, no. 1047, 24 June 1893,

Phantasmagorical effects: theatrical performance as part of a show entitled La nonne sanglante, mid 19th century

Albrecht Dürer, Underweysung der Messung, 1575

1960s who were infatuated with the make-believe world of opera. In one famous performance of the ride of the Valkyries, clouds were painted on pieces of glass and passed in front of electric lanterns that acted as projectors. Although the riders were motionless mannequins, the illusion created by glass and lanterns made it look as though they flew through the sky. The singer and the spectator were connected in the same way actors and moviegoers are connected today, except for the fact – and this is a considerable difference – that there was no intervening medium between the singer and the spectator.

Among 19th-century performing arts, story-based theatre and opera in particular prefigured the cinematic special effect known as transparency. Thus, it appears that this device originated well before the birth of cinema. In fact, it could be seen as the first modern device for creating an illusory representation of reality. From as early as the 18th century, phantasmagoric shows used devices quite similar to our 20th-century cinematic techniques to stage daydreams, nightmares and many other kinds of apparitions.

Metaphorically speaking, a literal definition of the word might lead us to suggest that perspective – an organizational principle of visual codes and symbols – is a product of the method known as *mise au carreau*, whereby a transparent template is used to divide the image into equal-sized squares, as seen in Dürer's famous work. Except that, in this case, the transparency of the glass, the projection that connects the portraying eye to the portrayed subject is geometrical and abstract as opposed to technical and concrete.

In 1874 Fulgence Marion wrote a piece entitled *L'optique* ("Optics"). The chapter entitled *Les merveilles de l'optique* ("Amazing Optics") reveals the secrets of how apparitions are made to appear – not through projected images, but rather by some combination of shadows, translucence and two-way mirrors. Apparently, the ghosts would be more visible if the theatre were kept dimly lit.

Spotting the Illusion

But what does transparency mean in cinematic terms? Paradoxically, although the term implies invisibility, the technique is most often easily detected by audiences. Theoretically, it should deceive the eye, through a sort of *trompe l'oeil* effect, but Hitchcock and his technicians did not appear too concerned with concealing it.

But how can transparencies be recognized? How do viewers, including those unfamiliar with cinematic techniques, spot this particular special effect? For there is little doubt that, of all the cinematic devices, transparencies are among the most recognizable. What alerts the spectator to the fact that a background apparently stretching to infinity is, on the contrary, limited – not by natural or technical restrictions on our vision, but rather by a screen, a veil? This veil both obstructs our view and acts as a substitute for reality by revealing a mere portion of the whole. The veil also delimits the performance space by creating a quasi-intentional illusion of infinity, especially in the case of a landscape or cityscape projected behind the actors.

How can we know when a transparency is being used? Sometimes the image on screen is more grainy; there is a slight difference in pigmentation, making the colours more saturated than elsewhere in the shot. The quality of light is also different; sometimes overexposed, since the background has to be lighter so that when it is refilmed on the set, the lighting will be the same for both the backdrop and the actors, who must necessarily be adequately lit.

The outline of the frame within which the background is projected frequently fluctuates or vibrates. The outline of car or train windows – indeed, the windows of any vehicle through which we see a landscape passing by – often shimmer, and are sometimes subject to solarization.

Although Agnès Minazzoli, writing in *La première ombre,* is concerned less with transparencies than with similarities, she nevertheless captures its visual hallmark: "An image with a movable outline and fluid lines, which seems to vanish before our eyes, to disappear from sight, always moving and changing; fundamentally indeterminable."[2]

Another way to spot transparencies is to look for a strange artifice in the actors' movements – one that cannot be explained by the fact that they may actually be walking on the spot on a sort of treadmill. Their bodies are immobile but the background, projected onto a screen, moves behind them and creates small but sudden frame shifts. The actors are cutout figures against the backdrop of a place where they may never have set foot. The gesticulating figures are superimposed on a far-off background that is supposed to signify a context close at hand or a setting within easy reach. The outline of their bodies is "cropped," to use a term employed by photojournalists, meaning that the figures seem to be "pasted" onto a flat background.

[2] Agnès Minazzoli, *La première ombre* (Paris: Éd. de Minuit, 1990), p. 115. (Free translation.)

This is why transparencies always contain a certain dreaminess, an element of oneiric reserve. Indeed, I believe filmmakers use it with exactly that, dare I say, "perspective" in mind.

A background created via transparencies is always faintly unstable; the instability comes from the fact that it has been filmed not once, but twice.

A Troubled Representation

It is not just the world within the film, but also the attempt to create a plausible reality that becomes troubled as the viewer watches the film. Transparencies instill the spaces they represent with a sense of unease. Suddenly, part of the picture no longer fits in with the rest. This "aggregate" use of space can be compared to the approach used in first-century Roman paintings (as described by Erwin Panofsky), and is in marked contrast to the modern, systematic use of space in the Renaissance that followed.

When we look at Panofsky's examples of aggregate space, we are struck both by the evidence of continuity between the two areas and by the signs of separation between them. The space created by a transparency, and the studio image that encompasses it, constitute aggregate space, a disturbed kind of homogeneity. The untimely tremors along the boundaries between these two kinds of images correspond to what Panofsky calls "depth intervals." Commenting on Pre-Pompeian paintings of "real" interiors and "real" landscapes, Panofsky writes: "The artist suggests extension in depth simply by arranging several strata of scenery one behind the other, indicating the depth intervals that would ordinarily separate them by means of intersections of different size that are, however, not readable in reference to shortened horizontal plane. Here we have a method that, to create the illusion of space, proceeds somewhat violently; in a uniquely negative manner, so to speak, the various layers of depth seem as a result to enter into *simultaneous* relations of *juxtaposition* and *postposition.*"[3]

I believe his comments provide a good description of how a transparency is perceived, its visual effects, and the *simultaneous* juxtaposition and postposition of elements.

In most cases, transparencies are a trap, a distraction to the viewer. The bottomless depth meant to recreate perspective artificially actually ends up confusing it and diverting the

[3] Erwin Panofsky, *La perspective comme forme symbolique* (Paris: Éd. de Minuit, 1981), p. 82. (Free translation.)

viewer's attention from the action. A background – natural or urban – that is created by the use of transparency is a miniature documentary in the fictional whole, a sort of "portable nature," or "excerpts from nature," to quote August Wilhelm Schlegel, who proposed these terms as he reflected on the status of landscapes in the interior "vedutes" done by German Romantic painters such as Carl Ludwig Kaar or Caspar David Friedrich. I am thinking in particular of a remark made by Louise, the character in Schlegel's *Tableaux,* as she argues with Reinhold and Waller: "I find it surprising, given its size, that this marvellous painting should be completely devoid of grandeur or charm, and that a modest siren song is its only means of drawing people into its reality. I believe it is because the painting – a charming miniature – recreates reality in the manner of a *camera obscura.*"[4] Hitchcock's German influences, which I will discuss below, can also be detected in his habit of treating landscape as remote, not just in geographical terms, but as though it were a distant part of the picture, occupying the farthest visual point. The scenery constitutes the background to the other representational planes, an abutment to vision, yet continues to be one of the many *accessories* in the overall composition. Whenever there are figures in Friedrich's paintings, the landscape is merely background, in every sense of the word. Instead of physical space, we notice the space conveyed by the person's gaze as he stares into the distance, and this impression is similar to the one elicited by landscapes created using transparencies in Hitchcock's films. Part of the films' suspense resides in the gap that separates and unites the actors and the space in which they move. For if the background is created by a transparency, this gap is uncertain, perturbed by visual phenomena that could potentially mimic the effects of a daydream *(North by Northwest, Vertigo, Strangers on a Train, The Thirty-nine Steps).*

These short sequences – sometimes forward tracking shots through city streets, or panoramic views of the countryside from a train window – that unspool behind live performers have no fictional value other than to provide a setting for the story, and no documentary value either. Like elevator music, the worst of them show a complete disregard for diegetic concerns. A reminder of reality, captured through a window visible behind the actors, transparencies create two levels of illusion, the first one being the cinema itself. If these images are common ones, they could be used indiscriminately in any film of a certain genre. In many cases, they are filmed by a "second unit," without the performers, thus creating the necessity for combining the two.

[4] August Wilhelm Schlegel, *Les tableaux* (Paris: Éd. Christian Bourgois, 1988), p. 5. (Free translation.)

I would like to conclude this list of ways to spot a transparency by mentioning that the technique is frequently used in train scenes. In some of Hitchcock's, and other directors', films, the transparency is scarcely visible. The countryside, shot at the same time as the actors in the foreground, really does seem to roll by in the background. Given that they are projected onto a transparent screen, surely transparencies by their very nature would have to be invisible. What, then, can we watch out for, if we want to spot an aggregate, a non-homogeneous space between the talking actors and the countryside in the background?

Sometimes, the only way is to view the sequence frame by frame, slowly, using an editing bench or a videotape recorder. Then, the artifice stands out, and we see that the moving panorama framed by the train window has been edited separately. The continuity of the moving image on a platform is suddenly interrupted, and the scene cuts to another shot. In other cases, the transparency is revealed, not through a break in the sequence of images, but rather through the same images, repeated in a loop. (This is especially noticeable during the long seduction scene between Eva Marie Saint and Cary Grant in the dining car in *North by Northwest*; the same landscape and tunnel are repeatedly seen.)

We have not come far, it seems, from the little toy theatres of the early 20th century in which, by turning a handle, the cardboard scenery was set in endless, repetitive motion at the back of the set. Nor are we far removed from the panoramas that were popular at the end of the 19th century, some of which were equipped with a landscape on a roll that allowed the armchair traveller to visit famous, exotic and spectacular places. In that sense, transparencies arise out of 19th-century means of portraying the spectacular, well before modern film production techniques came into being. They therefore lie somewhere between a practical tool and a discursive form – and this, in fact, is true for all devices used to codify representation.

I will discuss the impact that this *special effect* has on our senses in terms of an organizational principle posited by Gilles Deleuze and Félix Guattari in *Mille plateaux*: "It involves two kinds of organization; the one mechanistic, the other expressive."[5] Seen in this light, transparency becomes an expressive means of organizing reality. In other words, it is far more than merely a practical solution to the difficulties of shooting a film on location, or a simple method of reconstituting a particular kind of scenery.

[5] Gilles Deleuze and Félix Guattari, *Mille plateaux, Capitalisme et schizophrénie* (Paris, Éd. de Minuit, 1980), p. 625. (Free translation.)

57

If transparency constitutes an expressive means of organization, it does so in terms of various parameters, the most obvious of which are as follows:

- its place in the story (beginning, middle, end);
- its more or less frequent use (scarcity or systematic repetition);
- the conspicuous and deliberately gratuitous way it is used, which may be considered symptomatic;
- the amount of discretion with which it is used.

Even these few signs of expressiveness – and there are many more – elevate transparencies from the status of an ordinary special effect to that of a conscious aesthetic choice. Transparencies are a fusion of a machine, an *installation* (as used to refer to the works of contemporary artists), and a visual technique that creates a semblance of reality without erasing the illusory device that created it. In that sense, transparencies are somewhat akin to Yves Bonnefoy's description of the Roman Baroque period (with which transparencies doubtless share a number of conceptual and perceptive similarities, particularly with respect to the vaulting found in large Counter-Reformation churches). He said: "These two sensations – of faith and disillusion, of the absolute and the relative – are experienced simultaneously."

Here we have an apt definition for what I choose to call the *uncertain reality* of a transparency. Yves Bonnefoy's comment about the existence of presence and disillusion and their simultaneity echoes a key concept found in Panofsky's writings. In fact, because transparencies are an attempt to create a homogeneous space between pre-photographed reality and actors performing "in the present" in front of the camera, they are also in a sense an attempt to create a homogeneous time frame. This new and unique creation unites the prerecorded, temporal (slightly unrealistic) setting and the characters' actions (sometimes crudely superimposed) in a way that subjects the viewer to the kind of flickering common in the field of perceptive psychology.

We see, then, that there are two time frames being portrayed and brought together in one setting, a setting where the figures in the foreground and the scenery behind them are conjoined. Transparencies are all about time. Indeed, the very essence of transparencies is this temporal gap that our willing suspension of disbelief reduces to manageable proportions.

Hitchcock's Insistent Use of Transparencies

Exactly how prevalent was Hitchcock's use of transparencies? I believe it was in *Young and Innocent* (1937) that he first explored their full potential, drawing out elements of drama and poetry, narrative verisimilitude and a curious mixture of mockery and self-analysis. The significance of this film in terms of its masterful and entirely ungratuitous use of cinematic techniques will be discussed in greater detail further on.

For now, I will look at how Hitchcock's use of this effect evolved over the course of his career. I will begin by running sequentially through the films comprising his oeuvre, then return to certain key works.

If *Young and Innocent* stands out as one of the first and most astonishing uses of transparency, it is also significant for its experimentation with an opposite kind of technique. I am thinking in particular of the spectacular moving camera shot through the grand ballroom. This final crane shot resolves the suspense through a truly brilliant piece of mise en scène.

Within a year – and the proximity is surely not coincidental – Hitchcock produced *The Lady Vanishes,* in which a transparency contains both the mystery and the key to resolve it. In the condensation on the train window, the kidnapped woman writes her name and, later, a tea label miraculously appears there.

Rebecca (1939), *Foreign Correspondent* (1940), *Suspicion* (1941) and *Saboteur* (1942) all use transparencies in a self-consciously dramatic, at times excessive or voyeuristic, way. The obvious contrast between the realistic details of the "canned" world and the artificiality of the entire fictional environment unsettles the viewer. *Shadow of a Doubt* (1942), with Joseph Cotten's famous fall/disappearance between two trains, provides an important glimpse of how this technique would be used in subsequent films, such as *Spellbound* (1944) and *Notorious* (1945). Although the effects of transparencies are more concrete in these films, they still create strong, poetic repercussions, evoking intoxication, paranoia and unconscious perceptions. Significantly, *The Paradine Case* (1947), *Rope* (1948) and *Under Capricorn* (1948) all bypass the technique. In fact, these last two films use the properties of transparency in a more direct way: for example, the picture window overlooking the city in *Rope,* or – and Jean-Louis Schefer's essay in this catalogue enlightens us on this subject – the window that reflects Ingrid Bergman's face in *Under Capricorn*.

Transparencies are once again strikingly obvious in *Stage Fright* (1950) and *Strangers on a Train* (1950), and may be considered an important structural element for these two stories based on lies, an exchange of murders and the transference of guilt.

I Confess (1952), *Dial M for Murder* (1953) and *Rear Window* (1953) appear to resort less frequently to this type of trick shot; it is used more subtly, or rarely at all. For dramatic as well as theoretical reasons, Hitchcock toned down his use of the device. One might almost say it went underground.

Although Hitchcock used transparencies in *The Wrong Man* (1956), an opaque realism predominates, which distracts the director somewhat from his obsessive representation of infinity. Even though *North by Northwest* (1958) used the technique, it is a mere visual game, a way to throw the viewer off guard. And in *Vertigo* (1957), it does not lend itself to any particularly symbolic interpretation, since James Stewart's agoraphobia is sufficient to create that optical, spatial gap, as does the voyeurism and necrophilia of Anthony Perkins in *Psycho* (1959). In these last two films, rather than being represented deceptively, space is created in a more directly physical way. Significantly, a number of the characters in *The Birds* (1962) and *Marnie* (1963) are *blinded* in some way. *Torn Curtain* (1965) and *Frenzy* (1971) hardly employ transparencies at all, since Hitchcock's collaborators on those films (and the cameramen in particular) balked at using the technique.[6] In addition, the subject matter of both these "later" films has little to do with the turmoil evoked by transparencies, the one notable exception being Paul Newman and Julie Andrews's coach trip at the end of the film. Their escape has something of a nightmare quality, and the landscape that unfolds through the transparency contributes to that atmosphere. As for *Frenzy,* the English landscape is less about dreams than it is about absolute, materialistic and visceral realism – at times almost scatological, as exemplified by the body amidst the sacks of potatoes.

The Creation and Importance of Hitchcock's Transparencies

Going back to the 1930s, a year before *Young and Innocent* was produced, *Sabotage* (1936) provides crucial

[6] "Burks left us in the lurch when we were shooting *Torn Curtain* because Hitch persisted in using that particular special effect. He was fed up with rear projection and stuff like that. And Hitch didn't even want Bob to go to Germany and shoot the background negatives." Interview with Albert Whitlock, *Cahiers du cinéma,* No. 337 (June 1982), p. 46. (Free translation.)

insight into the essential nature of transparencies in Hitchcock's work. This film really marks the starting point of the director's extensive use of this technique.

From *Blackmail* (1929), his first sound film, to *Sabotage,* Hitchcock's production style evolved considerably. *Blackmail* is based on the unseen, on a mystery that no illusion-creating machine can resolve. Behind a completely opaque curtain – the counterpart to the matte yet translucent one in *Psycho* – a murder is committed. Throughout the film, Anny Ondra is haunted by the portrait of a clown; she finally claws its mocking, hideous face in an outburst of rage. The opacity conveyed at every level of the stage direction is countered by a vertical perspective, an abyss-like portrayal of the environment revealed through truly masterful cinematography: the shot of the long and unusual ascent to the painter's loft, and the vertiginous fall in the stairwell after the murder. *Blackmail* uses real urban scenes, with a few, fleeting transparencies. Mostly, it is a world based on rock-solid, tangible elements. Ondra's attack on the clownish caricature brings this sharply into focus, as though her action summarized the theme of the whole film: the search for proof as a metaphor for generalized confirmation that reality really does exist. And this, in fact – much more than any narrative strategy deferring the solution to a mystery – lies at the very root of Hitchcock's suspense.

Murder! (1930) makes spectacular use of transparencies in the final scene. The criminal trapeze artist, whose sexual ambiguity is overstated by a befeathered costume worthy of a cabaret dancer, commits suicide high above the ring in the circus tent. The camera moves in for a close-up of his face and outstretched arms, supposedly gripping the trapeze bar beyond our view. In reality, it is the image flying past behind him that creates the impression of movement; the actor was probably motionless in the studio. I do not believe that this scene represents a different kind of special effect, called a *matte shot*, which combines parts from two separate images on the same film. This is the first time Hitchcock used a transparency to convey something other than the impression of movement relative to a motionless body or object. In this scene, the character's unease, his fear and fatal confusion, are heightened by the world improbably passing by beneath him. This world is rendered even more unreal by the appearance of two immobile faces, "superimposed" upon the circus background as it spins in front of the trapeze artist's fainting eyes.

This sequence of shots employing transparencies, appearing unexpectedly at the end of the film, causes an abrupt break with the rest of the film's visual reality, a distortion of the connections between fictitious character and viewer that had been established over the previous 80 minutes. Is it coincidental that this same film's protagonist, as he reflects on the relationship between real life and art, should evoke the ideas of Schlegel's Louise? Or is it coincidental that he should shave to the notes of the prelude to *Tristan und Isolde,* or that the film's conclusion should attempt to portray a character's soul in an operatic grand finale? Hitchcock's use of transparencies in *Murder!* is more reflective of his German influences than was the expressionism found in his first silent films.

The Lady Vanishes, 1938

The Skin Game (1930) seems to favour painted backdrops to create the illusion of natural or urban space. In a somewhat hallucinatory shot (which prefigures the studio installations of Syberberg's *Hitler,* 1977), the heroine gallops off on horseback toward the far side of an immense clearing, surrounded by enormous trees painted on a gigantic piece of canvas. Several minutes later, a sports car – driving carefully through the delicate studio scenery – pulls up outside a château, depicted as naïvely as one of Magritte's nocturnal creations.

Could *Number Seventeen* (1931) be Hitchcock's final expressionist manifesto, a sort of farewell to this long-standing influence, which delayed for another three years his return to the systematic use of transparencies in *The Thirty-nine Steps* (1935)? *Number Seventeen* creates a world of stairs, models, toys and shadows that seem to break free from the objects that cast them. Lang, Murnau and Dreyer look as though they have been robbed. Most of the story takes place in stairwells, which provide a vertical frame of reference for the threatened ascent, the breathtaking fall, providentially cut short by an array of ropes. Transparencies are of little use with such deep perspectives. The geometrical shadows of rungs and banisters cast on the walls seem to imprison everyone, irrespective of their apparent innocence or guilt. The race involving the car and the train is a confrontation between two monsters, reduced to the level of toys; in addition to their customary role, the special effects were specifically designed to accentuate this childlike view of the world.

Herbert Marshall in Murder!, 1930

If *Rich and Strange* (1932), *Waltzes from Vienna* (1933) and *The Man Who Knew Too Much* (1934) also have little recourse to transparencies, *The Thirty-nine Steps* makes

The Skin Game, 1931

full – albeit somewhat reticent – use of the technique's illusory properties. Six years before Joan Fontaine in *Suspicion,* Madeleine Carroll encounters her travelling companion (behind her glasses) in a train compartment. There is more "real" scenery in this film, although the landscape seen through the train windows is a transparency. In fact, this film contains the first of many train scenes providing "canned" vistas.

In *Secret Agent* (1935), Hitchcock pioneered a new technique that I have not observed in the work of any other director: the use of a transparency to follow a dancing couple and isolate them from the other dancers on the floor. In *Saboteur,* this same technique is used more brilliantly and effectively, but in *Secret Agent* it still seems at the experimental stage. John Gielgud and Madeleine Carroll have just begun dancing at a reception when, suddenly, a cut makes it appear as if their faces and upper bodies are moving independently from the blurred background. Because the lack of focus is unrelated to depth of field, the projected image is easily spotted. In *Saboteur,* in a comparable narrative situation, Hitchcock uses a transparency to great dramatic effect. Robert Cummings and Priscilla Lane decide to have a discreet tête-à-tête at a reception riddled with spies. The transparency that suddenly appears isolates them, spirits them away from the surrounding action and characters. This cinematic sleight-of-hand lends the situation an air of enchantment and, assisted by the tender words Cummings murmurs to his partner ("This moment belongs to me"), speaks to the viewer's subconscious. Masterfully and deliberately, Hitchcock uses the technique to clearly outline the main characters – as light draws objects out of obscurity – while the extras remain out of focus. This scene is a perfect example of the dramatic, poetic and visual power of Hitchcock's transparencies, especially during this part of the 1940s, which constitutes his first classic period.[7]

Saboteur ends with a scene that is a *comment* on transparencies' ability to be both a production technique and a forum where illusion and reality confront one another. During the final chase scene to the top of the Statue of Liberty, the saboteur tries to hide out in a projection room. As he enters, with the police in hot pursuit, he is silhouetted against the film being shown on the screen behind him. To the people watching the film, and to us, the viewers, he becomes an actor moving in front of a transparency. The saboteur shoots at the audience who, for a split second, cannot differentiate between reality and re-enactment.

[7] Refer to the division of Hitchcock's oeuvre into periods, below.

This is one of the most accomplished moments in the director's oeuvre, revealing incredible insight into cinematic theory.

Six years earlier, in *Sabotage,* Hitchcock had already created a comparable scene. A police officer, accompanied by the young boy who will subsequently be killed by a bomb, infiltrates the Verloc household to try and learn more about the husband's secret activities. One evening, he slips behind the screen of the movie theatre where Sylvia Sidney works. As the two actors pass behind the screen, the results are twofold. The viewers witness a truly amazing oneiric vision, and the characters spying on the spies are drawn into a dreamlike sequence of role reversal: that single act *exposes* both the film and the spies. (In the same film, Verloc the saboteur meets his superior in a room filled with aquaria. It is quite a treat to watch the spies hatch their plans against a backdrop of translucent water. This is also the source of Verloc's apocalyptic vision of the city collapsing under the weight of terrorist bombings.)

As stated previously, I believe *Young and Innocent* to contain one of Hitchcock's most astonishing uses of transparencies, for this is where the director starts to use the technique to convey psychological and emotional insights into his characters. A car trip frequently provides the context. In this film, Nova Pilbeam and Derrick de Marney are involved in a lengthy escape sequence in a car. The convertible and the two people inside it stand out against a background of landscape shots. The halting progression of the background makes it completely impossible to believe that Nova Pilbeam is actually driving. However, the goal of this famous sequence was to hypnotize viewers and, as far as possible, draw them into the adventure of these two young innocents.

At the end of the trip, our two heroes finally find the old tramp who will exculpate them. Hitchcock probably set up a treadmill (or possibly the actors are exceptional mimes) and filmed the characters from behind as they ran toward a background created using a transparency and that appeared to be advancing to meet them. This technique, reinforced elsewhere by the presence of toys in the establishing shots on the train and in the car, transports the action to a make-believe children's world, a world we know Nova Pilbeam was well acquainted with, given her large number of siblings. This breathless pursuit ends when the car goes off the road into the open pit of an abandoned mine. The fall abruptly shatters the illusion and

Nova Pilbeam, Derrick de Marney and Edward Rigby in Young and Innocent, 1938

contradicts the transparency effects; as the car plunges into a world with "real" scenery, it looks as though the illusion – which, although exaggerated, has been used to great effect by the director – has engulfed the actors. This alternation between the transparencies' featureless illusion and the car's emergence into the scenery is resolved in the final scene, now considered legendary. The camera tracks across the real world (which requires no transparency to give it depth) in a single, grandiose shot that connects the foreground to the background, ending on a close-up of the criminal's heavily made-up, twitching eyes. At the end of this masterful piece of mise en scène, the character's nervous tic mirrors the viewer's own uncertainty about the reality of the world he sees.

This final sequence, which has become a sort of emblem of Hitchcock's bravura directing style, leads into another significant component of that style – a style that many critics agree to call "classic."

A "Periodical" Oeuvre

It is exceptionally easy to divide Hitchcock's oeuvre into periods, since he admirably covers all the periods in the history of cinema. Between 1925 and 1928, he directed eight silent films influenced by German expressionism (e.g., *The Lodger*, 1926), the Hollywood exoticism of that decade (*The Pleasure Garden*, 1925) and the experiments with form prevalent during those same years (*The Ring*, 1927). In some ways, this period could be considered his "primitive" one. In it, we see early versions of the themes he would later develop more fully: the double, places of entertainment as crime scenes, and women typecast as a kind of Ophelia figure. The years between *Blackmail* (1929) and *Jamaica Inn* (1938) could be classified as the first classic period, the period of the British sound films, characterized by bold alternations between two kinds of space: the "real" space actually inhabited by the actors, and the illusory space systematically created through transparencies. The tension between the two culminates in the final scene of *Young and Innocent*, where the camera alternately captures actual space – both close up and far off – and an artificial representation of infinite space projected behind the actors.

On the set of Young and Innocent, 1938

During his British period, Hitchcock excelled at dizzying, dazzling shifts from long shots to close-ups, from viewing characters in a variety of locations (often via transparencies) to focussing fetishistically on certain parts of the body (e.g., Madeleine Carroll's legs in *The Thirty-nine Steps*).

Paradoxically, during this period, Hitchcock emphasized *cohesion* and *plausibility* in his films, as well as the distinctive *ethos* of each (this was how Eugène Souriau defined classical painting), setting these characteristics up in opposition to the immoderate proportions and pathos of transparencies. *The Thirty-nine Steps, Secret Agent, Sabotage, Young and Innocent* and *The Lady Vanishes* are unqualified masterpieces of balance between these two extremes. Hitchcock's art consists in thrusting us into an implausible world, only to pull us back through such minute attention to detail that the most insignificant events are infused with a second and more accurate realism.[8]

Rebecca is the turning point that, from a number of perspectives, links not only Hitchcock's British and American periods, but also his first and second classic periods. In the latter period, which continued until the production of *Strangers on a Train* (1950), Hitchcock's classicism becomes subtly tinged with oneiric elements that imbue his art with a disturbing otherness, to which the transparencies (as found in the following films) contribute in no small degree: *Suspicion* (1941), *Saboteur* (1942), *Shadow of a Doubt* (1942), *Spellbound* (1944), *Notorious* (1945) and *Strangers on a Train* (1950). Before she came to embody Rossellini's concept of modernity, Ingrid Bergman was the inspiration for these distinctive (Hitchcockian) traits.

The subsequent period could be categorized as Hitchcock's "modern" period. The narrative seduction of *I Confess* (1952), *Dial M for Murder* (1953), *Rear Window* (1953), *The Trouble with Harry* (1954) and *The Wrong Man* (1956) does not prevent their subject matter from being clearly stated. This attention to *what the film is trying to say,* as opposed to *what the film is about,* is one aspect of the film's "modernity." In this light, *The Wrong Man* could be seen today as a sort of delayed echo, coming five years later, of *Europe 51* and of its heroine's final withdrawal – whereas, in real life, Bergman had been living in Italy for quite some time. In these films, transparencies all but disappear, or are concealed, as mentioned earlier.

Two shots from the movie theatre scene (Saboteur), 1942

In my opinion, *Vertigo* (1957), *North by Northwest* (1958), *Psycho* (1959), *The Birds* (1962) and *Marnie* (1963) could all be grouped together to form a Mannerist period, characterized by iconographic and narrative repetition, distortion and anamorphoses, as well as by multiple identities and manipulation of time. Seen in this light, the plots are extremely intriguing: the female lead in *Vertigo* has a double; the main character in *North by Northwest* is a victim of

[8] Maurice Scherer, *Cahiers du cinéma,* No. 12, May 1952, p. 65.

mistaken identity, the female lead (and star) in *Psycho* is schizophrenically doubled and her early exit is worthy of Antonioni,[9] and Tippi Hedren is visibly transformed in *The Birds* and *Marnie*. The Symbolist arabesque here reached the height of its geometrical complexity, its elegance and its metaphysical ambitions. Saul Bass even created spiral-shaped logos based on it. Transparencies are used to maximum poetic effect, and the filmed universe is presented as a daydream.

The final, or "mature," period is the hardest to classify; it seems to lie somewhere between "Mannerism" and a certain academicism. The director's attempts at coming to terms with British culture (as exemplified by *Frenzy,* 1971) resulted in a period that, even today, is not fully understood. I am aware that my proposed "genealogy" of Hitchcock's oeuvre – the division of his works into the commonly accepted periods of art history – is somewhat forced, but the evidence in favour of my hypothesis is too strong not to advance it. Also, it may lead to a clearer perception of the evolution both within and of Hitchcock's oeuvre, and the role transparencies play in it.

The Semantics of Transparencies

But let us return to the late 1930s.

After *Young and Innocent,* Hitchcock produced *The Lady Vanishes*. This is one of Hitchcock's great "railway films," in which both subject and storyline are defined by transparencies. Miss Froy writes her name in the condensation on the train window, and then she is gone, sucked into the eddies of the soap opera–like narrative. The train rolls on through an illusory landscape. A tea label – visible proof that the vanished woman really did exist – sticks by chance to the windows separating the actors. In *Orpheus* (1951), Cocteau uses a glazier to metaphorically identify the device itself; similarly, Hitchcock gives greater emphasis to his favourite special effect by exploring its various semantic meanings: the literal and generally accepted sense of transparency, and the cinematographic sense.

A few years later, Hitchcock imported a considerable part of his "Britishness" to Hollywood. An aura of Victorian romanticism dominates *Rebecca* from the outset, and the visit to the ruined estate of Manderley affords a vision worthy of Böcklin or Hugo. This film, together with *Shadow of a Doubt,* is incontestably closest to Orson Welles' worldview. As we stand at the gates to Manderley, it is hard not to think

[9] This was one of then-scandalous narrative paradigms of *L'avventura* (1960).

of the "No Trespassing" signs posted at Charles Foster Kane's Xanadu. Also, Joseph Cotten's character in *Shadow of a Doubt* is strongly evocative of Welles's *The Stranger*.

In *Rebecca,* transparency in the material sense and transparency in the sense of cinematic special effect complement each other. For instance, Mrs. Danvers (Judith Anderson) disappears in a sheet of flame after having terrorized Joan Fontaine with her disquieting appearances from behind translucent curtains, yet this film also contains the first of Hitchcock's great seduction scenes to rely heavily on the powerful effects of transparency. As Max (Laurence Olivier) and Rebecca stroll through the pinewood by the sea, Hitchcock alternates between landscape shots (perhaps recreated in the studio) and scenes filmed in front of a transparency. In effect, the viewer is a witness to Olivier's thoughts, as they move between the previous Rebecca de Winter to the current "Joan Fontaine de Winter." This creates a wonderful, oscillating visual contrast between figures conjured up from the past and those existing in the present, and prefigures the analytical fluctuations of *Spellbound* (1944).

May Whitty and Margaret Lockwood in The Lady Vanishes, *1938*

Transparencies as the "Visual Unconscious"

In *Spellbound,* Gregory Peck, haunted by the guilt of having accidentally killed his brother, pretends to be a psychiatrist. Aside from a certain "psychoanalytic naïveté," which Hitchcock shares in this instance with other contemporary Hollywood directors, the film has a remarkable symbolic cohesion, due mainly to the director's use of transparencies. The ski scene, involving an enormous amount of technical intervention, verges on the ridiculous; we cannot help but laugh at the close-up shots of the actors' faces as they stand in the studio, bending and twisting in comical imitation of the actual movements.

The presence of white, snow-covered mountains conjures up what has been termed, in other contexts, the crystal-clear (!) mountain air. The images of immaculate slopes provide the resolution of Ingrid Bergman's laborious and darkly labyrinthine struggle to uncover Gregory Peck's secret. The snow here is another *tabula rasa* sullied by parallel ski tracks – tracks that lead to the spiked fence, buried deep in Peck's subconscious, on which his brother met his death as a child. The brilliant whiteness of the screen is also a strong presence here, prefiguring the red flashes in *Marnie*. Finally, the large expanses of white are like blank sheets of paper on which the author must write an ending to the story, thus resolving the mystery.

The space crisscrossed by the actors – bearing in mind Peck's phobia of stripes (forks, pieces of material, almost anything distresses him) associated with his repressed memories – this snow-covered expanse is literally identified with memory, which in turn becomes the "screen" on which repressed events are replayed. The snowy landscape rear-projected behind the actors gives the impression of an interminable descent into an abyss – according to Symbolist theory, somewhat akin to the journey a person makes into the depths of his soul. The skiers' forward motion is equated with the backward movement of memory toward the instance of repression. Such naïve inverse symbolism may appear laughable but, strangely enough, I feel it is precisely the overtly obvious and exaggerated use of the technique, and its emphatic, declarative function, that renders the sequence acceptable and makes the film beautifully, paradoxically, true. In *Spellbound,* the technique revealingly points to the traditional place occupied by the psychoanalyst, who sits, silently "back-projected," behind the supine patient.

This is doubtless why even the most strait-laced psychoanalysts were ultimately obliged to take Hitchcock seriously: they saw their position metaphorically reflected in the mise en scène.

The Layered Effect of Transparencies

Given that transparency works in both abstract and concrete terms, we can understand why it is the only technique that seeks to draw attention to itself, while simultaneously being accepted for what it is there to replace; namely, reality. It is also easy to understand the multiple associations linking the device to the portrayal of the unconscious, as well as why Hitchcock's work, halfway between reality and dreams, resorts to it so frequently. In his films, the transparencies reminds us that the screen is like the surface of an eyelid, which must be rubbed to ascertain that the world we see reproduced is, in fact, real; or, rather, the screen could be seen as a page on which *images are inscribed*. In this context, cinema is like an imprint of reality, a flat mould, a *bottomless abyss,* as Jacques Derrida has said.

Transparencies could be seen as a kind of duplication within the film itself, a symmetry of pictured pictures, the junction of two surfaces that, as they slide past each other, create a *conceptual* space in which the characters move and act. Therein, indeed, lies the inimitable nature of this technique: it creates a conceptual space that is entirely visual and hence intangible. However, this same space metaphorically points to an image that is, if not visceral, at least epidermal (possibly indicated by skin tones) and thus connected to our sense of touch.

This sense of layering, of "optical epidermis," is conveyed strongly in the final scene of *Shadow of a Doubt.* After Joseph Cotten and Teresa Wright's fight – which has overtones of the intense, passionate murderous embraces depicted by Rodin or Von Stück – Cotten is pushed off the train and onto the tracks just as a train appears, coming from the opposite direction. To the viewer's astonishment, he appears to fall out of the picture and dissolve into the intensified "grain" of the oncoming train, which is a transparency. But there is another sense in which Cotten's body seems to disappear between two superimposed images. This ephemeral composite leads us to the fullest realization of the phenomenon, as described by Panofsky, of the *postposition* of levels within the created illusion. Indisputably, *Shadow of a Doubt* is a pivotal film in which we see the greatest number of exclusively Hitchcockian visual elements, as well as a significant number of themes used in subsequent films, such as doubles, creepy stairwells in upper-middle-class homes, connections between food and dead bodies, women seen from behind, close-ups of objects that break up the depth of field that would normally be apparent, extremes of size, transitions from the widest long shots to the tightest close-ups, and so on.

May Whitty and Margaret Lockwood in The Lady Vanishes, 1938

In the latter context, Hitchcock's films are notable for the ways they undercut the effects of his obsessive use of transparencies. In *Shadow of a Doubt,* the brilliant opening sequence cuts from the establishing shots of the city to reveal Cotten, lying on his back in his room. This is comparable to any number of famous sequences: the initial one in *Psycho* (which also ends in a room, where we see Janet Leigh entwined with her lover); the high-angle tracking shot in *Notorious* that ends on Ingrid Bergman's hand clutching the key to the basement; the one in *Frenzy* in which the camera, after an aerial shot of the Thames, "falls" onto the face of a politician earnestly talking about urban ecological disasters. Although there are many others, the final comparison I will give here is the opening sequence in *Rope,* where the camera appears to draw back, taking us suddenly from an establishing, low-angle shot of the street to a medium close-up of a bay window with drawn curtains. These examples should illustrate the passionate aesthetic tension that pervades Hitchcock's work: a tension between establishing a space with actual dimensions via different camera angles, and his inclination toward illusion.

Hence the difficulty afforded André Bazin, who felt that film's primary ontological goal was to record reality rather than compose an image or reconfigure another reality.

Hence also the realization that the path from François Truffaut, Bazin's disciple, to Hitchcock is not as direct as we believe it to be today. Jean Cocteau, Truffaut's other mentor, used camera trickery to immense poetic effect. There is no doubt in my mind that it was Cocteau who introduced the director of *Fahrenheit 451* (1966) to the Hitchcock aesthetic, just as his book of interviews with the director of *The Birds* was almost finished.[10] What I would like to emphasize here, however, is the tension between two opposing states that sustains the work of the major figures in the first century of cinema, first Hitchcock, then Murnau, Welles and, today, Godard: their films swing between an openness to reality and a vision of the world that stipulates "laws concerning the world around us, and creates a model based on ourselves."[11]

Gregory Peck and Ingrid Bergman in Spellbound, 1945

Transparencies as a Form of Romantic Representation

The "troubled" world Hitchcock creates through his use of transparencies appears to the viewer as a series of strata: nature is falling apart, and confidence in its unity is being eroded. Occasionally, the space thus created falls into parallel, disconnected layers. I am always amazed by the extraordinary scene of the sinking plane at the end of *Foreign Correspondent* (1940). Was it shot in the studio, with a tank substituting for the ocean? Or are the survivors, crouched on the wing of the plane in the foreground, being shot against a transparency of turbulent water? I find this to be one of Hitchcock's most sublime, romantic sequences. The viewer is deprived of visual reference points, for there is no intermediate shot to connect the foreground (the slowly sinking plane) with the background (the majestic waves). The cinematography reminds me of one of Caspar David Friedrich's more "experimental" works entitled *Riesengebirge Landscape*,[12] in which one's gaze travels directly from the foreground to the background of the painting. In Friedrich's composition, the eye is drawn to the horizon,[13] just as it is in the shot from the film, where it is irresistibly attracted by the heaving swell at the back of the image. An actual spatial hia-

[10] A full discussion of the interrelatedness of Bazin, Hitchcock, Truffaut and Cocteau exceeds the mandate of this essay. I will subsequently undertake a full examination, to be printed elsewhere.
[11] Schlegel, p. 57. (Free translation.)
[12] About 1830, Kunsthalle, Hamburg.
[13] According to a description of the painting by Elysabeth Decultot in *Peindre le paysage* (Paris: Du Lérot éditeur, 1996).

tus emerges between the realistic details and the overall unreality of the scene. Indeed, the contrast between the two quite possibly defines romantic painting as celebrated and analysed by Schlegel, and also recalls the above-quoted remark made by Maurice Scherer (the real name of Éric Rohmer, who was a great admirer of Murnau).

Scenery as Analogy for the Soul

Having looked at the role of transparency in a cinematic image, and discussed its effects on perspective, we have seen that, paradoxically, it both blocks our view and extends it through illusion.

In *Suspicion* (1941), transparencies are used in the final sequence to convey the characters' irredeemable ambivalence. From the very outset of the film, Cary Grant has behaved like a Don Juan; the upper-middle-class Joan Fontaine suspects him of trying to poison her. We know that Hitchcock had wanted to give the film a more shocking ending but that, for a variety of reasons, he chose to end it on a happy note. All the same…

Caspar David Friedrich, *Landscape in the Riesengebirge,* about 1823

As the car drives at high speed along the base of the cliffs, the rocky walls are seen as a transparency behind it. Grant's face is sombre, impassive; Fontaine looks terror-stricken, as she reflects on her companion's possible murderous intentions. The uneven road is close and, since it is a transparency, simultaneously far away. The film's closing sequence ends with a kind gesture, as Grant grabs hold of Fontaine to prevent her from falling out of the open car door. Calm is restored at every level: feelings, action, music, the story told by the film. "Now it's my turn to take care of you," says Fontaine, but Grant refuses to become involved with her again. As the two get back into the car, the viewer cannot help but conclude that they will go their separate ways. The camera provides a rear view of the two actors, sitting side by side in the car, with Grant's arm lying gently across Fontaine's shoulders. At that point, we conclude that the couple will overcome their suspicions, although Grant's embrace does contain a faint hint of a stranglehold. In the final long shot, we see the car driving away toward a vast landscape dotted with enormous trees and clouds. These objects are not, in fact, created via a transparency, but are painted on a gigantic studio backdrop. They seem stiff, frozen in the sort of stereotypical representation seen in bad paintings on the walls of public buildings. This terrifying portrayal of reality *troubles* the couple's newfound unity and makes the viewer doubt their future happiness.

The setting for this final sequence is, in some respects, the exact opposite of a transparency: the canvas backdrop is opaque; the artificial reality it recreates is immobile. It is a manufactured setting, however, with a function similar to that of a transparency. Through its portrayal of something akin to what Schiller called *Seelenlandschaft* (or, scenery as analogy for the soul), it illustrates Hitchcock's aesthetic preference for constructed sets; transparencies make a similar connection between landscape and the soul.

In *Marnie* (1963) Hitchcock uses a comparable organizational principle to end the film: after working through the origins of her maternal repression, Marnie leaves her childhood home apparently "cured." At that moment, our eye is caught by a strange motility at the end of an alleyway and some astonishing, almost imperceptible, surface movement. What we are actually seeing is a picture of a harbour (the source of Marnie's prostitute mother's customers), painted on an immense studio backdrop. Raphaël Delorme's painting entitled *Woman and Steamship* (1928), shown in this exhibition, recalls the disturbing strangeness produced by this "theatrical faux pas," which calls Marnie's recovery and the happy ending into question and confirms the "unresolved nature" of her repression.[14]

Hitchcock clearly believed that reality was intrinsically opaque, and this strongly held belief is exemplified by the visual limitations of the fake décor. This statement leads us to a discussion of *The Wrong Man* (1956), which is fanatical in its examination of the themes of opacity and visual limitations. I have always been mesmerized by a detail that, although insignificant, clearly must have obsessed Hitchcock. Henry Fonda is taken to a number of stores where the owners have been attacked and robbed, in order to be identified as the perpetrator. He is driven there in a police car, through whose windows we see a maze of city streets created using transparencies. After this *via dolorosa,* during the first cross-examination scene, Fonda – wrongfully accused – sits with his back against a wall in which there is a strange crack. Regardless of the changes in framing or camera angle during the cross-examination, this stain, this disintegration, this blot on the wall points inescapably to the imperfect nature of our world. Belief in Fonda's innocence is fatally undermined by this detail, which is echoed later in the film by the mirror, broken in the throes of Vera Miles's madness.

If Hitchcock's illusory world, in front of which the actors play their parts, is troubled by the transparencies, the

[14] The hunt sequence and Tippi Hedren's horseback ride with Sean Connery are reminiscent of the ski sequence in *Spellbound*: in both films, the actors' physical gestures are grossly exaggerated, and the dialogue more suited to an analyst's couch.

painted or imperfect backgrounds have an equally troubling effect. The wall's torn epidermis in *The Wrong Man* is yet further evidence of Hitchcock's layered reality.

The other film that deals with visual limitations, with the impenetrable nature of reality, is obviously *Rear Window* (1954). There are few transparencies in this film, since the subject and the scenery are one and the same: a closely watched façade that necessarily requires no special effects.[15] The film plays on the themes of sight and perspective, voyeurism and mise en scène. This is perhaps the film in which Hitchcock asks (himself) the most hard-hitting creative questions about the distinction between everyday vision and artistic vision; that is, how artists organize the world through their art.

The final scene of Marnie, 1964

Transparencies as Entertainment

In the preceding film, *Dial M for Murder* (1953), transparencies are evident throughout, and particularly so in the window shots where the commissioner is watching the street. Like *Rear Window, Dial M for Murder* is a sort of *Kammerspiel,* in which the action takes place entirely in the same location, whence the characters look out over the city. (Hitchcock often developed a theme or a special scenic effect over two – or sometimes more – films. *The Birds* and *Marnie,* for instance, are indelibly linked, through the images of winged destruction associated with Tippi Hedren.)

In *Dial M for Murder,* the transparencies are barely noticeable. Only after careful observation does it become clear that the street where Grace Kelly and Ray Milland are walking does not inhabit the same space as the apartment. It (the image of the two actors in the street) is a transparency, marked by the slight trembling of the fence that separates the building from the street, as well as by small differences in grain and colouring. What if Hitchcock had filmed Kelly and Milland in the studio, from the window of an apartment? Would that have affected the action or the plot? I believe it would have, for although the viewer is probably unaware of the technique, he may perhaps perceive it at an unconscious level. The characters, whose movements are *projected* in the background, *troubled* in appearance and aspect, are themselves filled with doubt and uncertainty. Their conversation deals with a misunderstanding involving keys surreptitiously taken and substituted for others. In real time, we watch as they are baffled, change their minds, become resigned and suppress the

[15] The windows on the opposite wall could be seen as small, separate screens in front of which the main characters stand out ... transparently.

voice of conscience. The director's reliance on a transparency in this scene definitely reflects the characters' mental state, but its implications go beyond the psychologically significant to include the aesthetically complex. The commissioner in the film is watching a spectacle in the topographical as well as the narrative sense. Within the film, he also is watching the drama unfold; as the suspects' stories become confused, he is literally dissecting them on a screen. In *Dial M for Murder,* the dramatic necessity of the transparencies is dazzling, their effectiveness significantly unfathomable.

Stage Fright (1949) is probably the only other film in which Hitchcock had used transparencies in such an intrinsic way. The film's opening sequence is unforgettable: Richard Todd and Jane Wyman are (once again) driving along a road. Todd tells his companion that he is "on the run" and asks for her help. The scene is shot from the front of the car's hood while the landscape rushes by behind the actors' backs in an extravagantly implausible way. The technique is patently obvious, and constitutes a premonition of what the rest of the film tries to disguise as long as possible: namely, Todd's falsehood. In fact, the entire film swings between truth and lies, between a portrayal of reality and the emotions portrayed therein, between theatre and life. In many respects, of all of Hitchcock's films, this is the one most reminiscent of Jean Renoir. Incomparably, transparencies resonate at every semantic level in *Stage Fright,* sounding the interconnections between theatre and life with the image of Marlene Dietrich's partially veiled face, clouded by the knowledge of her own duplicity.

Ray Milland in Dial M for Murder, 1954

Donald Spoto commented that Hitchcock often set his romantic scenes in automobiles, and that this was one of the factors that encouraged his use of transparencies. But *Notorious, North by Northwest* and *Family Plot* (1975), for instance, show scenes that go beyond passion and literally intoxicate the viewer, drawing him into recklessness. In *North by Northwest,* Grant, drunk from the bourbon he has been forced to drink, drives madly down a steep road. In *Family Plot,* Bruce Dern loses control of his car because the brakes have been tampered with. In both cases, the landscape behind the actors dissolves in a maelstrom that has no relation to the speeding cars. Disconnected from the actors' movements behind the wheel, the transparencies swirl behind them and draw the viewer, visually, into the centre of a vertiginous spiral. Of course, the effect is not accidental. Placing the viewer at the centre of a spiralling world is a delightful challenge for this showman, this fun-fair enthusiast. Hitchcock had this to say regarding the final scene of *Strangers on a Train*: "This was a most complicated sequence. For rear projection shooting there was a screen and behind it an enormous projector throwing an image on the screen. On the studio floor there was a narrow white line in line with the projector lens and the lens of the camera had to be right on that white line. The camera was not photographing the screen and what was on it, it was photographing the light in certain colours; therefore the camera lens had to be level and in line with the projector lens. Many of the shots on the merry-go-round were low camera setups. Therefore you can imagine the problem. The projector had to be put up on a high platform, pointing down, and the screen had to be exactly at right angles to the level-line from the lens. All the shots took nearly half a day to line up for each setup. We had to change the projector every time the angle changed."[16]

Jane Wyman and Richard Todd in Stage Fright, 1950

Spoto remarked: "The final effect of this sequence is terrifyingly vivid."

The characters in the foreground struggle to throw one another off the merry-go-round platform. As they roll around, it looks as though the horses' hooves might crush them. The exaggerated artifice of transparency reduces the world to a stage set made of toys, and the entire film becomes a sort of ghost train.

North by Northwest, 1959

The Ultimate Transparency: Full Circle Back to Painting

I have not said much about *Notorious,* where transparencies are used to simulate, among other things, the swerves of a drunken Ingrid Bergman behind the wheel. In this film, Hitchcock takes the art of the transparency to new heights. During her drive, presumably at dusk, Hitchcock fashions a veritable visual labyrinth in the far recesses of the image containing one of his most elegant "layered shots." The actors are shot from behind. Through the windscreen, the rear-projected scenery seems to rush toward the car. (In the studio, the parked car was shaken by prop men to simulate the effect of a bumpy road.) A police motorcycle appears in the rearview mirror. This is one of Hitchcock's most strikingly layered images, thanks to the Chinese box effect created by progressively larger, framed objects (a precursor of the façade in *Rear Window*). The frames (windshield, rearview mirror and screen outline) conform to the three criteria mentioned in Panofsky's quote at the beginning of this essay: simultaneity, juxtaposition and postposition. The viewer cannot help but won-

[16] Donald Spoto, *The Dark Side of Genius: The Life of Alfred Hitchcock* (New York: Ballantine Books, 1993), p. 347–48.

der about the actors' apparent location. Where are they, exactly? Between which strata of the image? Such questions are bound to affect the viewer's suspension of disbelief and, given the compressed perspective in this scene, the story's credibility necessarily suffers. However, Hitchcock's use of transparency does help us grasp the nature of the relationship between Grant and Bergman: a deep and uncontrollable passion, destroyed by a political order (represented by the police) that forces them to feign indifference. This car sequence leaves no doubt as to what the stakes in that relationship will be, and the famous balcony kiss scene merely confirms the premonition. The balcony where Grant and Bergman embrace, before redefining the terms of their contract and their mission, overlooks an ocean bay; the telltale iridescence of the balcony railings reveals that the view has been created with a transparency. Grant's refusal to continue the relationship causes Bergman to return to the bottle. When Grant surprises her in this alcohol-induced stupor, her face is slightly grainy and out of focus behind a light veil, as though her image were projected onto the back of this translucent piece of material. Such moments are surely not accidental. Great artists have always experimented with the tools of their trade. Hitchcock often used the transparent properties of certain materials to either blur the outlines of objects or bring them into focus. I have always felt that this preoccupation was in some way connected to his use of transparencies.

The inability to ascertain which space the actors inhabit confers an increasing sense of otherness on the mise en scène, and this impression is at its strongest in *The Birds* (1962). In the sequence of the children running from the school, under attack by the crows, Hitchcock achieved one of his most spectacular oneiric creations. The nightmare is at its most frightening, worse than anything in Dalí's surrealist bric-a-brac. The faces of Tippi Hedren and the schoolchildren are filmed in close-up. Although we can't see their bodies, they are presumably running on the spot to simulate flight. The nearby background of houses and fences is obviously a transparency behind them. Then, mechanical birds swoop down on the heads and shoulders of the children. But, strangely enough, there is hardly any attempt at verisimilitude. The birds are barely recognizable as such, as they dart in all directions, like lines slashing across the screen. They appear as shadows, quick brushstrokes, black, almost shapeless forms that momentarily obscure the characters' faces or pass behind them. Their omnipresence makes it impossible to know whether the birds are in a film being projected onto a translucent screen behind the actors, or part of a scene shot in the studio and subsequently superimposed on the master – a technique combining elements of animation and photography. This sequence represents one of the farthest points of deconstruction achieved by Hitchcock, and the landscape projected as a transparency represents a troubled background against which we see the tortured faces of people whose eyes constitute the ultimate targets.

Paradoxical and Innocent

Jacques Aumont

... was the man who, when it came time to thank his "agent," Lew Wasserman, could think of nothing better to offer as a parting gift – the epitome of luxury (DeLuxe-ury, if you will) and poor taste – than his own portrait as painted by Bernard Buffet. No doubt biographers too often retain only anecdotes, for lack of any discernible meaning to ascribe to them. But it remains that Hitchcock was not a painter: that the Klee and the De Chirico in his collection are to be understood as undeserved riches (in the case of the Klee, this was avowed; in that of the De Chirico, I am being presumptive). A pack rat – but for all that, according to companions-at-table and witnesses for the defence, the World's Greatest Host, never hesitant to spend on pleasures that he then shared – Hitch was anything but one's idea of a painter, of an artist. Godard was being ironic, seeking to shock, when, in chapter 4A of his *Histoire(s) du cinéma,* he dubbed Hitch *THE ARTIST*.

Let us say that Hitchcock was something of an informed art fan, who cared about value, acknowledgement and respectability. This art fan mattered to his films as much as, but no more than, the family man – responsible, faithful, making sure to act the clown in private to amuse his daughter, his wife and his friends. As for the images in his films, whenever they allude to the history of painting, Hitchcock reveals himself to be an academic. They are always too clean, too precise: the imagery in *Under Capricorn,* which was the darling of French critics, is sickly-sweet; the oneiric iconography of *Spellbound* does not help at all (even in Hollywood, the "ready-made" aspect of this type of dream did not go unnoticed: witness Donen and Kelly's satirical reworking of it in *Singin' in the Rain*); after that dalliance with Dalí, things are no better (e.g., the unbelievable backdrop of the fateful alleyway in *Marnie*); the canvases painted by his characters, on those unfortunate occasions when they happen to paint, are just as tacky – just as Place-du-Tertrian, to be precise – as all the other canvases of Hollywood fiction: massacres of Utrillo, at best a vague echo of Dufy (Minnelli's films contain some frightful examples of this). There is little difference between the works of the painter character in *The Trouble with Harry* and those of Joseph Cotten in *Portrait of Jennie*; between the portrait of Carlotta Valdés in *Vertigo* and Gene Kelly's paintings in *An American in Paris*. This is the opposite of Godard repainting, with a palette knife, a necessary Matisse or an approximate de Staël, quite prepared to sully his film in the manner of a child leaving inkstains on a smock. (Of course, I am not questioning that these Hollywood canvases function as perfectly appropriate narrative devices.)

The riddle of Hitchcock, then, is this: How could a filmmaker who lacked a compelling opinion about painting have demonstrated such a feel for imagery – if we accept that the cinema in general, during the years when Hitch was a master of the genre, had managed to fill, both in terms of the public imagination and of imagery, a void left by painting? To get at the answer – that there is indeed imagery, but not quite so directly pictorial imagery – we will have to take a circuitous route.

Close-up, Fetish, Clue

The nightmares in *Spellbound* and in *Vertigo* are truly nightmarish. Their iconography – a hodgepodge of found objects, surface surrealism, a surfeit of symbols – descends from the catch-all psychoanalytical clichés so prevalent in Hollywood from the late 1940s to the late 1950s. In a way, this represents the worst period of the Hitchcockian oeuvre (but not his worst films): that which exposes the boundaries of everything that made him fascinating – "control of the universe,"[1] and so on. In fact, this is his true "control of the universe" period, marked by an orgy of know-how, of craftsmanship, of surehandedness, of virtuosity – yet too gratuitous, something quite other than the childlike, innocent and fairly profound jubilation of the English adventure films or the euphoric despair of the great masterpieces that began with *Vertigo*.

At the same time, there is the datedness of all attempts at exegetic analysis of the dreamscapes and dizzying images in Hitchcock (no matter which school of thought, Paracelsian or Freudian, is summoned), whereby fairly unwieldy doctrines or theoretical suppositions are applied, and films such as *Spellbound, Rope,* even *Strangers on a Train* and *Under Capricorn* (each respectively superior to the first two) become flexible, complacent objects – because they are sufficiently dated in their use of these stylistic passages to achieve period effects (period furniture is usually fake).

For example, fetishism and the close-up: must a close-up give rise only to this agreed-upon idea? And what, exactly,

[1] "Contrôle de l'univers" is the title of the segment dealing with Alfred Hitchcock in Jean-Luc Godard's video and book series *Histoire(s) du Cinéma* (Paris: Gallimard/Gaumont; New York: ECM New Series, 1998).

can be fetishized? Just about anything: Marnie's purse, standing in during one shot for a vagina sewn up tighter than those in Buñuel; the key to the wine cellar in *Notorious* (the key to both alcohol- and drug-induced dreams and to Alicia Huberman's [Ingrid Bergman] chaste albeit paradoxical faithfulness); the Jívaro shrunken head in *Under Capricorn*; the tiny razor, a poor little penis, in *North by Northwest.* Anything can be "translated" if one relies on dictionaries, but the fetishist school of thought certainly leaves room for the Hitchcockian fascination with women's necks and silken hair, which hints at something deeper: something sensual and enigmatic (the living core of an image).

What matters in Hitchcock's films is not the close-up, nor is it the Object: rather, it is the indifference of the Object (or indifference *to* the Object, which could be literally anything), as long as it permits certain actions – a violent, sudden, arbitrary bringing-together, for instance. A superb example is seen in *Mr. and Mrs. Smith* (a not-so-Hitchcockian film, incidentally), with a shot that starts at the far end of the room and ends on Annie's (Carole Lombard) eye: a single, furious eye belonging to a face hidden under the sheets – not so much foreshadowing the close-up on Marion Crane's eye at the conclusion of the *Psycho* shower scene as analogous to Renoir's virtuoso tracking shots. And Hitchcock generally eschews the fetishist close-up (that of the avant-gardists), preferring a dynamics of close examination, of indexation – of delight in the Roving Eye (as occurs repeatedly in *Easy Virtue).*

Clement Greenberg wrote: "If the avant-garde imitates the processes of art, kitsch, we now see, imitates its effects." The Hitchcockian close-up is neither avant-garde nor kitsch. It does not aim to attract attention to itself as a composition, as a rhythm of light, as did the whole of the avant-garde tradition in photography, especially the German school, right up to Eisenstein, who inherited its lessons for the cinema. Nor does it seek to "be artistic" (photogenic), like Jean Epstein's close-ups. It does not ironically illustrate the devastating effects of light on an already ravaged face, as do those of Fassbinder. The Hitchcockian close-up is the time taken to pay visual attention to something – nothing more, nothing less. (A somewhat caricaturish demonstration is provided by the point-of-view shot of John Ballantine [Gregory Peck] drinking the glass of milk in *Spellbound*.) When Hitchcock was born, the Roving Eye was still a painterly eye. He was among those who rendered it irrevocably cinematic.

Hitchcock is not interested in graphical or plastic "formalism," either in his close-ups or in his most dizzying camera movements (e.g., the aerial crane shot that plunges all the way down to the key in the hollow of Alicia's hand in *Notorious,* or the expansive dolly shot that ends on the twitching eye of the murderous drummer man in *Young and Innocent,* rather than the somewhat telegraphed balletic movements of, say, *Rope* and *Under Capricorn*). Only rarely does he deliberately seek a kitsch effect: one example is the simulation of the sunset in *Rope,* for which a combination of lights, dimmers, kilowatts and carefully timed manipulations was used to create as artificial a result as possible. The relationship to objects is not formalist, then; it is something else – something quite simple that is merely the logical consequence of the decision to take a cinematic approach. Objects are what must be seen; to see them, it is necessary to move closer; to move closer means to see them in their fundamental Otherness – in other words, to transform them into something else: an inner world that is unexpected, fantastical, childlike, realist.

Symbolism

Some of Hitchcock's images are virtually inescapable, starting with his physical image, which he stubbornly and patiently manufactured, and wished to be identified with that of the *imagemaker* ("A filmmaker isn't supposed to say things. He's supposed to show them"; film is more than "photographs of people talking," etc.). His appearances in the teasers of the TV series *Alfred Hitchcock Presents* were emblematic: his silhouette became an empty image, a trademark, at a time when he was selling his name – just as often and for just as high a price – to help sell magazines (e.g., *Alfred Hitchcock Mystery Magazine*) or, potentially, anything at all. Every Hollywood actor who worked with him recalled the same powerful image – obese Buddha + careful Cockney diction + caustic, scatological wit – and his biographers could not fail to diagnose the phenomenon as overcompensation for an inferiority complex. Here was a flawless brand image, at a time when the laws of advertising were not yet fully mastered.

Hitchcock as imagemaker? Without a doubt, and the Godardian view is not that different from the preceding ones ("We've forgotten […] what […] Joel McCrea was going to do in Holland […] but we remember […] the sails of a windmill ," etc.). At once true and false, like all the images of Hitch that were his trademark. Where do the images come from? From painting, and its history? Certainly – on condition that we do not confound the movement of profound re-entry with the froth of time, or coincidences with contingencies. Unconscious obsessions? Unquestionably – but since these

Leon M. Lion and John Stuart in Number Seventeen, 1932

obsessions are apprehended solely through their images, and rightfully so, we know nothing about them (unless we are to believe, as in *Spellbound,* that a group of parallel lines on a white background can be traced back to some repressed "archetypal scene" – that of the London police station playing, biographically, the role of permanent MacGuffin).

The films and their exegeses are superimposed, inextricable – piles of "Freudian" clichés that necessarily miss all targets (in *Number Seventeen,* because the detective is blind, are we to conclude that he has an Oedipus complex?). This is something a little different from a painter of canvases (even if I can easily accept how one can discover, or theorize, that he extended the range of the painter's Roving Eye, as well as, in another way, extended some element of the Symbolist movement), or a frustrated, vaguely perverse man sublimating his filthy urges (or else he shares this with all the American directors of European origin – as if the trip to the United States had made them all fodder for psychoanalysis and heirs to culture in spite of themselves). It seems to me that there are other resolutions at work in the Hitchcockian enterprise: a project to conceptualize the positioning of the human subject within a group, with all its affects, but according to other concepts, different in nature and in origin – pre-Freudian concepts, for those who enjoy teleology – concepts that unmistakably come straight from the 19th century.

Hitchcock as heir to the 19th century? Though this might seem a vague description, it at least leaves room for the imagination. A descendant of the Symbolists? Perhaps, if one considers Symbolism as the great forgotten movement, subsumed by the Fauvists and Cubists (in painting), and the Dadaists and Surrealists (in literature and poetry). Cubism, as an avant-garde avatar of artistic painting, is cited only fleetingly through Hitchcock's lens, in *Suspicion* (and even then, from the perspective of a latter-day Picasso); Fauvism is absent, although its dying embers can arguably be detected in the canvases seen in *The Trouble with Harry*; Surrealism comes courtesy of Dalí. What remains, then, is a considerable Symbolist legacy – as demonstrated fairly irrefutably, scientifically, humorously and imaginatively in this Montréal exhibition.

Hitchcock as Symbolist, then, is the ideal comparison – except that one cannot really conceive of a Symbolist who does not resort to specific symbols, a Symbolist defined as such only through his use of a generalized symbol, that of the Soul. Hitchcock has no symbols – if the definition of symbol is the restriction of an image to one, and only one, meaning. I don't believe in the razor – nor, while we're at it, in the

Psycho knife. It seems to me that Francis Vanoye is more just when he relates that knife (and the ones in *Sabotage* and *The Thirty-nine Steps,* as well as a few others), via Conrad, to Dostoyevsky and *The Idiot.*[2] Godard and De Palma, as well, had a clearer view than did the Lacanian analysts: the former, in contenting himself with the observation that Hitchcock's films leave us with the haunting memory of objects that signify nothing and whose very names fade or cease to exist; the latter, by re-introducing those objects, and aspects of their "archetypal scenes," in his infinitely varied works of fiction and gestures – which, in their own way, also deprive them of any possible meaning (a *Psycho*-inspired shower appears in all of De Palma's films, but never as the site of an actual murder; the knife is never phallic; and so on).

Hitchcock's cinema is all about this presence, this obsession with the presence of certain objects that appear, unexpected, shifted, too-sharply delineated, their contours so clear that they become unwatchable, almost out of focus, refusing to symbolize anything at all (and, in that refusal, concurring with a project descended from Symbolism – which, according to my conception of it, is not symbolic either, not in this strict sense). They are usually simple objects; objects that people have used for a long time and that rarely serve more than one purpose – knife, scissors, handbag, bottle, key, eyeglasses, even a windmill. They can almost be traced as far back as the elementary objects glorified by one of Hitchcock's obvious spiritual ancestors, G.K. Chesterton – objects so simple that they can serve any purpose. When the artisanal, a fortiori industrial, object finds increasingly specialized uses, it loses any human relationship to the world (a nostalgic-ontological argument not so different from the Heideggerian reflection on "the Thing"). Single-purpose instruments are more refined, of their type – but the all-purposeness of older objects was a *Weltanschauung*: it referred to a law, at once moral and metaphysical. In a world of excessively specialized objects, our vision has become well and truly fantastical; we no longer see anything of the real world: "We see as in a vision a world where a man tries to cut his throat with a pencil-sharpener; where a man must learn single-stick with a cigarette; where a man must try to toast muffins at electric lamps, and see red and golden castles in the surface of hot water pipes."[3]

Simple objects, or objects considered to be simple (there is no difference), have no symbolic value save a conventional, superficial value. Thomas Carlyle: "Of Symbols, however, I remark farther, that they have both an extrinsic and intrinsic value; oftenest the former only. What, for instance, was in that

[2] Francis Vanoye, "Histoires de couteaux ou Comment détailler les femmes (Dostoievski, Conrad, Hitchcock)," *Cinéma et Littérature, Cahiers du RITM* (Paris: Université Paris-10, 1999), p. 197–206.
[3] Gilbert Keith Chesterton, *What's Wrong with the World* (New York: Dodd, Mead and Company, 1910), p. 148.

clouted Shoe, which the Peasants bore aloft with them as ensign in their *Bauernkrieg* (Peasants' War)?"[4] And indeed, what about everyday objects? What of the "clouted Shoe," what of Van Gogh's boot, stripped of the millions of dollars that it is worth today, and reduced to its simplest expression? This is an old notion of the strong symbolicity of ordinary objects – a symbolicity accessible to simple folk and peasants. Only an erudite, pedantic fool like Carlyle's Professor Teufelsdröckh could fail to discern it. (Today, professors argue in other ways – witness the squabble of professors Derrida, Heidegger and Schapiro over poor old Vincent's footwear.)

Things in Hitchcock's films, when the camera eye moves close to them, remain things, and they remain simple things. They are produced neither as Freudian-Teufelsdröckhian symbols, nor for comic effect – I don't imagine anybody ever really believed the phallic train anecdote, and as for the rest, Hitch put it very well: "There are no symbols in my films." As a result, they are intrinsic signifiers – that is how they symbolize, and they do so more profoundly than any kind of extrinsic symbolism. They signify that they are, and that they are enigmatic; that, just like the world in general, they cannot be apprehended through science, even less through culture and language, and only via an act of innocence and youthfulness, via an act of faith and of belief – belief in the world, childlike amazement at the world because it is what it is, and not a specific religious belief; we are not (necessarily) on Catholic ground here.

Blindness

Detectives Hodgson and Benson in Suspicion, 1941

[4] Thomas Carlyle, *Sartor Resartus* (Oxford World Classics), ed. K. McSweeney and P. Sabor (London: Oxford University Press, 1988), p. 168.

Doctored vision – vision that is inadequate because it is forever and hopelessly located on the underside of appearances (the wrong side of the mirror) – is the great Chestertonian theme: it is that of *The Man Who Was Thursday,* whose characters would be worthy of inclusion in Hitchcock's spy films; that, more subtly, of the Father Brown mysteries; that of *Four Faultless Felons* or *The Return of Don Quixote,* with their radical conception of faith and the meaning of life. Father Brown's secret is that he unmasks the criminal by becoming a criminal – by being able to see things as the criminal saw them. For the criminal is not a sick man: he *wants* to be a criminal. Seeing things through the criminal's eyes is not a question of psychological finesse. Criminality is not a psychological reality; it is a more radical reality, an ontological Other – this is why it takes a priest or an innocent to grasp it. Basically, Father Brown decides once and for all to replace psychology (vain, not very scientific, good only for providing excuses) with anthropology. In understanding the human condition, he discovers what is real, and therefore what is excusable (albeit fundamentally, impersonally), about crime.

The inspired detective, then, stands in contrast to the police in that the latter are incapable of noticing anything whatsoever. The short-sighted investigator, the unimaginative, insensitive flatfoot, the detective subjected in advance, practically *committed,* to error, is an eminently Hitchcockian figure, and one doesn't have to look far to find examples. In *Family Plot,* two police detectives drop in on Adamson at the very moment he is plotting with Joe Maloney, and then depart, blissfully ignorant that they have just visited a criminal. Fifty years earlier, the policeman in *The Lodger,* bereft of the most basic intuition, made mistake upon mistake; we could also mention the policemen in *North by Northwest* who fail to notice the red-capped Thornhill (Cary Grant) in the Chicago station, those in *Spellbound* who leave the living room without realizing Ballantine is there, ffoliott's brother, in *Foreign Correspondent,* who works at Scotland Yard and ruins everything, and many others.

Henry Fonda and "the right man" in The Wrong Man, *1956*

So why are the police in Hitchcock's films so blind? Because they believe that the putative criminal looks like a criminal – that he resembles the police sketch of him. The point is, the criminal is precisely the one man who never resembles a criminal (this is the theme of the very first Father Brown mystery, which on this basis introduces the delightful character Flambeau, hardened criminal and mischievous chameleon who, once unmasked, reforms and becomes almost saintly). And why are spectators of Hitchcock's films likely to be blinded? Because they try to see too far beneath appearances. It may seem easy to claim that the opposite is true. But no: both the characters' and the spectators' mistake stems from not recognizing reality. Hitchcock's best films construct a reality not at all unlike the "hidden" reality that Chesterton was aiming for: a reality in which simple objects and simple criminals share the same belief that there is a Truth in the world – contingent on one basic rule being respected, and that is that appearances mean nothing. (Carefully considered, this is the opposite of Hercule Poirot, who absolutely believes that appearances speak – they speak an encrypted, difficult language, which requires a specialist, preferably one with a doctorate in multiple languages and appearances, to convey their message; moreover, that interpreter, like all interpreters, is more often than not indiscreet, an embellisher, who occasionally can even be suspected of having translated the message any old way. I refer readers here to Pierre Bayard's unmatched analysis in *Qui a tué Roger Ackroyd?*[5])

Psycho, 1960

[5] Pierre Bayard, *Qui a tué Roger Ackroyd?* (Paris: Éd. de Minuit, 1998).

Hitchcock's mysteries are never whodunits (food for the Poirots of this world). The mystery lies not in "who has done it"; even less, in "why it was done" (the elegant theory of the MacGuffin takes care of that); rather, it lies in "how it was done." How is it that a slice of reality has been removed and hidden from view? How is it that reality can be made to gleam enticingly, as in a mirror (in this case, the title of one Christie mystery, *They Do It with Mirrors,* could not be more apt)? How are we to distinguish the good appearances from the bad? Characters disappear *(The Lady Vanishes)* and reappear unexpectedly and inexplicably (the eponymous Lady is already sitting at the piano in the Foreign Office when the heroes finally get there). Objects disappear as soon as characters need to find them again (the liquor bottles in the cabinet at the Townsend mansion in *North by Northwest*). Criminals look like, and enjoy the status of, honourable men (Herbert Marshall, his alter ego James Mason, the jeweller kidnapper in *Family Plot* and, of course, the distinguished Scotsman of the *Thirty-nine Steps*). And heroes appear to be criminals, like the Chestertonian hero; only a female gaze – that of a young girl whom we assume to be a virgin and marriageable – can discern his underlying quality: this man is in fact not a criminal. On the contrary, he is something of a saint: he is intent on seeming to commit a crime, but his true aim is to rescue someone who is in great danger but doesn't know it (and, indeed, will never even be aware of being rescued[6]).

Ivor Novello in The Lodger: A Story of the London Fog, 1927

(The title character in *The Lodger* appears, ambiguously, to be a criminal; in fact he is a hero, a saint – only the young girl, to whom he is bound by the handcuffs that "condemn" him, understands this. By dint of sticking close to the killer, the lodger, in the end, identifies with him. He is the most inspired of Hitchcock's investigators – and here too this is highlighted by the fact that all the other characters are so blind: the father does the dishes and fails to see the broken biscuit; the mother pricks up her ears, revealing that she can hear, but does not see; the crowd is quite simply blinded; finally, the illuminated title of the magazine, *Golden Curls,* is shown once more, in the background of the final shot, where none of the characters sees it.)

Plausibility

[6] Such is the schema presented, for example, in *Four Faultless Felons,* where the devoted young men function metaphorically as humanized, miniature Christs (the French translation is aptly titled *Les Quatre petits Saints du crime* – "The four little saints of crime").

Hitchcock also knew how, when it suited him, to use manufactured objects – industrial objects, even – such as the helicopter in the *Thirty-nine Steps* and the plane in *North by Northwest*. And these objects are always diverted from their real function: the plane, rather than spray insecticide over fields of crops, sprays bullets; the windmill blades turn backward; the rustic gas oven in *Torn Curtain* is used to cook a most unusual pig. Hitchcock did not fear the special-purpose object as did his great precursor, Chesterton. The filmmaker displayed a sort of greed, a sensualist, childlike side that enabled him to ascribe less importance to the things with which he played; but he wanted the chance to have fun with them, to change them, to draw them back to the wonderful versatility of primitive objects. If he could not get as much out of an airplane as he could from a knife, or as much out of an oven as he could from a fire, at least he could make them do things they were not originally designed to do: spray with bullets, asphyxiate. We remain, at ground level, in the realm of what is terrestrially possible; with the diversion comes a poetic shifting.

The same applies to the stories Hitch told – they are plausible, but not completely so: "our old friends, the plausibles" are not our friends. In fact, they wind up so chopped-up, sliced into tiny portions, that they are barely discernible in their entirety; the Hitchcockian plot is an essential but complex moment (*Mad* magazine was just short of the truth with its parodic take on the master of suspense, "Alfred Hatchplot"). We see here the classic opposition between the French conception of the novel, as in Balzac or Flaubert, and the English one: Henry James, for example (since there is an element of James in Hitchcock, as noted long ago by Raymond Bellour and more recently by Donald Spoto), but also Melville and Conrad (in fact Conrad's *The Secret Agent* was the source material for Hitchcock's *Sabotage*).

There is the persistent idea of the world apprehended via an experience of impenetrability; the world is a mystery because it is opaque, either because there are no longer any readable signs in the world (James), or because the world is indeed woven with signs, but we perceive only their flip side (Chesterton) and cannot understand. Despite the fact that he worked with so many different screenwriters and producers, Hitchcock was able to develop this idea fairly systematically. It is the inspiration for the espionage/travel film, whose characters cross some vaguely, underlyingly hostile country where, even more unexpectedly, they encounter sudden fits of sympathy and freely given assistance (see, among others, *The Man Who Knew Too Much*). The experience is in itself strange, and the travellers, in essence, confront the unknowable – landscapes, customs, distances, discrepancies between map and territory, between names and places (Alt-na-Schellach, in *The Thirty-nine Steps,* is more mysterious than Marrakesh), improbable languages, that of the Ruritanians in *The Lady Vanishes* or the Latvian in *Foreign Correspondent* – and are led to seek the Great Unknown: that which, like the Man Who Was Sunday in

Chesterton's allegory, changes in appearance, manner, value, meaning and size, even as we get closer to it. This is the framework of the *Thirty-nine Steps, Foreign Correspondent* (in part), *Young and Innocent, The Man Who Knew Too Much, Rich and Strange* (in part), *North by Northwest* and *Family Plot* (his last film consciously revisited *North by Northwest* – they were both scripted by Ernest Lehman – with its similar scenes, the fateful rendezvous, and so on).

The only invention that the Hitchcockian corpus added to its literary model is that of having sullied the investigating hero with something of the mystery of the person he is investigating. There is no better example, from this point of view, than the figure of George Kaplan – the "zero function" or "null function," to borrow a phrase from the heyday of Lacanian (and therefore, unwittingly, Heideggerian) analysis. This idea of the *figura nullius* is tailor-made for the unlucky character played by Cary Grant: the Hero flung *(geworfen)* into the World, who can do nothing but collide with the incomprehensible, in one way or another. Who, against his will, finds himself attracted by the signifying void, the signifier of the void. (In *North by Northwest,* it is not only the name of Kaplan that is a signifier of this void: the names of the professor and of the man at the Highway 41 crossroads go conspicuously unspoken; of the latter, all we know is that he "can't say it is [Kaplan], 'cause it ain't"; even Thornhill's name is cleverly mispronounced by Eve when she is asked to reveal it to the policemen outside the train.)

Hitchcock as hermetician, then? Indeed – but not, to quote a foolish description that has been made more than once, decked out in full magician/sorcerer regalia. Hitch was no hack alchemist on a quest for a philosopher's stone. Rather, he was a decoder who had cast aside his kabala (or, perhaps, a Symbolist who had restricted himself to the care of the Soul). At the beginning of *The Lodger,* appearances are once again deceiving. A police car seen from behind, its twin windows revealing the silhouettes of two cops' heads, becomes a face – an effect often seen in comic strips of the same period. Shortly thereafter, the crowd that discovers the first body is suddenly confronted by a ghostly murderer, which is nothing more than the reflection, in a distorting mirror, of a man bundled up in a coat – *ænigma in speculum.* Consequently, when the eponymous lodger does arrive, it is an effortlessly mysterious introduction, achieved in two shots that, paradoxically, *push back* our vision.

Here Hitchcock shows affinities with Béla Balázs and his notion of physiognomy. Cinema does not show the world as it is; it is not a phenomenological art (it was the succeeding generation of critics and filmmakers, Bazin, Bresson and Rossellini, that believed this). Cinema shows the world seen through a filter, seen as a vision may be seen: as endowed with a face – one might as well say a soul. Symbolism. One is reminded of Balázs's writings on "the face of things": his idea that the close-up is terrifying, because this "face" is more closely and clearly read; his theory of the exchange of qualities between animate and inanimate in film, and so on. All this is seen in Hitchcock,[7] wedded, with each successive film, to that other – more banal – intuition: that the world does not signify, is not to be read, but has a director (God, if you like, but the Hitchcockian god is terribly abstract, a hidden enunciator). The idea is brutally incarnate in his last film: Blanche and Lumley are riding in a taxi, planning their search for the missing heir; at the first intersection, the enunciator-master takes them down another road, introducing the woman who crosses their path and ends up leading them to the Unknown Someone – an ironic comment on the arbitrary nature of narrative, of mise en scène, of the management of coincidences. Providence does not play much of a role here (the same is true of just about all the happy endings in Hitchcock's films, almost always underscored in some ironic manner, from the drummer man's sniggering confession in *Young and Innocent* to the shot of the train in *North by Northwest*).

The starting point for the French critics' 1954 squabble over Hitchcock, which in the end led to his elevation to the rank of auteur, was the observation that his work was marked by an obsessional thematic: that of the *faux coupable,* or "wrong man." From there, Rohmer and Chabrol deduced that, since everyone in the Hitchcockian universe was potentially guilty, this must mean that his is a universe of Original Sin: everyone is guilty because everyone is fallen. The paralogism was crude, and its interpretation, not subtle enough to endure. But the obsession with that theme is very real: we do not see the truth, but the falsehood, because we see the flip side of real things, as in the conclusion of *The Man Who Was Thursday*: "Shall I tell you the secret of the whole world? It is that we have only known the back of the world. We see everything from behind, and it looks brutal. That is not a tree, but the back of a tree. That is not a cloud, but the back of a cloud. Cannot you see that everything is stooping and hiding a face? If we could only get round in front –"[8] Appearances are deceiving because they are the underside of reality. For Chesterton, the obverse is reserved for divine vision: "*posteriora videbis.*" It is so for Hitchcock, as well, but his version takes on an existentialist tinge: the world is simply opaque, antisignifying. In *Revenge,* one of the episodes in the TV series *Alfred*

[7] And, again, in Chesterton, where he remarks that we have nothing to fear from the natural world, but we do start to worry once we project human faces or forms onto nature (a tree is not frightening, but a tree that we take for a fantastical human is). See *Heretics* (New York: John Lane Company, 1905).

[8] Chesterton, *The Man Who Was Thursday: A Nightmare* (Beaconsfield: Darwen Finlayson, 1969), p. 177.

Hitchcock Presents (which one can term "rough drafts" of his universe), a woman "recognizes" a man as her rapist, then another, then another, indefinitely: her madness is the exacerbation of our perceptual condition – we think we recognize, but the recognition comes entirely from us; it is pure illusion.

Hitchcock as the softcore version of Chestertonian paradoxalism, then. For the Catholic writer, the paradox was a point of doctrine, starting with the theological virtues: faith, hope and charity – which consist in believing in the unbelievable, hoping for the unhopable, and forgiving the unforgivable, and are thus necessarily happy, as opposed to the ancient virtues, which are simply human, and somewhat sad.[9] (Chesterton converted to Catholicism because nothing that had been written against it, it seemed to him, held water. I shall leave the historical link to J.H. Newman and the Oxford Movement, etc., unexplored, for this goes beyond Hitchcock.) Chesterton's fictional works are enigmas fashioned from this knot: that that which is the most plausible is the most improbable (unless it is the reverse that is true). Hitchcock provides the vulgate: what we see has meaning, but does not mean what we think. For instance, signs are provided at the start (the eventual murderer's twitch in *Young and Innocent*), then stripped of their meaning; or, situations are created that are fundamentally paradoxical and impossible (Roger Thornhill searching for himself, under the name George Kaplan; the young man in *Young and Innocent* who, having managed to evade justice, is summoned by a policeman to take part in his own manhunt, etc.).

James Stewart and Kim Novak in Vertigo, 1958

The Couple

The paradox to end all paradoxes, and one that is as central to Hitchcock's universe as it is to Chesterton's, is the couple – or a certain vision of the couple, at least. For this we must hark back once again to the 19th century – to 1857, to be precise, and Flaubert's "I *am* Madame Bovary," and to 1855, and Wotan's (and, up to a point, Wagner's) "I am Brünnhilde." The inexpiable sin of Madame Bovary, of Brünnhilde, of women, is that they fail in love – but in the exclusive love of the Father, of the tyrannical or jealous Husband. The punishment is banishment from Paradise – Brünnhilde transmuted into a perishable body by the terrible, desolate damnation of Wotan; La Bovary ending her days in dereliction, of both body and soul.

Hitchcock oscillates between one and the other of these melancholy maledictions; if Woman is idealized so much, it is only so that one day she may be damned – precisely

[9] Chesterton, *Heretics*.

because she was idealized. The perspective in this case is decidedly un-Christian, contrary to the opinion of many writers. It is not the Fall, not the temptation of the Serpent or of the Apple. Not Eve. It is a more archaic, pagan damnation that, in its representation, is at once a "psychologization" and a symbolization of sadness (the father's, the daughter's; the husband's, the wife's). The man is hurt not so much because he has been deceived, but because the woman is not equal to the task: *"Zu gering wärst du meinem Grimm"* ("Were you too insignificant to make me angry?"), sings Wotan ironically. And yet, paradoxically, enigmatically, the man who exiles and who damns is, at the moment at which he utters that damnation, always a feminized man: Charles Bovary, Wotan, Scottie Ferguson, Sam Flusky.

Moreover, we know that the woman always proves to be stronger, and manages, if not to reverse the situation, at least to wield partial decision-making power therein. Brünnhilde chooses her own form of torture; the Magic Fire that engulfs her is her own invention, and it shatters the god's too-weak heart. The moment of banishment is one of the most beautiful love duets in all of 19th-century opera: the majority of Verdi's duets are kitschy – schmaltzy, even – by comparison. As Brünnhilde advances toward the place of her dormition, Wagner's score, for the only time, incorporates a quasi-Verdian theme: Wotan's love theme, which is heard as he embraces his daughter (*"Der Augen leuchtendes Paar, das oft ich lächelnd gekost"*; "That bright pair of eyes that often I fondled with smiles"). Then the music again becomes Germanic, sublime: the theme of love becomes intertwined with that of slumber; then comes the incantation to fire. Similarly, in Hitchcock, there is desire, weakness and melancholy in the way Scottie turns his back on Judy forever. (Bernard Herrmann made no mistake: his score for *Vertigo* quoted abundantly from Wagner's *Magic Fire* theme.)

"I think the fact of being chained together has more to do with sex than anything else."[10] Critics have often remarked on the recurring image in Hitchcock's films of the couple handcuffed or otherwise bound together (indeed, the French distributor of *Notorious,* at a time when English film titles were still translated in France, made an inspired choice: *Les enchaînés,* or "the chained ones"). *Notorious* contains some of the most beautiful images of this tying-up of the couple, this linking that *is* the couple. Notorious, indeed, is this first of many long kisses filmed in a continuous shot (not a *plan-séquence,* or sequence shot, which is something different – just as a held note in music is not the same as a cadence): two-and-a-half minutes of Cary Grant and Ingrid Bergman going from bal-

[10] Quoted in Dominique Auzel, *Alfred Hitchcock* (Toulouse: Editions Milan, 1988), p. 29.

Robert Donat and Madeleine Carroll in The Thirty-nine Steps, *1935*

Anne Grey in Number Seventeen, *1932*

Young and Innocent, 1938

---

[11] I beg my readers not to interpret anything in this discussion as echoing the theme of symbolic "castration," which I believe to be utterly foreign to the Hitchcock universe.

[12] William Makepeace Thackeray, *Vanity Fair: A Novel Without a Hero* (New York: Bantam Books, 1997).

[13] Chesterton, *What's Wrong with the World,* p. 66–67.

cony to telephone to front door in an unbroken clinch. The image would be repeated, with variations, in *Under Capricorn, Spellbound, To Catch a Thief* and *North by Northwest*: the man pulls the woman close to him, unable to break it off; although he loves her, he sacrifices her (or will eventually, or already has) to something that he cannot help (marriage, a reason of State). It is the age-old conflict – Christian and Roman (Catholic) – between the Law and the Home. Naturally, Hitchcock was Catholic (as was Ford). Yet the image of embrace, of attachment, is the radical image of the man who, at the very moment that it is his duty to turn his back, is unable to do so – he makes a decision rooted in affection, which does not preclude virility but, rather, feminizes it.[11]

Usually, men should be attached to the women they love. So that they never leave them, and do not go off alone in search of adventure, far from any home, perhaps – but especially so as to signify an ontology of the couple: the woman has hold of the man, the better to succeed in the most paradoxical enterprise of all, that of marriage. "And oh, what a mercy it is that these women do not exercise their powers oftener! We can't resist them, if they do. Let them show ever so little inclination, and men go down on their knees at once: old or ugly, it is all the same. And this I set down as a positive truth. A woman with fair opportunities, and without an absolute hump, may marry *whom she likes*. Only let us be thankful that the darlings are like the beasts of the field, and don't know their own power. They would overcome us entirely if they did."[12] This makes for an interesting reading of the fable that is *The Birds*: in the film, Melanie is expressly linked to evil spells – a blonde witch to the black birds. But can she not, more simply, be viewed as a bird herself – say, a linnet – birdbrained but stubborn, who *wants* the man she has chosen, and who, for once or for a while, is quite aware of her power?

Or, for a more prosaic view, we can turn again to Chesterton: "[T]he success of the marriage comes after the failure of the honeymoon. [...] Two people must be tied together in order to do themselves justice. [...] If Americans can be divorced for 'incompatibility of temper' I cannot conceive why they are not all divorced. I have known many happy marriages, but never a compatible one. The whole aim of marriage is to fight through and survive the instant when incompatibility becomes unquestionable. For a man and a woman, as such, are incompatible."[13] The lone Hitchcockian incursion into the comedy of remarriage, American-style, was not exactly persuasive. A excessively slick film with an excessively impersonal script, *Mr. and Mrs. Smith,* apart from a few details, could easily have been made by anybody else: say, directed by George Cukor and starring Cary Grant and Irene Dunne. Hitchcock's overall treatment of the issue of marriage, though, does coincide with this notion of the couple as that which must struggle in order to stay together. Handcuffs are but the figurative form of this intrinsic struggle, the figure of the incompatible made compatible. Classic cinema, especially English-language cinema, is rife with agitated, tormented, difficult couples. Hitchcock always rendered his couples as systematically paradoxical – there is no "missus," no image of a "regular girl"; he expected his scriptwriters to furnish images of this paradox, and himself invented such images, of which handcuffs and other material chainings-together are but the most frequently recurring examples.

Other more sophisticated images involve "visual sensuality," and sight as an agent of knowledge of the flesh – young female characters defined in terms of lingerie: Joan Fontaine dares not touch Rebecca's undergarments, and in so doing becomes a Hitchcockian, not just a Selznickian, character. A more obvious reference is Grace Kelly's skimpy nightshirt in *Rear Window,* a stream of silk spilling out of her overnight bag, which James Stewart hardly dares touch: women's daring; boys' shy virility. (And here again, we see the particular hue of Symbolism à la Hitchcock.)

This, too, is distilled in his final opus. The young woman in *Family Plot* is an irredeemable materialist who thinks only of eating and fornicating and liberally peppers her speech with sexual allusions, from "crystal balls" to "the only bird I'm gonna hold"; she has no self-control. The young man, on the other hand, submits to social order – he thinks only of getting the job done and coming off as a good boy. Misogyny? No. In her way, Blanche is sympathetic, strong-willed, efficient and not without charm; it is just that she must be as visibly incompatible as possible with *her favourite.* Hitchcock's women, in general, exhibit a sexual boldness equal to that of Hawks' heroines (however sassy they may be). The anecdote about Grace Kelly (related in the Truffaut book) is justly famous, but even in Hitchcock's British period the young women in his films were sexy blondes, not hesitating to put their bodies into play, and at the forefront (one example among many: Nova Pilbeam pinching Derrick de Marney's ears in *Young and Innocent,* ostensibly to wake him up after his fainting spell).

An altogether different treatment is reserved for incestuous couples: Fisher and his daughter *(Foreign Correspondent)*; Eve and Vandamm (James Mason) *(North by Northwest)*; Judy and her "handlers" *(Vertigo)*; Marnie and Mark Rutland (Sean Connery). Girl-women, all controlled by mature men, at once virile and fragile (one casting error excepted: the once and future James Bond, too muscular and unequivocally hirsute[14]). Incest: another 19th-century theme to go with stuffy bourgeois families, Victorian- or Napoleon-III-era sexual repression, and the soon-to-emerge, but still latent, Oedipus complex. Siegmund and Sieglinde, Wotan and Brünnhilde; the Brontë sisters; Henry James; Fernand Khnopff and his sister. The most compatible couple in all of Hitchcock are Charlie and Uncle Charlie in *Shadow of a Doubt* – and they come to a bad end.

Banished women; feminized men, miserable in their banishing; "incompossible" men and women, for whom incest is the extreme limit and, in a sense, an allegory; determined women, sure of their own bodies as well as of the bodies they desire; boyish men, comfortable with camaraderie (that of college, that of war – later, of the Cold War – and that of gentlemen's clubs) but not with eroticism; men and women chained together by something other than passion: by some sort of instinct. Handcuffs symbolize all this, to be sure, but so do certain stereotypes: Brylcreemed boys; airy blonde girls.

Cosmetics

The "control of the universe" formula, for all its rugged perfection, did not spring from Godard's (oral) pen by chance. "Control of the universe" is a devilishly modernist idea. From Duchamp's readymades to Léger's extolling of the exhilarating, humanizing and modernist values of advertising, of its graphic design and its proliferative virtue, the first two decades of the century just past (the century of cinema) were about the search for a formula that eventually enabled art not to enslave or alienate minds, exactly, but to become obvious and indispensable for those minds. Hitchcock, born 10 years after Duchamp and 30 years before Warhol, was the artisan of a sort of mainstream version of this enterprise.

The Symbolist image is the image of something immaterial, invisible, an ideal, an Idea. The Symbolist symbol is that which "in art, as in mathematics, [...] makes it possible to discuss a function on an unknown quantity – or, more appropriately, an unknown quality such as the ultimate meaning of life."[15] (Symbols of fidelity, melancholy, Sundays, sanctity, art; of all the anti-industrial values imagined in late-19th-century Europe.) The Hitchcockian image does not aim for this usual notion of Symbolism, but rather aims to symbolize the world; Hitchcock knew full well that cinema is not allegorization, but interpretation, of the world, and that if images have the power to symbolize (for they must be constructed with that aim),

[14] Years later a televised ceremony honouring Hitchcock (the American Film Institute Life Achievement Award) was to record a pathetic encounter between the director and the actor, during which Connery had to repeat his name over and over, and became increasingly disconcerted as Hitchcock did not recognize him. Excessive testosterone display...
[15] Michael Gibson, *Symbolism* (New York: Taschen America, 1997).

then that power is not metaphorical but figurative, and, simultaneously, realist (another paradox).

Take the imagery of ascension, heights, vertigo – being in High Places: in *North by Northwest,* the cliff over which Thornhill dangles and the plane from which Vandamm plans to "dispose of" Eve; in *Foreign Correspondent,* the famous plane crash sequence, and the clock tower in London whence the spy falls to his death; in *Vertigo,* the mission bell tower; in *Saboteur,* the fall from the Statue of Liberty; in *Mr. and Mrs. Smith,* the stalled amusement park ride. All these scenes produce plenty of sensations (dizziness, anguish, hands clammy with cold sweat) and no direct symbols (only a singularly twisted mind would see Scottie repeatedly ascending the bell tower as a metaphor for premature ejaculation): up does not equal the sky, down does not equal the ground, or hell; ascent is not an ascension to heaven, descent is not damnation, and so on. This is so obvious that, on those occasions when Hitchcock did allow himself a foray into this type of facile symbolism, it is immediately apparent and, as a result, the film is considered a failure, almost unworthy of inclusion in his filmography. An example is provided by *Downhill,* in which Roddy Berwick (Ivor Novello) is first overwhelmed by imposing stone surroundings, then descends to the lowest of the lower depths, spiralling down escalators and elevators in a Tube station, until the film's conclusion, where he re-ascends, up a modest staircase and in a burst of light, to return to polite society and the bosom of his family: the effect is fairly ridiculous – rife, indeed, with "symbols," and not very Hitchcockian at all.

Hitchcock's images are paradoxical in that they are both abstract and concrete. We return again to the 1920s, Balázs, and the Germans. For Balázs, the raw material of cinema, the "filmic subject," is not reality; it is a "reading," a transformation of reality already in progress – this is the intrinsic potential of film language. Cinema is incapable of reproducing "simple reality"; it can only "read" it, interpret it; symmetrically, in terms of its relationship with literature, film can legitimately appropriate only that which, in the literary source, is already filmic (and which is more easily found in minor literary works).

Through all its stages, therefore, cinema is a producer of meaning: Balázs argues that the camera is "productive," scissors are "inventive," the eye "senses," and so on – and this insight culminates with his idea of a "face" that the cinematic process ascribes to that which is filmed, whether it is animate or inanimate.[16] Hitchcock's cinema is never naturalist, any more than it is Symbolist, because he began making films in 1925, when cinema was conceived of as a deliberate inter-

[16] See Balázs' "The Visible Man, or The Culture of Films" (*Der sichtbare Mensch, oder die Kultur des Films*, Wien-Leipzig: Deutsch-Österreichischer Verlag, 1924).

The Thirty-nine Steps, 1935

Robert Donat
in The Thirty-nine Steps, 1935

[17] A more vulgar occurrence is reported by Donald Spoto. To an actress who simpered: "Mr. Hitchcock, what do you think is my best side?" the director responded, without looking at her, "My dear, you're sitting on it." (Donald Spoto, *The Dark Side of Genius: The Life of Alfred Hitchcock*, New York: Ballantine Books, 1983), p. 283.

pretation, systematically produced – an interpretation without a theoretical system (this has nothing to do with the attempts at exegesis). An interpretation whereby the interpretee is replaced by an interpretant that is just as impenetrable, just as enigmatic: the interpretation is not a clarification. Faces are not clear images. Indeed, there is a Hitchcockian obsession with taking faces for something else (e.g., "asses for faces," a famous line from *Frenzy,* or the more euphoric version: Ingrid Bergman's face as a laughing baby's backside[17]).

The cinema of Alfred Hitchcock is that of someone who started to make films during the 1920s, the heyday of Expressionism (which some have attempted to read as an avatar of Symbolism). His images are not symbols, but images that interpret the world, conferring upon it the equivalent of astonishment, of childlike wonder. "Not an art, not a technique, a mystery" – almost none of the critics who commented on *Histoire(s) du cinéma* perceived that Godard meant "mystery" to mean mystery in the full Christian sense of the word: the mystery of Christian charity, the mystery of Christian joy, the mystery of Christian childhood, naïveté and innocence, even though Hitchcock was a poor Christian (to say nothing of Godard). Hence the importance of Chesterton: not as some sort of spiritual father, influence, or philosophical/theological/ideological foundation, but as a reminder to take seriously the childlike solemnity, the natural liturgy, the joyous amazement of cinema as an instrument for reading the world.

In fact, if there was one writer who influenced Hitchcock, and indelibly so – having the lifelong impact that only an author read during one's adolescence can – it was not the Catholic polemicist that was Chesterton. It was John Buchan, a Colonel-Blimp, dyed-in-the-wool imperialist if there ever was one – and the epitome of contempt for the foreigner, the stranger, the Jew – but who invented, in Richard Hannay, a hero without fear and beyond reproach (the genuine antithesis of the meek, stay-at-home Alfred Hitchcock) and was an ingenious imagemaker: his every turn of phrase summoned forth a whole world of evocative imagery whose magical universe is at once more real than real and more dangerous than the most twisted labyrinth. The cinema of Hitchcock is no more than the lengthy unfurling of all those sensations felt as one exits childhood, and there are myriad elements in Buchan's three "war" novels that, right through to the end of Hitchcock's career, were to serve as material for his own works of fiction. From *The Thirty-nine Steps* (1915) comes the assassination of the foreign diplomat, the all-powerful leader of the enemy forces hiding behind the face of an English aristocrat, the sheer menace of the empty countryside.

"The free moorlands were prison walls, and the keen hill air was the breath of a dungeon"[18]: another sort of paradox, more facile, more novelistic (soap opera–esque, even), more ironic and shattering than those of Chesterton – more suited to the yarn-spinning mind of the younger, the middle-aged, and the older Alfred Hitchcock. From *Greenmantle* (1916) comes the whole *Mitteleuropa* atmosphere: the cosmopolitan passenger trains, the Orient of T.E. Lawrence, the fascination (in spite of it all) with German efficiency and rationality. And from *Mr. Standfast* (1919) comes this disturbing piece of information, whose lineage in Hitchcock is so apparent: the man who must, in the name of a higher morality and heroism,[19] allow the enemy to woo the woman he loves (for which some imbecilic critics tore *Notorious* to pieces).

Michael Chekhov in Spellbound, 1945

(Hitchcock could not be as Catholic as Chesterton was, and not only because he was not – far from it – as daring or droll a theologian. The writer is able to discourse upon religion in the arena of concepts, while the filmmaker unceasingly confronts images, representations. The Catholic religion is already rife with representations; it *is* representation. This is doubtless the reason for the weaknesses of Hitchcock's clergymen characters: the priest in *I Confess* or the cardinal in *Family Plot,* for instance. To find another cinema that replies to the ironic, paradoxical, practically desperate theological-ontological vigour of Chesterton, I feel we can look to only one other obsessional filmmaker, who is both a close and distant cousin of Hitchcock: Buñuel.)

The Thirty-nine Steps, 1935

"I now attempt to come to a sort of synthesis, to underline, along with the symbolism of the setting, the fundamental characteristic of the locale of the action." It was not Hitchcock who uttered these lines, but Wieland Wagner.[20] But it could well have been Hitchcock, were it not for the fact that, since he is not required to respect a text filled with almost-sacred symbolism, the filmmaker commands the dosage of symbols that he can choose to add to (or withhold from) a "fundamental characteristic," which is his main task in the cosmetic design, i.e., the manufacturing of the trappings of reality, that is proper to him. Are the obsessional images in Hitchcock symbols, then? They are less symbols than they are fundamental traits of adornment and reading of the world. I believe this is the foundation from which one must appreciate the director's Symbolist affiliation: as always in cinema, that affiliation retroactively transforms that which it inherited. The glass of milk (taken upstairs by Cary Grant in *Suspicion,* drunk by Gregory Peck in *Spellbound,* mentally superimposed over the oversized cup of coffee in *Notorious*) is an amenity, a happy blob of white froth (Fassbinder certainly

[18] *The Thirty-nine Steps* (1915), in *The Complete Richard Hannay* (London: Penguin Books, 1993), p. 44.
[19] The title here comes from the name of one of the allegorical characters in John Bunyan's *Pilgrim's Progress,* an ersatz pseudo-storybook Bible reading – a glorification of Christian values in daily life.
[20] Antoine Goléa, *Entretiens avec Wieland Wagner* (Paris: Pierre Belfond, 1967), p. 49. (Free translation.)

saw it as such, with his wonderful figurative commentary in *Veronika Voss*), but hardly a symbol. (A symbol of what, anyway? Purity? Vice? The fundamental concealment of poison beneath innocence? And why not, while we're at it, the Fall!) And must we absolutely read dangerous spectacle – lethal in the case of *The Thirty-nine Steps* and *The Man Who Knew Too Much,* risky in that of *Torn Curtain* – as the most orthodox of "archetypal scenes," when it is so natural to respond above all to the paradoxical image of closure painted in that spectacle, with the open stage enclosed by its wings? Etc., etc. "Symbolist I am, but I do not deign to use symbols": such could be the proud and ironic motto of the great Alfred.

Conclusion

The great Christian imprecators of the early 20th century and the inter-war period – Chesterton, of course, but also Bloy, Péguy, Bernanos – raved innocently about "what was wrong with the world" with no thought of self-censorship, because they could not imagine that free speech might unleash catastrophe. We should perhaps rework Adorno's aphorism to observe that what is no longer possible after Auschwitz is not so much art or poetry (which have adapted and survived perfectly well) as innocent imprecation. The "political correctness" that stifles us today is the terrible price paid for such impossibility. Hitchcock remains an auteur – an artist, if you like – who predates that impossibility. His protest against National Socialism *(Secret Agent, The Lady Vanishes, The Thirty-nine Steps, Foreign Correspondent)* was identical to his disgust for Communism *(Torn Curtain, Topaz)*; but by the time of these two later films, innocence and simplicity had already been lost. The happily ambiguous, impenetrable or antisignifying signs of the early days had become ponderous symbols. The Alfred Hitchcock that I imagine is the earlier one: paradoxical and innocent.

I shall offer two images, two portraits without allegory, as examples: the first is contained in a seemingly innocuous line of dialogue from an episode of *Alfred Hitchcock Presents* (entitled *Banquo's Chair*), describing the very British pastime of birdwatching: "A number of worthwhile qualities are called into play: planning based on knowledge and experience, a considerable amount of care and stealth, and the most acute observation and attention to detail, of course."

Or, if you prefer a purely visual image, there is that of the very last of Hitchcock's famous cameo appearances, in *Family Plot*: a black silhouette behind a door at the Barlow Creek registry office, just above the quite legible inscription: *Registrar of Births and Deaths.*

Ingrid Bergman's reflection in Under Capricorn, 1949

Hitchcock's Female Portraits

Jean Louis Schefer

The portrait is not what Hitchcock's films are about; rather, it is their starting point, a state to which they periodically return, a part of their dreamlike structure.

Although there are secret stories within Hitchcock's films, they are not hidden, but rather on the surface; in fact, they are a surface. Whether the stories are about love, devotion, idolatry or fidelity, they are embodied by figures in a portrait. (Only one does not conform to type: *Psycho* is the story of a young man who carries on an imaginary relationship with his dead mother and who, spurred on by her jealousy, kills any woman who tries to seduce – i.e., symbolically kill – him.) But the woman in the picture frame is barely alive; almost completely immobile, she merely sustains a pose. The events of her life can be compared to those of a picture: she endures, deteriorates, is reframed and affected by changes to the backdrop. Because of her power to captivate, she acts as both a catalyst of, and a hindrance or impediment to, the action.

The figures on Hitchcock's "canvas" constantly fall into ingenious emotional traps and become distracted by images. Is this how Hitchcock creates such beautiful, subtle female portraits? Or does the film itself represent an act of portraiture, through its corrections and alterations, its ability to capture the subject's essence and soul as art historians repeatedly tell us paintings do? I believe his films embody the output of two equally graceful periods: the skilful character studies of 17th-century writing, which represent such an artful blend of literature and psychology; and the mane or aura surrounding the painted figure, which can be seen as a product of the 19th-century bourgeois rendition of space, or 18th-century parlour paintings by Quentin La Tour and Chardin, for example. In this respect, Hitchcock's oeuvre resembles classic pastel compositions in its choice of subjects, attention to detail (the sheen on eyes, hair and skin), colour and quality of lighting and materials. In *Vertigo,* he "draws" Kim Novak over and over again in pastel colours: somewhere between chalk powder and mascara. In fact, in keeping with her role as the painting's understudy, she is the most obviously made up of all Hitchcock's female stars, the one he "paints" best. Her most successful incarnation is the one recreated by James Stewart, where her image is shown, miraculously triumphant, floating in the hotel room. But this image is one that has been repeatedly reworked through successive dabs and brushstrokes. It is, in effect, a masterpiece of what Proust called idolatry: happy memories of the unquestioning adoration a child feels when its mother comes to say goodbye before going out to dinner in a fancy restaurant. The image of that angel of eventide in Hitchcock's oeuvre is presented as childhood nostalgia. The joys of adult idolatry miraculously transport us back to remembered scenes of childhood consolation. In Hitchcock's films, the famous kisses fit into that emotional context: they are at once a presentiment of, and a consolation for, the loved one's departure.

Kim Novak in Vertigo, *1958*

In *Vertigo,* the camera dwells repeatedly on Kim Novak's face, missing, pursuing, creating and recreating her. The time expended on this exemplifies almost completely the film's qualities of duration, pause or delay. Kim Novak consistently appears in shades of grey and ash blonde, running through a gamut of greens: the yews and bougainvilleas in the Spanish cemetery; a flower-covered wall where the florist's tender greens predominate; her green Jaguar; the powdery green of the hotel room, and so on. The red damask of the restaurant walls, on the other hand, is either the backdrop to the portrait or the surrounding frame. We see Kim Novak's silhouette framed twice: once in a mirror and once in a doorway.

These are well-dressed images. Eva Marie Saint's black suit, her red cocktail dress with the dark-blue pattern, the deep-blue cardigan dress, her lovely grey gloves, the straight orange dress she wears in the final scene are straight out of a painting, especially as they interplay with eyes, blonde hair, carriage. As with all Hitchcock's female characters, her gait is smooth, the upper body immobile, so that the image remains unchanged. But here again, what sort of choices do they represent? Women are consistently depicted as phantoms and forbidden images: a hallmark of epics rather than novels. The wife or mistress of the father-king (whether good or evil, he is always a type of King Mark) is always Isolde, beloved of the young chevalier (*Spellbound, Notorious, Under Capricorn, Dial M for Murder, The Trouble with Harry, Vertigo, North by*

Grace Kelly in Rear Window, 1954

Northwest, etc.). Only once did I hear Isolde's theme from the second act of Wagner's *Tristan*: it plays as Cary Grant and Eva Marie Saint kiss on the train.

Only one of these possible images remains unexploited by the recipient of a woman's seductive attentions, and it is perhaps the most perfect image of them all: Grace Kelly in *Rear Window*. James Stewart, the photographer, has no interest in painting. Rather, he is obsessed with finding a missing scene in a story, and he stares at the place he is convinced it happened through his telephoto lens. He is obsessed with repeating the scene to try to find the missing image in the drama that took place in the apartment across from his. He does not focus on Grace Kelly. She is not even really in his film, and she is certainly never at the right distance to provide him with a good image; rather, she is a presence, a style, a perfume. Laid up with a broken leg, James Stewart is fussed over by his "nurse," but his mind is elsewhere, on his role as a spectator, on the ending that he will provide for the lost film, the vanished action, of which he has witnessed mere snippets. He must recapture the elements that are missing from the actual sequence of events, recreate the tragedy, replace the vanished victim with one he can see through his camera lens.

Hitchcock's characters are blessed with a particular charm that is the epitome of seduction. It emanates from them, making them in some ways vulnerable, yet also demanding a response. Their charm is a cry for affection, tempered by modesty, refinement or good breeding.

The extraordinary charm of Hitchcock's characters – both men and women – is a miracle of refinement and culture. Charming people possess discretion and a certain humility; those with subtle charm exude a kind of smugness at their social superiority, a secret delight in aesthetic inequality. Charm (that indefinable quality in their gestures and taste) separates the protagonists – those in the foreground – from the extras, and produces either reserve or animation in the background figures. Yet another factor that distinguishes the protagonists from the extras: the latter all proceed with their regular, everyday lives. That is to say, in most cases, they have jobs.

The occupation or obligatory employment of the protagonists is just for show. They are thrust into the action willy-nilly; they resent it, resist it, stubbornly obstruct it. The intrinsic flaws found in most of Hitchcock's characters prevent the action from moving forward. The extraordinary (or even ordinary) events that overtake their lives upset them, and doom them to a series of faux pas.

Who are they, anyway? The director's choice of roles is supremely ironic: the main characters are idlers, people who temporarily or permanently lack any sort of job or occupation.

The characters portrayed in Hitchcock's colour films are the very opposite of those in detective stories: neither police officers, investigators, criminals nor spies. Some of these roles can be found in Hitchcock's British films, in which a certain youthful hero-worship or social conscience produced a taste for adventurous professions: *Young and Innocent, The Lodger, The Thirty-nine Steps, The Lady Vanishes, Foreign Correspondent, Saboteur* – almost all of them are similar in plot and subject matter to the contemporaneous films of Fritz Lang.

A few of his later films *(Dial M for Murder, Shadow of a Doubt)* portray playboys.

The action is neither instigated, directed nor concluded by the characters' courage, feelings or physical strength: it is simply something that happens to them. James Stewart and Cary Grant are clumsy idiots, distracted charmers, aesthetic connoisseurs who, like art collectors, cultivate an ideal of beauty. What is the motive behind their actions? Michael Wilding, James Stewart and Cary Grant are forced into action because they are in love, and the object of their affections eludes them. It eludes them because it has been set in motion.

Part of the old-boy network, members of private clubs, they are the type of men who are attracted to an image and pursue it. During their pursuit they discover or create variations in the image: degradation, idealization, alterations in angle or profile, costume changes and so on.

Both instigators and puppets of the action, these heroes make us aware of the *object's painterly qualities*. It is precisely these qualities that weaken them, blind them, and lead them on – to what sort of exploits? Their "odyssey" can hardly be considered more fateful than Orpheus's quest for Eurydice. And the music that accompanies them on their journey? As mentioned above, the background music to Cary Grant and Eva Marie Saint's first kiss is three long notes borrowed from Isolde's theme in *Tristan*.

I will briefly touch on the figures in the extraordinary group portrait made in *The Trouble with Harry*. Who are the women in it? Mildred Natwick, who has her hair done in a grocery store; Shirley MacLaine, who initially appears as a tall, elegant figure in a tight skirt, quickly changes to an unflattering dress that draws attention to her adolescent features, her delicious pouts and smiles. The central theme of the film is a group portrait, in which connections and complicity are created by the presence of an extra body: a presence in the undergrowth, an empty space, a stumbling block, a question mark that won't go away.

What is the natural state of these characters? An indeterminate pose adopted from time to time, as though they were sitting for a portrait. The soul, rendered visible through charm, is nurtured in repose.

But the fact that these professional idlers cannot manage to hold the pose is precisely what makes the stories so amusing. Like the painter's model shooing away a fly, the characters' actions and gestures are clumsy.

The plot or action involves a suspension of regular activities, a sort of temporary abdication of social obligations. What we are left with is the physical being, clothes, an air of refinement overlaid with a sense of irony, an amused observance, a certain distraction. Once he is no longer constrained by the everyday obligations of a job, the character returns to the credulity of adolescence, placing greater trust in images and appearances. In so doing, he falls prey to those images, becomes ripe for seduction.

The roles the actors portray are extremely ambiguous: the plot, the sequence of events, a hankering for adventure all take place on a kind of perpetual Sunday afternoon – a time for going to museums or amusement parks. Experience has taught us that idle moments such as these form the real subject matter of portrait paintings, that a vague lack of purpose is eternalized in portrait galleries, that aimless strollers participate in a solemn kind of rite. As the visitors traipse around the gallery, the figures in the paintings gradually come alive; the girlfriend, the former mistress pales in comparison. We even see a faint, malicious shadow on the beloved one's upper lip. In short, the figures in the paintings caricature the people who face them.

This place of suspended time is inhabited by images that have been brought to life: a life of untrammelled illusion created by the procession of images, icons and hosts, the ceremonial floral arrangements on temporary outdoor altars (e.g., the florist's scene in *Vertigo* where the sacristy seems to provide a view of the altar).

The image captured by the painting does not convey the action, plot, story or climax in its entirety, nor does it altogether influence them. Rather, it is the connection between them, a means of correcting the subject or the focus.

A portrait can also be something of a mixed pleasure. What is it, after all, but a catalogue of cold, detached beauty that one man, in whatever role or perspective he chooses to adopt, has taken the time to assemble. How are these changeable beings perceived? They are not sex objects, per se: these women are more admirable than desirable, and they all conform to a certain notion of elegance. (Hitchcock taught them how to carry themselves in high heels and tight skirts, how to take small steps, swaying their hips slightly, their upper body immobile except for a slight swinging of the arms, almost floating above the ground.) Most of them are traps, operating within the confines of an initial, seductive image. Others are lost and degraded images that a stranger – being himself merely a product of society – will restore. In *Under Capricorn,* for instance, Michael Wilding heals Ingrid Bergman's wounded self-esteem, which masquerades as amnesia.

Ingrid Bergman and Michael Wilding in Under Capricorn, 1949

Although this view of Hitchcock's women generally holds true, there is one notable exception: Grace Kelly, in spite of her charm and excessively perfect outfits (Stewart's only reproach to her is: "You are too perfect, as usual") cannot manage to seduce James Stewart except by placing herself squarely in his field of vision. Unless she takes the place of the vanished woman within his viewfinder, unless she is prepared to become both potential and substitute victim in the missing scene from the crime "witnessed" by her friend, she is unable to distract him from his "photographic" idée fixe. Stewart is obsessed by cinema, by the logical progression of a scene from which, because he fell asleep, several frames are missing. Basically, his job consists of imagining or recreating that scene. The only "portrait" he paints is of the murderer entering his apartment, of him blinding his attacker, like an overexposed piece of film, with a burst of light from his flash. These extraordinary images unfold spasmodically on a brilliantly coloured background.

Hitchcock's most striking (some would say almost incomparable) portraits are of Ingrid Bergman, to whom he gave his finest roles. Whether in *Under Capricorn, Spellbound* or

Notorious, she displays her truly wonderful smile – compassionate, childlike, inherently refined; her eyes, with their distraught plea for understanding and the emotion contained in those full lips; the kind yet haughty profile; the temples that seem so fragile in the beautifully sculpted face. Hitchcock's extraordinary achievement lies in allowing the movements and gestures of this sovereign lady of cinema to convey her passionate languor, her undeniable charm. Ingrid Bergman is definitely the only woman in Hitchcock's films who is suffering, lost, drunk or poisoned, and doubtless also the only one capable of displaying fervour and agitation, deeply intelligent irony and reserve. What kind of love does she inspire? An excessive devotion that, for once, is not directed at an image but rather at a soul, and the particular kind of terror a man who loves his sister might feel. This regal, statuesque presence who moves with such grace and languor always plays a tortured soul that must be sheltered and protected.

She's the only one who, rather than being a mere image of perfection, has a body and soul that are both equally desirable – and this body is like a face; the only one whom others assist because she is oblivious to the beauty of this body, because she is without vanity, because, in the many scenarios where she is poisoned by a governess or a stepmother, she is unaware that the soul of this body has gone astray.

It is ironic that Charles Adare (played by Michael Wilding) – unlike James Stewart in *Vertigo* – should end up playing the role of wardrobe master. This somewhat vain young man, whose snobbish attitude obscures his intelligence and sensitivity, parades Lamartine's disappointing image before us. He is a powder-puff dandy who, through flightiness, boredom and lack of useful abilities, tries his luck among the nouveaux riches. Although his attempts at refinement initially appear merely ridiculous, his devotion to a tarnished beauty becomes the film's central theme. A restored portrait, a face, a sense of style, a legitimate reign are all part of the rehabilitation of an image that puts an end to Flusky's (Joseph Cotten) and Henrietta's (Ingrid Bergman) unhappiness. The concentration on appearances, the attention to a well-balanced, harmonious portrait are such that we almost forget the reasons for their misfortune: unconfessed guilt, a false accusation and social inequality.

Hitchcock's delicacy of perception, the artful intelligence of his portraits, enables him to transform a face, a form, into the role itself; a role that, as the events unfold, is never more than a development of the portrait's potential. His portraits are beautiful, unflinching, ironic, and yet also limited – or, rather, contained – by the role itself. For herein lies the paradox we have already guessed: his portraits do not represent types, characters or fictitious personalities – for who remembers those? Rather, they are portraits of the actors themselves. The story told by the portrait is believable because it possesses the "novelistic impatience" of the striking character descriptions written in the 17th century by Saint-Simon and Retz, who wrote about real people fulfilling fictitious court duties. The author's novelistic impatience does away with part of the character; what remains is tainted by indecision, an out-of-focus-ness whose actions are out of step with the painting.

Scenes where "portraits" are being cleaned or restored are essential to Hitchcock's films, for one element in the story must remain unchanged, secure. That element is the beloved one, the woman whose image is conjured up in dreams (the living portrait in *Vertigo,* Lady Flusky in *Under Capricorn,* and many more). Unlike Byzantine icons, this image is not an object of cult worship, nor is it repainted when the occasion requires. The image is closely guarded, however, becoming the object of often fatal devotion; this is so in all of Hitchcock's films, including the extraordinary *Shadow of a Doubt,* in which the young Charlie Newton lives for and suffers by the idealized portrait of her uncle, played by Joseph Cotten. In fact, the image of the beloved one originates within itself and, through its essence or soul, provides the only constant in the entire story of images, and more often the not, the story is about what happens to it. No matter that the image recedes, disintegrates or is untrue, time stops only when it is not being pursued. The portrait's impact is perhaps the film's only resounding blow, the one truly melodic note.

When Henrietta Flusky tells Charles Adare that she has lost her mirror, he shows her her reflection by placing his overcoat behind a plate-glass window: a fleeting portrait, created by a magician's sleight-of-hand, that reveals the distraction in her features, and is one of modern cinema's most touching moments. You offer me your face and I give you back your reflection. This coat I hold behind the glass, the darkness it creates, forms the backdrop upon which I paint your face, then give it back to you. From the moment that incomparably sweet, reverent gesture takes place, the entire film is gradually reduced to Adare's gift of the image and the restoration of Flusky's portrait.

These scenes go beyond the narrative just as a painting contains stories that are unable to unfold on their own, to represent the passage of time, to make people walk or figures glide. A painting is not a story frozen in time, but a composite of enigmatic identities. What do Hitchcock's films have to do with the science of portrait painting? The living image knows whence it came; the diseased, mendacious, amnesiac image (a prototype without an image or an image separated from its prototype) generates a story, a form of "portrait therapy" serving to verify the accuracy of its representation.

The charming nonsense from *The Trouble with Harry* is more of an artist's sketch than a painting. In it, we see only group portraits, against a background of autumn landscapes: undergrowth, river, green New England pastures. The subject who poses involuntarily is dead, yet nevertheless able to start and enliven conversations, create partners and friends, arrange a declaration of love at a Boy Scout's treasure hunt and so on. The body is a mysterious hot potato that each person believes he has killed inadvertently, in his thoughts, in his dreams. Although silent, it confers on the detailed tableaux a sense of intimacy. In fact, it is the key to the painting's success: the young artist miraculously sells his work, there is room for everyone in the composition – thus cancelling a short outing to snap some pictures: souvenirs of the first hint of autumn and the end of summer vacation. Conversations in the park, whispering in the bushes, enchantment along tree-lined paths, magic spells, misunderstandings. This autumn tableau has all the elements of a Shakespearian interlude: the scent or music from *A Midsummer Night's Dream.*

Henry Kendall and Joan Barry in Rich and Strange, 1932

Alfred, Adam and Eve
Alain Bergala

Creation, evil and guilt are recurrent themes in Alfred Hitchcock's work. Throughout his career, the prolific film-maker was haunted by key episodes in Genesis, which served both as textual (narrative) and visual (figurative) matrices for his plots. As Jean Bottéro notes, the stories in Genesis tend to follow a basic cause-and-effect sequence: "Each of the episodes recounts a misdemeanour, usually followed by a terrible chastisement."[1] Adam and Eve disobey God's orders and are banished from the Garden of Eden. Cain murders his brother Abel and is condemned to a life of endless wandering. Humanity grows corrupt and violent, and God brings on the Great Flood, eradicating everyone, with the exception of Noah, his wife and their immediate family. Once the earth has been repopulated, humans again commit a grave error, starting to build the Tower of Babel in an attempt to reach heaven. To punish this show of excessive pride, God makes everyone speak different languages, so they can no longer understand one another and are forced to go their separate ways.

In the first of his famous interviews with François Truffaut, Hitchcock vividly recalls one aspect of his schooling at Saint Ignatius College: "It was probably during this period with the Jesuits that a strong sense of fear developed – moral fear – the fear of being involved in anything evil. I always tried to avoid it. Why? Perhaps out of physical fear. I was terrified of physical punishment. In those days they used a cane made of very hard rubber. I believe the Jesuits still use it. It wasn't done casually, you know; it was rather like the execution of a sentence. They would tell you to step in to see the father when classes were over. He would then solemnly inscribe your name in the register, together with the indication of the punishment to be inflicted, and you spent the whole day waiting for the sentence to be carried out."[2]

Doubtless, this childhood memory was carefully reconstructed for the purposes of the interview. Nonetheless,

[1] Jean Bottéro, *Naissance de Dieu (La Bible et l'historien),* Folio Histoire, No. 49, (Paris: Gallimard, 1986). (Free translation.)
[2] François Truffaut, with the collaboration of Helen G. Scott, *Hitchcock,* rev. ed. (New York: Simon & Schuster, 1984), p. 25–26.

the sequence of events clearly holds a prominent place in Hitchcock's artistic enterprise: evil (a real or imaginary misdeed) gives rise to an almost unbearable suspense, in anticipation of the inevitable punishment to come.

The repetitive sequence of crime and punishment in Genesis, as typified by Jean Bottéro, made an indelible imprint on the Jesuit schoolboy's imagination. Hitchcock the filmmaker would "restage" the Biblical episodes in an entirely personal manner, however. In *Rich and Strange, Lifeboat* and *I Confess,* the Flood gives rise to Adam and Eve's expulsion from the Garden of Eden. In *Suspicion, The Birds* and *Torn Curtain,* an equally haunting scene recurs: Adam and Eve are shown at a distance, making agitated gestures on a hilltop in the Garden, from which they are soon to be expelled. The worried observer (audience) is too far away to see or hear whether the couple are locked in embrace or in a violent struggle.

Rich and Strange (1932) is one of Hitchcock's most revealing explorations of his anxieties, which he would later learn to skilfully mask with impeccably smooth and intentionally spectacular productions. The film starts off as a marital comedy, in the vein of *An Affair to Remember.* A married couple (Fred and Emily Hill) board a luxury cruise liner, hoping to put some thrill and excitement into their lives. Each will try to provoke the other by having an affair with a potential rival: Fred with an adventuress (the "princess") and Emily with Commander Gordon. For an hour, the film shows humorous scenes of the couple's attempts to jettison their relationship. Then, all of a sudden, Hitchcock changes his tune. Without warning, the audience is plunged into an entirely different scenario that bears very little resemblance to the previous comic scenes. The new scenario does, however, closely follow the scriptural account of the Flood and Adam and Eve's expulsion from paradise. This is the first time of many that Hitchcock will use these archetypal stories as a creative vehicle to explore unsettling personal themes.

After Fred discovers that his "princess" was a con artist and Emily decides not to run off with Commander Gordon, they use the little money they have left to buy a ticket home – this time on an "ordinary" ship. The Flood takes the form of a collision in a heavy fog. As the ship starts to sink, all of the passengers flee, except for Fred and Emily, who are trapped in their little cabin, surrounded by water on all sides. In a scene reminiscent of a Fritz Lang movie, the water seeps into their room under the door while they

Joan Barry in Rich and Strange, *1932*

Joan Barry and Henry Kendall in Rich and Strange, *1932*

prepare to die. Miraculously, however, they wake up the next morning to find themselves still alive on their deserted Ark – the new primordial couple. However, the 37-year-old Hitchcock does not let his survivors off the hook that easily. Far from being washed of their sins, Fred and Emily are just as guilty as Adam and Eve after the Fall.

Adam/Fred shouts "Ahoy! Ahoy!" to make sure they really are the only people left on board, stranded in the middle of the ocean. Then suddenly Eve/Emily realizes, to her dismay, that they are still in their pyjamas: "Fred, hadn't we better go and find some clothes or something?" she exclaims. "Someone might come!" In the ludicrous scene that follows, they rush into a cabin and emerge a few seconds later, each wearing part of an officer's uniform. "That's better," she says, with undue relief. *"And,"* says the Bible, after Adam and Eve have tasted the fruit from the forbidden tree, *"the eyes of them both were opened, and they knew that they were naked; and they sewed fig leaves together, and made themselves aprons."* Once they are dressed, the couple come across a very real-looking corpse that introduces a sinister element into the comedy. Emily realizes that the corpse is the man who was sitting next to her at dinner the night before. For the first time, she and Fred become aware of their mortality and perhaps their responsibility for this shipwreck-punishment. By implication, their flirtatious games have caused this catastrophe and the death of the man at their feet. Their sexual curiosity and failure to obey the law of marital fidelity have led to their downfall. At this point, a sound makes them turn around: emerging from behind a door is a black cat, like them an abandoned creature on this Noah's Ark. All that remains to complete the Biblical narrative sequence is for them to experience the Tower of Babel – a disconcerting "otherness" – which happens immediately afterward. To punish humans for their proud attempt to build the tower, God scrambled their language, so they could no longer *"understand one another's speech,"* becoming completely alienated from one another. In Hitchcock's film, this alienation takes the form of a Chinese junk that sails up to the wreck. No sooner have the couple boarded the junk, than the remains of the ship disappear beneath the waves. They find themselves among a people whose language and customs they cannot understand (the Chinese watch impassively as one of their crew gets tangled up in a rope and drowns). The culinary customs and social rituals of this foreign culture are equally shocking (the English couple greedily devour a dish they soon discover to be the black cat, and Emily watches in horror as the strangers splash a newborn baby with a bucket of salt water). This radical alienation is the last of their trials before they return to their cosy, if somewhat drab, existence in London. Having survived no less than the Flood, expulsion from the Garden of Eden, and "post-Babelian" alienation, they are finally able to rebuild their relationship, once threatened by the forces of sexual temptation. Back to their normal lives, she plans to have children and he, to get a promotion at work. The fact that Fred and Emily's story was co-written by Alfred and Alma sheds light on the autobiographic nature of this meditation on marital commitment versus adultery. Stanley Kubrick revisited the same theme in his last film, *Eyes Wide Shut* (a cross between Hitchcock and Buñuel), the plot of which is eerily close to *Rich and Strange.*

In *Lifeboat,* released 12 years later, God visits his diluvial wrath on humanity in the form of a tornado. All of the passengers in the lifeboat are certain their hour has come, when an enormous downpour literally floods the screen. At this point, the "bad" man (Kovak) puts his arm around the "bad" woman (the journalist, Constance Porter), and gallantly cries, "We might as well go down together, right Connie?" before passionately kissing her. A fade-out signals the death of everyone on board. When the storm subsides, though, Noah's Ark emerges intact, marking the dawn of a new human era. As the sun rises over a calm sea, the camera counterpoises two new dyads: the "pure" couple (the sweet nurse, Alice, and the shy radio operator, Stanley), who are sitting under a canvas sheet, and the defiant sexual couple (Connie and Kovak), who are joined in their desire and contempt (she is cynical, he is sceptical). The "good" couple are in a state of Edenic bliss. In these hellish surroundings, they have discovered their own small paradise under the canvas sheet, protected from the elements and prying gaze of the others. Later on, they agree to marry without even knowing each other's last names, as if they have become the primal human couple. Stanley's first amorous gesture is childish: he unties the ribbon of string in Alice's hair. This gesture – a man loosening the coiffed hair of an alluring woman – recurs frequently in Hitchcock's work, symbolizing surrender to sexual desire.

By the time *I Confess* was released in 1953, exactly 21 years after *Rich and Strange,* Hitchcock had significantly refined his personal "restaging" of the Flood and Adam and Eve's expulsion from Paradise. Systematically inverting the chronology of the Biblical account, the critical scene in *I Confess* occurs in a flashback. A priest, Father Michael Logan (Montgomery Clift), and a married woman, Ruth Grandfort (Anne Baxter), are summoned by the police to a confrontation of witnesses. The case under investigation is the murder of a blackmailer lawyer named Villette, whose killer (the church caretaker) has confessed his crime to Father Logan. Since the latter is bound by the Confessional Seal, he refuses to testify. It is therefore Ruth who reveals that she had been blackmailed by Villette and then proceeds to explain why. Before the war, she was madly in love with Michael, who was not yet a priest. During his long absence, he wrote her a letter asking her not to wait for him. After he stopped writing altogether, Ruth ended up marrying her employer, Pierre Grandfort. The day after Michael returned from the war, they went for a walk in the country. In this scene, Ruth does not tell Michael that she is married. At one point, she interrupts his talk of the war by pulling him toward her and kissing him; immediately a storm comes up and a heavy rain starts falling.

We then see them running across a huge field in the pouring rain toward the Ark (a small house). This race (which Godard refers to in his *Histoire[s] du cinéma*) is filmed in three shots, from three fixed points. Each time the couple run away toward the shelter, the camera immediately catches up to them; and again they race ahead, as if struggling to avoid the camera's gaze. But Adam and Eve cannot escape this all-seeing god who, in the blink of an eye, is at their side. Like the wolf in the story of *The Three Little Pigs*, they try in vain to enter the main (brick) house and the wood barn, finally taking shelter in a flimsy-looking summerhouse, exposed to the elements. As in *Lifeboat,* the man's first gesture is to touch the woman's hair, brushing the wet locks off her forehead. At dawn, radiant sunlight heralds a fresh new world. The first man and woman wake up to the beauty of creation and smile at each other. Their Edenic bliss is short-lived, however. From a distance, the owner (Villette) comes striding toward them, before Ruth has time to hide. As she recounts, "A man came walking down through the garden […]," echoing the Biblical narrative: *"[…] they heard the voice of the Lord God walking in the garden in the cool of the day: and Adam and his wife hid themselves from the presence of the Lord God amongst the trees of the garden."* Ruth goes on to describe how Villette did not initially know who she was, but apparently knew she was a woman, because he started making insulting remarks to Michael, who became infuriated and knocked him to the ground. At this point, Villette recognized Ruth to be Mrs. Grandfort. Calling her by her married name, he laid bare her secret to Michael, showing the future priest how he had been ensared by her seductive charms. Villette's arrival shatters the couple's illusory Garden of Eden, as both become aware of their guilt. Once again, Hitchcock does not allow his creatures to emerge from the flood washed of their sins. On the contrary, they are just as guilty – and aware of their guilt – as Adam and Eve on their banishment from the Garden. Michael's violence toward Villette sets off a chain of evil which culminates in the latter's actual murder by the caretaker. On a deeper level, Villette's murder probably fulfils an unconscious desire on the part of the illegitimate couple (doubly illegitimate, for she is married and he has become a priest in the intervening years), although neither would dare admit as much, even to themselves. Hitchcock's "wrong man" always knows deep down that he is ontologically guilty, although not necessarily of the crime of which he is accused.

Another compelling "archetypal" scene that frequently surfaces in Hitchcock's work is that of a couple arguing on a small hill. An unexpected wind comes up, accompanied by dramatic music. The image is reminiscent of 15th-century Italian paintings of Adam and Eve being chased from the Garden of Eden – Massacio's fresco in the Brancacci chapel in Santa Maria del Carmine, Florence (1425) and Fra Angelico's *Annunciation* altarpieces at the Prado in Madrid (1430–32) and at the Diocesan Museum in Cortona (1433–34).

Compared to the rest of the film, this image always looks "primitive," matching the figurative innocence and simplicity that marked the beginning of the quattrocento style. Hitchcock deliberately uses artificial-looking props (transplanted trees, for instance) to recreate a "naïve" landscape – one is reminded of the "cardboard" rocks of Giotto. Eden, for him, is not an Akkadian "plain" or a Sumerian "fertile ground"; rather, it is a small, fairly arid hill, covered by only a few spindly trees or hedges. Fra Angelico's *Annunciation* altarpiece at Cortona offers the closest model for these stylized studio landscapes in which a man and woman, outlined against the sky, confront one another.

This powerful image surges unexpectedly in Hitchcock's work, breaking up the continuity of the film (in *Suspicion,* the image creates a brutal figurative hiatus), like some irrepressible psychological urge the filmmaker is unable to control. As soon as the story approaches the dangerous waters of original sin, the film is suddenly sucked up in a

Tommaso di ser Giovanni Cassai Masaccio, *Adam and Eve Expelled from Paradise,* 1424–1428

maelstrom: Hitchcock willingly surrenders all homogeneity, irresistibly drawn into scenes that shatter the order and harmony thus far established in the script.

Julien Gracq has most clearly elucidated the manner in which these primal images haunt the creative imagination. "The artist," he writes (speaking of writers and poets), "is driven by an obsessive impulse that is articulated through certain repeated images or *movements.* These expressions are usually very simple, which means they can take on a thousand different forms, and still carry the same resonance. The images evoke a very special, powerful type of emotion. We sense them instinctively, from a distance. Even before we see them, we are filled with anxiety and foreboding. [...] One has the impression that, in approaching these unavoidable urges, [the writer] is filled with hesitation, fear, even panic – as if they were a personal abyss, a call to self-annihilation."[3]

In *Suspicion* (1941), this "artificial" image surges without warning, violently contrasting with the shots preceding and following it. One truly has the impression that Hitchcock is being unrelentingly drawn into his "personal abyss." Once again, the film starts off as a blithe romantic comedy. While travelling on a train, a rather prim young woman from a good family, Lina McLaidlaw (Joan Fontaine), meets an older man of leisure, Johnny Aysgarth (Cary Grant), whose amorous exploits provide endless fodder for the local gossip pages. The following day, Johnny stops by Lina's house with some friends, under the pretext of escorting her to church. At the church gate, though, he tosses a coin to determine their true destination and then leads her astray on an impromptu walk. The scene that follows clashes strongly with the previously peaceful tone of the film. The rupture is accentuated by sudden strident music, suggesting an imminent murder. The couple are on top of a hill beside two scraggly trees. A strong wind has risen, shaking the trees and tugging at their clothing. Lina, whose bag and hat are lying on the ground, appears to be struggling with Johnny, trying to fight off what seems, from the audience's limited perspective, to be an attempted murder. It is impossible at this distance to hear what they are saying, especially since the music is predominant on the soundtrack. In the next shot, however, the camera has leapt to their side, and their voices can suddenly be heard very clearly. The wind has miraculously died down, and the disturbing music has been brusquely replaced by a sentimental melody. "Now what did you think I was trying to do?" Johnny inquires sardonically, "Kill you? Nothing less

[3] Julien Gracq, *Préférences* (Paris: José Corti, 1989), p. 58. (Free translation)

than murder could justify such violent self-defense!" When Lina asks him to let her go, he remarks, "Oh, I'm just beginning to understand – you thought I was going to kiss you, didn't you?" When she tremulously asks, "Weren't you?" he laughingly replies, "Of course not! I was merely reaching round you, trying to fix your hair." The film's "bloody moment" has lasted all of one shot. In an instant, order is restored and the previous gentle tone resumed. But the episode has introduced a note of confusion and ambiguity into the story: a doubt that will plague Lina for the rest of the film (did he want to embrace or kill her?). It is almost as if Hitchcock, in temporarily "losing control" of his art, were revealing the deep anxiety he undoubtedly felt during the filming of the scene. The image of the couple on the hill surfaces in at least three other films: *The Birds, Torn Curtain* (in its purest form) and *Notorious* (a more diluted version).

In each case, the powerful, eruptive image reveals both Hitchcock's "personal abyss" and his driving creative force. Both figuratively and literally, it signals an overflow of emotion and carries all the intensity of a primal or archetypal situation. The observer, who is forced (by the camera) to watch the scene from afar, without being able to hear what the man and woman are saying to one another, is like a little boy watching *the* archetypal scene: his parents engaged in an argument. Unable to decide whether he is witnessing an act of violence (an attempted murder or rape), or an act of love from which he is excluded, the boy is filled with anxiety. A way for the adult filmmaker to overcome this anxiety is to project it, in all its intensity, onto a scene, making the viewer share in the child's experience. One is reminded of how Marnie, in the film of the same name, "sees red" when she is distressed, although this subjective vision is not, strictly speaking, limited to her viewpoint. The audience, which sees *all* the shots in red at these tense moments, is "infected" by Marnie's anxiety.[4] Hitchcock knew better than anyone (perhaps with the exception of Buñuel) how to use cinematographic language to draw his viewers into a character's turmoil.

It is interesting to note that Hitchcock uses the archetypal image of Adam and Eve's expulsion to "tone down" or depersonalize his intense psychological investment in these sequences. The camera's capacity to defy spatio-temporal laws, instantly breaching the gap between the observer and the figures on the hilltop, offers Hitchcock a means of psychologically overcoming the distance between himself and his parents. Like an omnipotent god,

[4] Hitchcock invites viewers to identify with a distressed character by making the latter's subjective reaction "contagious." For instance, a "wrong man"'s dizziness at the moment of his incarceration is conveyed, not in the shots corresponding to his point of view, but in the entire frame that contains the character.

the filmmaker has found the perfect tool with which to "breach the gap" of time and space, and thus avenge the little boy's frustration: he fulfils his desire to see and hear (and even participate in) what is going on. According to the well-known Hitchcockian theory, a person filming a couple making love is inevitably drawn into a ménage à trois.

Let us return to *Suspicion* for a moment. The intensity of the enigmatic scene on the windy hilltop immediately abates when the camera lens captures the couple up close. Now that his creatures are no longer trying to escape his control or talk behind his back (cf. the Tower of Babel), the angry creator is appeased. One is reminded of God's wrath in Genesis when his newly "enlightened" children try to hide from him: *"And they heard the voice of the Lord God walking in the garden in the cool of the day* [a breeze, which in Hitchcock's interpretation, becomes a storm or sudden, violent wind]*: and Adam and his wife hid themselves from the presence of the Lord God amongst the trees of the garden."* In *Suspicion* and *The Birds,* the trees are too thin to hide behind and Hitchcock, the jealous god, does not even allow his subjects a second shot to run away from him: he is instantly at their side, camera and microphone at the ready. On the hilltop in *Suspicion,* Adam immediately starts playing with Eve's hair, undoing her tightly wound braid and sticking it up behind her head like a feather. As we have already seen in *Lifeboat,* this gesture symbolizes surrender to physical temptation. Hitchcock was fascinated by this image, an adept inversion of classic portrayals of Adam reaching to take the

apple offered by Eve (even if here, the man is the true temptor). Once the tense moment in *Suspicion* has passed, the couple descend the hill, back to reality. When they reach Lina's house, Johnny stays at the gate and watches her walk away toward the front door. Just before reaching the door, she overhears her parents through the open window, saying that she will probably end up a spinster. The moment Lina hears this terribly definitive assessment of her undesirability, Hitchcock catches the back of her head in a tight close-up: her hair is neatly tied up again in a bun. She turns to face the camera, visibly offended, and (along with the audience) makes the surprising discovery that the man she has just refused to kiss is standing less than a metre away. She abruptly puts her hand around his neck and kisses him. In this instance, both Hitchcock and the man magically "cross the gap" and appear before the woman, allowing her the opportunity to yield to the temptation she resisted, and ease her vexation and desire.

In *The Birds* (1963) Hitchcock returns with insistence to this image of the couple on the hill. The scene is perfectly inverted: this time it is the woman (Melanie) who is the stranger. Her arrival in the isolated village of Bodega Bay is preceded by gossip-column reports of her wealth, frivolous nature and questionable "big city" morals. Corruption follows in her wake. Although she is no Anita Ekberg, rumour has it that she, too, swam naked in a fountain in Rome the previous summer.

The Adam-and-Eve scene on the hill takes place at a critical juncture in the storyline: just before the birds launch their first attack on the children at Mitch's little sister Cathy's garden birthday party. After the scene in which Mitch and Melanie confront one another and then apparently become reconciled, evil suddenly strikes the innocents. The rapid succession of the two scenes clearly implies a relation of cause and effect.

The archetypal scene is filmed on top of a sparsely vegetated dune from which, at low tide, several branches of a river may be seen, strongly evoking the four branches of the river in the Garden of Eden. Mitch and Melanie leave the party to walk up to the top of the dune. In a very abrupt 180° transition, they suddenly find themselves face-to-face in an empty, stylized landscape, as if they were the first couple, alone together at the beginning of time. They are initially filmed from a distance and, as in the archetypal scene in *Suspicion,* the viewer cannot hear what they are saying (the soundtrack is completely silent). Then, as they approach the camera, Hitchcock "switches on" their dialogue, as if they were suddenly very close. The director's decision appears completely arbitrary, without the slightest concern for realistic effect. In this instance, it is the soundtrack (the sudden return from silence) that allows him to magically breach the gap that separates him from the object of his desire. The jealous god has become a soundman, able to tune into his creatures' conversation at will.

Mitch, in this scene, remains perfectly still – literally "rooted" to the spot – his bottle and glass in hand.[5] Melanie, however, keeps moving away and returning like a yo-yo. On three occasions, she turns her back to him, offering a perfect view of the back of her neck and bun. Good-natured Mitch is attracted to this worldly woman, but is determined to resist her charms. This distrustful Adam will not surrender without a fight to the seductive Eve, who insists she is not the "bad" woman she is rumoured to be, recounting her respectable weekly routine in detail. One is reminded of the creation story in Genesis, except that Melanie's day of rest is, of course, Friday (the day of Venus). In her efforts to persuade Mitch of her innocence, she even explains, in an angry tone, the cause of her rebellious behaviour: her mother abandoned her when she was 11 years old. The first time she turns away, showing Mitch (and us) the back of her neck, she alludes to her time in Rome as a confused period in her life ("it was very easy to get lost there"). Although she has already told Mitch that the famous fountain story was largely untrue (she was

[5] Contrast this with the scene in *North by Northwest* (1959) where Cary Grant, who realizes that Eva Marie Saint is playing a double game, remains motionless while she gesticulates in an attempt to justify herself.

actually pushed, fully clothed, into the fountain), the incident, like Adam and Eve's eating of the fruit, revolves around a shameful discovery of nudity. The second time she turns is when she describes the departure (and guilt) of her mother. We will never know if this Eve – who, at these moments, doesn't dare meet the gaze of the man she has fallen in love with, is sincerely aware of her guilt and is trying to make amends – or whether she is a consummate actress, skilfully using her art to overwhelm Mitch's defenses. Mitch, who knows only too well how a mother can affect the life of her child, appears to believe Melanie and seems to be at the point of surrender. At this point, they descend the dune and re-enter society, under the resentful gaze of the two women who have loved Mitch for a long time (Annie Hayworth and Mitch's mother). Immediately afterward, the birds launch their first organized attack, against the children at the birthday party. Mitch's surrender, reminiscent of Adam's surrender to Eve, is immediately punished by an unfair, jealous god, who makes innocent victims pay for the crime that has been committed. Typically, Hitchcock shrouds the moment in ambiguity. After giving Melanie plenty of time to justify her actions, ask for forgiveness and convince us of her innocence, he confirms her ontological guilt (she is rich and frivolous and wants to seduce a naïve man) by juxtaposing the scene with the massive punitive attack by the birds.

In a later and long underrated film, *Torn Curtain* (1966), released 25 years after *Suspicion,* Hitchcock realized his most definitive reconstruction-reversal of the Adam and Eve scenario. To perfect his adaptation of the haunting Biblical episode, he not only cast Adam and Eve, but also the third character, Yahweh Himself. This last portrayal is a "negative," in which all the original sequences are systematically inverted: Cain's murder of Abel precedes the fall of Adam and Eve; a duplicitous Adam, who has assumed a false identity so as to escape the watchful gaze of the apparatchik who controls their fate, is the one who tempts Eve to taste the fruit of knowledge. It is this complete reversal that allows the story to logically end on a happy note. The political message is very clear: the communist "paradise" must be escaped at all costs (even murder). The firm and rather unpleasant political stance of this film afforded Hitchcock his most effective means of retaliation against the psychological anguish the archetypal image had been causing him for so long.

Professor Michael Armstrong (Paul Newman) is a renowned nuclear scientist who pretends to defect to the "other" side in order to extract a secret formula from an East German professor. His fiancée/assistant, Sarah Sherman (Julie Andrews), who accompanies him to East Berlin, is not aware of his double game and believes he really has betrayed the United States. On their arrival, Michael is assigned a security guard who goes by the dubious name of Gromek. Gromek clearly takes himself for Michael's German brother: he once lived in New York, he chews gum incessantly and he tries to act like Edward G. Robinson. Gromek follows Michael everywhere he goes. At one point, thinking he has thrown his keeper off his scent, Michael takes a taxi to an isolated farm where he meets his contact from the π network who is to arrange his and Sarah's re-crossing of the Iron Curtain once he has obtained the formula. Just before leaving the house, Michael is dismayed to see that Gromek has followed him and knows his secret. He has no choice but to kill this false brother, which he does with the help of the German woman in the farmhouse. As in the story of Cain and Abel, the murder is committed in the middle of the country.

Shortly afterward, the famous Adam-and-Eve scene takes place between Michael and Sarah, partway up a hill. They know they are being watched from a distance by the political agent, Karl Manfred, who has arranged Michael's transfer to the East. Michael reveals to Sarah that he has not in fact defected, but is playing a double game to fool the communists. As in the Fall story, the scene revolves around access to "forbidden" knowledge, although in this case, Adam is the one who has had the first taste. Instead of causing immediate punishment and suffering, however, the revelation triggers an outpouring of love and grace. Once Sarah's eyes are opened to the truth, she weeps with happiness, while romantic music accentuates her emotions.

One has the impression that Hitchcock has discovered a way to exorcise the anguish and guilt he always associated with this compelling scene. In psychological terms, the filmmaker's third attempt at reversal is a success: by remaining more faithful than ever to the original account in Genesis, he manages to end the story on a satisfying note.

In the scene preceding the confrontation on the hill, a tense Sarah is interrogated about Michael's work by an Areopagus of scientists in a university amphitheatre. When she refuses to speak and turns to yell at Michael, "You're the one who sold out – you tell them!", the scientists decide to let her fiancé have a word with her in private. The couple walk away from the others along a path leading up a hill. The scene could be titled "from one hill to another": from the Areopagus (the learned assembly that gathered on the hill of Ares) to Hitchcock's hill in the Garden of Eden. The setting is entirely incongruous: a studio hill directly inspired by Renaissance paintings of Adam and Eve's banishment from the famous garden. Manfred, who respects Michael's wishes by remaining at the bottom of the hill, cannot hear what the couple are saying to each other. Hitchcock films them from Manfred's point of view: two miniature figures silently arguing on the hilltop, gesturing like figures from a quattrocento painting. Never has the filmmaker remained so faithful to his pictorial models as when he shamelessly perverts the original Biblical account in this scene. At the same time, he remains very close to the story of the Flood, the implication being that, in the middle of the Cold War, five years after the construction of the Berlin Wall, God's new elect are none other than the American people.

After making a series of angry, frustrated gestures, Sarah appears to calm down. At the same time, sentimental music wells up. Hitchcock then cuts from the long shot to a close-up of a tearful Sarah, smiling with relief as she exclaims "Oh, Michael!" But her fiancé, who has not forgotten that their lives are still in danger, cautions her to be careful, as he gestures toward Manfred below, who is straining to see what is going on through his thick-lensed glasses, trying to guess what they are talking about. Hitchcock then proceeds with a quite literal evocation of the famous passage cited earlier: " [...] and Adam and his wife hid themselves from the presence of the Lord God amongst the trees of the garden." After another explicit shot in which the couple are framed on either side of the "tree of knowledge," separated into two symmetrical halves on the screen, Michael pulls Sarah behind a clump of bushes where, hidden from the eyes of the "father figure," they passionately embrace one another, caught in extreme close-up by Hitchcock's famous "third camera," and "transported" by the music.

Contrary to the Biblical account, where nothing can escape the knowledge and wrath of God, this Edenic scene has a happy ending, even though Michael and Sarah have yet to surmount other obstacles in their path. For the moment, Manfred appears to have been taken in by Michael/Adam's little play. Even though the noose continues to tighten around Michael's neck (on a tip from the taxi driver, the secret police have just uncovered Gromek's makeshift grave in the farmyard), he and Sarah will succeed in crossing the Iron Curtain and will finally be able to get married, her trust in him restored after the revelation in the Garden.

The childish traits of Manfred, who looks more like a big baby than a serious "father figure," reveal much of the personal story behind Hitchcock's creative exploitation of the Biblical account. Hitchcock is the child who, worried and powerless, watches his parents' lovemaking/confrontation from afar. Armed with a camera and microphone, however, the adult filmmaker can finally take complete control of the situation, instantly breaching the gap of powerlessness, guilt and incomprehension, and openly joining the Edenic couple in their happy, shameless embrace.

Martin Balsam in Psycho, 1960

Hitchcock the Metaphysician

Gérard Genette

This letter, addressed by Gérard Genette to the Cahiers du cinéma *(No. 52, Nov. 1955) and commented on by François Truffaut ("since we're invited to, why not end with a little metaphysics?") was written, according to its author, as a hoax; a deliberate attempt to stir up the Hitchcockian interpretative debate. Beyond responding to the zealous views of a reader whose letter appeared in issue No. 50, Genette's analysis targetted the famed interpretations of Claude Chabrol and Éric Rohmer, well before they were published in 1957. The hoax that supposedly inspired this letter is rapidly effaced by the critical brilliance of the admirable author of* Figures *(1966, 1969, 1972),* Mimologics *(1976),* Palimpsests *(1982),* Narrative Discourse Revisited *(1983),* Fiction and Diction *(1991) and the two volumes of* The Work of Art *(1994 and 1997), all published by Éditions du Seuil. That is why I persuaded Mr. Genette at length to let us republish his letter, annotated by François Truffaut ("We wanted to print this superb analysis in its entirety, as a fitting conclusion to this chapter of the Hitchcockian exegesis").*

D.P.

Mr. Editor,

I wish to tell you that, as a faithful reader of the *Cahiers* and a great admirer of Hitchcock's work, I was both delighted and disappointed to read the letter signed J.M., published in issue No. 50.

Delighted, because I feel this letter has finally sparked a meaningful debate on Hitchcock by planting it in its natural terrain: theology. Disappointed, because I find your correspondent to be guilty of certain inaccuracies that lead me to suspect he might belong to the Society of Jesus.

Mr. J.M. very rightly claims that Hitchcock is anything but Puritan. However, he insists on referring to the filmmaker as "moral," comparing his position to that supposedly held by the likes of Bourdaloue. Furthermore, your correspondent appears to fall prey to the common confusion between Puritanism and Jansenism, leading us back into a fray we hoped to have put behind us. As much as I consider it absurd to speak of Hitchcock's Puritanism, I find it both legitimate and necessary to speak of his theology – which is not perhaps that of Port-Royal and Pascal (then again, the *Interview with Mr. de Sacy...*), but is at least that of Saint Cyran and Jansen, and finally (to go straight to the heart of the matter) that of Saint Augustine himself.

I do not believe that Hitch's attitude toward his heroes stems any more from an ethics of Evil (like that of Fritz Lang) than it does from criminology (cf. Hawks in *Scarface*)[1]; rather it may be traced to a metaphysics of sin, one that, from every perspective, refers to the dialectic of grace. Because sin presupposes grace just as much as grace presupposes sin. Stripped of its polemical qualities, this orthodox statement perhaps captures the essence of Jansenist theology in its rigorous adherence to the original Christian message, as Mr. Orcibal recently demonstrated in his talks at the École des Hautes Études.

I would not call Hitchcock a "prodigious moralist" for the simple reason that he is not a moralist (especially not one who, in the classic French tradition, has been raised on casuistry), but rather a metaphysician.[2]

Even his humour is metaphysical, not unlike that of renowned fellow countrymen John Donne and Andrew Marvell. It is insufficient to say that Hitchcock does not despise his heroes; he does not even condemn them, because he sees them as carrying the burden of sin even before they openly acknowledge their guilt. The crime they commit (or supposedly commit) invariably bears the stain of Original Sin.

Critics have too often neglected to point out that the true culprit in *Rear Window,* whose final punishment Hitchcock never reveals, is not the "criminal" in the plot, but rather the witness (the "voyeur"), because he is the one who has committed the real sin of gaining forbidden knowledge. One could see this extraordinary film as a point-by-point retelling of the original story in Genesis, particularly in its treatment of the couple, characterized not by eroticism (in the sense of erotic fulfilment) but rather by frustration on every level, including the erotic. The two lovers are unhappily trapped in an earthly paradise from which they try to escape (she, through her penchant for beautiful clothes, he, through his love of food) until finally, they are confront-

[1] It is even less inspired by the type of Greek fate mythology embraced by Huston or Becker in *Touchez pas au Grisbi* ("Honour Among Thieves"), or by other, lesser, talents who have sought to revive the ancient tragedies. Hitch has far too Christian a sense of destiny to become ensnared by the Fates.

[2] Which might explain why, in various interviews, he has been largely disinterested in answering his admirers' deliberately *moral* questions. These questions were not, as previously thought, above him, but rather beneath the complexity of his work.

ed by true temptation in the form of the Tree of Knowledge. All of the elements from the Biblical account are present, including the Fall, which Hitch mercilessly portrays to the letter; even the Woman's corrupting role is subtly evaded until the critical point, and only then does the temptation become irresistible. Thus, the lovers are joined, not in love, which is only for the blind ("If God exists, we must love Him, not his creatures"), but in the pathetic complicity of Sin. While physically, they embrace each other, in fact they are embracing their mutual downfall, misery and spiritual destitution ("And the eyes of them both were opened, and they knew that they were naked").

In a less explicit but equally clear manner, films such as *Rebecca* or *Suspicion* lead us from earthly crimes back to Original Sin by showing the guilt of the man as necessarily coexistent with the curiosity of the woman. I do not think it paradoxical to say that Laurence Olivier would not be retrospectively guilty of murdering Rebecca if Joan Fontaine had not insisted on solving the mystery of her death. And what is the plot of *Suspicion,* if not an implacable demonstration of the link between suspicion and crime, between knowledge and Sin, to the extent that a renunciation of the one all but eradicates the probable existence of the other?

There are doubtless as many examples of these theological undercurrents as there are Hitchcock movies; they are an essential feature of the filmmaker's creative project. We need look no further than *Rope,* where the criminals are lured into crime, not by the temptation of financial gain, but by a theory. The last images of the film show the young men's former housemaster (the true culprit) concluding that all theories are the work of Satan.

How then does one distinguish between Hitchcock's victims and executioners, the guilty and the innocent? Crimes are never perfect because they are always reversible (the explicit message of *Dial M for Murder*) and they are only reversible because they are universal. Hitchcock's murderers are almost always disarmingly charming. No matter what they do, the audience finds them "likeable," and rightly so, because they are not really any guiltier than the supposedly innocent characters. Let us recall what is possibly the most appalling and beautiful image in cinematic memory: the scene from *Strangers on a Train* where, just before committing his "crime," the murderer allows himself the gratuitous pleasure of bursting a child's balloon with his cigarette. The boy, brutally deprived of his childish happiness, turns toward the man (the audience) with an expression neither of anger nor even surprise: as if he knows only too well that he deserved this cruel prank. After all, wasn't this "innocent" victim the one who, just a few seconds earlier, brandished his ludicrous but symbolically aggressive toy pistol at the "executioner"? In Hitchcock's game, there are no guilty players because there are no innocent players either. Such is the implication of this striking episode, which most viewers (according to my research) find "implausible."

It would appear that Hitchcock's "morality," which has nothing to do with the common meaning of the term, is tied to the purest and most rigorous strain of Christian metaphysics.[3] Not the debased, perverted, moralizing message of Puritanism or of Protestantism as a whole; nor the worldly casuistry of the 17th-century French Jesuits, rightly denounced by Pascal. Rather, as historical chance would have it, Hitchcock takes his moral inspiration from Jansenism, a tradition dating back to Thomas Aquinas and Saint Augustine before him. This tradition teaches us not to play with Sin: the fall-grace dialectic can only be resolved at the Last Judgment, an endless horizon toward which Hitchcock's heroes advance, *smiling.* Can we ever know whether this smile is one of resignation to Infernal misery or certitude of Heavenly pardon?

It is futile, in my view, to insist on the lessons a modern viewer can draw from reflection on these subjects. For Hitchcock's terrifying reality only reflects the even more terrifying reality of Christianity.

Much remains to be said about these matters. The *exegesis* of Hitchcock's work – a project the *Cahiers du cinéma* have embraced with suitable passion – has only just begun. I would be very grateful if you could publish this letter, in spite of its aggressively partisan tone, because I think these things need to be said, and yours is the only magazine in which one can say them.

Sincerely,

Gérard Genette, Paris

[3] Here we can see one of the reasons why Hitch denies having an underlying "message" in his work. There is, properly speaking, only one message: the divine message. Human artistic creations do nothing more than illustrate, popularize or parody this message. Hitch might well say that he is interested only in telling "stories." That is because every story is a version of The Story, the divinely comic tale of human tragedy.

Hitchcock: Eating and Destruction

Pierre Gras

Vivien Merchant and Alex McCowen in Frenzy, 1972

Frenzy, 1972

A cosy domestic scene: the table is set, the evening meal has been served, a husband and wife exchange small talk. While the man eats, the woman remains standing at the table or by the stove. Alfred Hitchcock creates this tableau twice in 35 years, reusing in *Frenzy* (his last British film, made in 1971) the dinner scene from *Sabotage* (1936). Given the director's well-known tendency to transcend the ordinary – i.e., to infuse his audience's most familiar associations with the spectacular – it is not surprising that, in *Sabotage,* the evening meal of Mr. and Mrs. Verloc (played by Oscar Homolka and Sylvia Sydney) should turn into a murder scene. Fascinated by the kitchen knife, the wife picks it up and thrusts it into her husband. Nor should we be surprised that, as Inspector Oxford (played by Alec McCowen) eats his dinner and talks to his wife in *Frenzy,* the scene should gradually be taken over by invisible corpses with bulging eyes, whose murderer the inspector is trying to track down.

The palpable presence of invisible corpses is a key element at both meals. In *Sabotage,* it is Stevie, Mrs. Verloc's younger brother who has been accidentally blown up by a bomb he was unwittingly carrying. The explosion is the climax to a suspense sequence that critics called sadistic and that, in response to the accusation, Hitchcock publicly deplored for the rest of his life. Although Hitchcock rarely adapted the works of well-known writers, this film (with some slight changes) follows the two main plotlines of Joseph Conrad's novel *The Secret Agent*: a child's shocking death in a burst of light and torn metal, and the dinner where Mrs. Verloc – more confused than vengeful – is gradually drawn to murder. Mr. Verloc, the one who gave the child the bomb, seems more preoccupied with his dinner than with any thought of defending himself. In *Frenzy,* Hitchcock dissociates sound from image so that, while we hear the inspector's wife putting her husband on the trail of the real murderer, we see him staring at the cadavers on his plate: greasy pork trotters, small quail bodies, fish staring fixedly at him from the soup. Hitchcock was always a perfectionist, and in the intervening 35 years his directing style had evolved. In 1936 he filmed a pivotal scene in an understated way; the lack of emphasis allowed the spectator to retain some sympathy for Mrs. Verloc. In 1971 he took a weak scene (helping the police find a murderer whose identity the spectator already knows) and gave it a startling new twist by making a concrete connection between dead bodies and food.

Anny Ondra's murderous hand (Blackmail), 1929

Through conspicuous repetition, through a brilliant formalistic retelling by this masterful director, Hitchcock's obsession returns. In his oeuvre – in which he pursues an uncluttered directing style and plays like a conductor on the spectator's feelings – food has a significant role. The relationship between dead bodies, garbage and food is a constant in his work, from his earliest film (*Blackmail*, 1929) to *Frenzy* (1972). In *Blackmail*, the knife the young heroine uses to kill her would-be rapist is an obvious choice, since it is close at hand in the seducer's apartment; it also points to Hitchcock's obsession when it reappears in the familiar guise of a bread knife at the family supper table. At this point, as in *Frenzy*, the character and the audience are forced to acknowledge the murder weapon when it resurfaces in conversation, in an auditory device typical of the earliest sound films.

A number of films from Hitchcock's Hollywood period re-examine the theme of food. The plot of *Rope* (1948) is built around a chest in which two students have hidden the body of a friend they killed for a lark. The chest is consistently visible at the cocktail party to which they invite the dead boy's parents and friends; it even serves as an ersatz buffet table. Clearly, the two murderers are trying to have the body symbolically eaten: the victim is both absent (the guests exclaim over the victim's disappearance) and present through the act of symbolic cannibalism.

The dialectic of presence and absence, the concept of bodies reappearing in other forms, is also dealt with in *Psycho* (1960), but in a more indirect way. Norman Bates's mother has one spirit (which belongs to Norman) and two bodies: her own, which has been stuffed in order to prevent decay, and her son's, through which she acts. Food is introduced in a striking way, but its presence unfailingly adheres to a certain narrative logic, such as when Marion and Norman, surrounded by stuffed animals, eat sandwiches before the famous shower scene. There are two possible ways of getting rid of the body: through internal-

Edith Evanson and James Stewart in Rope, 1948

ization (eating) or externalization (veneration). Once Marion has been murdered, her body becomes a waste product (presaged on screen through the image of a toilet seat), wonderfully conveyed by the spiral motif, which encompasses both the young woman's blood draining out of the tub and the camera's backtracking from the drain toward the henceforth immobile eye of the corpse.

In one sense, *Torn Curtain* (1966) returns to the somewhat prosaic realism of Hitchcock's British period with the murder of police officer Gromek (Wolfgang Kieling) in the kitchen. The sequence is slow, heavy, sinister, and also trivial in the deliberate use of such domestic items as a knife, saucepan and stove. At its most basic level, to kill is to transform a body into food. A scene that was filmed, but never used, methodically pursued Hitchcock's obsession with food.[1] After the crime, Armstrong (Paul Newman) meets Gromek's brother in a factory. The brother uses the same kitchen knife to cut a piece of blood pudding, which he gives to Armstrong, saying: "Could you pass this on to my brother; he loves this stuff." Once again, Hitchcock's sardonic humour urges the character to finish the job: "You've killed him; now you have to eat him!"

In film after film, their obsession with food impels the characters to define themselves through their relationship to dietary customs and habits. The police officer in *Sabotage* disguises himself as a fruit vendor to spy on the terrorist Verloc. In *Frenzy,* the "wrong man" is a barman, while the real murderer has a produce store where he hides his victims' bodies among the bags of potatoes. However, the greater prevalence of bodies in Hitchcock's postwar films (*Rope, Torn Curtain, Psycho*) should not necessarily be seen as a metaphor for World War II exterminations. An explicit connection between dead bodies and food had already been made in Conrad's *The Secret Agent* (published in 1907). The novelist likens Mr. and Mrs. Verloc's final meal to a funeral rite for the young brother that, because he has to replace the child's missing body, leads Verloc to his death.[2] In another even more direct passage, Conrad has Inspector Heaton examine the child's remains at the autopsy. As he searches through the muddy scraps of what was once Stevie Verloc, blown up in a blinding flash at the turning point of two centuries, Inspector Heaton stares at the autopsy table with (as Conrad tells us), "a calm face and the slightly anxious attention of an indigent customer looking over what might be called the by-products of a butcher's shop with a view to an inexpensive Sunday dinner."[3]

[1] François Truffaut, *Le cinéma selon Hitchcock* (Paris: Seghers, 1975), p. 348.
[2] Joseph Conrad, *The Secret Agent* (London: Penguin Popular Classics, 1994), p. 205.
[3] Conrad, p. 79.

Conrad, a conservative, spiritual writer, was deliberately attacking the materialistic violence of the czarist and imperialist regimes. He was also criticizing modern philosophy's belief in the primacy of the idealist through the "Nietzschean" tirade delivered by the professor, a terrorism expert who feels justified in murdering total strangers because he believes they are vile.[4]

There are many different explanations for the obsession with food found in Hitchcock's films. The primitive drive for food was used as a form of psychological manipulation to keep the audience alert and provide a variety of fertile associations. The use of everyday objects as murder weapons was yet another means of getting the audience involved. The heroine in *Blackmail,* Mrs. Verloc in *Sabotage,* and Professor Armstrong in *Torn Curtain* are all driven to kill almost in spite of themselves. The fact that they use the same familiar object – a kitchen knife – as a murder weapon allows the audience to identify with them and makes their characters more sympathetic. Finally, there is a typically Hitchcockian confrontation between dietary materialism and the director's Platonic ideas. Juxtaposed with films where dead bodies are omnipresent (as caricatured in *The Trouble with Harry*), there are a whole series of films from the 1950s in which the imagined presence of the dead body plays a major role. Other than *Rope* (mentioned above), these would be *North by Northwest* (in which Roger O. Thornhill, played by Cary Grant, must pretend to be George Kaplan, who is in fact a made-up spy), *Vertigo* (in which Kim Novak twice takes on the role of Madeleine, the ideal fantasy wife,[5] and *Psycho* (in which Norman's mother lives on through her son's spirit and body).

Frenzy, 1972

Hitchcock wanted to incorporate his view of the body as garbage and people as immaterial beings in other projects as well. He told Truffaut of his plans to make a documentary about 24 hours in the life of a city.[6] This film – with no police drama, no cast and no suspense – was going to be about the food cycle. He obviously felt it was important to explain how the food that is brought to market in the morning is bought, eaten, digested and excreted into the sewers. As he said, he wanted to show "what people do to good things. Your theme might almost be the rottenness of humanity." In other words, Hitchcock wanted us to see man's predatory behaviour toward nature and those around him. Taken in this context, *The Birds* could be seen as an inversion of the food chain, used to underline the truth about humanity.

[4] In *Rope,* another professor, James Stewart, also has "Nietzschean" ideas, which his criminally minded students put into practice.
[5] Truffaut, p. 359.
[6] Truffaut, p. 343.

Among his unfinished projects, Hitchcock's Platonic idealism manifests itself in his desire to adapt *Mary Rose,* a play by *Peter Pan* author Sir James Barrie.[7] In the play, the young mother escapes her cumbersome body and the onset of old age by disappearing, only to reappear in spirit form to her descendants before vanishing forever in a burst of light. Ultimately, the body is able to go through a final metamorphosis and reappear as a waste product of industrial idealism.[8] There, I believe, lies the real meaning behind a scene Hitchcock told Truffaut he had wanted to include in *North by Northwest*. While Thornhill and a foreman have a conversation next to an automobile assembly line, elsewhere on screen we see parts gradually being added on to a chassis. When the vehicle is complete, the foreman opens the door and a dead body falls out, apparently sprung from nowhere: an anachronistic waste product of the industrial age.

An obsession with food, the idealist fantasy, the question of figuration and Christian incarnation all come together. Hitchcock wondered how actors, with their corruptible flesh, could bring these spiritual entities (i.e., his characters) to life. In this regard, the Platonic scenes serve as a counterpoint to the cannibalistic ones. The idealized Madeleine's pure perfection, as recreated by Scottie,[9] is the opposite of a female corpse with bulging eyes and dangling tongue, buried under a mound of muddy vegetables. Seen as a whole, Hitchcock's oeuvre is a lengthy incantation in which corruption and divinity are endlessly superimposed, inevitably separate and forever conjoined.

[7] Truffaut, p. 343.
[8] Truffaut, p. 343.
[9] Madeleine first appears to Scottie in a restaurant: for men, the ideal woman is also a "choice morsel."

The bomb in the omnibus Sabotage, 1936

Hitchcock's Objects,
or the World Made Solid

Sally Shafto

[1] Andrew Sarris, "Alfred Hitchcock," *The American Cinema: Directors and Directions 1929–68* (New York: Dutton, 1968), p. 58–59.

[2] In referring to Hitchcock's early films as English, I follow Charles Barr, for whom these films are specifically English, not British. Barr here parts ways with the two earlier studies devoted to the first period of Hitchcock's career: *Hitchcock's British Films* (Maurice Yacowar, 1977) and *Alfred Hitchcock and the British Cinema* (Tom Ryall, 1986). See Charles Barr, *English Hitchcock* (Moffat, Scotland: Cameron & Hollis, 1999), p. 6.

[3] Sidney Gottlieb, "Early Hitchcock: The German Influence," *Hitchcock Annual 1999–2000*, p. 100–30; Bob Thomas, "Alfred Hitchcock: The German Years," *Action*, Vol. 8, No. 1 (Jan.–Feb. 1973), p. 23–25; Kirk Bond, "The Other Alfred Hitchcock," *Film Culture*, No. 41 (Summer 1966), p. 30–35.

[4] See Barry Salt, "From Caligari to Who?" *Sight and Sound*, Vol. 48, No. 2 (1979); and Jacques Aumont, "Forme et déformation, expression et expressionnisme," *L'œil interminable: cinéma et peinture* (Paris: Séguier, 1995), p. 197–222.

[5] The phrase is borrowed from Georg W. Költsch, "Expressionnisme – Le monde n'est pas solide," *Figures du moderne 1905-1919, L'expressionnisme en Allemagne* (Paris: Musée d'art moderne de la Ville de Paris, 1992), p. 58–62.

[6] Godard makes this comment in chapter 4A of the *Histoire(s) du cinéma*: "We've forgotten why Joan Fontaine leans over the edge of the cliff, and what was it that Joel McCrea was going to do in Holland. We don't remember why Montgomery Clift was maintaining eternal

"Hitchcock's films abound with objects as visual correlatives – the missing finger in *The Thirty-nine Steps* [...] the milk chocolates on the assembly line in *Secret Agent*, the knife and time bomb in *Sabotage*. [...] Hitchcock's objects are never mere props of a basically theatrical mise-en-scène, but rather the very substance of his cinema."
– Andrew Sarris[1]

The original, self-imposed brief of this article was to consider Hitchcock's English films[2] and their relation to German Expressionism. Much, for instance, is often made of Hitchcock's stay in Germany in the mid-1920s, and the fact that he had the chance to watch F.W. Murnau while the latter filmed *The Last Laugh* (1924). Ultimately, however, playing the game of detecting Expressionist influences in Hitchcock seemed a dead end, or as the director himself might say, a red herring. On the one hand, the topic has been ably tackled by Sidney Gottlieb.[3] On the other hand, the transfer of the term "Expressionist" from painting to film is by no means unproblematic.[4]

Still, it is possible to regard Hitchcock's dramatic use of light and shadow, his repetitive use of stairs, ladders, images of the double and dark foreboding landscapes, as Expressionist elements. But what seems decidedly counter to Expressionism where "the world is not solid"[5] is Hitchcock's focus on objects. The very solidity of his objects belies the shimmering inchoate aura of Expressionism. Godard expresses this idea succinctly in his *Histoire(s) du cinéma* when he comments that the only thing one remembers in a Hitchcock film is its objects.[6] Godard's extended passage cites only Hitchcock's American films, but he could have cited his English films too.[7]

In filmic language, Hitchcock's objects are often presented in close-ups. His English films frequently begin with such a shot, a *pars totalis*, and that annunciative position declares its significance.[8] *Number Seventeen* opens mysteriously on a close-up of a branch blowing in the wind. The camera then moves left and down to focus on a hat being carried along in a gale. Subsequently, an establishing shot reveals a man trying to catch up with his Stetson, a visual metaphor forecasting the audience's difficulties in keeping up with the generic mayhem of *Number Seventeen*. The opening shot of *The Man Who Knew Too Much* displays travel guides to Switzerland, orienting the film's first locale. Even the much maligned *Waltzes from Vienna* begins with such a shot: a horn underscores the title, announcing that this will be a film about music. *The Thirty-nine Steps* opens on an illuminated billboard of a music hall, as the camera pans across the sign displaying each individual letter. Ninety minutes later, the film reaches closure by returning to the same milieu.

The relation of part to whole is particularly evident in the opening shots of *Blackmail* and *Sabotage*. The former, opening on a close-up of a spinning hubcap, continues with a police van speeding through the streets. This same montage, indicating a chase, will be repeated at the film's climax. *Sabotage* opens with a dictionary entry of the film's title. Close-ups of a naked light bulb are followed by a shot of London at night brightly lit. We are then shown the light bulb again, now dimly flickering, until eventually it goes out. Dramatically, the film thus begins with an act of sabotage.

In *The Ring* two athletes compete in a boxing ring. The ring of a boxing match is intimated already in the film's opening shot of a drum being beaten. It suggests that a drum roll will accompany the announcement of a winner and a loser. Here Hitchcock portrays a love triangle (two men and one woman). Outside and inside the ring, Bob and Jack compete for the attentions of Nelly. Both attempt to bind her to them by gifts of jewelry. During the marriage, as Jack slips the ring on her finger, Bob's bracelet portentously slips down her arm, indicating her indecision about the two men.

Hitchcock's next film *The Manxman* continues this geometric emphasis. *The Manxman* opens on a close-up of a Catherine wheel, iconographic symbol for St. Catherine's martyrdom. The wheel's three spokes suggests the film's triangle (Kate, Pete and Philip) and forecasts the inexorable suffering of all three. This visual motif is repeated in the scene of the lovers' tryst in a mill, where Kate and Philip are first framed outside by the turning water mill. Inside, Kate sets in motion another wheel (a millstone), indicating her agency in the ensuing tragedy. An ellipse indicating the first

silence, or why Janet Leigh stopped at the Bates motel, or why Teresa Wright still loves Uncle Charlie. We've forgotten what it was that Henry Fonda wasn't entirely guilty of, and why exactly the American government had hired Ingrid Bergman. But we remember a handbag. But we remember a bus in the desert. But we remember a glass of milk, the sails of a windmill, a hairbrush. But we remember a row of bottles, a pair of spectacles, a sheet of music, a bunch of keys, because through them and with them Alfred Hitchcock succeeded where Alexander, Julius Caesar, Hitler, and Napoleon had all failed, by taking control of the universe. Perhaps there are ten thousand people who haven't forgotten Cezanne's apple, but there must be a billion spectators who will remember the lighter of the stranger on the train, and the reason why Alfred Hitchcock became the only *poète maudit* to meet with success was that he was the greatest creator of forms of the twentieth century, and it's forms that tell us finally what lies at the bottom of things; now, what is art if not that through which forms become style." Jean-Luc Godard, *Histoire(s) du cinéma,* trans. John Howe (Paris: Gallimard/Gaumont; New York: ECM New Series, 1998), p. 11.

Godard had already expressed this idea in 1980 in an interview with the newspaper *Libération,* following the death of Hitchcock. Godard noted that: "If you ask people to recall a film by Hitchcock, without fail they will describe for you an image, or even an object that struck them. A pair of shoes, a cup of coffee, a glass of milk, Bordeaux wine bottles." See Jean-Luc Godard, "Alfred Hitchcock, un poète maudit qui eut un succès commercial immense," *Libération,* 2 May 1980, p. 12–13. (Free translation.)

[7] Godard was not the first to make this observation. Already in the 1956 Hitchcock issue of *Cahiers du cinéma,* Philippe Demonsablon enumerated many of the recurring objects in the Hitchcock universe. See Philippe Demonsablon, "Lexique mythologique pour l'œuvre de Hitchcock," *Cahiers du cinéma,* No. 62 (Aug.–Sept. 1956), p. 18–29, 54. And in 1968, Andrew Sarris reiterated this point; see the epigraph at the start of this essay.

The Ring, 1927

lovemaking of Phil and Kate is followed by a close-up of the millstone turning, a reminder that what has just occurred will have irrevocable consequences. Finally, the iconographic motif of the wheel/circle will be returned to in the scene immediately following Kate's suicide attempt. The shot is an extreme close-up of Philip's circular inkwell, as he draws his pen to sign his first document as Deemster.

Easy Virtue, like *The Manxman,* also begins with a shot of especial narrative significance. The film's credits appear over the silhouette of a camera. (It is immediately followed by a close-up first of a newspaper, then of a judge's wig: these two shots will be repeated just before the film's finale, thus creating a rhyming frame around the narrative). At several critical points in the film, Hitchcock returns to the camera. The jury's verdict is displayed over the camera silhouette; exiting the courtroom, Larita is approached by a swarm of photographers; registering in a hotel in the south of France, she imagines a camera and the publicity she will attract, and promptly decides to take an assumed name; in the home of her second husband's family, she is frightened by the sight of a camera on a table; finally at the film's end, the newly divorced Larita walks out of the court-room and declares to the horde of photographers awaiting her: "Shoot, there is nothing left to kill." Thirty years before Michael Powell's *Peeping Tom,* Hitchcock equated the camera with a murder weapon.[9]

The Skin Game, in contrast, deviates from this pattern of opening on a close-up of an object. But that film's highly restricted use of the close-up signals its significance. Following the film's prologue, a series of 12 rapidly alternated close-ups (some repeated) underscores the rhyming binary established already in the synecdochic naming of the two warring families: Hillcrest, suggesting an alliance with nature, and Hornblower, suggesting an alliance with both noise and machines.

[8] See Claudine Delvaux, "Propositions pour un système des objets (en gros plans) chez Alfred Hitchcock (1ʳᵉ partie)," *Revue belge du cinéma,* No. 10 (Winter 1984–85), p. 61–71. In the same issue, see also "Alfred Hitchcock: le truc des accessoires géants," p. 57, and "Alfred Hitchcock: le gros plan avant la chute ou le raccord à bout de bras," p. 59.
[9] Powell, of course, was the stills photographer on *Champagne* and *Blackmail.*

Very often, an object impels a Hitchcockian narrative. At the outset of *Young and Innocent,* a woman is strangled with the belt of a mackintosh. The missing raincoat in fact propels Robert's flight from the police, because he thinks (wrongly) that it offers the proof of his innocence. In *The Lady Vanishes,* the discarded label from a packet of tea convinces the musician Gilbert that Iris is telling the truth. Subsequently, their discovery of Miss Froy's pince-nez prods the young couple forward in their search for her. In *Easy Virtue,* a decanter links present time (courtroom trial) to the time under investigation (when Larita was sitting for her portrait). The search for a stolen necklace motivates the confusion of *Number Seventeen*. Finding a tattered glove on the premises of the murder, the Scotland Yard detective in *Blackmail* realizes that his girlfriend has been there. In *The Thirty-nine Steps*, a hand missing the top joint of its little finger is the telltale clue to Richard Hannay that he is in the presence of his enemy.

What do these objects tell us about Hitchcock? Writing of Godard, for instance, critic Georgia Brown once aptly observed that "each of his films is a small museum lovingly tended."[10] The same could be said for Hitchcock's films as well. But whereas Godard's films, beginning with his citations of Renoir, Picasso, and Klee in *À bout de souffle,* are decidedly highbrow, early Hitchcock is a more varied and sundry affair. The sum of Hitchcock's objects reveals not Godard's Musée des Beaux-Arts but rather a homely *Wunderkammer,* epitomized by Ben in *Number Seventeen*.[11] Ordered to display the contents of his pockets, the wisecracking Cockney reveals a handkerchief, a string, a sausage, a baby picture and half a "fag." (Later, when questioned about his sausage, Ben comments wryly: "What do you think it is? A Christmas cracker? Back in the larder you go.")

Hitchcock's faith in objects manifests his most fundamental idea on filmmaking; i.e., that the cinema is predominantly visual, an art of monstration. In 1936 the director wrote: "A film has got to be ocularly interesting and above all it is the picture which is the thing. I try to tell my story so much in pictures that if by any chance the sound apparatus broke down in the cinema, the audience would not fret and get restless because the pictorial action would still hold them!"[12]

His ideas here correspond to those of the German philosopher Ludwig Wittgenstein, who declared in his first major book, the *Tractactus-Logico-Philosophicus*: "That which may be shown need not be said." Published in 1921 but composed during World War I, Wittgenstein's tract accompanied the shift from an Expressionist worldview to that of the *Neue Sachlichkeit* (New Objectivity). *Neue Sachlichkeit* made its critical debut in painting in 1925, when Hitchcock was in Berlin.[13] That same year Wilhelm Michel wrote: "We are dealing with a new *objectivity.* [...] We are dealing with a discovery of *things* after the crisis of the ego."[14] In painting, the New Objectivity frequently represented portraits: sitters accompanied by various objects of the world, as in Christian Schad's *Half Nude* (1929). This painting of photographic verisimilitude offers us a wealth

[10] Georgia Brown, "His Life to Live," *The Village Voice,* 10 May 1994, p. 58.

[11] In his English films, Hitchcock only rarely included easel paintings. When he did, they were invariably family likenesses, as in the female portraits decorating the lodger's room in *The Lodger,* Larita's society portrait in *Easy Virtue,* the portrait of one of Philip's forebears in *The Manxman,* and the military portrait of Brodie in *Secret Agent.* Ancestral portraits continue to play a significant role in Hitchcock's American films, as is evident in *Rebecca, Saboteur, Suspicion* and *Vertigo.* The post-Cubist canvas that attracts the assistant inspector's gaze twice in *Suspicion* obviously deviates from this tendency. Stephen Heath reads this painting in his article "Narrative Space," without, however, quite pushing his analysis far enough. In fact, Hitchcock's inclusion of this painting subtly underscores the ambiguity of Cary Grant's character (that is, legible as a still-life, the painting remains abstract). The painting is a neat reminder of abstract painting's problems in reception, and perhaps signals that Hitchcock was just at that time beginning his own art collection, which included more than a few examples of abstract painting. See Stephen Heath, "Narrative Space," *Screen,* Vol. 17, No. 3 (Autumn 1976), p. 68–72.

[12] Alfred Hitchcock, "Close Your Eyes and Visualize!" *Hitchcock on Hitchcock: Selected Writings and Interviews,* ed. Sidney Gottlieb (Berkeley: University of California Press, 1995), p. 247. Originally published in *Stage* (July 1936), p. 52–53.

[13] In 1925, Gustav Hartlaub presented an exhibition at the Mannheim Städtische Kunsthalle under the title "Neue Sachlichkeit: Deutsche Malerei seit dem Expressionismus." In Berlin, Hitchcock worked as assistant on Graham Cutts' *The Blackguard.* While working at the UFA studio, he had a chance to watch both F.W. Murnau on the set of *The Last Laugh* and Fritz Lang on the set of *Metropolis.* See Donald Spoto, *The Dark Side of Genius: The Life of Alfred Hitchcock* (New York: Ballantine Books, 1983), p. 72–77.

[14] Wilhelm Michel, in the journal *Deutsche Kunst und Dekoration*

Christian Schad, *Nude Bust,* 1929

of closely observed detail: pillow creases, hair under the model's arm, a necklace of variegated stones, and even the veins in the model's breast.

Hitchcock's objects suggest a faith in physicality. Such an interest is also evident in *Neue Sachlichkeit* painting, where objects and firm outlines are distinctly favoured, offering a substantial counterweight to the more flimsy physiques in Expressionist painting. Hitchcock's ample silhouette, regularly objectified in his cameo appearances, recalls the zaftig sitters in the drawings of George Grosz. Even his apparent disposition for eating suggests a certain faith in physical presence.

What else might Hitchcock's focus on objects possibly mean? Closer to home, it suggests the contemporary interests of British documentary filmmaking. Raymond Durgnat observes: "It must be remembered that realism in the '30s was a rarer and more difficult achievement, that the director couldn't just point a TV camera in the street. He had first to notice certain details, love them enough to remember and recreate them, and lastly to slide them deftly into the thriller context."[15]

In *Blackmail,* the director even jokes about his documentary interests. After the arrest of the first criminal, we are shown a large close-up of a fingerprint. Later, the off-duty detective Frank will ask his girlfriend to go to the movies with him. But Alice has seen everything worth seeing. Frank persists: "You haven't seen *Fingerprints.* I'd like you to see that. It's about Scotland Yard. It might be amusing. They're bound to get all the details wrong." Alice, though, is well informed, and her reply tops his: "I don't see why. I did hear they'd got a real criminal to direct it, so as to be on the safe side." Her rejoinder aligns the art of filmmaking with criminal activity, and reminds us that for this film Hitchcock guaranteed "authenticity" by hiring a retired Scotland Yard chief to play the detective sergeant.[16]

Sabotage literally teems with documentary detail, here conveyed not by close-ups but by general ambiance: the greengrocer's next door to the Bijou cinema offers a convincing front to the undercover agent Ted and recalls Hitchcock's own childhood milieu; an aquarium that houses enormous turtles in the London Zoo provides the spectacular backdrop for Verloc's clandestine meeting; Professor Chatman concocts his explosives in a bird shop where he must occasionally contend with customers dissatisfied because their birds won't sing. Likewise, the opening scene of the return

(1925), quoted in Ursula Zeller, "Neue Sachlichkeit," in *The Dictionary of Art,* ed. Jane Turner, Vol. 22 (London and New York: Macmillan and Grove, 1996), p. 922.

[15] Raymond Durgnat, *The Strange Case of Alfred Hitchcock, Or, The Plain Man's Hitchcock* (London: Faber & Faber, 1974), p. 29–30.

[16] In the film, ex–Detective Sergeant Bishop of Scotland Yard is credited as the Detective Sergeant.

of the fishermen in *The Manxman* seems keenly observed. Such vivid details stay with the spectator.

Hitchcock himself occasionally advanced a Freudian association for his objects. Asked by Truffaut about the frequency of handcuffs in his films, he replied that they were fetish objects.[17] As usual though with Hitchcock's rhetoric, his response is an artful dodge, the canny reply of a lapsed Catholic who has adjusted to our secular times. Still, his pronouncement serves to move this inquiry onto another plane. Calling his objects fetishes suggests their ritual, magical quality, and reminds us that *Neue Sachlichkeit* was also alternatively called Magic Realism.[18] It reminds us too that Hitchcock was trained by the Jesuits.[19]

Occasionally, Hitchcock's objects even have a kind of magical quality, as in for instance the Bible that deflects the bullet from Hannay's body in *The Thirty-nine Steps*. In *Murder!,* a close-up of a weather vane turning is a talisman as well as a clever pun (weather vane for Handel Fane) pointing to the identity of the murderer, Fane. The indeterminacy of the weather vane's direction is a neat visual trope for this man's confused sexual and racial status: he is a transvestite and a half-caste.

Like other Catholic orders, the Jesuits are dedicated to declaring the supremacy of Jesus Christ. They are also adept at casuistry. Focussed on the hereafter, they are skilled in the here and now. Unlike the monastic orders, the Jesuits do not live sequestered from the world. Celebrated teachers, the Jesuits may have failed to convey any abiding religiosity to the young Hitchcock, while nevertheless conveying a deep faith in the thingness of the world to him. The ability of the Jesuits to partake of the things of this world while remaining an intellectual elite makes them, let us say, the Hollywood of the Catholic orders.[20] In addition to their teaching mission, these Christian soldiers were also celebrated missionaries.

Despite the missionary zeal of the editorial board of the journal *Close Up* (1927–1933), film in England in the 1920s and 1930s never received the prestige it had in France, Germany and the U.S.[21] English society, resolutely class-bound, held onto a rigid, binary idea of high and low culture.[22] It is well known that Hitchcock resented the English denigration of the new medium. English society may have ensured his emigration to the U.S., and the Jesuit legacy may have enabled him to negotiate masterfully between the demands of commercial filmmaking and the constraints

[17] François Truffaut, with the collaboration of Helen G. Scott, *Hitchcock,* rev. ed. (New York: Simon & Schuster, 1984), p. 47.
[18] See Wieland Schmied, *Neue Sachlichkeit und magischer Realismus in Deutschland 1918–1933* (Hannover: Fackelträger Verlag, 1969).
[19] Between October 1910 and July 1913, Hitchcock studied at Saint Ignatius College in London. See Spoto, p. 22–35.
[20] Agnès Gerhards, *Dictionnaire historique des ordres religieux,* foreword by Jacques Le Goff (Paris: Fayard, 1998). Gerhards notes: "Teaching became the principal activity of the order, and it became the principal teaching congregation of the Catholic world. The Jesuits became the 'intellectual gurus' and the trainers of the intellectual elite," p. 351. (Free translation.)
[21] It is worth noting that *Close Up* favoured productions from France, Germany and Russia. Although its publication (1927–33) coincided with Hitchcock's first English films, the journal was lukewarm in its reception of its native son – never, for instance, reproducing a still from one of his films.
[22] Spoto, p. 205–06.

of High Art. It is precisely such a negotiation, for instance, that has always eluded Godard.[23]

Hitchcock's biographer, Donald Spoto, observes that already as a child the filmmaker had a distinct visual orientation, at a time when English education was predominantly literary.[24] As a Catholic, Hitchcock belonged to a distinct minority in England and, most likely, his Catholicism encouraged his preoccupation with images. The Catholic faith is, after all (and in contrast to the variant of Protestantism, the dominant religion of England), fundamentally visually demonstrative. In Catholic doctrine, persuasion is frequently achieved by demonstration. After the Resurrection, Christ encouraged one of his disciples to regard and to touch his stigmata to recognize that he was indeed the risen Saviour. The Catholic mass, frequently animated by the colourful robes of the priest, is based on monstration: during the ceremony, bread and wine are transformed into the body and blood of Christ. Occurring over a period of four nights and three days, *The Thirty-nine Steps* emphasizes monstration, and the Passion of an innocent man. Offering refuge to the spy Annabella on a Friday evening, Hannay offers her a meal. As a good Catholic, he holds up for her inspection (and ours as well) a substantial filet of haddock, a reminder of a once important custom in Catholic households. Monstration figures too in the bronze we see in Hannay's apartment. The sculpture represents a male figure that cries out and points, and its emphatically deictic gesture indicates that Annabella's assassins have entered through the window.

Not surprisingly, Hitchcock's belief in the visual affected his attitude not only to what is shown but also to what is heard. The Hitchcockian use of sound frequently seems emphatic and evidentiary, as for instance in *The Lady Vanishes,* the sound of the bumbling Englishman bumping his head repeatedly on the eave of the maid's room where he is staying, or more ominously and significantly, in *Juno and the Paycock,* the sound of a machine gun firing its round twice, while on the image track we see a close-up of a statue of the Virgin Mary with the Christ Child. Distinct and contained, these sounds convey a strong sense of physicality.[25]

Blackmail was the first English talkie, and like René Clair's trilogy of the same period, it is a hybrid, both incorporating the new technology while also revealing its atavistic origins in the silent cinema. The first diegetic sound (a shattering windowpane) occurs nearly five minutes into the film, and the first dialogue, three minutes later. The emphasis on the

[23] Always on the fringes of commercial filmmaking, Godard has occasionally courted the idea of working in a Hollywood-style production. *Le mépris,* his film that most closely approximates this goal, was originally to have starred Kim Novak and Richard Burton. In the early 1980s Godard toyed with the idea of shooting in Hollywood. Entitled *The Story* and starring Diane Keaton and Robert De Niro, this project later became *Passion,* filmed in Switzerland. Colin MacCabe, *Godard: Images, Sounds, Politics* (London: BFI, 1980), p. 25, 32.

[24] Spoto, p. 20.

[25] It seems likely that Hitchcock was an important influence on both Tati's and Godard's interest in *musique concrète.*

soundtrack of the shattering glass intimates its narrative significance. Accompanying the arrest of an anonymous criminal, this same sound will be repeated at the film's dénouement when the blackmailer, accidentally slipping atop the glass dome of the British Museum, falls to his death. *Blackmail* offers a striking counterpoint of what is shown and what is heard. During the celebrated scene at breakfast, Alice nervously fingers the bread knife while a visitor drones on about the inappropriateness of killing with a knife. The neighbour's incessant repetition of the word *knife* "stabs" Alice, and she jumps out of her seat. Wishing to dispense with dialogue, Hitchcock had what might be called a visual approach to sounds.

A strong partisan of images, Hitchcock also frequently suggests the affinity between sound and image, vividly expressed by the General's malapropism in *Secret Agent.* After he and Ashenden are trapped in a belfry whose bells are ringing, the General later tells Ashenden that he is "still blind in one ear." This affinity is also expressed in the telepathic crosscutting between the murder of the Englishman Caypor and the escalating whining of his dachshund.

Hitchcock's belief in the supremacy of the visual over the aural also deeply affected his attitude toward language. Spoto notes that the filmmaker was deeply inarticulate.[26] Often masked by dialogue-happy scenarists,[27] that muteness is nonetheless strongly conveyed by his titles. In their terse directness, the Hitchcockian titles have a sort of obdurate "objectness" about them. Eighteen of his over 50 titles are but a single word: *Downhill, Champagne, Blackmail, Murder!, Mary, Sabotage, Rebecca, Suspicion, Saboteur, Lifeboat, Spellbound, Notorious, Rope, Vertigo, Psycho, Marnie, Topaz, Frenzy.* And this list is considerably lengthened if one also includes his titles comprising a substantive with its definite article.

If Hitchcock was an engaged advocate of the image, he also knew and frequently acknowledged that appearances frequently deceive, that in fact the visible is not always what it seems. Reading the visible correctly, Hitchcock seems to say, is a vital life skill. It is a skill and a lesson that his Catholic education would certainly have reinforced (to get to Paradise one has first to negotiate successfully the pitfalls of this world). In *Young and Innocent,* this moral is clearly put forth. Looking at the unconscious Robert, Erica remarks: "Is he guilty? ... I shouldn't think so – he doesn't look like a criminal." The officer in charge chides her: "Don't let looks influence you, young lady."

[26] Spoto, "Preface," p. xii.
[27] Spoto notes that the coming of sound forced upon Hitchcock an unhappy dependence on writers. "For Alfred Hitchcock, putting images into words was a terrible chore; polishing dialogue was tolerable – creating it was an almost impossible task." Spoto, p. 112.

These early films are filled with false appearances, like the trick bottom of the coffer that allows Signor Doppo to escape in *The Lady Vanishes.* In *The Thirty-nine Steps,* Pamela is coerced by Hannay's gun, hidden in his pocket, which turns out to be only a pipe. In the same film, the Professor tells Hannay that "My existence would be jeopardized if people were to realize that I am not what I seem." In *Number Seventeen,* Ben and the detective find a body that they mistakenly think is a corpse. In the same film, the gangster's moll is an elegantly dressed deaf and dumb woman who turns out to be neither deaf nor dumb: it was only, as she later reveals, the cheap trick of a crook.

In *The Lady Vanishes,* Iris remarks the visual incongruity of a nun in high heels, and correctly realizes that something is indeed amiss. Thanks to her boyfriend, Alice in *Blackmail* is particularly privy to the world of detection, but she is considerably less astute than Iris and therefore less fortunate. In a chillingly memorable line, Alice tells her would-be rapist: "I always think a girl knows when she can trust a man." In *Secret Agent,* a leather button found in the clenched hand of the dead organist mistakenly convinces the General (and Ashenden too at first) that Caypor, whose jacket is missing just such a button, is the murderer.

Under Capricorn, 1949

So many of the Hitchcock narratives feature a detective at work, a metaphor for a Pilgrim's Progress. Like an art historian, a detective is one focussed on observing objects and telltale clues. In *The Lady Vanishes,* Iris is only an amateur sleuth, but she is indefatigable. Her suitor, Gilbert, admiringly comments that she has no manners and that she is always seeing things! Hitchcock's brief stint of art history in night school could not equal the formal training in the same subject that F.W. Murnau had enjoyed.[28] Still, Hitchcock was clearly a quick study, and on the set of *The Last Laugh* (a film with no intertitles) he learned to narrate a film entirely with images.[29] Hitchcock himself urged his audiences to see his films "at least three times, in order to pick out all the details and the intention behind them, and in order to get deeper into things."[30] Hitchcock's focus on objects goes beyond their narrative function, suggesting in turn his complex vision of the world.

[28] At the University of Heidelberg, Murnau studied art history with Professor Carl Neumann, a former student of Heinrich Wölfflin. See Angela Dalle Vache, *Cinema and Painting: How Art Is Used in Film* (Austin: University of Texas Press, 1996), no. 14, p. 258.
[29] F.W. Murnau, "The Ideal Picture Needs No Titles," *Theatre Magazine,* Vol. 47, No. 322 (1928). In a 1966 interview Hitchcock discusses the "tremendous influence" of *The Last Laugh.* See George Angell, "The Time of My Life," *BBC Home Service,* 30 July 1966: Tape No. TLO 634/725.
[30] Hitchcock, quoted in Spoto, p. 37.

Hitchcock's objects, according to Godard, succeed where Cézanne's apples failed. Confined to the highbrow culture of museums, Cézanne's apples affect only the select few. Against such a Jansenist view promising salvation to an elect, Hitchcock's objects are enclosed in cinema's *Wunderkammer,* its transubstantiation of ordinary objects reaching millions. Hitchcock's objects (and by extension his sounds and titles too) lodge themselves indelibly into the spectator's memory. André Bazin, who championed the cinema over painting precisely because the former was an art of the masses, did not recognize Hitchcock for what he was: the Seventh Art's most able apostle.[31] In order for Hitchcock to fulfil his destiny, he had to leave England for Hollywood. If, as many think, the cinema is the 20th century's secularized religion, then Hitchcock is clearly its most successful missionary, and his objects have become our new relics.

[31] See André Bazin, "Hitchcock contre Hitchcock," *Cahiers du cinéma,* No. 39 (Oct. 1954), p. 25–32 (special Hitchcock issue).

The Symbolist Woman in Alfred Hitchcock's Films

Julia Tanski

*Eva Marie Saint in
North by Northwest, 1959*

"Women are like suspense ... the more imagination there is, the more emotion there is."
– Alfred Hitchcock

"Interior: Shaw and Oppenheim Galleries. Close shot of the back of Eve's neck and plunging back of black and red dress. Light on the blond hair. Camera moves slowly away to a larger take. Vandamm's fingers moving over the soft flesh of Eve's neck. Camera draws back to include Eve seated and her face moves ever so slightly to the right, giving a hint of her profile."

The blond, perfectly coiffed hair, the beautiful figure and face creating a distance that coincides with that in her eyes, characterize what we have come to expect of a Hitchcockian woman. This shot of Eva Marie Saint in *North by Northwest* is a perfect example of the way Hitchcock introduces his actresses to us: a "fetish-y" zoom in on the particularly elegant body parts – the ankles, the neck, the hands, the lips. The profile. With this combination of a readily definable woman and the camera treatment, Hitchcock created a canon, an internationally recognizable figure. We find this curvy, wavy woman in the angles and boxes of a train compartment and the skyscrapers of New York City. Hitchcock likes to heighten the contrast of what formally makes up a woman's body to that which makes up a man's and his world – trains, airplanes and urban skylines.

Hitchcock's world is varied, from a neo-gothic one based in London's fogs and in secluded, shadowy parts of the British countryside, to a more streamlined, contrasted, urban one. Hitchcock's formative years were spent surrounded by the remaining influences of Symbolism, which were visible in the films of the day (*East Lynne,* 1913, Bert Haldane[1]) as well as in the literature (*The Secret Agent* and *Heart of Darkness* by Joseph Conrad). The sharp, incrusted shadows of architectural sites like London Bridge and

[1] Donald Spoto, *The Dark Side of Genius: The Life of Alfred Hitchcock* (New York: Ballantine Books, 1983), p. 57: "In 1913 William George Barker's production of *East Lynne* [...] attracted the patronage of thousands [...]. It was the first British six-reeler (running time over an hour) and it told of a brutal murder."

the Parliament, and the lamp-lit streets, stalked by Jack the Ripper, of London itself are so many latent traces of Symbolism.

During the period that he was assistant director to Graham Cutts, Hitchcock worked on multiple aspects of the film-making process, including the designing of sets and promotional images that give pertinent examples of the formal aspects of the Symbolist vocabulary that existed in his work. The celestial stairway in a scene from *The Black-guard,* curving upward with crowds on either side, is similar in form and in celestial effect to a painting by Edward Burne-Jones, *The Golden Stairways* (1880). The trade show advertisement for *Woman to Woman* and the poster present a woman in an oriental, feathery show costume bending toward the viewer, very similar to the attitudes and ornamentation of the women that Gustav Klimt painted (*Nudas Veritas,* 1899). Stylized flowers, feathers and figures were part of Art Nouveau, the dominant style of the 1920s, which infiltrated the film industry, and were reinforced by the art history courses Hitchcock attended at night school[2] and his likely visits to London's art museums. Edgar Allan Poe,[3] whose poems clearly evoke the eerie dark staircases and heavy red velvet curtains that set the stage for the nightmarish psychological trips of Symbolism, was a direct source of inspiration to Hitchcock.

Hitchcock's suspense and the MacGuffin are neat labels that have been used to try to define how a viewer is made antsy in his seat. While watching a Hitchcock film, one is transported to another dimension. *North by Northwest* takes us all around the United States, but the most important trip is in the head of this man and his being chased, as if in a dream, running nowhere and screaming to no one, with no real identity. In *Rear Window* and *Lifeboat,* we spend the whole film in one place, and yet we travel to worlds as dark and sulphuric as hell itself. The role of women exemplifies these dreamscape films as it does Symbolist culture.

Symbolism[4] described the deepest colours of the human soul. Within a context of humanistic response to Industrialization and to the constant rise of a complacent bourgeois class, these artists dug into their own national traditions as well as others, to find inspiration. The classical world in its pureness, the medieval, spellbound universe, and the everyday object became sources of inspiration. Symbolism was an all-encompassing phenomenon in the years from 1886 through 1905.[5] It was all-encompassing in

[2] Spoto, p. 38.
[3] "Why I Am Afraid of the Dark," *Hitchcock on Hitchcock: Selected Writings and Interviews,* ed. Sidney Gottlieb (Berkeley: University of California Press, 1995), p. 142–45.
[4] For a complete understanding of Symbolism, see *Lost Paradise: Symbolist Europe,* exhib. cat. (Montréal: The Montreal Museum of Fine Arts, 1995).
[5] Jean Clair, "Introduction," *Lost Paradise: Symbolist Europe,* p. 18.

The Lodger: A Story of the London Fog, 1927

the sense that, willfully Wagnerian, it touched on a number of artistic media, from literature to the decorative arts to painting to photography. "It was to halt the growing ascendancy of a world evidently disillusioned and godforsaken, but also devoid of all magic, good or bad, that Symbolism employed its sorcery – visual, musical and poetic. Could words, colour, sound, succeed in reuniting what science had torn asunder? It was art as the final bastion against loss of meaning, art for art's sake as the ultimate response to the emptiness of appearances."[6] .

The Lodger, played by Ivor Novello in 1926, enters his rented rooms and takes a look around. The paintings on the walls are all of women with long, flowing hair, full lips and a distant look in their eyes. The similarity to the Rossetti/Burne-Jones canon cannot be denied. On the mantle, we see a reproduction of the painting by Burne-Jones, *Perseus Series: The Rock of Doom* (1884–1885). This type of woman, which the lodger must remove from his view, will not be as easily dismissed for Hitchcock himself, as the blond, unattainable woman played in this film by "June" will haunt him until the end of his career. In what seems at first a cut-and-dried story (boy loves girl, girl plays hard to get, boy and girl will get married), there enters, via the newspapers, a smog-veiled stranger, taking the young blond woman by the hand into a world of dark mystery and stranglings, shadowy staircases, dim-lit medieval buildings, a bench under a lamppost, a potential lynching. And then boy is proven innocent, and boy and girl prepare to get married. The full circle is completed again. We find ourselves dipping in and out of the fantastic world of Hitchcock much the same way as a viewer can, standing in front of Dante Gabriele Rossetti's *Bocca Baciata.*

The Lodger: A Story of the London Fog, 1927

The portraits used in *The Lodger* are symptomatic of a kind of shot that Hitchcock will often use in his vision of women. The close shot of Eva Marie Saint at the auctioneer's in *North by Northwest* ends with a profile, an idealized beauty presented to us in the pure tradition of Western art from the Renaissance to modern times. James Stewart's first long look at Madeleine in *Vertigo* is also a stop-action profile shot. The references to Western art in a portrait shot are visible also in the Madonna-esque image of Anny Ondra in *The Manxman,* when she presents herself before her Judge and Lover with a shawl over her head. Or the daughter of the farmer in *The Farmer's Wife,* at her wedding banquet. How could we forget Mrs. Bates sitting up at her window in *Psycho,* much like Whistler's mother in

[6] Clair, p. 18.

Symphony in Grey? This same attitude is used again for Claude Rains's mother in *Notorious*. Portraiture itself plays a big role in Hitchcock's films. Carlotta Valdés in *Vertigo* and a family member of Rebecca's in *Rebecca* come to life in the films. In fact, we can point to a few portraits used in Hitchcock's films – Alida Valli in *The Paradine Case* (above her bed at the country mansion), Barbara Bel Geddes in *Vertigo* and Ann Todd also in *The Paradine Case.* Hitchcock uses these portraits within his overall treatment of women, to create a strong image that he can then build up and then knock down. In *Notorious,* Ingrid Bergman is lovelier than ever before.[7] But she is the fallen woman, the adventurous woman, the weak woman, the strong woman, the adored woman. At the same time, Hitchcock literally prostitutes her, portrays her as an alcoholic and drugs her at the end.

Alida Valli in The Paradine Case, 1947

In *The Glove,* Edgar Allan Poe creates a delirious poem stemming from a single idea: the hand of the woman he loves. As Redon, Rackham, Beardsley, Martini, Previati and many other Symbolist artists pay tribute in their illustrations of Poe's work, Hitchcock was also inspired by him.[8] His specific shots of a foot or legs, a luxurious mane of hair or the back of a woman's neck, testify to this inspiration and become part of his female "fetish." In the famous Hitchcock/Truffaut interviews, while discussing *Marnie,* he states that he was especially attracted by "the fetish idea." These close-up images can signify a point in time, a prelude to death.

Tippi Hedren in The Birds, 1963

Hitchcock's women are screens on which infinite metamorphoses are played out. In *Blackmail,* Anny Ondra, after killing the painter, walks endlessly through the night, in a somnambulistic trance; Hitchcock gives us a close-up of her legs at the beginning, fresh, with white stockings – and afterward at dawn, with muddy shoes and stained stockings. The legs become a device to show the progression of time. In the beginning of *The Birds,* when Tippi Hedren crosses the street in her straight skirt and high heels, causing her to walk literally like a bird, her legs and feet become a metaphor for the whole film and transform this lady into a hybrid figure, a death-sorceress figure, as stated in the café scene after the gas station explosion when the mother of two children screams at her, "You are the cause of all this, you witch!" Grace Kelly's offered neck, embellished with a diamond necklace, takes a central position in the scene in *To Catch a Thief* where she and Cary Grant proceed to put the energy of the background fireworks into their physical desire. Tippi Hedren's hair becomes a

[7] Éric Rohmer, *Hitchcock* (Paris: Éditions Universitaires, 1957), p. 89: "If the director extensively kneaded the soft dough, rich in minute resources, of his actors (this is perhaps the most beautiful creation of Bergman), then the scenario […]." (Free translation.)
[8] Gottlieb, p. 142–45.

pivotal element of her disguise in *Marnie*, the colour of it drained out in the shower before a new colour is applied. In *Vertigo*, Madeleine's hair colour is not only important, but the way it is tied up, in a chignon, is symbolic of the movement, the scenario and the psychosis of the film. We literally fall into this whirl, as Madeleine fell into San Francisco Bay.

The similarity of *Vertigo*'s story to *Bruges-la-Morte* by Georges Rodenbach is striking. This tale by the Belgian Symbolist author, written in 1892, relates the story of how a widower's grief and the death itself of his beloved become perfectly entwined in the mirror-like water of Bruges and its grey streets. During Hugues Viane's long walks by the canals, from which fog reaches up to the medieval architecture, creating geometrical cloud forms, Jane emerges and becomes the dead wife in his mind, much like Judy becomes Madeleine as Scottie Ferguson follows her through the winding streets of San Francisco. Both men become obsessed by "that pastel hue, those eyes with pupils dilated and sombre amid mother-of-pearl [...] that hair peeking out at the nape of her neck [...] the colour of amber and cocoon, a yellow flowing like text."[9] These men create their dream-like worlds and at the centre is the female figure, in her ambiguous, unattainable state. Women become mirages toward which Hitchcock lunges, but never catches (*Bruges-la-Morte*, 1892, book cover by Fernand Khnopff).

Fernand Khnopff, *Who Shall Deliver Me?*, 1891

The empty gaze that characterizes the some of the women depicted in Hitchcock can be linked with a marmoreal quality. Statue-like women in their cold death, or in their irradiated mesmerization, like *Who Shall Deliver Me?* by Khnopff, are recurrent in Symbolism. Starting from an objectively distant representation, they succeed in evoking colours and perfumes, and in ringing our souls. Khnopff's female figure is represented in a simple composition – her figure on the left, taking up the whole first field, a scattered space behind her with three openings and cobblestones on the ground. Her startling red hair and blue eyes incite a first look. The égide-like pendant around her neck reflects a cloudy, "Mirror, Mirror on the wall" revelation. The doorway opens to a shadowy, uncertain future and coincides with the mystery of the scene. The trance-like gaze of this figure gives the impression of another world inside what is physically represented, an idea enhanced by the accoutrements and the title of the painting itself, a title taken from a poem by Christina Georgina Rossetti, Dante Gabriele's sister. This same mysterious world that exists

[9] Georges Rodenbach, *Bruges-la-Morte* (Brussels: Labor, 1986), p. 29. (Free translations.)

under the skin and yet is indicated by the eyes, the upright calm of the woman, can be found in Hitchcock's heroines.

Anny Ondra in *Blackmail* emerges from behind the curtain surrounding the bed of the painter she has just killed. She stands there with her knife, taken from the table next to the bed, in a mesmerized freeze. She has touched death and been the cause of it. White becomes black as the scene advances. We see her in black next to the white of the tutu, object of the innocent game that ended tragically. She physically enters a different world, walking blindly through the night of London, having crossed over the line into a world of death and sin. We see her face to face with her own image when she reaches her apartment.

We see Ingrid Bergman, in a white dress with pleats falling to the ground like the lines of a column, evoking in period and material the ancient Roman statue, Julia Domna, next to her in a promotional still for *Notorious,* and similar in its lightness and grace to *Symphony in White* by Whistler, which Bergman was paging through on the set. Grace Kelly is presented to us for the first time in *To Catch a Thief,* in a strapless, blue dress enhancing the cold, austere primness of her character. The passionate kiss that she gives Cary Grant at the end of the evening, however, surprises us by introducing us to the dual quality of this princess, illustrating almost word for word a fantasy of Hitchcock's that he strives to fulfill in choosing his leading ladies: "We're after the drawing-room type, the real ladies, who become whores once they're in the bedroom."[10]

Ingrid Bergman on the set of Notorious, *1946*

Moulding his women is a genuine preoccupation for Hitchcock. As he states in an article entitled "How I Choose My Heroines," "[…] I have to consider whether my potential heroine is sensitive to direction. In other words, whether she is the kind of girl I can mold into the heroine of my imagination."[11] This idea of creating and bringing to life an object by the force of one's imagination and love is identical to that of Pygmalion, also a favourite of the Symbolist artists. Burne-Jones dedicated a whole cycle to it *(Pygmalion and the Image)* as did Franz von Stuck *(Pygmalion).* *Vertigo* is based on this tale, the moulding and coming to life of a dreamed or dead woman. Ingrid Bergman, in a scene cut from the final version of *Spellbound* – dressed in a Greek-inspired costume, all in white, complete with her blond hair tied up with a ribbon in a swirl on top of her head – actually breaks out of her statue mould. In *Spellbound,* Ingrid Bergman is a multifaceted woman. She metamorphoses from the beautiful, severe doctor fantasized

[10] François Truffaut, with the collaboration of Helen G. Scott, *Hitchcock,* rev. ed. (New York: Simon & Schuster, 1984), p. 224.
[11] "How I Choose My Heroines," Gottlieb, p. 75.

Edward Burne-Jones, from the series "Pygmalion and the Image," *The Hand Refrains,* about 1868

about by her fellow psychiatrists to a schoolmarm, to this other-worldly figure who develops in the dream of Gregory Peck and breaks it into pieces. This same evolution occurs with Tippi Hedren in *The Birds.* She is first presented as a rich, conniving socialite, then becomes an evil sorceress and, at the end, evolves into a frail and broken woman. These transformations speak of the woman in Hitchcock's films and mind: she is presented as we have come to know her – cold, unattainable – and through the film she grows wings and flies, on her own, beyond the mould, taken out of even Hitchcock's reach.

Bill Krohn, in his recent book *Hitchcock at Work,*[12] finds evidence to back up his premise that Hitchcock worked with more improvisation than he would have liked us to believe. It is the same for his female characters. He creates an order from which the different elements have the freedom to grow and evolve. His most memorable actresses are all very skilfully chosen and groomed, and then they bloom into their own. Suzanne Pleshette, in a recent interview states, "If we needed freedom, he gave us freedom […]." In this same interview, Tippi Hedren talks about the function of the storyboards, which were accessible to everyone on the set: "That was helpful if you had something technical you had to do, but I don't ever recall anything having to do with an emotional scene being boarded."[13]

Mallarmé, when describing his *Hérodiade*, said: "She is a being purely dreamt, and absolutely independent of History." He owed his inspiration to "that divine name, 'Hérodiade,' sombre and red, as a pomegranate." As he was inspired by the "clay" of his work – a word – and from this word grew a ripe fruit, Hitchcock started with an actress and she became a flower, a statue and a bird. No matter how heavily charged the name, Hitchcock's women go beyond their initial mould to become his fantasy, and then ours. In defining Hitchcock's characters psychologically, Raymond Bellour notes that "the difference which appears due to woman is nothing but the mirror effect of the narcissistic doubling that makes possible the constitution of the male subject through the woman's body […]." We can say the same for the director himself, and for his viewers as well.

[12] Bill Krohn, *Hitchcock at Work* (New York: Phaidon Press, 2000).
[13] Greg Garrett, "Hitchcock's Women on Hitchcock: A Panel Discussion with Janet Leigh, Tippi Hedren, Karen Black, Suzanne Pleshette and Eva Marie Saint," *Literature/Film Quarterly,* Vol. 27, No. 2 (1999).

Such Stuff As Dreams Are Made On:
Hitchcock and Dalí, Surrealism and Oneiricism

Nathalie Bondil-Poupard

"*All* that we see or seem
Is but a dream within a dream"[1]
– Edgar Allan Poe

A certain critic once bemoaned the "lack of rigour displayed by those who insist on seeing the mark of Surrealism just about anywhere, in Hitchcock or Fuller, as needed. Yes, Surrealism has left visible signs of its influences in all fields, but one should resist the temptation of trotting it out to fit any situation. Were it truly everywhere, it would be nowhere."[2] In fact, one might say instead that Alfred Hitchcock was everywhere, but was above all himself. In alluding – whether consciously or not – to his many and varied aesthetic influences, from Romanticism to Expressionism, from Symbolism to Surrealism, he appropriated, assimilated and transcended them. Such is the hallmark of any great artist. And with the centenary of his birth just past, exegeses of the Hitchcockian oeuvre show no signs of waning. Here I shall examine the Surrealist dimension of his films, his collaboration with Salvador Dalí,[3] and the role of dreams in the filmmaker's works.

America in the Throes of "Acute Dalinitis"

When Dalí left Europe for the United States, he was turning his back on parochial squabbles (he had been banished from André Breton's Surrealist group) and on wars, period. He saw before him a new and vital country: America was hungry for Dalí, and Dalí was hungry for money and glory (and didn't try to hide it). New York's Museum of Modern Art devoted an exhibition to him in 1940. From social soirées to the windows of chic boutiques, Dalí's works and his "happenings," which were ahead of their time, quickly made him *the* Surrealist artist and celebrity of the moment.

Fresh from the success of *Gone with the Wind* in 1939, David O. Selznick had brought Hitchcock to Hollywood and put him under contract; he was eager to repeat the critical

[1] Edgar Allan Poe, "A Dream Within a Dream," in *Selected Poems* (London: Bloomsbury Publishing, 1999), p. 94.
[2] Alain Virmaux and Odette Virmaux, *Les surréalistes et le cinéma: Anthologie* (Paris: Seghers, 1976), p. 6. (Free translation.)
[3] The essential bibliography for the *Spellbound* dream sequence is: Donald Spoto, *The Art of Alfred Hitchcock: Fifty Years of His Motion Pictures* (New York: Anchor Books, 1976), p. 151–59; and James Bigwood, "Solving a *Spellbound* Puzzle," *American Cinematographer,* Vol. 72, No. 6 (June 1991), p. 34–40. I extend warm thanks to Mr. Bigwood for his assistance. On Surrealism in Hitchcock, see Michael Gould, *Surrealism and the Cinema (Open-Eyed Screening)* (South Brunswick and New York: A.S. Barnes and Company; London: The Tantivy Press, 1976), p. 97–116.

and commercial success of their initial collaboration, *Rebecca* (1940). He showed the director a treatment based on the novel *The House of Dr. Edwardes,* by James Beeding. The story, after extensive reworking by Hitchcock and screenwriter Ben Hecht, became *Spellbound.*[4] In the November 20, 1945 edition of the *Dalí News,* the artist's self-promotional publication, Dalí recounted: "My movie agent and excellent friend, FeFe (Felix Ferry), ordered a nightmare from me by telephone. It was for the film *Spellbound.* Its director, Hitchcock, told me the story of the film with an impressive passion, after which I accepted. (Hitchcock is one of the rare personages I have met lately who has some mystery.)"

Some years earlier, Dalí had been approached to work with Fritz Lang, to design a dream sequence for a film produced by 20th Century Fox. Lang walked off the set after only a few days' shooting, however, and the Dalí sequence was dropped. The film was completed and released in 1942 as *Moontide,* directed by Archie Mayo. In Selznick's eyes, Dalí's scandalous "phallic frescoes" made for a bonus selling proposition: he could get a publicity stunt and an artsy dream sequence for his new picture in one fell swoop – quite the bargain!

Hitchcock, too, insisted that the dream sequence in *Spellbound* be included: "I requested Dali. Selznick the producer had the impression that I wanted Dali for the publicity value. That wasn't it at all. What I was after was [...] *the vividness of dreams* [...] [A]ll Dali's work is very solid and very sharp, with very long perspectives and black shadows. Actually I wanted the dream sequences to be shot on the back lot, not in the studio at all. I wanted them shot in the bright sunshine. So the cameraman would be forced to what we call stop it out and get a very hard image. This was again the avoidance of the cliché. All dreams in movies are blurred. It isn't true. Dali was the best man for me to do the dreams because that is what dreams should be. So that was the reason I had Dali."[5] As ill fortune would have it, Hitchcock didn't get the effect he wanted; the sequence ended up being shot in a studio using sets and painted miniatures, and thus fell short of the director's initial intentions. Had these been respected, the sequence may have resembled the experimental short films that Maya Deren was making at the time, such as *Meshes of the Afternoon* (1943–59) and *At Land* (1944). Strongly influenced by Surrealism, her Jean Cocteau–esque oneiric visions were composed of sun-blasted, arid, barren landscapes.

Few direct accounts of the Hitchcock–Dalí collaboration are extant, although many production stills, as well as the artist's

[4] The script tells the story of Dr. Constance Petersen (Ingrid Bergman), a psychiatrist in an asylum, who falls in love with "Dr. Edwardes" (Gregory Peck), the newly hired director. She soon learns that he is actually a mental patient with a pathological fear of parallel lines and the colour white, and may also be an amnesiac imposter, "John Ballantine," accused of having killed the real Dr. Edwardes. Constance is convinced of the young man's innocence and, with the help of her former teacher, analyses his strange dreams. Together they uncover the repressed trauma at the root of "J.B."'s condition, and identify Dr. Edwardes' true killer.

[5] *Film Profiles: Alfred Hitchcock,* interview with Philip Jenkinson for BBC TV, n.d. (Emphasis mine.)

original works, do survive. Patricia Hitchcock O'Connell recalls that her father got on very well with Dalí during the shooting. The two men – Dalí was five years younger than Hitchcock – shared a knack for self-promotion; if one was an exhibitionist and the other, discreet, both were nonetheless charismatic personalities who cared equally about their respective audiences and popularity. And they were both complex, violently contradictory men: desire and fear were mainsprings of Dalí's as well as Hitchcock's art. The two displayed similar obsessions with food, as a metaphor for the world defined in terms of attraction and repulsion: Hitchcock dreamt of filming the metamorphoses of a meal, from a restaurant to the sewers of a city; Dalí dreamt of an edible habitat, with walls made of bread, and chocolate chairs. Lautréamont, Poe and Freud were key references for both. There is no doubt that they were kindred spirits: "I got along wonderfully with Hitchcock, and set to work, but FeFe telephoned me: 'they adore all that you are doing at the Selznick studios, but I want to caution you, for the moment they want to use you only in small drops.'"[6]

The dream sequence as originally planned[7] comprised five key set pieces, corresponding to the locales imagined by Dalí: 1) Gambling Hall; 2) Rooftop/Chimney; 3) Ballroom; 4) Desert; and 5) Pyramid.

The Protocol of Dreams

In addition to his customary imagery (ants, grand pianos, anthropomorphic landscapes, "melting" wheels, and the like), Dalí reused a whole slew of Surrealist props. He imagined, in his notes on a preliminary sketch of the image that he thought would best function as a conclusion to the gambling-hall sequence, a "cockroach with an eye glued onto its back moving across the blank cards," and marching metronomes "precisely synchronized in *opposing* directions." He also indicated that "the eye could reappear and serve as a dissolve into the wheel in the chimney scene."[8] In this Prévertian inventory, we can identify, in turn, Man Ray's *Indestructible Object* (1923), set down on the four corners of each table in the gambling hall, and tables and chairs perched on women's legs – Surrealist furniture-objects recalling Kurt Seligmann's stool or a Meret Oppenheim table (both from 1938). The deadly deck of cards was an allusion to Cocteau's film *Le sang d'un poète* ("Blood of a Poet," 1930), while the masked assassin in a suit could have stepped out of a painting by Giorgio De Chirico or René Magritte. The biblical statue (not used in the final cut of the sequence), for its part, was a favourite device of the Surrealist cinema and

[6] Salvador Dalí, *Dalí News,* 20 Nov. 1945, p. 2.
[7] See the details of the sequence in the excerpt from the original script, p. 411.
[8] James Bigwood, "Solving a *Spellbound* Puzzle," *American Cinematographer,* Vol. 72, No. 6 (June 1991), p. 39.

of Poetic Realism: a modern version of Lot's wife, petrified for all time. There were other allusions, too: the ancient wrestlers and doomed lovers can be traced back to Man Ray's short film *Les mystères du château de dé* ("Mystery of the Castle of Dice," 1929) or Marcel Carné's *Les visiteurs du soir* ("The Devil's Envoys," 1942), or the anthropomorphic mineralogies of Magritte and Dalí.

The Surrealists relied heavily on the symbolic power of the eye: closed to the deceptive appearances of reality, but open to the inner worlds of dreams (Man Ray's painted eyes) descended from Symbolist art (Odilon Redon). The Dalí dream sequence in *Spellbound* affords amusing analogies to a drawing by the 19th-century French illustrator and caricaturist J.J. Grandville, another touchstone for the Surrealists. The work, entitled *Crimes et Expiations,* is a representation of a nightmare. Grandville wrote: "Is it the nightmare of a man tormented only by the thought of committing a crime? Or is it the dream of a murderer who, in a fever of the brain, is pursued by remorse?"[9] Proceeding by free association of images, it tells the story of a flight, to be read from the top to the bottom of the page, along a dizzying S-curve: a murder is committed beneath a cross; the cross becomes a fountain; the blood, water; the victim's hand, the hand of justice; the scales of justice, the eye of justice; the eye widens horribly, while the killer tries in vain to flee: "At the same time a thousand other eyes of a shape similar to that one watch him and greedily throw themselves on him. [...] Are these the thousand eyes of the crowd drawn by a rumoured imminent spectacle of torture?"[10]

Jean-Jacques Grandville, *First Dream: Crimes and Atonements,* 1847

Yet another undeniable borrowing in the Dalí dream is the shot in which a myriad of unblinking, voyeuristic eyes advance toward the spectator and observe the depraved woman offering herself to the gamblers. It is virtually identical to Freder's feverish hallucinations of the Evil Maria dancing half-naked for a dumbfounded male audience at Yoshiwara's in Fritz Lang's *Metropolis* (1926–27). This, too, is a nightmare vision. Dalí, who had seen *Metropolis,* admired Lang's marriage of grandiose spectacle with the worst theatricalism of historical painting: "Oh! Fritz Lang! Who seeks spectacle in the most inhabitual and grandiose scenes, and insists on that unique emotion which titillates the flesh."[11] The wounded eye is also a Freudian component of the Oedipus complex, a symbol of castration and of parental authority – the Eye of God. With his image of the scissored eye, Dalí was clearly alluding to his own prior work with Luis Buñuel in the opening sequence of *Un chien andalou* ("An Andalusian Dog," 1928): to the woman's eye

[9] Annie Renonciat, *La vie et l'œuvre de J. J. Grandville* (Courbevoie: ACR Édition internationale, 1985), p. 281–82 (emphasis mine). The drawing is one of two entitled "Deux rêves: Crimes et Expiations," which appeared in the *Magasin pittoresque* in July 1847. (Free translation.)
[10] Renonciat, p. 281–82.
[11] *Gaceta Literaria,* 15 Dec. 1927, in *Salvador Dalí: Rétrospective 1920-1980,* 18 Dec. 1979–14 Apr. 1980, exhib. cat. (Paris: Centre Georges Pompidou, Musée national d'art moderne, 1979), p. 65. (Free translation.)

– in fact that of a shaved and made-up calf – slit by a razor blade just as the moon slips behind the clouds. The eye under attack is a symbolic Surrealist motif, as seen, for example, in the work of Alberto Giacometti – *Pointe à l'œil* ("Point to the Eye," circa 1932) – as well as that of Hitchcock, who in *The Birds* (1963) warns us: "If the birds decide [...] with the millions that they are, to go for everybody's eyes, then we'd have H.G. Wells' *Kingdom of the Blind* on our hands!"

Copy/paste/invent: in the end, the sequence unfolds as a dreamlike collection of borrowings and reminiscences – a typically Dalinian puzzle with "Arcimboldesque" overtones.

The Lost Scenes

The first of the two lost scenes in the *Spellbound* dream sequence, designed by Dalí and filmed by Hitchcock, takes place in a ballroom: "In one of the scenes of my 'sequence,' it was necessary to create the impression of a nightmare. Heavy weight and uneasiness are hanging over the guests in a ballroom. I said to FeFe: 'In order to create this impression, I will have to hang 15 of the heaviest and most lavishly sculpted pianos possible from the ceiling of the ballroom, swinging very low over the heads of the dancers. These would be in exalted dances poses, but would not move at all, they would only be diminishing silhouettes in very accelerated perspective, losing themselves in infinite darkness.' FeFe communicated the idea which was accepted with enthusiasm by Hitchcock. They passed the idea along to the experts, because in Hollywood there are many, many experts to perfect everything. Some days after I went to the Selznick studios to film the scene with the pianos. And I was stupefied at seeing neither the pianos nor the cut silhouettes which must represent the dancers. But right then someone pointed out to me some tiny pianos in miniature hanging from the ceiling and about 40 live dwarfs who according to the experts would give perfectly the effect of perspective that I desired. I thought I was dreaming. They maneuvered even so, with the false pianos and the real dwarfs (which should be false miniatures). Result: The pianos didn't at all give the impression of real pianos suspended from ropes ready to crack and casting sinister shadows on the ground (for another expert imitated the shadows of the pianos with false shadows projected with the aid of a very complicated apparatus) and the dwarfs, one saw, simply, that they were dwarfs. Neither Hitchcock nor I liked the result and we decided to eliminate this scene. In truth the imagination of the Hollywood experts will be the one thing that will ever have surpassed me."[12] The expert in question, apparently, was Hitchcock himself – for, at the very beginning of his career, as set designer for the film *Die Prinzessin und der Geiger* ("The Blackguard," 1925*)*, he had employed exactly the same technique, using little people to create forced perspective!

"I'm beautiful, O mortals, as might be a sculpted dream"[13]

Ingrid Bergman recalled the second lost scene: "It was a wonderful, twenty-minute sequence [far shorter, in fact], that really belongs in a museum. The idea for a major part of it was that I would become, in Gregory Peck's mind, a statue. To do this, we shot the film in the reverse way in which it would appear on the screen. They put a pipe in my mouth, so I could breathe, and then a statue was actually made around me. I was dressed in a draped, Grecian gown, with a crown on my head and an arrow through my neck. Then the cameras rolled. I was in this statue, then I broke out and the action continued. We ran it backward, so it would appear as if I became a statue. It was marvelous."[14]

Dalí produced sketches for the actress's costume, which he described as a "draped gown made of very, very thin *white wool*," with a "gold necklace, plain except for a gold arrow nailed to its centre, which holds up the drapes"; this "arrow necklace symbolizes the *obstacle* between the two lovers." Another design – which in the end was never used – was a pair of "folding wings" with a "mechanism for opening and closing" that would be deployed when the actress turned into the statue. Dalí wanted the winged statue to crack, with "ants crawling in and disappearing into the *crevices*"; they were to symbolize "life taking refuge inside the statue" and were another reference to *Un chien andalou*. According to Hitchcock, though, since it was impossible to have Ingrid Bergman covered in ants, this "strange idea" of Dalí's was abandoned.

The surreal image of woman as statue, as disquieting muse, as antique marble goddess *à tiroirs,* as Venus de Milo revisited, was graven in the imagination of the Surrealist painters – Dalí, Magritte, Paul Delvaux; in film, she became the figure of Destiny (?) in Cocteau's *Le sang d'un poète,* and that of Truth in Carné's *Les enfants du paradis* ("The Children of Paradise," 1945). In *Pandora* (1951) she remains the eternal idol: the director, Albert Lewin, a collector and lover of paintings, set out to make a film with a Surrealist ambience, and drew inspiration from the works of Delvaux. Women became

[12] Dalí, p. 2.
[13] Charles Baudelaire, "The Beauty," in *Selected Poems from "Les Fleurs du Mal,"* trans. Norman Shapiro (Chicago and London: University of Chicago Press, 1998), p. 35.
[14] Spoto, p. 158.

Greek statues, hewing to the new canons of fashion invented here and there by Dalí, or De Chirico, for prestige magazines like *Harper's Bazaar* and *Vogue*. Dalí, especially, here touched upon the fantasy of the marmoreal, unattainable woman, an ideal that never manifests itself – extremely common in Hitchcock, and so marvellously recreated by his costume designer, Edith Head. The filmmaker's muses – Ingrid Bergman, Grace Kelly, Tippi Hedren – with their long, immaculate dresses, have statuesque figures. Significantly, Constance Petersen is referred to as an "iceberg" by her colleagues at the asylum in *Spellbound*.

"What is all that drivel?"[15]

With principal photography completed, Hitchcock and Dalí had both left the set of *Spellbound*; the former was in England, the latter in New York. David O. Selznick was in control. Following a preview of the film in September 1944, the audience comments included: "Dream sequence very good. Why didn't we do it in Technicolor?"[16] The producer intervened decisively, writing on October 25: "The more I look at the dream sequence in *Spellbound,* the worse I feel it to be. It is not Dali's fault, for his work is much finer and much better for the purpose than I ever thought it would be." He found, however, that Dalí's paintings did not photograph well enough, and decided that their dreamlike qualities needed to be reinforced – but without distorting the paintings, for the artist's contract with the studio contained restrictions to this effect. Selznick complained about the utter lack of imagination in the photography, lighting, sets, and so on. He cabled Hitchcock on November 13, 1944: "I have Menzies working on dream sequence corrections and think we will have something very exciting."

William Cameron Menzies was one of Hollywood's most brilliant production designers, having conceived the sets for Raoul Walsh's *The Thief of Bagdad* (1924) and *Gone with the Wind,* among others. He had previously worked with Hitchcock on the huge sets for *Foreign Correspondent.* The films he made as a director (e.g., *Things to Come,* 1936) were forerunners of the modern science fiction genre. Answering Selznick's appeal for help, Menzies designed new storyboards for the dream sequence. On December 19, Dalí's agent wrote to the producer, telling him that his client wished to see the dream sequence, and was willing to submit new drawings at no charge. Felix Ferry: "I want you to realize how anxious he is that his work in this first American picture should be perfection. He is so anxious that the entire work have the usual Dalí quality." Time was short: the New York

[15] Spoto, p. 158.
[16] All documents cited without reference hereunder are from the Selznick archives at the Harry Ransom Humanities Research Center, University of Texas at Austin.

premiere of *Spellbound* was scheduled for April 1, 1945, and Selznick was losing patience. Parts of the dream sequence were reshot between October 1944 and January 1945: according to the script and storyboards as reworked and designed by Menzies, in the "weird deserted place" conceived by Dalí, "J.B." (Gregory Peck) runs toward Constance (Ingrid Bergman), seated behind a desk; suddenly she disappears; then he is chased through the "uphill-downhill" dreamscape, a huge pair of wings beating over his head. In fact, this was not a new sequence, but merely an adjustment that made better use of Dalí's designs. In the end, Menzies' revisions were abandoned, and Selznick wrote, on February 14, 1945: "I am not surprised that Bill Menzies does not want credit on the credit sequence in *Spellbound*. [...] Whatever other reasons Bill may have for not wanting credit, as far as I am concerned the sequence is a severe disappointment." Ingrid Bergman: "[P]ractically the whole of the scene was 'lost' in that limbo of the film world known as the cutting room floor. Salvador Dali's relationship with David O. Selznick cooled rapidly."[17] The final credits for the dream sequence read "based on designs by Salvador Dali," with James Basevi getting credit for art direction.

What happened to the lost scenes, then? James Bigwood writes that Hitchcock swore he never shot the statue scene, yet photos from the set show that he did; and according to an acquaintance of Hitchcock, who was a serviceman at the time, the film was screened, before its premiere, with the full dream sequence intact. No trace of the lost scenes remains today, except for an oft-reprinted photograph acquired by the Museum of Modern Art, New York – apparently a frame enlargement from an 8-mm negative – corresponding to one of the shots that had been excised; its origins, however, remain obscure. In the end, amnesia claimed victory over the persistence of memory.

Dalí's Works

Dalí had been paid $4,000 for his work on the picture and, in addition, wished to retain ownership of all his designs; each was worth $500 at the time. Selznick was not pleased: "I think the Dalí deal is absurd, that we have been jockeyed into a silly position and that this is probably the first time in history that an artist has been paid more than top price for his work in order for him to keep his work [...]."[18] In the end, the production retained exclusive distribution rights to the works, and enjoyed 50% ownership of all sketches and paintings along with a "right of selection": Selznick, Hitchcock and Daniel T. O'Shea were to receive one canvas each. And

[17] Ingrid Bergman and Alan Burgess, *Ingrid Bergman: My Story* (New York: Delacorte, 1980), p. 160.
[18] Letter of 4 Aug. 1944.

Dalí, his agent hastened to say, would "be delighted to dedicate to [Selznick] personally any one of the sketches [he liked] best."

Five original works by Dalí, used as matte paintings in the dream sequence, were carefully preserved by the production company. They were catalogued as follows: 1) *The Eyes* (from the gambling sequence); 2) *The Man Falling Off the Roof*; 3) *The Pyramid* (from the "uphill-downhill" sequence); 4) *The Vista*; and 5) *The Single Eye.*[19] The five works were painted on panels, in muted tones of monochrome grey, in keeping with the black and white of the screen; the picture area had the same dimensions in each. Dalí kept at least three of them; the edges of the panels were not trimmed and his annotations are still visible. These three paintings remained part of the artist's estate and are still preserved at Figueiras; the other two were given as gifts and are now in private collections. Their edges were removed for framing. Dalí dedicated one sketch, *Horseman on Death,* to Hitchcock, and gave him *The Eye,* which the director kept in his possession until he died; as for *The Man Falling Off the Roof,* the only painting signed by Dalí, it may have been given to Selznick.

The same letter mentions seven other Dalí sketches, both large – and small-format – although the Selznick promotional campaign for *Spellbound* boasted of a hundred such drawings. Lastly, two huge set backdrops, painted in black and white on muslin, were designed and executed under Dalí's supervision. They were preserved for many years at the Grosh Scenic Studios, although one of them was unfortunately coloured for use in a subsequent production.

Critical Reaction

Spellbound met with considerable success. Critics received the film well, singling out Ingrid Bergman's performance for particular praise and, although the Dalí sequence failed to generate the added publicity value that Selznick had hoped for (Dalí was already old hat, according to popular magazines), it was by and large well received, save for a few ironic comments: "Ingrid goes to work with a five-foot shelf of Freud, abetted by Salvatore [*sic*] Dali dream sequences to prove it ain't so"[20] or "of course, there's that dilly of a Dali dream sequence with curtains and staring eyes, and a man in a mask, and some people playing cards across a table that would have trouble getting into Grand Central. Stuff to keep you awake at night, and no wonder the guy who dreamed it needed a psychiatrist."[21]

[19] Letter of 10 Jan. 1945. Another painting from the abandoned ballroom sequence is known to exist, but its whereabouts are unknown. There is apparently no mention of it in the Selznick archives.
[20] Lee Mortimer in the *Daily Mirror*, n.d.
[21] Leo Mishkin in *The Morning Telegraph*, n.d.

"Celluloid Freud"

The idea of making a film about psychoanalysis was Selznick's. He had himself been in therapy recently, as had the scriptwriter, Ben Hecht. The producer's analyst, Dr. May E. Romm, served as scientific adviser for the screenplay. Selznick's pedagogical aims are fairly clear in the prologue to *Spellbound.* In fact, he wrote, with regard to possible troubles with the censor: "I think it should be pointed out to Breen that it is no cheap titillating sex subject, but a serious attempt to go into psychiatrist problems [...] since the nation is going to be faced with probably millions of psychiatrist problems." And later: "an education [...] in psychiatry is of great importance to the mental and moral health of the public."[22] At the time, Freud (who had died five years earlier) and psychoanalysis were beginning to be much discussed by the general public. With soldiers returning home, people wanted to know more about the traumatizing effects of war. In 1945 John Huston directed a documentary on the subject, *Let There Be Light,* which was banned for its intense realism.

Spellbound, 1945

There could have been no better choice than Dalí to illustrate a dream recounted by a patient on a psychiatrist's couch. The painter shared the Surrealists' admiration for the author of *The Interpretation of Dreams,* and had even met him once: "During the Surrealist Era, I wanted to create an iconography of the inner world – the world of wonder, of my father Freud. I managed to do so."[23] Indeed, "Dalí inflected his artistic orientation according to his profound interest in, and knowledge of, Freudian psychoanalysis; indeed it is based on his exploration of the unconscious, expressed in painterly terms, that he created his contribution to Surrealism. [...] To this end, he employs a resolutely naturalist technique, visible as much in his brushstrokes, so precise and impeccable, as in the representation of his images, executed in as concrete and photographic a fashion as possible."[24] Dalí was the right artist to render the unsettling Otherness of Freudianism, to create, for Hitchcock, imagery that was as realistic, clear and convincing as it was surreal, bizarre and striking.

The film is rife with more or less explicit references to Freud, or at least to Freudian iconography. The actor who plays Constance's former analyst, Michael Chekhov, is a caricature of Freud, with his erudite, paternal bearing, Germanic accent, round spectacles and white goatee. The film toyed with sexual references and played fast and loose with the censor, which was alarmed at such lines of dialogue

[22] Letter of 22 May 1944.
[23] Preface to the catalogue of the 1958–59 exhibition at the Carstairs Gallery, in *Salvador Dalí: Rétrospective 1920-1980,* p. 366. (Free translation.)
[24] Harriet Janis, "Paintings as a Key to Psychoanalysis," *Art and Architecture,* Los Angeles, Feb. 1946; also quoted in *Salvador Dalí, Rétrospective 1920-1980,* p. 127.

as "mass *sex* menace," "airing your *frustrations,*" and "mechanism of your *libido.*"[25] The pool that Constance draws on the tablecloth with her fork resembles a vagina; the image of the brush plunged into the shaving cream could not have been much more explicit; the same is true of the straight razor, erect and phallic.

The critics, though, weren't fooled: "The sponsors assure us that *Spellbound* is the first attempt to present psycho-analysis 'roundly and scientifically' in a feature film. They appear to have taken considerable pains to get a psychi-atrist's advice about their film; they even sought the sur-realist assistance of Mr. Salvador Dali for some of the 'dream sequences.' All the same, psychiatrists will not be taken in and others should not be. To put it bluntly, this film plays old Harry with psycho-analysis. It is like most Hitchcock films, one of mystery and adventure."[26] Indeed, Hitchcock did not intend to "educate" his audience, though he did share Dalí's interest in the work of Freud. The director did not hold the film in the highest regard, calling it "just another manhunt story wrapped up in pseudo-psychoanalysis."[27]

Dalí in Hollywood

During the 1940s, as Hollywood turned its gaze increas-ingly toward art, in conjunction with the influx of European directors steeped in turn-of-the-century, old-world culture, the European Surrealist cinema revealed itself to be little more than a bunch of films "on paper" – a collection of unfilmable scripts. The output was laughable compared to the initial expectations (the only exceptions being the twin Buñuel–Dalí masterpieces, whose power has not dimin-ished over time). The failure of this collective undertaking was attributed to meagre financial resources and public indifference, although this is understandable given the paradoxical and suicidal stance that advocated art without compromise (whether commercial or aesthetic), ever sub-versive and revolutionary – when in fact these were works bankrolled by patrons who had few affinities with the film industry.

Dalí, along with Cocteau, was in the prisoners' dock. Philippe Soupault accused them both of being cheats: "I say without reservation: Cocteau and Dalí have steered the Surrealist cin-ema away from its pure wellspring, from its true vocation."[28] Ado Kyrou, who, incidentally, unjustly devalued Dalí's contri-butions to *Un chien andalou,* condemned *Spellbound* for its superficial surrealism: "The dream sequence that Dalí created

[25] Letter of 19 May 1944 to Selznick from Breen of the Motion Picture Producers & Distributors of America.
[26] The "London Film Critic," in the *Manchester Guardian,* 18 May 1946.
[27] François Truffaut, with the collab-oration of Helen G. Scott, *Hitch-cock*, rev. ed. (New York: Simon & Schuster, 1984), p. 165.
[28] From a 1965 interview quoted in Virmaux and Virmaux, p. 81. (Free translation.)

for Hitchcock's commercial film *Spellbound*. Elementary Freudianism and cheap baubles are within easy reach of any lingerie shop window decorator or purveyor of chintz. Dalí, who at the time was an immensely talented painter, had already begun to display vague desires to take up these lucrative crafts."[29] The same judgment without appeal was handed down by Georges Ribemont-Dessaignes: "For some time now Dalí appears to have downgraded the Surrealist doctrine to the level of fashion; he is now employed in Hollywood, but all he is doing is holding an everything-must-go Surrealist rummage sale, and Surrealism is passé anyway."[30] The gavel had fallen.

So, was Dalí nothing more than a special-effects man, a counterfeiter of Surrealism? Can an haute couture designer who makes the switch to ready-to-wear no longer pretend to be making art? For all that, the Dalí dream sequence in *Spellbound* remains unique and, well, spellbinding. It is Alice telling us about her dream in a childlike universe; it is the set dressing for the narrative space of dreams – we are a long way from the automatic process of irrational images, as defended by the "guardians of the gate." Dalí, who was leery of the visual rhetoric of a cinema tempted by the avenues of abstraction, designed the sequence as one would a theatre set, with painted miniatures. (Forced perspective, in fact, was a technique dating back to Renaissance theatre.) The result was more graphic than cinematographic, more akin to Dalí than to Hitchcock. We barely notice the Hitchcockian touch in the huge, winged shadow chasing after Gregory Peck in the "uphill-downhill" sequence, recalling the sinister shadow of a cloud dulling the whiteness of the snow-covered slopes in *Secret Agent* (1936).

No, Hitchcock was at the peak of his craft in this film with his brutal, powerful depiction of the horrible childhood memory that is at the root of the hero's psychosis: in just a few shocking shots, this nightmare vision conveys all the stark horror of the fateful accident, alternating between facial close-ups and fatal perspectives. Here, the visual rhetoric of film places this wordless sequence on the same plane as that of the baby carriage tumbling down the Odessa Steps in Sergei Eisenstein's *Bronenosets Potemkine* ("The Battleship Potemkin," 1925).

Dalí thus imported his usual iconography to the cinema, as opposed to adapting it to cinematographic techniques. The dream sequence resonates with the illusionist trickery of Georges Méliès (whose films were little known at the time, but would later be described as Surrealist). For Dalí, the

CRITIC'S DREAM SEQUENCE. Caused by the week's films—William Powell, Gene Tierney, Angela Lansbury, Vincent Price, John Hodiak, Eric Portman, Ingrid Bergman, Gregory Peck, Alfred Hitchcock

Critic's Dream Sequence, 1946

[29] Ado Kyrou, *Le surréalisme au cinéma* (Paris: Éditions Ramsay et Le Terrain Vague, 1963), republished 1985, p. 208–09. (Free translation.)
[30] From a 1946 article quoted in Virmaux and Virmaux, p. 294. (Free translation.)

golden age of "surrealist" cinema was born with the first silent films of the Italian school: "[A m]agnificent era of historic cinema with Francesca Bertini, Gustavo Serena, Tulio Carminati, Pina Menichelli, etc. A cinema so right, so marvelously close to the theatre, with the huge merit of offering us real and concrete documents of psychological disorders of every kind, of the true development of youthful neuroses, of the realization in life of the most impure yearnings and fantasies. All the rest is decadence."[31]

Dalí, who had thrown himself heart and soul into this commissioned work for *Spellbound,* did not emerge from the experience with the hoped-for satisfaction. After a number of abortive attempts, he turned away from filmmaking, saying: "I do not believe that the cinema can ever become an art form. It is a secondary form because there are too many people involved in its creation."[32] He would nonetheless take an increasing interest in optical illusions, stereoscopy and holography, among other forms. Outside of Andy Warhol, he is the painter who attempted the most forays into the realm of cinema. After his initial collaboration with Buñuel, Dalí's partners in Hollywood were not exactly poor choices: at the time, he could have done far worse than the Marx Brothers, Fritz Lang, Alfred Hitchcock and Walt Disney. All we can do today is lament the failure of these projects. For this reason, the dream sequence in *Spellbound* is in a way better than a testimonial: it was Dalí's only child in Hollywood, one of the first experimental attempts at making an "art film," and the father of that child was Alfred Hitchcock.

Animated Dreams

In Hollywood, Hitchcock's success in getting an artist like Dalí to design a dream sequence for a production aimed at mainstream audiences was pioneering. Hans Richter's avant-garde film *Dreams That Money Can Buy,* made in collaboration with Alexander Calder, Max Ernst, Fernand Léger, Man Ray and Marcel Duchamp, was produced just after *Spellbound,* in 1946. It too was promoted as a "Freudian Surrealist film" upon its release, and it too was attacked for being chintzy!

Hitchcock responded by collaborating with an American artist for the design of Scottie's (James Stewart) nightmare in *Vertigo* (1958).[33] John Ferren, who had moved in Parisian art circles between the wars, was a minor figure of American Abstraction whose forcefully coloured works evoked both Henri Matisse and Wassily Kandinsky. He was a

[31] Antonio Urrutia, with the collaboration of Catherine Iglesias, quoted in "Dalí and the Cinema," in *Homage to Salvador Dalí,* special issue of *The XXᵉ siècle Review,* New York, 1980, p. 144.
[32] From 1968, quoted in *Salvador Dalí, Rétrospective 1920-1980,* p. 353. (Free translation.)
[33] Dan Auiler, *Vertigo: The Making of a Hitchcock Classic* (New York: St. Martin's Press, 1998), p. 43–44.

friend of Hitchcock, who asked him to collaborate on the *Vertigo* nightmare in 1957. The director, who had a great fondness for Ferren's work, had already employed him for *The Trouble with Harry* (1955); the painter character's canvases in that film were executed by Ferren, and he in fact appeared as an extra in the film, as well as dispensing technical advice.

If the *Spellbound* dream sequence is firmly rooted in the Dalinian universe, the nightmare contrived by Hitchcock and Ferren was emblematic of the pure visual cinema that the director advocated: a parade of images without words, understandable by their sheer visual power, keyed to a rhythm that evokes the pumping of blood in the body, sustained by stridency of colour and simplicity of shape, with Bernard Herrmann's music the only accompaniment to this tempo. The shooting script was specific: the architecture of the San Juan Bautista mission was to be harshly lit such that all its details were visible; Scottie's drawn silhouette had to be very sharply delineated in black. The hallucinatory breadth of the imagery, the mesmerizing rhythm, and James Stewart's fixed, terrified stare all reinforce the verisimilitude of the nightmare, which the director was so determined to convey. The obsessive alternations of images, the visions clashing together in the coruscating dazzle of the nightmare realm, become so many polyptychs of symbols hidden in the subconscious.

Here Hitchcock blended the live-action image with the animated image. Whenever he sought visual inspiration, his technical inquisitiveness and penchant for experimentation led him to explore a very broad spectrum of sources. Cartoons and comic strips were an integral part of his visual designs for *Strangers on a Train* (1951), for example, and *The Man Who Knew Too Much* (remake, 1956). James Mason, incidentally, once said that Hitchcock viewed his actors as "animated props."

"The logic of your pictures [...] is rather like the logic of dreams"[34]

From very early on, the cinema had provided a means of exploring the twists and turns of the human soul. Later discoveries in the realm of psychoanalysis were an influence, to be sure, but to truly appreciate this filmic exploration requires an understanding of the cultural and aesthetic currents that had gone before, throughout the 19th century – from the Romantics' studies of passion to the Symbolists' plumbing of the murky confines of the Self.

[34] Truffaut, p. 260.

Georg Wilhelm Pabst's *Geheimnisse einer Seele* ("Secrets of a Soul," 1926) was among the first films to open these doors. As early as 1931, Fritz Lang relied specifically on the services of psychoanalysts and psychiatrists in developing the script of *M. ein Stadt sucht ein Mörder* ("M."), and he would later develop broader themes of dreams, fantasy and madness (see, for example, the Dr. Mabuse cycle) during his American period. Psychoanalysis emerged as a clear theme in Hitchcock's American period, too, at the very time that it began to exert a fascination on both the general public and the media.

This investigation into the heart of neuroses (a legacy of Lang) made *Spellbound* the first of Hitchcock's psychotraumatic thrillers,[35] a precursor of *Under Capricorn* (1949), *Vertigo, Psycho* (1960) and *Marnie* (1964), whose storylines are structured around psychotic or neurotic repercussions of a traumatic event experienced by one of the main characters. Even when a Hitchcock film is obviously fantastical, as is the case with *The Birds,* this surreal dimension provides, above all, a means for meticulous inquiry – a project to elucidate a psychological proposition. The director created novel visual and auditory effects to depict these mental terrors: striated whites in *Spellbound;* flashy reds in *Marnie*; the new imagery resulting from the engaging of visual artists for the nightmare sequences in *Spellbound* and *Vertigo*; and even new soundscapes (e.g., the theremin in Miklos Rozsa's score for *Spellbound* and the "electronic silence" of *The Birds*).

"Last night, I dreamt…"[36]

The oneiric dimension in Hitchcock's cinema can be understood not only in terms of his characters' neuroses, however; for those characters display obsessive relationships with houses, objects and people that exist outside this sphere. As in Lang, there are elements of the horror film in Hitchcock, emergent in psychoanalytical fairy tales in which haunted houses, bewitching paintings and the handles of locked doors are simultaneously attractive and terrifying. These are necessary objects of fantasy and icons of fear, becoming, for the audience, visual manifestations of their anxieties – expressed using the same visual vocabulary as in art. There is, for instance, a fascination with the pictorial double, which vampirizes the characters in *Rebecca* and *Vertigo* – it has Symbolist, Victorian underpinnings (Daphne du Maurier, Oscar Wilde) and was widely exploited by the Surrealist painters (Delvaux, Magritte). The dream sequences that serve as prologues in *Rebecca* and in Lang's *The Secret Beyond the Door* (1948) drew from the same sources as did

[35] Charles Derry, *The Suspense Thriller: Films in the Shadow of Alfred Hitchcock* (Jefferson, N.C.: McFarland & Company, 1988), p. 194–215.
[36] This is the opening line of Daphne du Maurier's novel *Rebecca* (London: Gollancz, 1938) and of Hitchcock's film adaptation.

Cocteau for his *La belle et la bête* ("Beauty and the Beast," 1946).

Hitchcock moved progressively away from "readable" dreamscapes, with their aesthetic and literary references to Symbolism or Surrealism, and created a protocol for his own dreams. His subjective camera rummaged around inside his characters' minds, capturing their reveries (*Rear Window,* 1954), their delusions *(Vertigo)* and their madness (*Strangers on a Train, Psycho, Marnie,* etc.). Indeed, Hitch had a disdain for verisimilitude: "There's nothing more stupid than logic. [...] I don't attach any importance to logic. None of my films is based on logic. Give me a bomb: and Descartes can go boil his head."[37] He added: "The area in which we get near to the free abstract in moviemaking is the free use of fantasy, which is what I deal in."[38]

Inventor of Surrealist Forms

In the following quote, Hitchcock seems to respond to Breton, who considered Edgar Allan Poe to be a "surrealist of adventure": "And surrealism? Wasn't it born as much from the work of Poe as from that of Lautréamont? This literary school certainly had a great influence on cinema, especially around 1925–1930, when surrealism was transposed onto the screen by Buñuel with *L'âge d'or* and *Un chien andalou,* by René Clair with *Entr'acte,* by Jean Epstein with *The Fall of the House of Usher,* and by your French academician Jean Cocteau with *The Blood of a Poet.* An influence that I experienced myself, if only in the dream sequences and the sequences of the unreal in a certain number of my films."[39]

Hitchcock dreamed in broad daylight. His razor-sharp, fantastical imagery – he himself said he sought to achieve these effects – was Surrealist. To lend a dreamlike depth to Scottie's stalking of Madeleine in *Vertigo,* he shot in harsh sunlight but through a fog filter, turning the streets of San Francisco into an Yves Tanguy reverie. The images in his films become *unreal* because, as in Dalí's and De Chirico's canvases, they are *too* real, too sharp, too well honed – achieving the same climate of paranoia found in the paintings of Edward Hopper. De Chirico and Hitchcock reveal affinities in their respective formal approaches. Their dramatically accelerated perspectives compress the ratios of scale between characters and their environments: in the colonnades of the Jefferson Memorial in *Strangers on a Train* and in the infinite iterations of the mission archways in *Vertigo,* we can see De Chirico's *La Grande Torre*

[37] From a 1963 interview in Oriana Fallaci, *Limelighters,* trans. Pamela Swinglehurst, new ed. (London: Michael Joseph Ltd., 1967), p. 93.
[38] Peter Bogdanovich, *Who the Devil Made It: Conversations with Legendary Film Directors* (New York: Ballantine Books, 1998), p. 531.
[39] From a 1960 article quoted in Sidney Gottlieb (ed.), *Hitchcock on Hitchcock: Selected Writings and Interviews* (Berkeley: University of California Press, 1995), p. 144.

("The Great Tower," 1913) and his metaphysical piazzas. The abnormal visual confrontations of monumental statues and tiny humans – the colossal Egyptian head in the British Museum in *Blackmail* (1929), the Statue of Liberty in *Saboteur* (1942), Mount Rushmore in *North by Northwest* (1959) – result in fantastical, destabilizing images. The sleeping Ariane of De Chirico's imagination, who dreams of an unsettling black locomotive appearing on the horizon, is an unwitting avatar of young Charlie, daydreaming in her bed when the train (which Hitchcock intentionally made very dark) carrying her evil uncle arrives in *Shadow of a Doubt* (1943). Both the filmmaker and the painter preferred the archetypal to the individual: the disquieting image of the state trooper with the dark glasses in *Psycho* is reminiscent of *Il sogno del poeta* ("The Dream of the Poet") or the *Portrait of Guillaume Apollinaire* (1914). And there is the Hitchcockian obsession with filming gloved hands and everyday objects – cups, glasses, eyeglasses – in the foreground, out of scale with reality, to perverse and unsettling effect: this recalls *Canto d'amore* ("Song of Love") and *The Serenity of the Scholar,* also from 1914. Sylvia Sidney, who starred in *Sabotage* (1936), once recalled that while shooting, Hitchcock seemed interested only in hands and objects.

Objects diverted from their usual functions, closed doors, windows onto courtyards: these, in the Hitchcock universe, are the keys to the interpretation of dreams, the unexpected answers – as in Magritte, where windows with curtains drawn conceal as many dreams as they do assassination attempts. What are we to make of *The Birds,* which Fellini called a poem without an end? The particular iconography that leads us to view the ordinary bird as a disturbing, cruel animal stems from the Surrealist painters: Max Ernst and his *Monument to the Birds,* Magritte and his *Companions of Fear,* Joseph Cornell and his boxes of stuffed birds.

With tongue only half in cheek, I leave you with the contention that the most Dalinian of Hitchcock's films is actually *North by Northwest*. The film, which even its creator admitted was like one long dream sequence (he compared it, incidentally, to a painting by Christopher Nevinson), is pure fantasy. The hero, a "wrong man" but a "right paranoiac," unjustly pursued, is caught up in the implacable logic of a delirious tale: along the way he encounters sphinx-like women, stands waiting in broad daylight beside improbably desolate fields, and gets lost in the anthropomorphized "face" of Mount Rushmore! Image and imagination, after all, are derived from the same word.

Saul Bass, *Opening credits of* North by Northwest, 1959

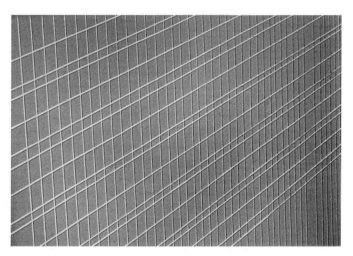

Saul Bass, *Opening credits of* North by Northwest, 1959

Hitchcock and Contemporary Art

Stéphane Aquin

Alfred Hitchcock's prestige in the eyes of other filmmakers is unequalled. To many of them, from Éric Rohmer and Claude Chabrol through to Gus Van Sant – via Brian De Palma, and not forgetting François Truffaut – he is *the* master. His films transcend the norms of usual production: they are Books of Cinema, master classes in the cinematographic art. They are there to be elucidated, followed, revisited and on occasion, perhaps, surpassed.

That same prestige extends far beyond the frontiers of film. Scores of artists in other disciplines have also studied Hitchcock, who unwittingly has become a fetishized reference in the realm of modern art, a sort of ideal representative of the cinema. Pierre Huyghe took up the task of doing a shot-for-shot video remake of *Rear Window,* named, aptly enough, *Remake* (1995); in this endeavour, he was merely following the example of Hitchcock himself, who allowed himself the luxury of revisiting *The Man Who Knew Too Much* and who at one time, quite soon after his arrival in Los Angeles, had seriously considered remaking *The Lodger, The Thirty-nine Steps* and *The Lady Vanishes.*

Another remake: that fashioned by Stan Douglas in his loop installation *Subject to a Film: Marnie* (1989), which recycles the scene in which Marnie stays late at the offices of Rutland and Co. to steal the key that will give her access to the safe.[1] The well-known cinephile David Reed, for his part, has reproduced Judy's and Scottie's bedrooms from *Vertigo,* substituting two of his own canvases for the nondescript paintings hanging above each bed – a substitution he applied within the film itself through digitally modified scenes that run in a continuous loop on the TV sets in each reconstructed room.[2]

A cult film if there ever was one, *Vertigo* has been referenced numerous times by conceptual artists. For *The Bridge* (1984), Victor Burgin restaged certain elements of Madeleine's attempted suicide beneath the Golden Gate

[1] Douglas, whose interest in the construction of cultural values is well known, examines the circular psychology of the eponymous character in *Marnie*: she is a passive subject of a camera that certain critics have denounced as a symbol of sexual domination. See essays by Scott Watson and John Fiske in *Stan Douglas: Monodramas and Loops,* exhib. cat., (Vancouver: UBC Fine Arts Gallery, 1992).

[2] Essays by Elizabeth Armstrong, Paul Auster, Dave Hickey and Mieke Bal in *David Reed Paintings Motion Pictures,* exhib. cat. (San Diego: Museum of Contemporary Art, 1998). Also interesting is the neo-Platonic analysis of these works in Arthur Danto, *After the End of Art: Contemporary Art and the Pale of History* (Princeton: Princeton University Press, 1997).

Bridge, in the process emphasizing the scene's psychoanalytical underpinnings. With *Ask the Dust: Vertigo, 1958–1990,* Cindy Bernard conducted an archeological examination of the same scene, as part of a wider project aimed at rephotographing famous locations from film history. More recently Bernard has reconstituted, as a computer model (*Location Proposal #2, 1997–1999),* each shot of another famous scene from the film: the one set amid the sequoias in the Muir Woods.

Vertigo also gets a nod in the work of Douglas Gordon; one of his photographs (*Empire,* 1998) shows the lighted sign of the Empire Hotel, where Judy Barton stays – installed for the occasion on a Glasgow street. In 1993 Gordon had hit upon the idea of projecting *Psycho* in slow motion so that its running time would be extended to a full day; the resulting installation was titled *24-Hour Psycho.* Stripped of its soundtrack, slowed down to the limit of tolerability, the film plays like a regression through the history of cinema, back to that threshold where the black-and-white frame haltingly becomes a moving image.[3]

The specific relationship between contemporary art and the Hitchcockian oeuvre was the subject of an exhibition organized by the Museum of Modern Art, Oxford in 1999, the centenary of the filmmaker's birth. The show assembled a number of the aforementioned works along with others that quoted Hitchcock's films or made explicit reference to them.[4] The fact that these works incorporated references or borrowings from Hitchcock rather than another director is not necessarily of particular significance. In many cases, these examinations of Hitchcock from other artistic perspectives are in keeping with a complex and lasting fascination with the cinema on the part of artists in other disciplines – a fascination whose many and diverse manifestations have been the catalysts for a variety of recent exhibitions.[5]

Beyond informed commentaries, tributes to the classics, veiled references, or enshrinements (sometimes inopportune) of Hitchcock, the filmmaker's most durable legacy in the art world is perhaps not to be found in those works that reference him explicitly, but rather in a certain way of looking at the world and of reconstructing its image. There exists a Hitchcockian gaze, one that no viewer can ever forget, and whose distinct qualities, like so many visual filters, have left their imprint on the other arts as well as on the cinema – even affecting how we perceive ordinary scenes in our daily lives. What adult today can look at a murder of crows and not think of *The Birds*?

[3] In a more recent work, he proceeds in opposite fashion, retaining only the Bernard Herrmann score for *Vertigo* as conducted by James Conlon, whose hands and eyes are filmed by Gordon (*Feature Film,* 1999). Douglas Gordon has repeatedly revisited the works of Hitchcock, most often with the aim of showing the power of Hitchcockian fiction (i.e., its ability to extend beyond its original incarnation, via our memories, and contaminate our relationship with reality): by sending letters to Lars Thorwald, the killer in *Rear Window,* asking him "What have you done with her?" (*A Souvenir of Non-Existence,* 1993); by affixing to a surface a quantity of postage stamps (each depicting Hitchcock) that would be necessary to send an object equivalent to the filmmaker's body weight from New York to Glasgow, by both air and surface mail (*Airmail White Portrait,* 1999; *Surface Mail White Portrait,* 1999). See essays by Eckhard Schneider, Lynne Cooke, Friedrich Meschede, Charles Esche and "a Friend" in *Douglas Gordon,* exhib. cat. (Hannover: Kunstverein Hannover, 1998).

[4] *Notorious: Alfred Hitchcock and Contemporary Art,* exhib. cat. (Oxford: Museum of Modern Art, Oxford, 1999). The exhibition catalogue contains essays by Kerry Brougher and Michael Tarantino. Artists exhibited included John Baldessari, Cindy Bernard, Victor Burgin, Stan Douglas, Christoph Girardet & Matthias Müller, Douglas Gordon, Pierre Huyghe, Christian Marclay, David Reed and Cindy Sherman; films by Atom Egoyan and Chris Marker were shown. Other artists not represented at this exhibition who have referenced Hitchcock include Marcel Odenbach (*Der Widerspruch der Erinnerungen,* 1982) and Mark Tansey (*Four Forbidden Senses,* 1982).

[5] Recent years have seen the exhibitions *Art and Film Since 1945: Hall of Mirrors,* Museum of Contemporary Art, Los Angeles, 1996; *Spellbound: Art and Film,* British Film Institute and Hayward Gallery, London, 1996; *L'effet cinéma,* Musée d'art contemporain de Montréal, Montréal, 1996; and *Cinéma Cinéma: Contemporary Art and the Cinema Experience,* Stedelijk Van Abbemuseum, Eindhoven, 1999.

Quantifying this Hitchcockian legacy involves more than a simple compilation of references. Even though it is multifaceted, that legacy is nonetheless founded on a certain number of identifiable procedures – visual paradigms[6] that serve to structure several contemporary works. Paranoid imagery, constructed so as to arouse suspicion and anxiety in the spectator, is among the most recognizable of these. In *Unapproved Road* (1992), for example, the Northern Ireland–born photographer Willie Doherty focusses his lens on his subject in the same way Hitchcock's camera would stubbornly pause to pick out an "ordinary" detail (the stuffed birds in *Psycho,* for example), provoking a feeling of paranoia – a feeling rendered all the more insistent by the fact that nothing in the frame, objectively, justifies it.[7] "So you gradually build up the psychological situation, piece by piece, using the camera to emphasise first one detail, then another," Hitchcock once explained, referring to the extended shots of the kitchen knife held by Mrs. Verloc in *Sabotage*.[8]

A corollary to this "paranoia of the gaze" is the fact that certain objects, because they are filmed in close-up or the camera lingers on them, become fetishized, and take on a decisive narrative power, not to mention specific sexual connotations – examples include the lighter in *Strangers on a Train* and Madeleine's hairstyle in *Vertigo*. In his diptych entitled *No* (1997), Eldon Garnet juxtaposes two fragmentary subjects that are equally fraught with meaning: the blood-flecked beak of a crow and the nude torso of a young woman, her pubis shaved. This association can be read as an intense and violent symbolic drama: a thematic conjugation of horror and sexuality with strong Hitchcockian overtones.

Another of these visual paradigms is that of the "reaction shot," masterfully employed by Hitchcock, and which consists in depicting an event by showing only a character's (or characters') reaction to it. Tony Oursler has pushed this idea to the limit with a series of pieces in which he projects, onto a sphere, the video image of an eye watching a film – sometimes a horror film, as in the case of *Seed* (1996), in which the hidden spectacle is the Nunnally Johnson psychological drama *The Three Faces of Eve*. Diane Arbus, for her part, took an approach that was at once sociological and poetic with her series of photographs of movie-house audiences, taken during the very period that gave birth to suspense à la Hitchcock. *Murder Witness,* from the film *New York Confidential* (1958), depicts a woman reacting in horror to a film, much as she might to a similar scene in the real world, and much as a murder witness in a Hitchcock film would.

[6] The term "visual paradigm" was coined by Bill Krohn. In his book *Hitchcock at Work,* he demonstrates how the director would employ such paradigms repeatedly within the same film to create visual and dramatic coherence. For example, in several scenes in *Notorious,* Hitchcock systematically used what Krohn terms "the evolving visual paradigm of 'the close-up of a detail revealing a hidden drama going on within the scene,'" going so far as to substitute this paradigm for the shots planned in the script when it came time to film a scene. Bill Krohn, *Hitchcock at Work* (London: Phaidon Press, 2000), p. 98.

[7] In a recent essay, Maite Lorès has pointed out a kinship between Doherty's work and film noir aesthetics. See Maite Lorès, "The Streets Were Dark with Something More Than Night: Film Noir Elements in the Work of Willie Doherty," in *Willie Doherty: Dark Stains,* exhib. cat. (Donastia–San Sebastián: Koldo Mitxelena Kulturunea, 1999).

[8] Alfred Hitchcock, "Direction," in Charles Davy, ed., *Footnotes to the Film* (New York: Arno Press & The New York Times, 1970), p. 8.

Hitchcock's cinema is a lesson in voyeurism. The central theme of a film like *Rear Window,* for instance, voyeurism also characterizes the very movement of the camera: Hitchcock's camera is an omnipotent eye that roves through space and penetrates all the way into the private realm of its subjects. Merry Alpern's series of photographs *Dirty Windows* (1994) proceeds from the same impulse; the artist set up her camera in a friend's New York City apartment and recorded, through the bathroom windows of a nearby sex club, multiple manifestations of crime, in its sordid and thrilling association of money, sex and drugs. In *Exhibition dans le nord de la France* (1992), Alain Fleischer revisited the theme of domestic voyeurism seen in *Rear Window,* but by projecting, onto the fronts of houses – temporarily transformed into public screens – the private scenes that they hide.

Gregory Crewdson, from the series "Natural Wonder," *Untitled,* 1992–1997

Voyeurism à la Hitchcock, as many commentators have noted, is the cinematic extension of an act of sexual control – as is the case, formally, when the camera in *Psycho* penetrates the hotel room to show Marion Crane (Janet Leigh) sprawled half-naked on the bed or, explicitly, in the same film, when Norman Bates (Anthony Perkins) peers through an orifice in the wall as Marion undresses. It is this gaze to which some of the photographs in Cindy Sherman's *Untitled Film Stills* seem to allude. Through this series, the artist, without citing any specific cinematographic sources, analysed and subverted the gender codes of Hollywood cinema.[9]

Beyond its formal constitution, the Hitchcockian gaze is characterized by a set of thematic fixations – "obsessions," to borrow a much-loved term from auteur theory. There is abundant literature on this topic, and numerous themes have been identified.[10] Outside these more informed circles, however, certain themes are more spontaneously and commonly associated with the work of Hitchcock: morbid associations of the Eros/Thanatos variety, for example, explored in many of his films but especially in *Psycho, The Birds* and *Frenzy,* and which find their echo in a number of works such as the aforementioned Eldon Garnet piece; haunted sites, the uncontested legacy of Symbolism, whose spirit permeates works like Holly King's *Place of Desire*; or the sudden intrusion of horror into daily life, or into a natural setting (of "disorder into order," as Hitchcock was fond of saying). Gregory Crewdson has exhaustively explored the latter issue in his series of photographs *Natural Wonder* (1992–1997), many components of which seem directly inspired by the Hitchcock universe. Crewdson himself explains: "In all of my

[9] Exhibition jointly organized by the Museum of Contemporary Art, Los Angeles, and the Museum of Contemporary Art, Chicago. See essays by Amada Cruz, Elizabeth A.T. Smith and Amelia Jones in *Cindy Sherman: Retrospective,* exhib. cat. (London and New York: Thames & Hudson, 1997).

[10] For a discussion on thematic analyses of Hitchcock, see David Sterritt, *The Films of Alfred Hitchcock* (Cambridge Film Classics coll.) (Cambridge: Cambridge University Press, 1993).

Sarah Morris, *Midtown-SOLO (9W57)*, 1999

photographs I'm very much interested in creating tension; between domesticity and nature, the normal and the paranormal, or artifice and reality, or what's familiar and what's mysterious. [...] I'm interested in using the iconography of nature and the American landscape as surrogates or metaphors for psychological anxiety, fear or desire."[11]

And in that we find yet another characteristic of the Hitchcockian gaze: it confers visual form – which can be figurative or abstract – on psychological states and their psychosomatic effects: blackouts, dizziness, hallucinations. In *Marnie,* the violent resurfacing of a repressed memory, that of the murder she committed as a young girl, causes the title character to quite literally "see red"; in *Vertigo,* Scottie suffers from dizzy spells that, in the bell tower at San Juan Bautista, become a geometric structure rushing away from the viewer at an accelerated pace; in *Suspicion,* the shadows cast in the foyer of the Aysgarths' home form a tentacular web symbolizing the psychological trap into which Lina (Joan Fontaine) feels drawn.

There is in Hitchcock a true geometry of anguish; its locus is the intersection of the visible and the abstract, and it can be related to that component of abstract painting that involves the depiction of altered states at the frontiers of perception. Vertigo was given precise geometric representation in the works of Bridget Riley, a contemporary of Hitchcock. A painter linked to the Op Art movement, Riley nonetheless invested her optical hallucinations with a psychological dimension, and the titles of some of her canvases of the time seem to bear this out: *Deny, Arrest, Tremor.*[12] In this regard, *Blaze 4* (1964) provides an almost palpable image of the abysses of vertigo. Closer to us in time are the abstractions of Sarah Morris, derived from the façades of Manhattan skyscrapers, whose obsessive gridlines suggest similar states. Perhaps not coincidentally, the famous Saul Bass title sequence in *North by Northwest* was structured in symmetrically inverse fashion: a dizzying network of lines gradually dissolving into the modern steel-and-glass architecture of a New York City building.

[11] See *Gregory Crewdson: Dream of Life* (Salamanca: Ediciones Universidad de Salamanca, 1999). Of particular interest are the essay by Darcey Steinke and the interview by Bradford Morrow, in which Crewdson states *Vertigo* is his "all-time" favourite film.

[12] See essays by Lisa G. Corrin, Robert Kudielka and Frances Spalding in *Bridget Riley: Paintings from the 1960's and 70's,* exhib. cat. (London: Serpentine Gallery, 1999).

Alfred Hitchcock and a watercolour by Rodin

Alfred Hitchcock: An Artist in Spite of Himself

Nathalie Bondil-Poupard

"Do you think of yourself as an artist?"
"No, not particularly."[1]

Nearly a half-century later, no one would oppose Éric Rohmer and Claude Chabrol's time-honoured contention that Alfred Hitchcock was "one of the greatest inventors of form in the history of cinema."[2] But what did Hitchcock himself think? What was it about his method that makes him comparable to an artist? What were the connections to art in his life, and on what bases can his life's work be likened to that of an illustrator, a painter or a composer?

Apprentice

In 1915 Hitchcock began attending evening classes in, among other things, art history, later complemented by drawing and painting classes. Soon he was carrying a sketchbook wherever he went, and studying the masters of English painting. From his office job at the W.T. Henley Telegraph Company (a manufacturer of electric cables), he was promoted to a position as a graphic designer in the firm's advertising department.

By 1920 he was a committed film buff, and was hired as a part-time title card illustrator by Famous Players–Lasky Corporation, which had recently set up shop in Great Britain. There he drew intertitles for several silent films, and made the acquaintance of George Fitzmaurice. A prestigious director of the time, Fitzmaurice became Hitchcock's first mentor: he, too, had studied painting, and believed that cinema had its affinities with the visual arts. The consummate professional taught the young apprentice all the rudiments of the craft, including how to plan a film shot by shot using drawings.

In 1924 Hitchcock travelled to Berlin's UFA studios to work as art director on the Michael Balcon–Erich Pommer co-production *Die Prinzessin und der Geiger* ("The Black-

[1] Peter Bogdanovich, *Who the Devil Made It: Conversations with Legendary Film Directors* (New York: Ballantine Books, 1998), p. 554.
[2] On this subject, François Regnault has devised an amusing checklist system. See "Système formel d'Hitchcock (fascicule de résultats)," *Cahiers du cinéma,* special issue, 1980, p. 21–28.

179

guard," 1925). There, Hitchcock was initiated into the pre-eminent cinema of the day, the German school, absorbing both the fantastical imagery of the Expressionists and the "visual readability" of the *Kammerspiel* ("chamberplay") films. By his own account, it was with *The Ring* (1927) that he began to experiment with "painterly" flourishes in his films.

Art Lover

Alfred and Alma Hitchcock appear to have begun collecting works of art around 1944,[3] the year *Spellbound* was produced, with the collaboration of Salvador Dalí. The painter gave the filmmaker a canvas executed for the film's dream sequence, entitled *The Eye,*[4] as well as a drawing with the inscription *Horseman on Death.* The Hitchcocks had similar tastes, and chose their paintings together. Although the collection was important to them, they were not what one would call avid collectors: their daughter, Patricia, does not recall hearing, as a child, any conversations about art, or her parents' collection. They owned a life-size bronze bust of their daughter wearing an evening gown, by the sculptor Jacob Epstein. Neither inherited any works of art, and neither resold any of their works. Hitchcock also regarded the collection as an investment: his financial advisers, for example, once recommended that he buy a painting by Jean Dubuffet but, in the end, he did not. There was a frustrating episode in 1970 involving the appraisal of a painting in his collection attributed to Pablo Picasso. Titled *Nature morte au buste,* it was declared by Picasso himself to be a fake – a copy of the original, which now hangs in the Thyssen-Bornemisza Museum in Madrid.[5]

The Hitchcocks' collection[6] encompassed a wide variety of styles, artists and subjects, but this was more revelatory of their social standing than of a concerted approach to collecting. The director once explained: "Alma knows much – too much – about me. [...] She knows that for a thriller-movie-making ogre, I'm hopelessly plebeian and placid. She knows that instead of reading mysteries at home I'm usually designing a built-in cupboard for the house; that I wear conservative clothes and solid-color ties; that I prefer talkative colors to somber ones in a room, properly introduced through flowers or fine paintings."[7] Their collection, while eclectic, was variable in both interest and quality, and included works on paper by minor English masters of the late 18th century. These were etchings, drawings and watercolours, decorative and pleasing

[3] I should like to thank Ms. Patricia Hitchcock O'Connell for having agreed to answer my questions.
[4] *The Eye* is not included in the archives: at the time, the unsigned canvas was apparently wrongly considered to be a "mere" film prop.
[5] Christian Zervos, *Catalogue raisonné de l'œuvre de Picasso,* Vol. 5, No. 372 (Paris: Cahiers d'arts/Freitag, 1952).
[6] I rely here on two sources from the archives of the Academy of Motion Picture Arts and Sciences, Margaret Herrick Library, Los Angeles: a list of 19 of the Hitchcocks' most prized works of art, drawn up for insurance purposes in 1970 by art dealer Frank Perls, and an inventory of the works in their two homes in Bel-Air and Santa Cruz.
[7] From a speech given in March 1953, quoted in Sidney Gottlieb (ed.), *Hitchcock on Hitchcock: Selected Writings and Interviews* (Berkeley: University of California Press, 1995), p. 52.

Fidelio Ponce De Léon, *Five Women,*
1941

to the eye, depicting picturesque scenes of English life, from the hands of such artists as Thomas Rowlandson, a prolific caricaturist and illustrator (five watercolours), Samuel Alken and George Morland (Hitchcock owned one Morland canvas, *Noonday Rest,* which was deemed worthy of inclusion on his insurer's list).

The Hitchcocks were mostly interested in works by modern artists. Latin American artists were much in vogue in the United States at the time, and the couple's acquisitions included *Seated Nude,* a lithograph by the noted Mexican painter David Alfaro Siqueiros, and *Voodoo Dancers,* by a Haitian artist, Enguerrand Gourgue. In one particular instance, the director used a painting from his own collection as a prop in one of his films: the set of *Rope* featured a canvas by the Cuban Modernist Fidelio Ponce de León, *Five Women* (1941), which Hitchcock had acquired just before the film was shot, and had displayed in his living room.

Among the Hitchcocks' most important acquisitions were a good number of paintings by Fauvists and Cubists (highly coveted at the time), and whose range of subject matter was perfectly characteristic of these artists' output. These painters were without exception colourists; their works, expressive and figurative. Alfred and Alma owned one of the many views of *Trouville* by Raoul Dufy (1935), as well as two canvases by Maurice de Vlaminck: *Route [de] village* and *Flowers in a Blue Jug.* The couple were particularly fond of Maurice Utrillo, and owned two of his paintings: *Rue des Abbesses* (circa 1928) and *Le moulin [de la Galette] en hiver* (circa 1936). Alfred was also a great admirer of Georges Rouault, whose Catholic sensibility he shared. Rouault was represented in their collection by a *Suaire* and a lithograph. They owned another painting in the same expressionist mould – a particularly beautiful work by Chaïm Soutine, *The Tree* (circa 1939), acquired in 1968 – and a canvas entitled *L'écuyère,* by the Cubist Albert Gleizes. The Hitchcocks also collected graphic works, among them abstractions by Claude Garache, nudes by Henri Gaudier-Brzeska, and three drawings by Marie Laurencin. They also owned a number of less figurative works by more contemporary artists, including Americans Darrel Austin *(Eclipse of the Moon)* and Milton Avery *(Winter Landscape),* as well as an abstract work by Pierre Soulages (dated 10.10.61). According to Patricia Hitchcock O'Connell, her father appreciated non-figurative compositions as long as they were pleasing to the eye, but was not interested in their meanings.

Chaïm Soutine, *The Tree,*
about 1939

A few works seem to correspond more specifically to Alfred Hitchcock's tastes and personality, such as the Auguste Rodin watercolour *Danseuse nue*. Rodin's sculpture *The Kiss,* incidentally, was one of Hitchcock's favourite works of art. Indeed, his camera would often spin around a pair of embracing lead actors as a gallery visitor might around a piece of high-relief sculpture. Hitchcock shared the sculptor's romantic sensuality. The filmmaker also owned a 1908 engraving, part of a famous series by the English painter Walter Richard Sickert, called *The Camden Town Murder.* Inspired by the famous 1907 death of a prostitute, who was found nude and strangled on the bed of her room in the North London borough of Camden Town, the engraving shows the killer and his victim sitting on the bed before the crime – she nude, he clothed. The work points up a typically British taste for crime – one that Hitchcock claimed as his own. Then there was his fascination for cubist painter Georges Braque's "birds series." Hitch ordered a huge mosaic based on this theme from the Galerie Maeght in Paris (it is said he would have preferred that the artist come and install the work personally at the back of his garden in Santa Cruz!); it was later dismantled after his house was sold. While it is obviously tempting to imagine connections between the Braque and *The Birds,* and by extension Hitchcock's fear of birds, the director never mentioned it.

Alfred Hitchcock with Strange Hunt *by Paul Klee*

Hitchcock owned three works by Paul Klee,[8] of whom he was especially fond. He once said: "I'd compare myself to an abstract painter. My favorite painter is Klee."[9] The paintings *Seltsame Jagd* ("Strange Hunt," 1937) and *Odysseisch* ("Odyssey," 1924) may have been acquired in New York, when he was beginning his collection. His passion for Klee appears to have been sparked by a painting he saw exhibited in London, but that he balked at purchasing, unsure of whether he could afford the asking price (600 pounds, no small sum at the time). This may have been the watercolour entitled *Man with Scythe* (date unknown).

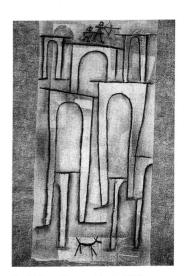

Paul Klee, *Strange Hunt,* 1937

Gallery Owner

Hitchcock would often use paintings in his films, not merely as props, but as stand-in supporting characters: in *Blackmail,* the clown portrait is employed by turns to comic and ironic effect, depending on the heroine's state of mind; here Hitchcock drew on the montage aesthetic of Slavo Vorkapich. Like Father Logan and the crucifix in *I Confess,* his main characters would often be confronted with moral authority in the form of an archetypal portrait –

[8] Here I should like to thank Ms. Constance Naubert-Riser for her assistance.
[9] Thomas Samuels, *Encountering Directors* (New York: Charles G.P. Putnam's Sons, 1972), p. 239.

Paul Klee, *Odyssey,* 1924

Alfred Hitchcock sketching a camera setup during the making of Spellbound, 1945

which is always immediately readable as such, though it may be very ordinary in its execution. There is the portrait of the judge in *The Manxman,* urging the liar to reveal himself; that of the soldier father in *Suspicion,* so controlling until his daughter disobeys him; there are the delirious portraits of a father detested by his son, in *Strangers on a Train,* and of a dead father who was too often absent from the home, in *The Birds*; and there is that of the wife who reminds her unfaithful husband of his conjugal duties and seems to communicate her own treacherousness to him with a pointed finger, in *The Paradine Case*. As in the films of Fritz Lang or Albert Lewin, a character's confrontation with the pictorial can be dangerous: in *The Lodger,* the visions of both angelic and perverse blondes are so unbearable to the eponymous character that he turns them inward to face the wall of his flat; and, of course, there are the portraits of Maxim de Winter's forebear and of Carlotta Valdés, invisible doppelgängers that vampirize the respective heroines.

Artist

Hitchcock's creative process has affinities with the other arts, particularly with painting and music, to which he would often refer with convincing coherence when asked to talk about his method. Imagining his method and style in terms of artists' tools makes for an amusing exercise.

Pencil
In Hitchcock's artistic campaigns, the first territory to be invaded was the draftsman's empty white page, itself so like a movie screen: "You see, the point is that you are, first of all, in a two-dimensional medium. Mustn't forget that. You have a rectangle to fill. Fill it. Compose it. [...] [W]hen I'm on the set, I'm not on the set. [...] I am looking at a screen."[10] Showing little regard for off-screen space, he would make sure to fill his "easel" with as much pictorial information as possible, while being subject to the following constraint: "A painter is able to choose the canvas size that fits his subject. (I happen to own a Dufy that was painted on a long, narrow canvas; but the subject is a harbor and therefore suitable.) Filmmakers, on the other hand, are bound by the screens available throughout the world."[11] Perhaps it was to break free of that constraint that his imagination and curiosity constantly drove him to explore new techniques and new creative tools.

It was important to Hitchcock that a filmmaker convey "the feeling that when you see [the film] on the screen you are

[10] Bogdanovich, p. 515.
[11] Samuels, p. 232.

watching something that has been conceived and brought to birth directly in visual terms."[12] Most of the scriptwriters who worked with him would tell of how they found it difficult to adjust to his unique creative approach, whereby he would devise scenes of immense visual power, but with no way of linking one to the next – so that what was supposed to be, say, a chase sequence would initially appear as a hodge-podge. Hitchcock once said that "cinema is simply pieces of film put together in a manner that creates ideas and emotions."[13] His primary objective was to "put things together visually; to tell the story visually; to embody the action in the juxtaposition of images that have their own specific language and emotional impact – that is cinema."[14] For Hitch, too much dialogue in a film smacked of filmed theatre, or photographs of people speaking, rather than the "pure cinema" that he advocated: "To me, a picture must be planned on paper. [...] In order to do this, you've got to have a visual sense. I never look through the camera; I think only on that white screen that has to be filled up the way you fill up a canvas. That's why I draw rough set-ups for the cameraman. [...] I could draw every frame of the finished picture. [...] After having completed this process, I leave it to the screenwriter to write his dialogue within the framework of the finished, agreed cinematic story line. [...] What mystifies me is why so many other filmmakers need to see things on the screen before they edit, whereas a musician can hear his music simply by looking at the notes and lines of his score. Why shouldn't we do the same? [...] Is a listener allowed to choose the notes he'll hear? If you free the spectator to choose, you're making theater, not cinema."[15]

This approach to pre-production was so crucial that Hitchcock would often repeat that a film was essentially "done" by the time shooting actually began. "You can improvise and you should improvise, but I think it should be done in an office, where there are no electricians waiting and no actors waiting. [...] Sometimes, I compare it with a composer who is trying to write a piece of music with a full orchestra in front of him. Can you imagine him saying, 'Flute, give me that note again, will you? Thank you, flute,' and he writes it down. A painter has his canvas and he uses his charcoal sketch and he goes to work on that canvas with a preconceived idea. I'm sure he doesn't guess it as he goes along."[16] It was thus up to the screenwriters to adjust to the visual demands of the director.

The outcome of this type of creative process, the focus on the gaze rather than on words, combines elements of

[12] "Direction," Gottlieb, p. 255–56.
[13] Samuels, p. 232.
[14] "Film Production," Gottlieb, p. 214.
[15] Samuels, p. 234.
[16] Donald Spoto, The Dark Side of Genius: The Life of Alfred Hitchcock (New York: Ballantine Books, 1983, p. 540.

expressionism and abstraction, where the shot and the frame are sovereign. Everything can be expressed visually, with the least possible reliance on dialogue, as in the silent films Hitchcock made at the beginning of his career. For instance, he would seek to capture a thought, a feeling, an emotion on the face or body of his characters, as a painter would. He would seek to show the invisible via the visible. In this light, as Bill Krohn has pointed out, *Notorious* and *Rear Window* are films about Ingrid Bergman's and James Stewart's faces. This study in portraiture can be traced back to the expressive faces in paintings of centuries past, which Hitchcock seemed to transfer to a new medium. His films can be said to resemble live-action comic strips, and he admitted as much.

Paintbrush
After conceiving of his subject in pictorial terms, with lines and strokes, then in terms of words and sentences, Hitchcock would compose his images and their timings, as a painter would: "[I]t's just like designing composition in a painting. Or balance of colours. There is nothing accidental [...]."[17]

Then he would devise his setting: "Settings, of course, come into the preliminary plan, and usually I have fairly clear ideas about them; I was an art student before I took up with films. Sometimes I even think of backgrounds first."[18] His rigorously constructed interiors were often anchored by staircases, which he found quite photogenic; of location shooting he said that "by using colors and lights in front of beautiful landscapes, I feel I am a painter."[19] He strove constantly to free himself from material constraints, to arrive at absolute mastery of his images and thus freedom in his art. The artifice of the matte painting, for instance, gave him the impression that his creative power was limitless: "The beauty of a matte is that you can become God."[20] Like any artist, he desired the freedom to make his own aesthetic decisions, without having to justify them: "I'm not interested in content. It disturbs me very much when people criticize my films because of their content. It's like looking at a still life and saying, 'I wonder whether those apples are sweet or sour.' Cinema is form."[21]

Hitchcock knew that he had a characteristic style, but one that was restrictive at the same time: "Like any artist who paints or writes, I suppose I'm limited to a certain field. Not that I'm comparing myself to him, but old Rouault was content with judges, clowns, a few women, and Christ on

[17] "On Style," Gottlieb, p. 294.
[18] "Direction," Gottlieb, p. 255.
[19] François Truffaut, with the collaboration of Helen G. Scott, *Hitchcock,* rev. ed. (New York: Simon & Schuster, 1984), p. 335.
[20] Bogdanovich, p. 488.
[21] Samuels, p. 233.

the Cross. That constituted his life's work. Cézanne was content with a few still lifes and a few scenes in the forest. But how long can a film-maker go on painting the same picture?"[22]

Palette

Hitchcock ascribed great importance to the use of colour in his films, but such use came in the form of expressionist flourishes, and was never random: "The film always has to deal in exaggerations. Its methods reflect the simple contrasts of black-and-white photography. One advantage of color is that it would give you more intermediate shades. I should never want to fill the screen with color: it ought to be used economically – to put new words into the screen's visual language when there's a need for them."[23] This colourist's concern was evident in Hitch's sets and costumes. He deliberately chose, for example, to film his macabre fable *The Trouble with Harry* amid the flamboyant fall foliage of the forests of Vermont. Future muse Grace Kelly recounted her first meeting with the Master, at the time of *Dial M for Murder*: "We talked about the clothes. [...] He wanted to go from a bright and colorful wardrobe to a drab and depressing one as the woman's fortunes changed."[24]

Commenting on this particular artistic application of colour, Hitchcock once described how he would have gone about shooting a murder scene had it been set in a tulip field in Holland: "The assassin – say it's Jack the Ripper – comes up behind the girl. The shadow creeps up on her, she turns, screams. Immediately we pan down to the struggling feet, in the tulip bed. We dolly the camera in to one of the flowers, sounds of the struggle heard in the background. We go right to one petal – it fills the screen – and, splash! a drop of red blood comes over the petal. And that would be the end of the murder."[25] Chabrol would later shoot a murder scene in *Le boucher* (1970) in a similar manner, with blood dripping onto a buttered slice of toast.

The decision to use, or not use, a particular colour prevailed even as a fundamental principle, influencing, for instance, the choice of film stock: "I made *Psycho* in black and white purposely to avoid the blood. Red would have been unpleasant, unnecessary. [...] Color should start with the nearest equivalent to black and white [...] color should be no different from the voice which starts muted and finally arrives at a scream. In other words, the muted color is black and white and the screams are very psychedelic color you can think of starting, of course, with red."[26] Even his

[22] Truffaut, p. 319.
[23] "Film Production," Gottlieb, p. 214.
[24] Spoto, p. 367.
[25] Bogdanovich, p. 509.
[26] Samuels, p. 236.

composer, Bernard Herrmann, explained that in scoring *Psycho* for violins only, he was trying to write "black-and-white" music.

Musician

Where Hitchcock would describe the work that went into a shot in terms of painting or drawing, the restrictive running time of a film led him to comparisons with music: "Pure cinema is complementary pieces of film put together, like notes of music make a melody."[27] In fact, in his famous cameos, he was quite willing to portray himself as a musician carting around a cello or double bass, humorously choosing these "portly" instruments as musical doubles. "Construction to me, it's like music. You start with your allegro, your andante, and you build up."[28] Tippi Hedren has told of how, one day on the set of *The Birds,* the actors were amazed to find a musician with a drum on hand for the shooting of the climactic scene of the birds attacking the house in which the characters have barricaded themselves – to convey the intensifying tempo of the winged onslaught, the drummer was asked to beat out a particular rhythm, since both the birds and their accompanying sound effects were to be added in later. He said: "I myself, use musical terms when I direct. I say, 'don't put a great big close-up there because it's loud brass and you mustn't use a loud note unless it's absolutely vital.' Cinema is the orchestration of shots."[29] Hitchcock explained that the scene in *Psycho* in which Detective Arbogast is brutally stabbed in the eye as he climbs the stairs in Mrs. Bates's house was so effective because "the shock comes [. . .] in relation to the sudden change in size. From a high angle to a big close-up. It's orchestration again, you see?"[30] And did he not once say that, when shooting *Psycho,* he had the feeling of playing with the audience's emotions like an organist playing on his keyboard?

Hitchcock became a musician when it came to designing his sequences: "[O]rchestration is perhaps the best simile for a film, even to the parallel of recurrent themes and rhythms. And the director is, as it were, the conductor."[31] In this way, he would fashion all manner of double situations, from the clever symmetries after the opening credits in *Shadow of a Doubt* to the stylistic exercise of *Family Plot,* where his aim was to merge two seemingly unrelated story lines into one, in symmetrical and inescapable fashion. Often he would weave together two independent rhythms in parallel; for example, a chase sequence inherent to the film script with a symphony concert and clashing cymbals

[27] Bogdanovich, p. 522.
[28] "On Style," Gottlieb, p. 298.
[29] Samuels, p. 234.
[30] Bogdanovich, p. 544.
[31] "Film Production," Gottlieb, p. 216.

187

(The Man Who Knew Too Much), or with a film screening *(Saboteur)* or a theatrical production *(The Thirty-nine Steps)*.

Cinema Is Art; Hitchcock Its Artisan

If Alfred Hitchcock firmly believed that, because of its ability to communicate with audiences around the world, the cinema was the 20th century's most innovative art form, he himself never hid the fact that he was a commercial moviemaker, subject to all the attendant production constraints and on-set compromises. And yet, it is well known that he did all he could to avoid such annoyances, by crafting his films in advance, designing them within a framework so rigid that it left only the barest room for improvisation (a famous anecdote has it that producer David O. Selznick found it impossible to cut *Rebecca* in any other way than that which Hitchcock had devised, so tightly were the shots connected, leaving no room for "play"); in this way he imposed his artistic freedom, his mastery of his craft.

Hitch found the analogy with artists flattering, but preferred to compare himself to a master craftsman: "Take a person like Picasso, you know, who does double profiles and has gone through cubism and God knows what, but he knows every muscle in the human body. If you ask him to draw the figure of a man or a woman, there wouldn't be a muscle out of place. You've got to know your craft in order to express your art."[32] This is what was most important to him: "Learn the art and craft of filmmaking on paper first as a composer learns the technique of writing music. Master every aspect of it in theory and then put what you've learned into practice."[33]

[32] Bogdanovich, p. 555.
[33] Laurent Bouzereau, *The Alfred Hitchcock Quote Book* (New York: Citadel Press, 1993), p. 157.

Hitchcock in Quebec

Robert Daudelin, director of the Cinémathèque québécoise, here offers us an essay that attests to the historical importance of Hitchcock's work. Preserving prints of films, but also preserving the memory of how those films are received by the public, is well and truly the role of the ideal film archive.

Simon Beaudry, for his part, recounts a remarkable episode in film history: the making of I Confess *in Québec City.*

Alfred Hitchcock and crew members during shooting of I Confess, *1953*

Tippi Hedren in Marnie, 1964

Marnie: Early Testament?

Robert Daudelin

In 1965 I was a young critic writing for a small Montréal-based film magazine where Hitchcock was much adored, and it fell to me to write a review of *Marnie*. (The house rule was that whoever showed the most enthusiasm had first crack at writing about any new film.)

Here is that review, complete and unexpurgated (!), as published in *Objectif 65,* Issue 31 (February-March 1965).

In Marnie, *you have* L'arrivée d'un train en gare *and* Hiroshima mon amour; Greed *and* Rio Bravo. *In* Marnie, *you have cinema as craft – with its sixty-strong artisans on set, heavy machinery at their service – and cinema as art – just one man in his intimate surroundings, speaking to another. In* Marnie, *you have cinema as entertainment (and cinema is always entertainment, no matter how metaphysical you want to get with it), and cinema as novel. In* Marnie, *you have the sheer magic of cinema: the unmatched intimacy of one man seated amongst two thousand others gathered to share in a work with an intensity that no book, no painting will ever be able to summon.*

Marnie *never ceases to amaze: with each viewing, one realizes that a certain scene, vaguely remembered the first time, is now laden with hidden bounties; that a certain gesture made by one of the characters, a gesture that earlier seemed trivial, unnecessary even, finds elucidation in its logical relationship with a certain other one, and so on. And though we have long been acquainted with Hitchcock's touch, his consummate skill, with* Marnie *the Master's art has scaled new heights.*

Directing, which is more than an art, is here revealed to be a science. Each scene illustrates an equation that, in the end, is solved, via a balance that could not be more "necessary." Indeed, it is through his stunning faith in its very nature that Hitchcock's mise en scène is admirable: the goal of the director is to bring characters to life – characters who are imaginary in the eyes of the audience (who are themselves quite real, and therefore demand reality). Now, the prime virtue of Hitchcock's directing style is that it is functional; in other words, it serves the characters. Each scene therefore unfolds as follows: character + situation = viewer, for mise en scène is in fact the bridge between character and viewer.

Because film directing is based on characters and is foremost a function of their existence, it follows that a relationship of balance should develop between the two, with the characters provoking the mise en scène and the mise en scène enhancing the characters. From this perspective, it becomes entirely logical that Marnie *should be not only Hitchcock's most perfect film, but also his most moving.*

But such considerations, as justified as they are likely (!) to be, render us liable to wrest Marnie *away from its true perspective. Indeed, the film's stunning perfection, this art that now seems to know no bounds, is above all the result of the work showing a greater openness to its audience. Hitchcock's art is nothing like a laboratory experiment – the most skilful scene or the most complicated camera movement is still rooted in only one indivisible aim: to heighten the viewer's awareness of the character's plight. The finest scenes in* Marnie *can thus be analysed quite soundly from the point of view of the audience and its curiosity. A good example of this type of construction is the depiction of the Strutts' arrival at the reception before the hunt: the entire scene is encompassed in a slow tracking shot from the top of the stairs to the front door, where a butler is announcing the guests to Marnie's young sister-in-law. As the camera progresses forward, the doorbell rings and two guests appear – up to the precise moment when the camera frames the door and, with a final ring of the doorbell, the fateful couple, the Strutts, are ushered into Marnie's home. This scene, one of the finest in the film, responds to a sense of unease that the audience feels already; the forward tracking shot engages them, the better to give them the key to that unease.*

The repeated use of short shots has a similar function: to provoke, as it were, the audience into paying closer attention – to provide anchor points for their receptivity. There are abundant examples of this in Marnie: *the foot sliding the key into the grille at the bus station, the shoe on the floor during the theft sequence, Sean Connery's finger on the word* red *during the nighttime "therapy session," and so on.*

The structure of a number of scenes also attests to these preoccupations, the best example doubtless being that showing the first kiss between Marnie and the publisher, in his office. The scene begins with a fairly exacting setup: a survey of the setting, the opposite placement of the characters, the simple intelligence of the space. When the thunderclap arrives, the audience is already acquainted with the setting; their attention is immediately drawn to the principal content of the scene. Hitchcock then assembles a series of shots that follow one another logically up to the extreme close-up as the two mouths meet. A classic montage, to be sure, but one whose logic gains a supple, efficient quality: the final kiss becomes a necessity – not only dramatic but formal, even.

Tippi Hedren in Marnie, 1964

This mastery, moreover, is so non-gratuitous that the viewer may well fail to notice it. One of the most amazing moments in the film occurs when Marnie, after her husband has left, goes down the stairs to telephone her mother. This is presented as a very long and beautiful tracking shot, but one that we are oblivious to because Hitchcock, wishing to focus our attention on Marnie and her inner turmoil, keeps his lens trained on her face: it is only at the conclusion of the shot that we realize the virtuoso skills the director must have summoned to present his character to us in this way.

In fact, if there are scenes in Marnie that work less well, it is for similar kinds of reasons; one in particular that comes to mind is that in which Marnie, wearing gloves, is unable to take the money from the safe. To translate this physiological (as well as moral) inability, Hitchcock chose a series of rapid forward-backward movements that convey Marnie's powerlessness literally. The technique is obviously effective, but for once I would have appreciated it had Hitchcock left us greater freedom to choose our emotional reaction; personally I would have preferred a neutral shot, from which the drama would have emerged discreetly, almost fraudulently.

Marnie, *then, is an eminently public work such as I have attempted to define, but it is also a personal work that takes its place in the succession of great Alfred Hitchcock films, revisiting a number of his favourite themes: the "lost heroine" (*Marnie *is, in a way, a reprise of* Vertigo*), the "isolated mother," the "wrong man," the "secret country" (the Red Fox Tavern and the Garrett stables having already served as settings in* The Trouble with Harry, Psycho *and* The Birds*), "mysterious love" and so on. But* Marnie, *above all, is Mar-*

ion Holland, Margaret Edgar, Mary Taylor: a woman who has lost love, alongside whom we happily share in the struggle to recover it, to move beyond the pain encapsulated in the song we hear the children singing when Marnie visits her mother in Baltimore: "Mother, Mother, I am ill..."

This review, needless to say, hasn't aged all that well. I'm somewhat scandalized by its naïveté. And yet, after getting over the initial shock of its impressionistic style, and swallowing the fairly simplistic (and mythicizing) view of mise en scène on which the text was heavily dependent, I can't bring myself to make too harsh a criticism of my youthful enthusiasm!

There was no way of knowing, of course, in the spring of 1965, that *Marnie* was to be the last great Hitchcock opus. François Truffaut, though, writing in the 1983 afterword to the definitive edition of his book of historic interviews with the Master, could not fail to assess it in those terms: "Finally, in *Marnie*, the last picture to reveal Hitchcock's deepest emotions, can there be any doubt that Sean Connery, in trying to control, dominate, and possess Tippi Hedren by investigating her past, finding her a job, and giving her a job, is expressing Hitchcock's own feelings as a frustrated Pygmalion?"[1]

In hindsight – I did not see the film again until April 2000 – *Marnie* seems quite clearly to me to be Alfred Hitchcock's testament. Everything that came after, even the magnificent excesses of *Frenzy,* were merely blips in his career. The Master's oeuvre was well and truly complete with *Marnie,* a film in which Hitchcock insisted on leaving his signature on every shot.

Indeed, as Truffaut so pointedly reminds us, *Marnie* was the last film for which Hitchcock was surrounded by his legendary collaborators, cinematographer Robert Burks, composer Bernard Herrmann and editor George Tomasini; it was also the last film on which he was truly "calling the shots."

As for the fascination that the film's directing style held for this young film buff in the early 1960s, it is utterly justifiable, for *Marnie* functions as a veritable treatise in Hitchcockian mise en scène. All the techniques of which the old master was so fond – starting with rear projection, which is explicitly used and explicitly celebrated here, perhaps more than in any other film – are repeatedly drawn upon, and delightfully so. This only brings even more to light the filmmaker's founding philosophy: systematic rejection of

[1] François Truffaut, with the collaboration of Helen G. Scott, *Hitchcock,* rev. ed. (New York: Simon & Schuster, 1984) p. 346.

all naturalism, simplification of the actors' performances (as well as of their costumes and hairstyles), schematization of storytelling, theatrical stylization of the sets, and so on. Mise en scène here becomes a veritable *mise à plat* – a flattening. The canvas, rather than the stage or set, is the ideal mode of representation – right up to the final signature (as in the corner of a painting): the studio street complete with painted backdrop and saturated colours.

This exceptional attention paid to the craft of directing is all the more justified, given the script's admittedly flimsy, stupid premise. The mystery surrounding Marnie's character, explained away at the last minute via a simplistic detour into psychoanalysis, is hardly enough to sustain viewer interest. The further the film progresses, the more it becomes clear that Hitchcock's discourse is located/constituted elsewhere: in the very writing of the script, in all those cleverly constructed, and no less cleverly assembled, shots (like so many canvases, in fact). As often happens in popular cinema, as well as in popular music, the score doesn't matter so much – it's the interpretation that makes all the difference.

My Favorite Things, an ordinary little tune lifted from *The Sound of Music,* becomes a masterpiece in the hands of a John Coltrane. I am still willing to believe that the same can be said of *Marnie,* the testament of a great filmmaker who was also that "great inventor of forms."

Alfred Hitchcock with Anne Baxter, Renée Hudon and Lucien-Hubert Borne during shooting of I Confess, *1953*

Hitchcock in Quebec: Code of Silence

Simon Beaudry

After the 1951 triumph of *Strangers on a Train,* Alfred Hitchcock, then at the peak of his Hollywood career, found himself dithering over the subject of his next film. Still under contract to Warner Bros, wishing to explore the theme of guilt transference anew, the world's best-known filmmaker sifted through dozens of proposed story ideas. His choice, somewhat surprisingly, settled on a screenplay adaptation of *Nos deux consciences,* an obscure French play written in 1902 by Paul Anthelme, and for which Warners had bought the rights.

The plot hinged on a priest accused of a murder. He knows he is innocent, and knows who the true guilty party is – because he has recently received his confession. The crux of the storyline lies in a canon of the Catholic Church: the Confessional Seal. This rule forbids the reverend from divulging the identity of the real killer to police. To respect the wishes of the Church, he bears the heavy burden of indictment through to the final act.

While Hitchcock was doubtless attracted to the "wrong man" aspect of the storyline, his Roman Catholic upbringing most certainly piqued his interest for this tale, which had little resonance in the more liberal climate of postwar America. Three drafts by as many screenwriters would be rejected before Hitchcock finally decided, in the winter of 1952, to bring the story to the screen as *I Confess*. When the time came to choose a location in which to set the action, Hitchcock realized that, by its very essence, the story could not be told credibly in a country where Roman Catholic sacerdotal practice, no matter how strict, could no longer be expected to render a priest unassailable by the legal system. The director immediately began to search for a locale in which to film the story. After flirting briefly with the idea of shooting in Ireland, Hitchcock – probably inspired by the memory of a short stay in Canada with his wife Alma shortly after their arrival in North America – contemplated setting his latest suspense drama in the heart of the only non-English-speaking region on the continent: the province of Quebec.

In addition to its social and cultural characteristics, Québec City afforded Warner Bros, first and foremost, an important political advantage: for the previous four years, Hollywood had been abiding by the terms of an agreement reached with the federal government of its neighbour to the north, called the Canadian Cooperation Project.[1]

With the choice of Québec City finalized and approved by Warner Bros, Hitchcock journeyed there in March of 1952 to conduct extensive location scouting. He found the place brimming with religious icons; they were omnipresent in this city and society still under clerical control. Church steeples towering over every street corner, crucifixes ubiquitous in public spaces and private homes, the sight of hundreds of priests and nuns walking in the streets, the eerie moods created by the narrow, winding streets within the fortified walls of the Old City – all these features quickly convinced Hitchcock that the social context would boost the credibility of the entire storyline. It was an innocuous visual detail, however, that finally won the director over and persuaded him that Québec City was the right choice: to his amazement, nearly all the local priests still wore the cassock, whereas the Roman collar was by then the established clerical dress throughout the United States.

During his stay in Québec City, the director discovered a distinct society living against the tide of the rest of North America. The use of the French language constituted a formidable barrier to French Canadians' integration into the largely English-speaking continent. This isolation was supported by, among others, the Church, which sought to delay Quebec's entry into the modernizing postwar era. In 1952 the fertility rate of Quebec families was among the world's highest; school enrolment was substantially lower than that elsewhere on the continent; television had just been introduced but would not be widely implemented for some years yet; and the cultural ascendancy of France outweighed that of the United States. The province of Quebec was living under the yoke of an autocratic premier, Maurice Duplessis, who held his firm grip on power thanks in large part to the widespread support of the clergy. In short, Hitchcock had landed in a city that was North American as far as the pace of life was concerned, but foreign in its social and cultural workings. Given this context, Hitchcock was firmly convinced that the story of *I Confess* should be told in this geocultural framework.

[1] In the fall of 1947, following the massive decline in U.S. currency reserves at the end of World War II, Canada moved to curb imports of several U.S. goods, and also considered setting quotas on imports of Hollywood feature films. Since the 1920s, the major U.S. studios had considered Canada an integral part of their distribution territory – the "domestic market." The majors reacted very quickly to the Canadian move, and in January 1948, proposed a daring plan to promote Canada to the American public; the Canadian Cooperation Project was thus born on the spot. The agreement consisted of five key points, calling for, among other things, a greater number of Hollywood productions to be shot on location in Canada, and the purchase of Canadian productions for distribution in the U.S. market. The agreement was accepted by virtually the whole of the Canadian intelligentsia, and between 1948 and 1954 the major Hollywood studios shot no less than 38 feature films, in whole or in part, north of the border. The majority of these productions merely featured summary highlights of Canadian symbols that were already extremely well known abroad: Mounties, fur traders, "natural wonders," and so forth. From this perspective, Hitchcock's film, with its attention to authenticity and its urban setting, would prove to be an exception.

Hitchcock was mindful of moulding the plot of his film to fit the religious and social ethos of Québec City in 1952 and, during his location scouting trip, arranged a meeting with the Roman Catholic Archdiocese, intent on obtaining script approval as well as authorization to shoot in a number of locations that were on Church property. Worried Church officials suggested that a representative of the Archdiocese, Father Paul Lacouline, be appointed to the crew; Hitchcock accepted, and Father Lacouline became technical adviser to the production, through to the completion of shooting in Hollywood. A bon vivant, open to the arts and perfectly fluent in English, Father Lacouline undertook lengthy negotiations over every reference to the sacred that was to be included in the script. He was to recall later that the Archdiocese was initially quite reluctant to allow the shooting of a number of sequences inside Québec City churches. By dint of tact and diplomacy, Lacouline succeeding in convincing the clerical elite that Alfred Hitchcock was offering the city's Roman Catholic Church an extraordinary opportunity for self-promotion; after all, the plot of *I Confess* itself bolstered the image of the Church as completely above suspicion.

There were a number of disturbing details, however, that apparently escaped the clergy's censorship. In the aftermath of the War, many German refugees had settled in Quebec, which was controlled at the time by a Church that was anticommunist and generally insensitive to the Jewish cause; this appalling situation was one that Hitchcock himself hadn't even considered. Instinctively and unwittingly, Hitchcock was about to craft an artistic production that would become one of the works most emblematic of a period in Quebec history that many observers would later refer to as the "grande noirceur," or "great darkness."

Another locally recruited technical adviser was policeman Olivier Tanguay, who briefly guided Hitchcock in his consideration of legal and law-enforcement-related details in the film.

As to the rest, Warner Bros and Hitchcock enjoyed a great deal of support from the State, which, among other things, granted the production access to several locations, including the National Assembly buildings. Premier Duplessis himself was a firm believer in the power of motion pictures. A committed nationalist, he had authorized the creation of the *Office du film du Québec* (Quebec Film Bureau) a few years earlier, to counterbalance the National Film Board of Canada, which Ottawa had created in 1939. Headed by Bishop Maurice Proulx, the Bureau produced several dozen documentary shorts aimed at promoting Quebec both within its own borders and abroad.

On August 20, 1952, principal photography on *I Confess* finally got under way, causing quite a stir throughout Québec City. Dozens of extras were recruited for several scenes during the three weeks of location shooting. Ever the stickler for authenticity, Hitchcock had already cast certain supporting roles that he specifically wished to be played by French Canadians. A number of Quebec actors thus had the chance to work with the master. Renée Hudon, a young drama student, was chosen to play one of the two witnesses to the murder. She later recalled that she got the part quite by chance, after scores of young women from the area had filed in and out of a room at the Château Frontenac hotel, where auditions were held, to no avail. Hitchcock had wanted to find two young girls with no previous training as actors for these parts. At the time, however, children fluent in both French and English were extremely rare in Québec City; young Renée Hudon, like a fellow student who was chosen to play the second witness, was studying performing arts, and so was hired. In casting the adult roles, Hitchcock was assisted by Paul L'Anglais, the founder of the only large film production company established in the province, Quebec Productions. Ovila Légaré, whom Hitchcock admired tremendously, won the part of the lawyer, Villette, and Gilles Pelletier was chosen to play Father Benoît, the vicar of Father Logan's parish. The lead roles went to Montgomery Clift as Father Michael Logan and Anne Baxter as Ruth Grandfort, the woman who secretly loves him. Baxter was forced upon Hitchcock by Jack Warner at the last minute: she replaced Anita Björk, a young Swedish actress who had been dismissed by the studio. Warners had feared a public scandal after learning that the actress had had a child out of wedlock just before her arrival in the United States.

Strangely enough, Montgomery Clift had made a French-Canadian acquaintance long before coming to Québec City to star in *I Confess*. One day in 1945, as the actor strolled through New York's Grand Central Station, he had come upon a young man seated on a suitcase, sobbing uncontrollably. His name was Brother Thomas, and he was a young monk on his way home after having taken his vows of perpetual poverty, celibacy and obedience in an American abbey. "Home" happened to be a monastery near Québec City.

Brother Thomas had missed his train and, since he couldn't speak English, had no idea how to go about exchanging his ticket. Clift, who spoke French, approached him and asked what it was that was troubling him so. The young monk explained everything, and the actor offered to help: he took care of changing the train ticket.

In the years following their meeting, the two corresponded regularly. "Brother Thomas lives in a state of grace," Clift would say, full of admiration. In 1952, before the shooting of *I Confess,* Clift visited the monastery where Brother Thomas lived and spent five days there. The monk took the actor under his wing, showing him how to say a rosary and "walk" the Way of the Cross properly. Thomas even managed to convince Clift, who still had his doubts, of the absolute inviolability of the Confessional Seal. It was also during his stay at the monastery that Clift learned to master the hand movements that a priest would make. Clift felt that properly conveying the "priestly gait" was of crucial importance to his acting, and he managed to integrate it perfectly. In fact, François Truffaut would comment in his 1962 interviews with Hitchcock that "[…] Montgomery Clift is always seen walking; it's a forward motion that shapes the whole film. It also concretizes the concept of his integrity."[2]

Alfred Hitchcock with Father Paul Lacouline, technical advisor, on the set of I Confess, *1953*

Self-portrait (caricature), dedicated "To 'Père'" by Alfred Hitchcock during shooting of I Confess, *1953*

Brother Thomas's friendship with Montgomery Clift was to continue after the shooting of *I Confess* in Québec City. Thomas attended the actor's funeral in 1966; at the time, he was himself dying of cancer. After the ceremony, he reportedly told Clift's relatives that he wished to remain anonymous in any future biographies of the actor.

Throughout the shoot, Hitchcock put the particularities of Québec City's urban landscape to good use. In the first few minutes of the film, the ferry crossing between Lévis and the *vieille capitale* serves as an establishing shot under the opening credits; the long staircases connecting the Lower Town to the Upper Town provide the setting for the director's inevitable cameo appearance; and a myriad of one-way arrows marking the narrow, winding streets of the Old City point straight to the scene of the crime. A number of low-angle shots of civic and religious monuments are featured throughout the film, lending an atmosphere of foreboding to the urban setting. As was his wont, Hitchcock was able, in a very short time frame, to take full advantage of all the visual elements provided by his shooting locations.

[2] François Truffaut, with the collaboration of Helen G. Scott, *Hitchcock* (New York: Simon & Schuster, 1984), p. 204.

If the urban setting served Hitchcock and his cinematographer well, it was another story when it came to the director's relationship with his actors. For instance, Clift's homosexuality was an open secret among the Québec City crew, and this was a cause of concern for Hitchcock. Father Lacouline recalls arriving on the set one morning and noticing that the left side of Clift's face was swollen, the result of an inopportune encounter in a bar in the Sault-aux-Matelots neighbourhood, not far from the city's imposing harbour; the establishment was a favourite watering hole for sailors on shore leave. The incident explains why a number of shots in the finished film favour the right side of Montgomery Clift's face: for once, this did not stem from an artistic choice or an actor's desire to be photographed from his "good side"!

Hitchcock was fascinated by the ambiguous sexuality of actors like Clift, and this was apparent in the early 1950s with *Rope* and *Strangers on a Train*. This curiosity even led him, on occasion, to forgo his disdain for the acting techniques propounded by the Actor's Studio, to which Clift hewed. At any rate, a female representative was secretly employed for the duration of the Québec City shoot, and was given the official title of "assistant" to Montgomery Clift.

Despite this enthusiasm for certain stars, Renée Hudon later recalled, Hitchcock lived up to his reputation for speaking only rarely to his actors. Doubtless because she was so young, Hudon was one of the only members of the *I Confess* cast to be pampered by the director: he would keep the girl amused and entertained by letting her ride on his shoulders as he imitated a galloping horse. Not only did Hitchcock fail to communicate with his actors, but he would also, quite often, fly into a rage on the set, with little regard for the disastrous consequences such tantrums could have on the remainder of the shoot. One morning, a few days before the studio portion of the production was due to wrap up in Hollywood, Anne Baxter arrived on the set late – and slightly drunk. In front of the entire crew, Hitchcock indicated to her that he would tolerate no further misbehaviour and would not hesitate to reshoot every scene in the movie that the actress had appeared in thus far. He told her he was quite prepared to use another actress should Ms. Baxter fail to meet his expectations.

Gilles Pelletier recalled an encounter with Hitchcock in his dressing room during the studio shoot in Hollywood. The Quebec actor professed amazement at how few takes were necessary for each scene. Downing a rum and coke, the director declared that, to him, a film shoot was like a party – his only real work came in preproduction. The filmmaker then revealed to Pelletier one of his secrets to successful shooting. After each take he would bellow, in his deep voice, "Sound, please!" Hitchcock explained to the young actor that, while it was impossible for him to immediately view the scene just shot, he could tell merely by listening to the audio playback of the dialogue whether the actors had got it right.

After a month of principal photography on location in Québec City and a further three weeks of shooting on Hollywood soundstages, the production wrapped in October 1952. Just four months later, Hitchcock was to experience one of the worst affronts of his career.

On the evening of the world premiere of *I Confess,* February 13, 1953 at the Capitol cinema in downtown Québec City, Hitchcock could not contain his indignation in the face of the cuts that had been demanded the previous week by the *Bureau de censure du cinéma de la province de Québec.* He declared: "So, there will be one version of *I Confess* for Quebec and another for the rest of the world!" Hitchcock's fury was all the more understandable in that the entire script had already been gone over with a fine-toothed comb and approved by the Archdiocese of Quebec. In fact, Father Lacouline remembered years later how he had had to obtain special permission from the Archbishop to attend the film's premiere screening. Controlled, through its advisory committee, by the Quebec Catholic Church, the province's censor board at the time was among the strictest in the world. Up to the early 1960s, it banned more films than the United States, the rest of Canada and England combined. In those days Quebec had acquired a reputation within the film industries of other countries as the most puritanical jurisdiction in the world. Many a filmmaker enjoyed referring to Quebec as the "homeland of the enemies of cinema." In the case of *I Confess,* the board demanded nine cuts, totalling 235 feet of film, or a running time of 2 minutes, 37 seconds. The scenes that the censor demanded be excised touched on three points that were deemed sensitive by the Church of the day: its public image (the scenes showing Father Logan being pushed and shoved upon his exit from the courthouse), morality (Anne Baxter reiterating her love for Logan with a kiss) and dogma (Logan refusing to answer the police's questions). Hitchcock was hardly the only one to taste the censor's medicine: the majority of films distributed in the province of Quebec at the time were cut, if not banned outright. It was not until the arrival of André Guérin in the early 1960s, and the later adoption of Bill 51 in 1967, that film censorship in the province disappeared completely – to the point where today, in a spectacular reversal, Quebec has become one of the most libertarian jurisdictions in the world where film distribution is concerned.

Despite the fact that Jack Warner was enormously happy with Hitchcock's latest endeavour, *I Confess* would not prove to be a box-office success, in Quebec or anywhere else. Roundly criticized by both critics and the public, neither of whom could believe the story of a priest who would willingly face the gallows in the name of the sanctity of Confession, the film remains, to this day, one of the master's least-known works. Hitchcock even confided to Truffaut: "we shouldn't have made the picture."[3]

On a visit to Quebec in the late 1960s, an Alsatian-born actor by the name of Buhr, who also did dubbing work and was a personal friend of Hitchcock, told Gilles Pelletier that the director was not fond of French Canadians. No doubt still infuriated over the censor board's actions, the master of suspense – despite the fact he had been very satisfied with the locally recruited actors and the assistance he had received during his stay in the *vieille capitale* – would never again have contact with anyone in Quebec. In an ironic echo of the title given to the French version of the film, *La loi du silence,* Alfred Hitchcock adhered until his dying day to a "code of silence" vis-à-vis Quebec.

[3] Truffaut, p. 204.

Catalogue

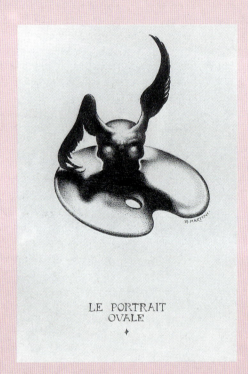

LE PORTRAIT
OVALE

✦

"Yet each man kills the thing he loves" (Oscar Wilde)

Hitchcock is above all an Englishman. His thoroughly British reserve and black humour have been frequently noted in films such as *The Trouble with Harry* or *Lamb to the Slaughter.* Hitchcock vividly captures the England of George V in his settings and characters: the mischievous boy in the Underground car in *Blackmail,* the crowd of spectators in *The Ring,* the throngs of curious onlookers in *Sabotage.* The filmmaker's characteristic blending of realistic detail with humorous touches – even in his rare period films, such as *Jamaica Inn* and *Under Capricorn* – is reminiscent of Victorian paintings in the style of William Maw Egley or George Earle.

But do we know enough about the origins of Hitchcock's dark romanticism, especially as it surfaces in his masterpiece, *Vertigo*? We might turn to John Everett Millais' hauntingly beautiful *Ophelia,* inspired by the great Shakespearean tragedy, which thoroughly infected the romantic sensibilities of Victorian England. Bathed in sorrow, Ophelia has the eternal appeal of a loved one whom death has claimed as a bride. She is not unlike those lost souls in *The Pleasure Garden* or *The Manxman* who, in a final act of desperation, throw themselves into the River Thames; or Madeleine, in *Vertigo,* who falls into San Francisco Bay – a beautiful siren, silenced by the water. Passing through the hands of Millais, Odilon Redon and Willy Schlobach, Ophelia is a romantic martyr who haunts the artist's imagination. Delicate and ethereal, she floats by in a watery shroud, eyes forever shut as the currents bear her where they will.

Conscious of Hitchcock's indebtedness to Millais for this image, English artist and writer Victor Burgin sees Madeleine with her flowers under the bridge as the filmmaker's modest erotic fantasy: available and consenting, the woman in the black dress is nonetheless unreachable, her eyes closed. She is Marnie with the blank stare; Marnie who is stripped and raped and almost drowns. England is famous for its ghosts and haunted castles: far from departing, the dead remain very present among the living. Hitchcock once said he would have loved to film J.M. Barrie's *Mary Rose,* the story of a young mother who dies and whose ghost pursues her lost child.

The dead woman is a tragic romantic obsession: "Do you believe that someone out of the past, someone dead, can enter and take possession of a living being?" *(Vertigo).* The portrait of Carlotta sucks the lifeblood out of Madeleine like that of Max de Winter's ancestor or that of Dorian Gray. The memory of Madeleine haunts Scottie in San Francisco, as Jane

Alberto Martini,
The Oval Portrait
(detail), 1905–1907

haunts Hugues Vianes in Rodenbach's novel *Bruges-la-Morte* (with its memorable frontispiece by Fernand Khnopff). Seeking their lost love in sleep, these wandering lovers dream of finding her perfect double, returned from the dead – a ghostly Madeleine lit up by a neon green hotel sign: "Oh ... how she looked like his dead wife!" (Rodenbach). In their secret worship, these men are caught in an ecstasy of violent, mournful passion. Scottie hates Madeleine and hates himself for loving her, yet "in watching Jane, Hugues thought of his dead love, his lips still warm from her embrace. In kissing this woman, he could bring her back. What had seemed forever lost could be reborn. He would remain faithful to Her, because she was the one he would embrace as he took her living effigy into his arms." In *Vertigo,* Hitchcock dreams of an ideal, unattainable woman, an absolute and necessarily tragic love, reminiscent of the poet Ernest Dowson's imaginary love for a London girl.

This quasi-religious love is similar to Dante's eternal passion for Beatrice (Dante Gabriele Rossetti). After she dies, he eventually finds her again, her head bathed in a halo of divine light and her eyes full of tears, as she comes to guide him through Paradise. The epitome of chaste Catholic love, Beatrice is the Chosen Lady, her spiritual beauty the Word of God. One is reminded of Edward Burne-Jones' *Fides,* a woman in whom Christian piety and love are combined to create an iconic effigy, timeless and intangible.

This romantic fascination transcends the physical. Death wraps the woman in eternal beauty: melancholy *Proserpine* (Rossetti), divided between the worlds of the living and the dead; sad Judy, true unrecognized love, and the adored but deceased Madeleine. The Pre-Raphaelites might have been attracted to Catholicism, but Hitchcock lived it. Like Rossetti, Burne-Jones or Millais, he has his muses, his own particular blend of ideal and sensual beauty "whose image changes yet unchanging seems." Rossetti's *Bocca Baciata*, new Eve with the apple, tells how "the mouth that has been kissed loses not its freshness; still it renews itself as does the moon" (Boccaccio).

Trembling lips and the silky feel of a lover's hair were the ultimate erotic fixation of the Victorian Pre-Raphaelites. Inheriting the tradition, Hitchcock is intent on capturing glistening fair hair, sensual caresses and passionate kisses in the closed frame of his lens. Each woman is at once a Madonna and a Mary Magdalene, a saint and a sinner. Julia Margaret Cameron was also fascinated by the unfathomable feminine Trinity of sensuality, idealism and beauty, capturing the ambivalence in her photographic portraits.

Unfortunately, the only possible conclusion of this romantic ideal, exalted by Tennyson in *The Lady of Shalott,* is death. Guilty lovers caught in the struggle between flesh and spirit – Paolo and Francesca, Lancelot and Guinevere, Tristan and Isolde, Madeleine-Judy and Scottie – are condemned: "It's too late. Look, it's not fair, it's too late! It wasn't supposed to happen this way; it *shouldn't* have happened. Let me go, please let me go! You believe I love you. And if you lose me, then you'll know I ...

I loved you and I wanted to go on loving you." Death drives their tragic fate, triumphs over their love (George Frederic Watts, Hunt). Scottie rediscovers Madeleine, only to lose her again, as Orpheus loses Eurydice for a second time. But isn't the cherished memory more beautiful than life itself? The parted lovers adorn the *Memento Mori* of their love with eternal memories. Like a chalice holding their precious tears, the sleep of death forever keeps their love sacred (William Blake Richmond).

Mirrors, masks and doubles – a game of reflections in which we hide and lose ourselves and then, like Alice, are drawn to the other side. In *Vertigo,* Scottie is cast into a reverie by the multiple mirror reflections of Judy, just as the Lady of Shallot gazes upon a mirror reflection of the outside world. There is also the Victorian theme of the broken mirror, which, in *The Wrong Man* or *Psycho,* offers a glimpse into madness, schizophrenia.

Thick clouds and fog sit heavy on London (Albert Goodwin) and Whitechapel. Each man has his mask, his terrifying double: Dorian Gray and his portrait; Dr. Jekyll and Mr. Hyde; a possible physician and Jack the Ripper; and Hawley Crippen, Charles Peace and John Christie – men whose sweet and shy appearances hide frustration, sadism and murderous intent – their appalling crimes laid bare across the British headlines. These characters held a fascination for the young Hitchcock, seated on the benches of the Old Bailey. Hitchcock, the amateur criminologist, avid reader of detective novels (Collins, P.D. James, Doyle, Wallace, etc.), frequent visitor to the Crime Museum in London. The list of murderers in his films is long: although they skirt the edges of the abyss, they are cultivated, intelligent and charming, because English crime is brilliant, methodical and secret. A chat with the neighbours in *Shadow of a Doubt* or a meal with friends in *Suspicion* are opportunities to indulge in a favourite British pastime: imagining the perfect crime.

Hitchcock avowed that the writer who had the most lasting influence on his work was the very British-like American, Edgar Allan Poe. In his youthful writings, Hitchcock freely plagiarized from the master of the grotesque: "I can't help comparing what I've tried to put in my films with what Edgar Allan Poe put in his novels: a completely unbelievable story told to the readers with such a spellbinding logic that you get the impression that the same thing could happen to you tomorrow." Implacable intellectual logic, steeped in Dark Romanticism. Poe's admirers are struck by the living nightmares into which his characters are plunged. Admirers including Aubrey Beardsley, Arthur Rackham, James Guthrie, Odilon Redon, Alberto Martini, Gaetano Previati – and, naturally, Alfred Hitchcock.

N.B.-P.

F. Fizzi, *Jack the Ripper, Famous Crimes,*
Vol. II, No. 15, 1888

R. Taylor, *Jack the Ripper, Illustrated London News,* 1888

Dr. Crippen is hanged at Pentonville prison,
London, Le petit journal, 1910 (23 November)

Anonymous, *Dr. Hawley Harvey Crippen (1862–1910) and his mistress*
Ethel Le Neve in the witness box, 1910

Albert Goodwin, *Saint Paul's from the South,* 1898

George Earle, *Going North, King's Cross Station,* about 1890

Dante Gabriele Rossetti, *Salutatio Beatricis (The Salutation of Beatrice),* 1859

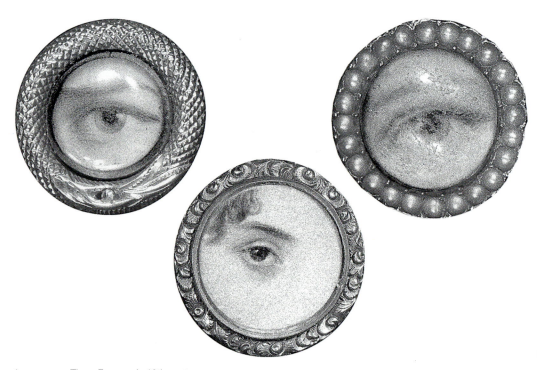

Anonymous, *Three Eyes,* early 19th century

Edward Burne-Jones, *Fides*, 1872

Ingrid Bergman in Under Capricorn, 1949

Ingrid Bergman and Joseph Cotten in Under Capricorn, 1949

Dante Gabriele Rossetti, *Bocca Baciata (Lips That Have Been Kissed)*, 1859

Julia Margaret Cameron, *The Three Sisters (Love, Peace and Faith),* 1868

Julia Margaret Cameron, *The Angel at the Tomb,* 1869

Walter Bird, *Ingrid Bergman in* Under Capricorn, 1949

Julia Margaret Cameron, *Alethea*, 1872

Roger Furse, Costume designs for *Under Capricorn*, 1949

Ingrid Bergman in Under Capricorn, 1949

Walter Bird, *Ingrid Bergman in* Under Capricorn, 1949

Dante Gabriele Rossetti, *Proserpine,* 1877

Kim Novak for Vertigo, 1958

George Frederic Watts, *Love and Death,* about 1874–1877

William Blake Richmond, *Sleep and Death Carrying the Body of Sarpedon into Lycia,* about 1875–1876

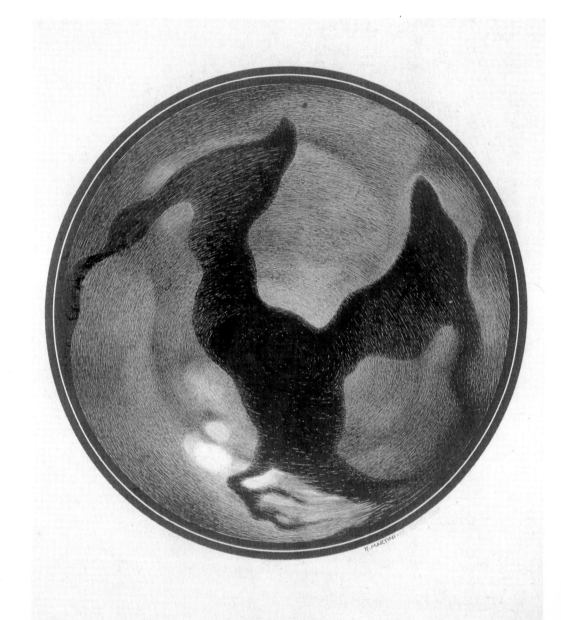

LE CORBEAV

Alberto Martini, *The Raven,* 1906

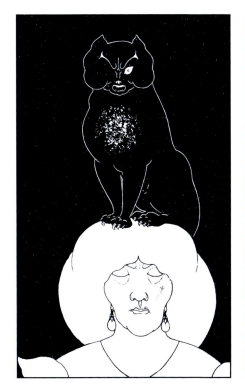

Aubrey Beardsley, *The Black Cat* and *The Fall of the House of Usher,* 1925

Arthur Rackham, *William Wilson,* 1933

Arthur Rackham, *The Pit and the Pendulum,*
illustration for the story by Edgar Allan Poe,
1935

COLLOQVE ENTRE MONOS ET VNA

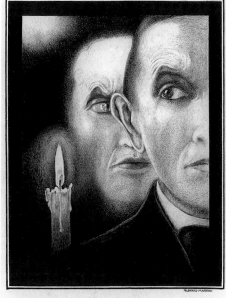

WILLIAM·WILSON
-E·A·PÖE-

Alberto Martini, *The Colloquy of Monos and Una,* Alberto Martini, *William Wilson,* 1936
1907

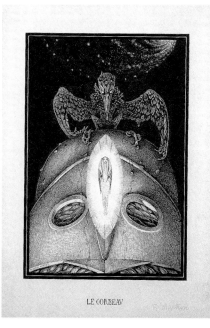

LE CORBEAV

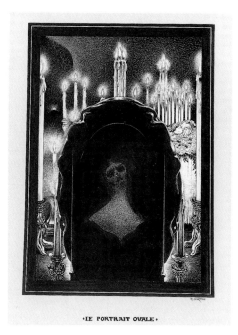

·LE PORTRAIT OVALE·

Alberto Martini, *The Raven,* about 1907   Alberto Martini, *The Oval Portrait,* 1908

CONVERSATION D'EIROS AVEC CHARMION

Alberto Martini, *The Conversation of Eiros and Charmion,* 1906

LE SCARABÉE D' OR

Alberto Martini, *The Gold Bug,* 1909–1910

Kim Novak and James Stewart in Vertigo, 1958

Alberto Martini, *The Tell-Tale Heart,* 1908

Philippe Halsman, *Tippi Hedren for* The Birds, 1963

Devant le noir Soleil de la MÉLANCOLIE, Lénore apparait.

L'œil, comme un ballon bizarre se dirige vers L'INFINI.

Odilon Redon, *"To Edgar Allan Poe,"* 1882
Before the black sun of Melancholy, Lenore appears

Odilon Redon, *"To Edgar Allan Poe,"* 1882
The Eye, like a Strange Ball that directs itself towards infinity

Le souffle qui conduit les êtres est aussi dans les SPHÈRES

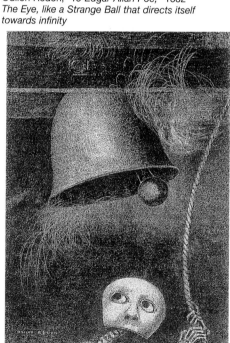

Odilon Redon, *"To Edgar Allan Poe,"* 1882
The breath which leads living creatures is also in the Spheres

Odilon Redon, *"To Edgar Allan Poe,"* 1882
A Mask Sounding the Death Knell

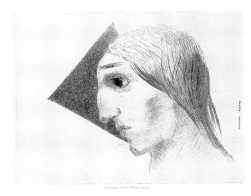

Odilon Redon, *"To Edgar Allan Poe,"* 1882
Madness

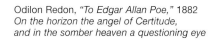

Odilon Redon, *"To Edgar Allan Poe,"* 1882
*On the horizon the angel of Certitude,
and in the somber heaven a questioning eye*

Anthony Perkins in Psycho, 1960

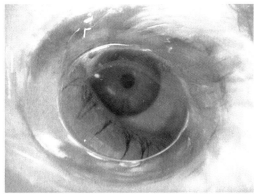

Janet Leigh's eye (Psycho), 1960

James Guthrie, *To the River, The Haunted Palace,* 1901 [1908]

Gaetano Previati, *A Descent into the Maelström,* 1890

Kim Novak in Vertigo, 1958

Anne Grey and John Stuart in Number Seventeen, 1932

Nita Naldi in The Pleasure Garden, 1927

Fernand Khnopff, *Illustration for Pol de Mont's* Iris, 1894

Fernand Khnopff, *Bruges-la-Morte,* about 1892

Victor Burgin, *The Bridge* (detail), 1984 Sir John Everett Millais, *Study for Ophelia,* 1852

Odilon Redon, *Ophelia,*
about 1900–1905

Willy Schlobach, *The Dead Woman,* 1890

Kim Novak pretends to drown herself beneath the Golden Gate Bridge (Vertigo), 1958

Joan Fontaine and Judith Anderson in Rebecca, 1940

Joan Fontaine in Rebecca, 1940

Judith Anderson and Joan Fontaine in Rebecca, 1940

William Holman Hunt, *My Beautiful Lady*
and *My Lady in Death,* 1850

Kim Novak in Vertigo, 1958

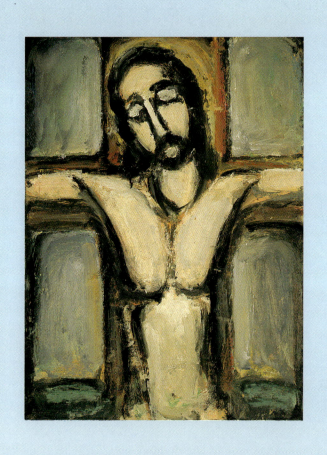

"I don't think I can be labeled a Catholic artist, but it may be that one's early upbringing influences a man's life and guides his instinct."

A.H.

(*The Dark Side of Genius,*
Donald Spoto)

Georges Rouault,
Christ Crucified,
about 1939

Montgomery Clift in I Confess, 1953

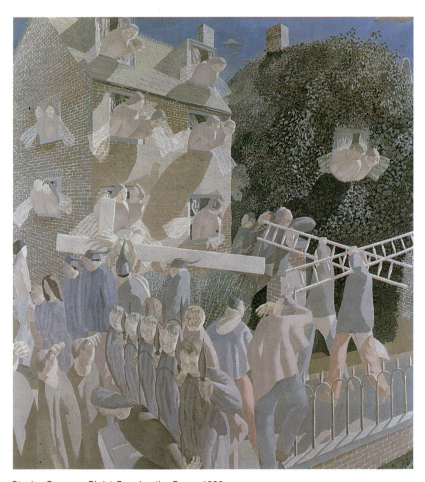

Stanley Spencer, *Christ Carrying the Cross,* 1920

Ivor Novello facing the mob
(The Lodger: A Story
of the London Fog), 1927

*Ivor Novello, June Tripp
and Malcolm Keen in*
The Lodger: A Story
of the London Fog, 1927

Topaz, 1969

Montgomery Clift in I Confess,
1953

Henri De Groux, *Study for The
Mocking of Christ,* about 1925

Edvard Munch, *Into the Forest,* 1915

Cary Grant and Eva Marie Saint in North by Northwest, 1959

Maurice Denis, *The Solitude of Christ,* 1918

The Manxman, 1929

All the World's a Stage...

The particular atmosphere found in places of entertainment – the noise, the dim lighting pierced by spotlights, the choreographed sequence of events – had fascinated Hitchcock ever since he was a boy. Throughout the 1920s, he was an avid fan of the London theatre scene. The plays he saw and the playwrights and actors he discovered during those years had a lasting effect on his creative output. The experience of going to the theatre – the performance itself, the suspense created by an actor playing to a live audience – remained imprinted on his memory. From his first film, *The Pleasure Garden,* whose title he borrowed from a London cabaret show, to the dance number that all but ruined Paul Newman and Julie Andrews's escape in *Torn Curtain,* theatres are often where the prelude or the conclusion to the actual story takes place. *The Thirty-nine Steps* best illustrates this confusion between spectacle and reality, and *Stage Fright* (with Marlene Dietrich as a third-rate actress) extends it by playing on the theme of deceit. Antonio Donghi's realist and magical puppets reveal the tragic, subconscious side to placing bodies on display, and the terror felt upon viewing such monstrosities in carnival shows or at the circus. The trivialized operatic finale to *Murder!* admirably conveys these contradictions.

The English artist Walter Richard Sickert painted a number of theatre scenes that focus on the relationship between the brightly lit stage and the semi-darkness of the house, the sideways view from the wings that encompass them both, the contrasts of light and darkness created by the footlights. Hitchcock had one of Sickert's paintings in his personal art collection. Perhaps he felt that Sickert had captured the ideal stage director's perspective, halfway between the actors and the audience, as shown in Guy Pène du Bois' delicate representations.

Sir Thomas Beecham, painted by Sickert in mid-gesture, was a leading conductor of the day when Hitchcock created the fateful clash of cymbals in the original version of *The Man Who Knew Too Much*. For the remake, Hitchcock's favourite composer Bernard Herrmann was at the podium.

Shooting the reactions of the audience rather than the performance itself was one of Hitchcock's trademarks. Similarly, when filming a crime, he tended to focus on the horror in the victims' faces.

Many of his films' final scenes point to the director's deep-seated doubt regarding the possibility of recreating truth through art, such as those that take place in a concert hall (both versions of *The Man Who Knew Too Much*), in front of or on a theatre stage *(I Confess, Blackmail),* in front of a

Felix Vallotton,
The Patriotic Ditty
(detail), 1893

cinema screen *(Sabotage, Saboteur),* above a circus ring *(Murder!),* on a merry-go-round *(Strangers on a Train)* or on an orchestra podium at a ball *(Young and Innocent).* The strong current of violence running through his stories and their dénouements in places of entertainment reveal, far more than Hitchcock's legendary black humour, a sense of disenchantment and a worldview tarnished by derision. The clown portrait in *Blackmail,* his first sound film, already points to these aspects of his *Weltanschauung.*

In the 1930s, during his English period, Hitchcock and several early 20th century painters – Vuillard, Vallotton, Sickert and Rouault – shared a taste for the boundaries created by light and shadow, the framework found in the theatre, circus and cabaret.

It should come as no surprise, then, that the director of *Vertigo* and *Rear Window* should perceive city streets, crime scenes – indeed, the entire world – as a kind of stage.

The building's facade in *Rear Window* is minutely examined by Hitchcock/Stewart's film/eyes, through his movie camera/still camera lens, creating so many small stages/windows that prefigure home television screens and contemporary video art. Stewart's voyeuristic performance has been – and will probably continue to be – an enduring inspiration to artists like Merry Alpern and Alain Fleischer. Conversely, the German trend known as *Neue Sachlichkeit* ("new objectivity") had already served as inspiration for the points of view found in Hitchcock's films (see the works of George Grosz).

As Herbert List has written, the mere act of watching turns the passing scene into entertainment. This encapsulates one of the few certainties of 20th-century art. In a photomontage that has become a modern icon, Herbert Bayer conflates all the elements of the best-known film about the compulsion to gaze: the facade of the apartment building (an inescapable facet of modern, urban life), the murdering hands, the obsessive vision.

D.P.

Walter Richard Sickert, *The Old Bedford:
Cupid in the Gallery*, about 1890

The Thirty-nine Steps, 1935

Walter Richard Sickert, *In the Cabaret at the End of the Pier,* about 1920

Édouard Vuillard, *Loge (Downstage at the Théâtre Antoine),* about 1895

Walter Richard Sickert, *Noctes Ambrosianae,* date unknown

Félix Vallotton, *The Patriotic Ditty*, 1893

The Pleasure Garden, 1927

Guy Pène Du Bois, *In the Wings,* 1921

Murder!, 1930

The Thirty-nine Steps, 1935

O.E. Hasse in I Confess, 1953

The Man Who Knew Too Much, 1956

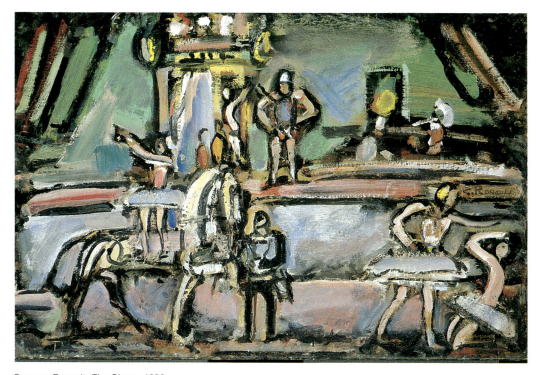

Georges Rouault, *The Circus,* 1936

Murder!, 1930

Antonio Donghi, *Equestrian Circus,* 1927

Wylie Watson in
The Thirty-nine Steps,
1935

Antonio Donghi, *The Cabaret Singer,* 1925

Anny Ondra and Cyril Ritchard in Blackmail, 1929

Anny Ondra in Blackmail, 1929

Esme Percy in Murder!, 1930

Walter Richard Sickert, *Sir Thomas Beecham Conducting,* about 1935

Bernard Herrmann in The Man Who Knew Too Much, 1956

Auguste Chabaud, *Hôtel-Hôtel,* 1907–1908

Mr. and Mrs. Smith, 1941

Paul B. Haviland, *Entrance to Luna Park,* 1909

Lighted advertisement (Blackmail), 1929

Downhill, 1927

Rich and Strange, 1932

The Bijou Theatre (Sabotage), 1936

André Kertész, *Circus, May 19, 1920, Budapest,* 1920

The fairground in The Ring, 1927

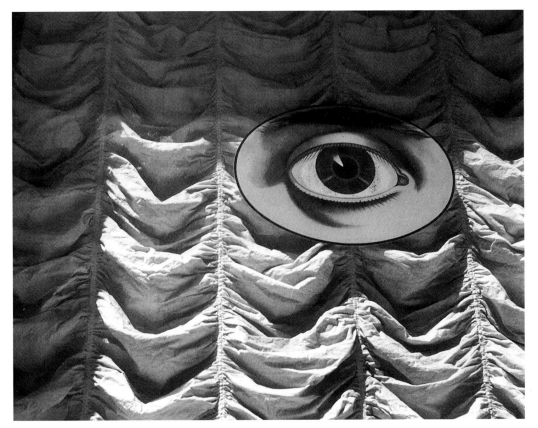

Herbert List, *Optician's Display,* 1936

John Gielgud in Secret Agent, 1936

Theo von Alten in Champagne, 1928

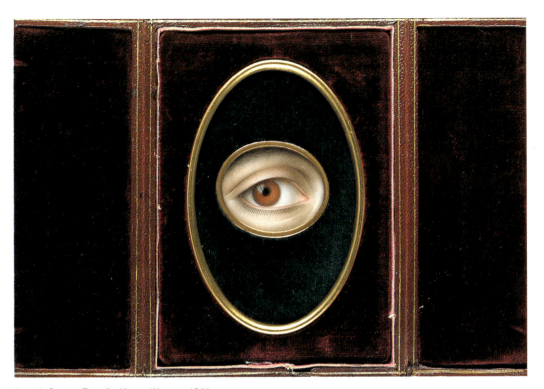

Joseph Sacco, *Eye of a Young Woman,* 1844

Ingrid Bergman in Notorious, 1946

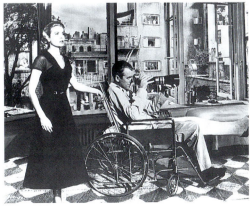

Grace Kelly and James Stewart for Rear Window, 1954

Herbert Bayer, *Good Night, Marie,* 1932

Herbert Bayer, *The Lonely Metropolitan*, 1932

George Grosz, *People in the Street,* 1915–1916

Sabotage, 1936

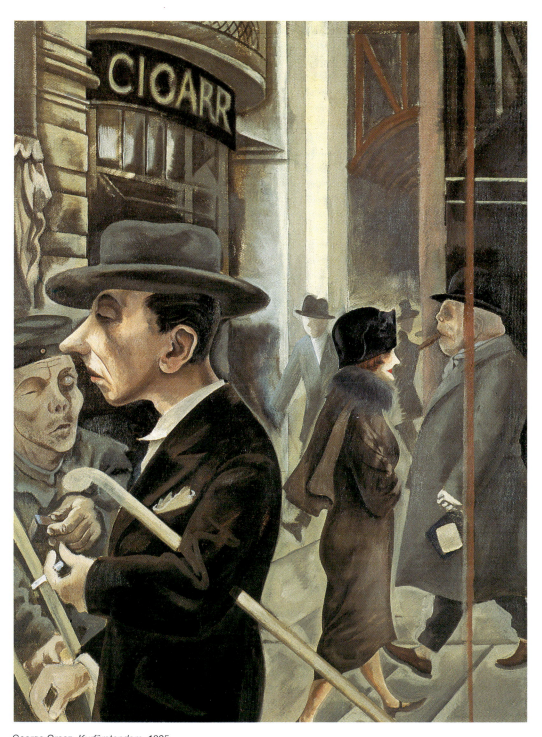

George Grosz, *Kurfürstendam,* 1925

René Magritte, *Edward James in front of* On the Threshold of Liberty, 1937

Alain Fleischer, *Exhibition in the North of France,* 1992

Merry Alpern, *Untitled No. 28,* 1994

Rear Window, 1954

Bill Brandt, *Portrait of a Young Girl, Eaton Place, London,* 1955

Rear Window, 1954

Women

The resemblance between the women Hitchcock chose to act in his films constitutes one of his oeuvre's most striking signature elements. Their main characteristics are their regular features, blonde hair, and a certain "icy coldness" that has become legendary. The roots of this ideal are far more ancient than the clichés dictated by the Hollywood dream factory. They go back to the aloof, ephemeral women of Dante Gabriel Rossetti or Julia Margaret Cameron.

From the 1950s to the mid-1960s, we witness the gradual entrenchment of an idealized prototype, embodied by four actresses who all point to a similar obsession, and bear witness to the search for an inaccessible image: Grace Kelly *(Dial M for Murder, To Catch a Thief, Rear Window),* Kim Novak *(Vertigo),* Eva Marie Saint *(North by Northwest)* and Tippi Hedren *(The Birds, Marnie).* It is as though the director had projected his Pygmalion-like designs onto the character of Scottie (James Stewart), who reconstitutes Judy, feature by feature – who, in fact, *moulds* her – in the image of the lost Madeleine (Kim Novak). Edith Head, Hitchcock's loyal costume designer, had this to say concerning Grace Kelly in *Dial M for Murder*: "Every costume was indicated when [Hitchcock] sent me the finished script. There was a reason for every color, every style, and he was absolutely certain about everything he settled on. For one scene, he saw her in pale green, for another in white chiffon, for another in gold. He was really putting a dream together in the studio." There could be no better description of the obsessive desire to create a prototype of the female body. In this exhibition, Franz Von Stuck and Auguste Rodin *(Éternelle idole)* declaim that enduring illusion.

Hair, the ultimate erotic fixation, contributes to the interchangeable nature of faces and bodies, of which so many fine examples can be found in art history: Leonardo, Rembrandt and Bonnard (to name but a few) all drew the same female features. Was Hitchcock trying to capture a single form that existed only in his imagination? He excelled at capturing his actresses unawares from behind, and filming the nape of their neck. Painters have often depicted their models from that viewpoint. Édouard Vuillard, Domenico Gnoli and other contemporary artists have used their own bodies to create implicitly erotic mises en scène (the works of Cindy Sherman provide another example).

Flowing, gossamer-like hair is captured in a spiral chignon, features are frozen into a profile as if stamped on a medal, and passionate contemplation leads from erotic fascination to violence and fetishistic

Grace Kelly for
Rear Window
(detail), 1954

dismemberment. Women in his films are idealized, fetishized, cut to pieces, drowned *(Frenzy)*. This process, combining erotic possession and murder, is a preoccupation of long standing that Hitchcock's stories merely revive: Fernand Khnopff, René Magritte and Man Ray have already said all the diabolical things there are to say on this subject.

Lusted after and aloof, icy and ostentatiously displayed, possessed and all-consuming, Hitchcock's women – sisters of Beata Beatrix, Lady Lilith and others – are an obvious Symbolist throwback, of the kind both idealized and feared by the Pre-Raphaelites. Their expressionless, sphinx-like faces vitiate all pathos. But behind the mask slumber animal cruelty and all-consuming nymphomania. There are Grace Kelly, the unattainable and unfaithful wife, a wholesome girl and a curious and perverse mistress; Kim Novak and Eva Marie Saint, both two-faced, lovers and spies, submissive yet calculating; Tippi Hedren, the enterprising bird-woman, enigmatic and kleptomaniac, sincere and profoundly deceived, evokes Dante Gabriele Rossetti's *Rosa Triplex* and Odilon Redon's and Edvard Munch's *Vampires*. Munch's lithograph *The Three Stages of Woman (The Sphinx)* epitomizes the metamorphoses that Hitchcock imposes upon the image and substance of womanhood.

But these "Symbolist women," resembling as they do certain Victorian prototypes – oppressive and oppressed, remote, haughty and steeped in cannibal-like passion – were preceded by other blondes who, although equally fascinating, embodied that schism between beauty and dangerous seduction to a lesser extent. Even before Kim Novak tried to drown herself in *Vertigo,* Ingrid Bergman had played an Ophelia-figure in *Under Capricorn,* whose flower-bestrewn hair stunned the Australians into silence. One hundred years earlier, the Pre-Raphaelite painter Ford Madox Brown, in *Farewell to England,* had painted the same British emigrants.

Ophelia is an element of Victorian iconography that, since his first silent films, has appeared throughout Hitchcock's oeuvre. The native woman in *The Pleasure Garden* (1925) drowns according to this scenario, a time-honoured cliché reworked by John Everett Millais' paintbrush, but which Redon, Man Ray and Khnopff later "disturbed."

Ingrid Bergman embodies another aspect of feminine "malleability": a marble-like immobility. A different kind of coldness, yet similarly reflecting the filmmaker/sculptor's ongoing obsession with the Pygmalion myth.

The conjunction of Anny Ondra *(Blackmail)* and Madeleine Carroll *(The Thirty-nine Steps)* precociously prefigured Ingrid Bergman's singular essence: somewhere between '30s-style haughty seductiveness (Meredith Frampton) and a tender sensuality, the face caught between "Victorian" reserve *(Under Capricorn)* and the radiance of awakened passion *(Notorious, Spellbound)*.

There are notable exceptions to the *sublime* blonde prototype, stunning brunettes whose features, devoid of all threat, diffuse exquisite innocence: Teresa Wright *(Shadow of a Doubt),* Margaret Lockwood *(The Lady Vanishes),* Laraine Day *(Foreign Correspondent)*...

D.P.

Fernand Khnopff, *Red Lips,* 1897

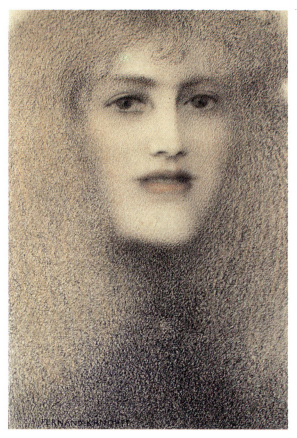

*The Lodger: A Story
of the London Fog,* 1927

Grace Kelly for Rear Window, 1954

Ingrid Bergman for Notorious, 1946

Fernand Khnopff, *On Animality*, 1885

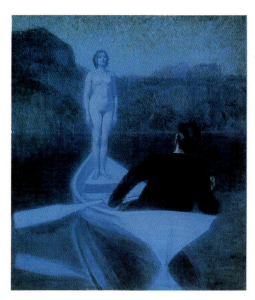

Ernst Stöhr, *The Woman,* 1898

Man Ray, *The Avignon Fort,* 1937

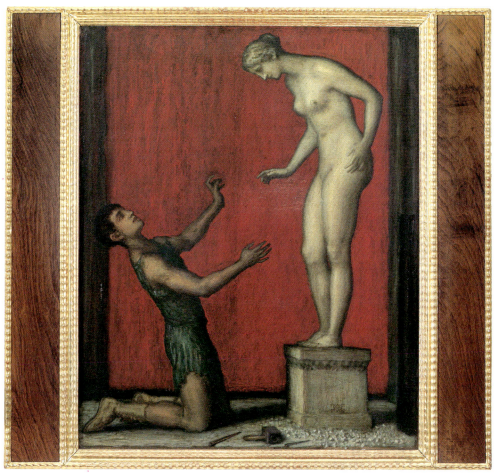

Franz Von Stuck, *Pygmalion,* about 1926

Auguste Rodin, *Eternal Idol,* 1889

Édouard Vuillard, *The Nape of Misia's Neck,* about 1897–1899

James Mason and Eva Marie Saint in North by Northwest, 1959

Domenico Gnoli, *Curly Red Hair,* 1969

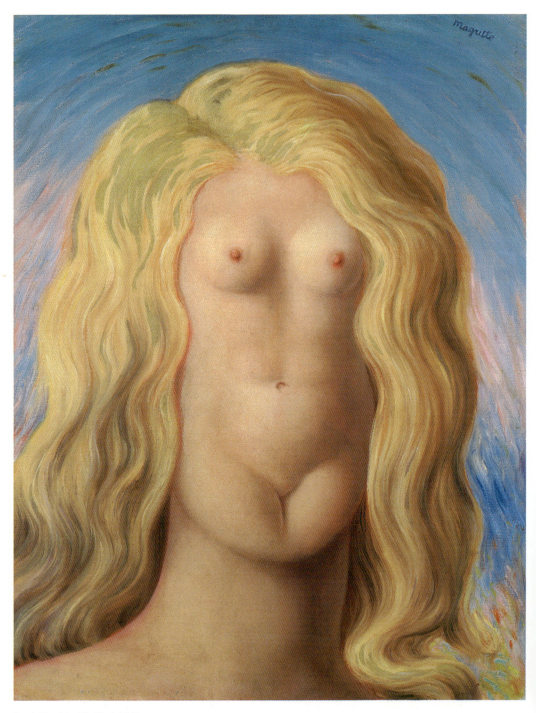

René Magritte, *Untitled*, 1941

Max Ernst, . . . *majestic,* 1929–1930

René Magritte, *The Rape,* 1945

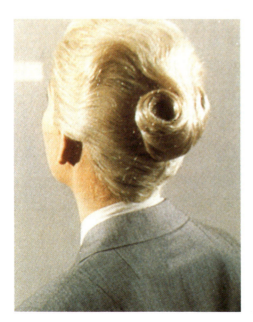

Kim Novak in Vertigo, 1958

Cindy Sherman, *Untitled (Film Still #81),*
1979

Kim Novak in Vertigo, 1958

Grace Kelly in To Catch a Thief, 1955

Eva Marie Saint in North by Northwest, 1959

Giorgio De Chirico, *Antique Woman,* design for *Vogue* (New York), 1937 (March 15)

Edith Head, *Costume design for* To Catch a Thief, 1955

Ingrid Bergman for Notorious, 1946

Ingrid Bergman for Notorious, 1946

Joan Fontaine *for Rebecca,* 1940

Meredith Frampton, *Portrait of a Young Woman,* 1935

Cecil Beaton, *Marlene Dietrich,* about 1935

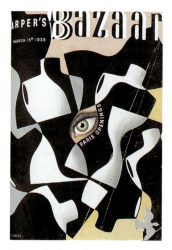 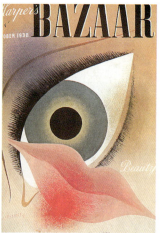

Cassandre (pseudonym of Adolphe Mouron), *Covers for* Harper's Bazaar
(New York), 1938 (15 March)

Herbert List, *Slave I*, 1936

Man Ray, *Restored Venus*, [1936]–1971

Janet Leigh in Psycho, 1960

Gus MacNaughton, Jerry Verno and Robert Donat in The Thirty-nine Steps, 1935

Marnie, 1964

Wilhelm Leibl, *The Corset* (fragment), about 1880–1881

Catherine Lacy's feet (The Lady Vanishes), 1938

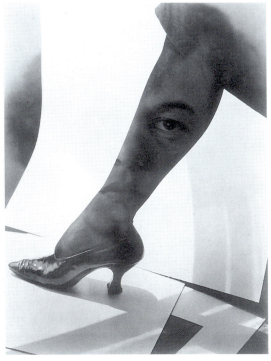

Alfred Stieglitz, *Dorothy True,* 1919

Betty Balfour in talent agent's office (Champagne), 1928

Alfred Hitchcock and Tippi Hedren on the set of Marnie, 1964

Margaret Lockwood in *The Lady Vanishes,* 1938

Tippi Hedren in The Birds, 1963

Clarence John Laughlin, *The Masks Grow to Us,* 1947

Joel McCrea and Laraine Day in Foreign Correspondent, 1940

Teresa Wright and Henry Travers in Shadow of a Doubt, 1943

Cary Grant and Eva Marie Saint in North by Northwest, 1959

Fernand Khnopff, *The Cigarette,* about 1912

Edvard Munch, *Woman (The Sphinx)*, 1899

Odilon Redon, *Haunting*, 1894

Desire and Double Trouble

The climax of a Hitchcock film, the narrative zenith, is often marked by an embrace. But, contrary to Hollywood "doxology," the lyrical languor of an entwined couple rarely comes at the end of his films, although he very possibly crafted the most exquisite kisses ever filmed. More often than not, the embrace's emotional intensity occurs at a midpoint in the story. Unlike other situations, filmed embraces require the presence of a "third party," and Hitchcock amused himself by using it to create a "ménage à trois": the man, the woman and ... the camera. How else can one explain the extraordinary eroticism of the embraces between Ingrid Bergman and Cary Grant in *Notorious,* between Kim Novak and James Stewart in *Vertigo,* or between Eva Marie Saint and Cary Grant in *North by Northwest*? Faces so close they seem to become one; the giddy pull of sensuality; every movement controlled by eager passion.

As it circles around them, the camera unites the lovers as an art aficionado circumambulates and encompasses a group of statues. *The Kiss* by Auguste Rodin invites the viewer to just such a voyeuristic experience. The filmmaker may well have been inspired by the scourges set in motion by the kisses of Dante's lovers, Paolo and Francesca. Could the quoting of music from Tchaikovsky's ballet *Francesca da Rimini,* in *Torn Curtain,* be proof of this? Interestingly enough, when it was first exhibited to the public, Rodin's sculpture was entitled *Paolo and Francesca.*

Edvard Munch, Emil Rudolf Weiss and René Magritte painted this same sensual abyss, into which the blinded and confused lovers fall headlong.

Absolute fusion, the fateful state of inseparable union that befalls Hitchcock's couples, leads inevitably to an act of sacrifice. Like Hector and Andromache, as illustrated by De Chirico, or Lancelot and Guinevere, as depicted by Julia Margaret Cameron, the couples in *Young and Innocent, Notorious, Under Capricorn, Strangers on a Train* and *Torn Curtain* resist the forces that threaten to separate them. The conjunction of their destinies goes beyond passing erotic attraction.

However, in Hitchcock's worldview, desire is a vector that can bring about disturbing reversals. Maybe the unique and idolized loved one will split (amoeba-like) and become many: Rossetti's *Rosa Triplex* shows a woman's features – prefiguring those of Hitchcock's heroines – multiplied, after the manner of Madeleine and Judy in *Vertigo,* or the innumerable faces of Marnie. Or perhaps sexual distinctions will dissolve in the heat of passion, so that one can no longer be distinguished from the other. In *Shadow of a Doubt,* young Charlie and her namesake uncle

Robert Delaunay,
Lovers: The Kiss,
1929

293

illustrate this daring metaphorical absorption, this exchange of identities, also represented by Picabia's *transparencies.*

Tampering with the differences between the sexes leads to further problems. Hitchcock excels at creating characters with doppelgängers that embody the complex contradictions of narcissism: auto-eroticism and the yearning for an unattainable idyll. Twinship is associated with death: the Charlies in *Shadow of a Doubt,* again, but also Ingrid Bergman and Gregory Peck in *Spellbound,* whose tightly knit embrace is threatened by the razor that can fatally separate them. Twinship also discreetly reveals the director's curiosity regarding homosexuality: both *Strangers on a Train* and *Rope* make a connection between attraction to one's own sex and a fascination with death.

Not surprisingly, there is another twist, as when embraces change from passionate to deadly. Lovers are also predators, and pursuing the object of one's desire may prove fatal. This kind of threat is here represented by the work of Max Klinger and Edvard Munch.

How can we distinguish love from danger in *Spellbound*'s famous movie poster motif? François Truffaut commented that Hitchcock's love scenes looked like murders; his homicides, like passionate embraces (see the works of Vallotton). Kissing resembles biting, desire is akin to voracity, sex is like cannibalism. Munch's *Vampire* and his *Kiss of Death* could well be referring to the intertwined lovers in *Spellbound.*

Are all embraces merely strangleholds extended to the entire body? Blurring the line between loving and strangling is pure Hitchcock.

The strangler's gesture is the same as that of a film director framing a shot with outstretched hands. Coincidence?

D.P.

Francis Picabia, *Aello,* about 1930

Ingrid Bergman and Cary Grant for
Notorious, 1946

Ivor Novello and June Tripp in The Lodger: A Story of the London Fog, 1927

Lillian Hall Davis and Ian Hunter in The Ring, 1927

Gregory Peck and Ingrid Bergman for Spellbound, 1945

Gregory Peck and Ingrid Bergman for
Spellbound, 1945

James Stewart and Grace Kelly in Rear Window,
1954

Montgomery Clift and Anne Baxter in I Confess,
1953

Grace Kelly and Cary Grant in To Catch a Thief,
1955

Auguste Rodin, *Fugit amor (Fleeting Love)*, 1881

Auguste Rodin, *Large Clenched Hand with Imploring Figure,* date unknown

Auguste Rodin, *The Kiss,* about 1916

Julia Margaret Cameron, *The Parting of Lancelot and Guinevere,* 1874

Emil Rudolf Weiss, *The Kiss,* 1899

René Magritte, *Duo,* 1928

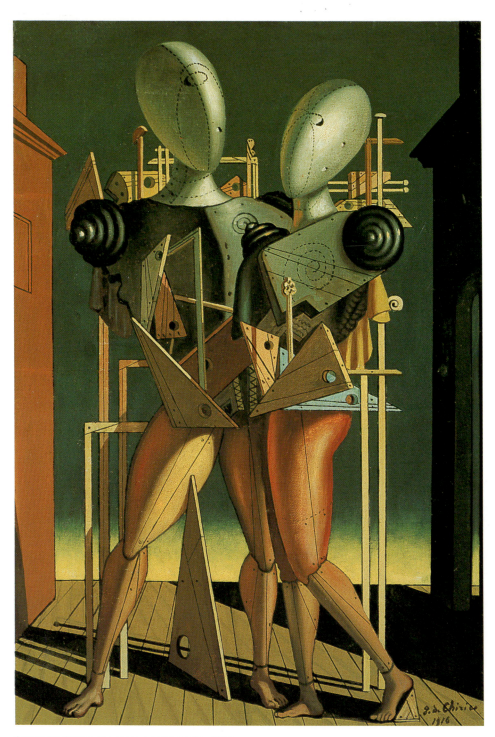

Giorgio De Chirico, *Hector and Andromache,* 1916

*Nova Pilbeam and Derrick de Marney
in* Young and Innocent, 1938

*Cary Grant and Ingrid Bergman
in* Notorious, 1946

Fernand Khnopff, *With Grégoire Le Roy: My Heart Longs for Other
Times,* 1889

James Stewart and Kim Novak (Madeleine/Judy) for Vertigo,
1958

*James Stewart and Kim Novak: Scottie between
Madeleine and Judy for* Vertigo, 1958

Herbert Bayer, *College Fashions, cover
for* Harper's Bazaar, 1940 (August)

James Stewart and Kim Novak for Vertigo, 1958

Dante Gabriele Rossetti, *Rosa Triplex*, 1874

Grace Kelly and Anthony Dawson for Dial M for Murder,
1954

Madeleine Carroll and Robert Donat for The Thirty-nine
Steps, 1935

Unsigned, *Anny Ondra and Cyril Ritchard for* Blackmail,
1929

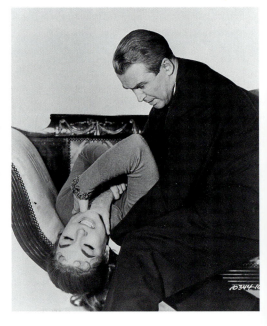

Kim Novak and James Stewart for Vertigo, 1958

Oscar Homolka and Sylvia Sidney for Sabotage, 1936

Teresa Wright threatened by Joseph Cotten for Shadow of a Doubt, 1943

Robert Walker in Strangers on a Train, 1951

Cary Grant and Eva Marie Saint in North by Northwest, 1959

Vera Miles and Alfred Hitchcock during shooting of The Wrong Man, 1956

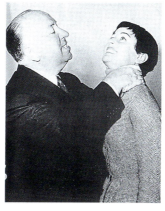

Alfred Hitchcock and Mary Scott during shooting of the television episode Mr. Blanchard's Secret, 1956

Alfred Hitchcock and Ingrid Bergman during the making of Spellbound, 1945

Félix Vallotton, from the series "Intimités I," *The Fine Pin,* 1898

Félix Vallotton, from the series "Intimités I," *The Lie,* 1897

Félix Vallotton, from the series "Intimités I," *Murder,* 1898

Félix Vallotton, from the series "Intimités I," *Print Pulled from the Destroyed Blocks,*
date unknown

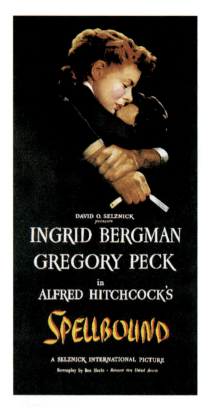

Unsigned, *Spellbound,* 1945

Max Klinger, *"Paraphrase on the Discovery of a Glove,"*
or *"The Glove,"* 1878–1881

Edvard Munch, *Vampire,* 1895–1902

Edvard Munch, *The Kiss of Death,* 1899

Disquiet

Surely uneasiness, and not suspense, is the overriding emotion felt by anyone watching an Alfred Hitchcock film. The suspense is merely the culmination of a whole disquieting process, requiring a meticulous and highly skilled dramatic preparation to attain the apogee of tension, the pinnacle of terror.

This feeling of Hitchcock-induced uneasiness is elicited by familiar places and everyday situations, although some trigger it more easily than others. Architecture, whether real or recreated in studio, was always a significant element in Hitchcock's work, as attested by the many pre-production sketches and models he used. The décor was influenced first by images from Dark Romanticism, and then "Metaphysical Surrealism."

Who could forget the many houses in his films in which the isolated inhabitant is immured as though in a tomb? The Neogothic castles, illuminated by flashes of lightning to resemble haunted sepulchres? Or the darkened apartment thresholds and series of doorways? Odilon Redon, Édouard Vuillard and Wilhelm Hammershøi have created powerful images of similar boundaries between light and shadow, where neuroses lurk (*Blackmail, Sabotage, Psycho, Frenzy,* and so on).

Carel Willink, Algernon Newton and Edward Hopper have all depicted hallucinatory, isolated haunted houses. The pictorialist photographer Alvin Langdon Coburn has "pre-faced" the home of the mummified Mrs. Bates. These sepulchral residences remain imprinted in the minds of contemporary artists, such as Holly King. Each of these houses conjures up mental images of endless corridors and a dark, phantom-ridden miasma. Today, Cindy Sherman and Willie Doherty have produced their own impressive versions, imbued with photography's sombre sensibility. But overwhelming anxiety is also outside, emanating from the dismal forests that undermine our mental stability (Max Ernst, William Degouves de Nuncque). The cyclical nature of time threatens the Edenic qualities of these forests *(Vertigo),* where cadavers lie concealed and apparitions are sheltered *(The Trouble with Harry).*

The influence of romantic ruin and abandonment (William Turner, Arnold Böcklin) on the director of *Psycho* and *Rebecca* is well known. But his works are also contemporaneous with the highly metaphysical and monumental tendencies of Surrealism. Indeed, from Léon Spilliaert to Giorgio De Chirico and Ralston Crawford, the generalized tendency toward monumentalization provided a representative and poetic bridge between Symbolism and Surrealism.

Léon Spilliaert,
Vertigo (detail),
1908

313

The otherness of the windmill blades, rotating contrary to the wind's impulse, draws Joel McCrea's attention in *Foreign Correspondent.* This scene – exemplifying the poetry in Hitchcock's work – draws upon an imaginative source that lies at the crossroads between Romanticism, Symbolism and Surrealism, as evoked by *Moulin à la pleine lune* by Georges de Feure.

How could the viewer ever forget those stupendous monuments (with their affinities to Léon Spilliaert), which, after a dizzying climb, become the stuff of nightmares *(Blackmail, Saboteur, North by Northwest)*? Those Neoclassical columns bearing down upon innocent and guilty alike, exacerbating the unhinging of their already confused minds *(Strangers on a Train)*? Or those sleepy or dead little towns inhabited by silent individuals whose features – obliterated through deceit, secrets or imagined indifference – are open to the obsessive creation of innumerable models *(Marnie)*?

Hitchcock's aim was to represent a diminished and disoriented humanity *(North by Northwest, Strangers on a Train, Saboteur),* similar to that of Italian metaphysical architecture of the 1920s (De Chirico). Commemorative function aside, there is something disturbing about these excessive proportions. They elicit a feeling of vertigo, and suggest a kind of inversion: the obliteration hinted at by Raphael Delorme, in a kind of foreshadowing of the final shot in *Marnie.*

Those places that allow the body to pass into another world, a world where it can change shape, are equally memorable. Such places make us uneasy either because time appears to stand still there, or because we might be confronted by a ghostly image of ourselves, like the melancholy hero in *Bruges-la-Mort,* lost in his recollections of a deceased woman, in a silent, mist-enshrouded city. Fernand Khnopff dreamed of bridges, indifferent to any Ophelias who might float past, as was the San Francisco bridge in *Vertigo,* revisited today by Cindy Bernard.

Through these encounters and metamorphoses, can we not perceive the likeness of that ultimate animal of fantasy and Surrealism, dangerous yet fragile, symbol of grace and aggression: the bird? At the beginning of the 20th century, Nikolai Roerich and Spilliaert, and, more recently, Gregory Crewdson and Eldon Garnet, reveal the darker side of such encounters. Through the lens of photographer Philippe Halsman, femininity, via an amalgamative evolution, will come to embody its own kind of threat, as exemplified by such women as Melanie in *The Birds,* or Marnie. The Surrealists accomplish the synthesis of these elements in a different way (Max Ernst). René Magritte's *Eaux profondes* provides an apt description of the "accuracy" of images through his depiction of "idealized," pseudo-antique features, severe masculine attire and a cold demeanour. The black bird becomes one with the woman who will not submit, creating a composite image of unhealthy frigidity: submissive and thwarting passion, Tippi Hedren becomes that woman in *Marnie.*

D.P.

Arnold Böcklin, *Ruin by the Sea*, 1881

I Confess, 1953

The Hillcrist home (The Skin Game), 1931

The ashes of Manderley (Rebecca), 1940

Joseph Mallord William Turner, *Dolbadern Castle, North Wales*, 1800

James Basevi, *Rebecca,* 1940

The Manxman, 1929

The Man Who Knew Too Much, 1956

Murder!, 1930

Alfred Junge, *The Man Who Knew Too Much,* 1956

Joseph Cundall (Cundall and Fleming), *Elz Castle,* about 1867

Fernand Khnopff, *Le lac d'amour, Bruges,* about 1904–1905

Charles Lacoste, *London Docks, Sunday Dawning,* date unknown

Algernon Newton, *The Deserted Factory,* 1941

Stage Fright, 1950

Carel Willink, *The Letter,* 1932

Edward Hopper, *North Truro Station,* 1930

Alfred Junge, *Young and Innocent,* 1938

Derrick de Marney in Young and Innocent, 1938

Edward Hopper, *Lighthouse Hill,* 1927

Alvin Langdon Coburn, *The Haunted House,* 1904

Anthony Perkins in Psycho, 1960

Holly King, *Place of Desire,* 1989

The house at night (Under Capricorn), 1949

The house at daybreak (Under Capricorn), 1949

Harland Fraser, *Shadow of a Doubt,* 1943

Dorothea Holt, *Shadow of a Doubt,* 1943

Alfred Junge, *The Man Who Knew Too Much,* 1956

Robert Boyle, *Shadow of a Doubt,* 1943

Blackmail, 1929

Downhill, 1927

Downhill, 1927

Anny Ondra in Blackmail, 1929

Number Seventeen, 1932

John Stuart in Number Seventeen, 1932

Leon M. Lion in Number Seventeen, 1932

Cindy Sherman, *Untitled (Film Still #51),* 1979

Spellbound, 1945

Odilon Redon, *"We both saw a large pale light,"* illustration for the French translation of Edward Bulwer-Lytton's The Haunted and the Haunters, 1896

Wilhelm Hammershøi, *Interior, Strandgade 25,* 1915

Sylvia Sidney in Sabotage, 1936

Sabotage, 1936

Édouard Vuillard, *The Two Doors,*
about 1891

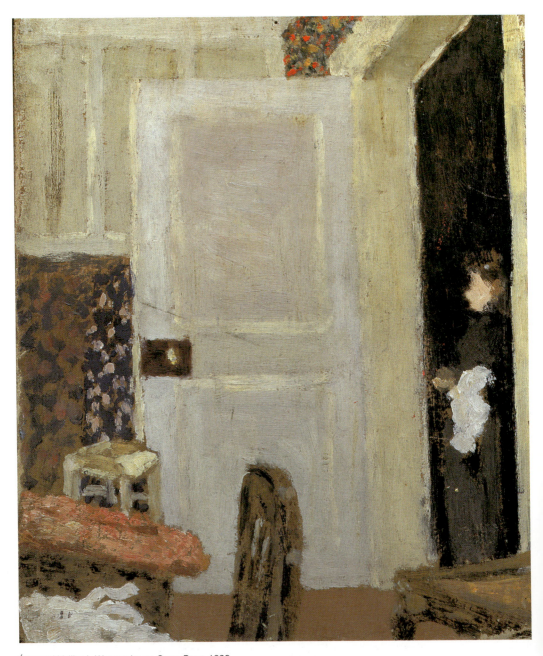

Édouard Vuillard, *Woman by an Open Door,* 1893

Anny Ondra in Blackmail, 1929

Alida Valli for The Paradine Case, 1947

Alvin Langdon Coburn, *Weirs Close,* 1904

Édouard Vuillard, *Perfect Harmony (Madame Gillou at Home),* 1931

The cast of Rope, 1948

Leopoldine Konstantin and Claude Rains in Notorious, 1946

Judith Anderson in Rebecca, 1940

Léon Spilliaert, *Wind,* about 1902

Judith Anderson in Rebecca, 1940

The Thirty-nine Steps, 1935

William Degouve De Nuncques, *Leprous Forest,* 1898

Headlights in the woods (Young and Innocent), 1938

Kim Novak in Vertigo, 1958

Max Ernst, *Vision Induced by the Nocturnal Aspect of Porte Saint-Denis,* 1927

Saboteur, 1942

Willie Doherty, *Unapproved Road*, 1992

Psycho, 1960

Janet Leigh in Psycho, 1960

Georges De Feure, *Windmill
by Moonlight,* date unknown

Foreign Correspondent, 1940

Raphaël Delorme, *Untitled (Woman and Steamship),* 1928

The Wrong Man, 1956

Marnie, 1964

Donald Calthrop chased through the British Museum (Blackmail), 1929

Donald Calthrop caught (Blackmail), 1929

John Rogers Cox, *Grey and Gold*, 1942

North by Northwest, 1959

Robert Cummings and Norman Lloyd in Saboteur, 1942

North by Northwest, 1959

Léon Spilliaert, *Pursuit,* 1910

Shadow of a Doubt, 1943

Cindy Bernard, *Ask the Dust:
Vertigo,* 1990

342

Ralston Crawford, *Whitestone Bridge,* 1939

Léon Spilliaert, *Night,* 1908

Ralston Crawford, *Overseas Highway,* 1939

Donald Calthrop in Blackmail, 1929

Ingrid Bergman in *Notorious,* 1946   *John Vernon and Karin Dor in* Topaz, 1969

The Man Who Knew Too Much, 1956   *Vertigo,* 1958

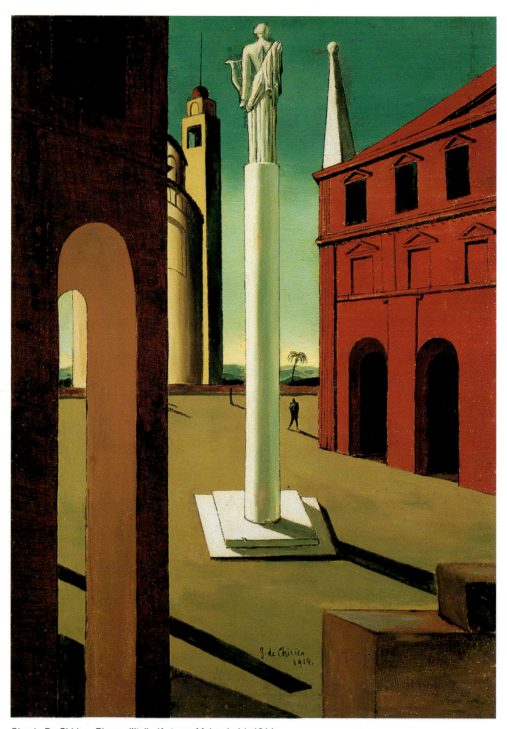

Giorgio De Chirico, *Piazza d'Italia (Autumn Melancholy),* 1914

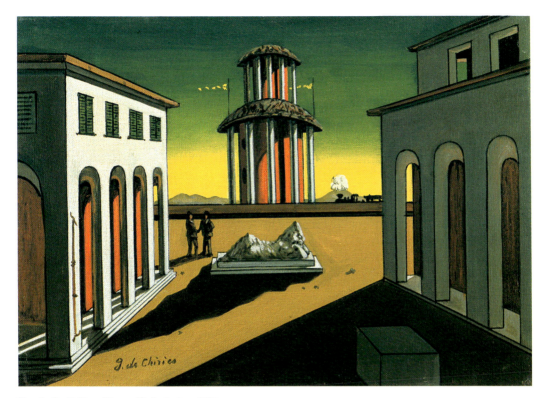

Giorgio De Chirico, *Piazza d'Italia,* before 1935

The Lodger: A Story of the London Fog, 1927

Robert Walker in Strangers on a Train, 1951

Léon Spilliaert, *Vertigo,* 1908

Claude Rains in Notorious, 1946

Léon Spilliaert, *Staircase,* 1909

Léon Spilliaert, *The Liner* or *The Strand,* 1909

Philippe Halsman, *Tippi Hedren for* The Birds, 1963

Anthony Perkins for Psycho, 1960

Philippe Halsman, *Tippi Hedren for* The Birds, 1963

Arthur Rackham, *The Seven Ravens,* 1900

Tippi Hedren in The Birds, 1963

Robert Boyle, *The Birds,* 1963

Harold Michelson, storyboards for *The Birds,* 1963

Max Ernst, *Forest Bird,* 1927–1928

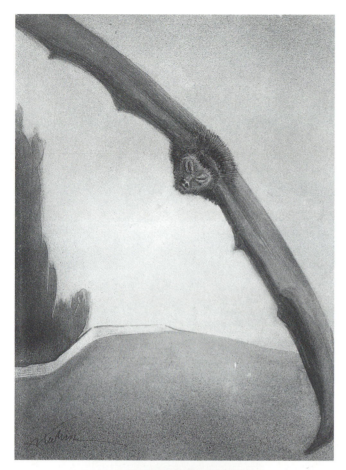

Alfred Kubin, *The Bat (Cemetery Wall),*
1900–1903

Léon Spilliaert, *Bird of Prey,* 1904

354

Georges Braque, *The Black Birds,* 1956–1957

Nikolai Roerich, *Ominous,* 1901

The final shot of The Birds, 1963

Eldon Garnet, *NO,* 1997

Gregory Crewdson, *Untitled (Birds around Home),* 1997

Philippe Halsman, *Tippi Hedren for* The Birds, 1963

René Magritte, *Deep Waters*, 1941

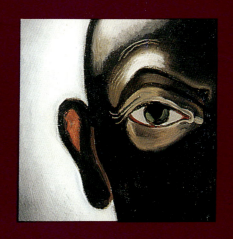

Sheer Terror

In *Psycho,* it is precisely what we don't see – Janet Leigh's bloody, naked body, hacked to pieces by a kitchen knife – that terrifies us the most. We could avert our eyes, but what good would it do? The object of our terror is not on the screen but rather in what Hitchcock compels us to imagine: a corpse, treated like a piece of meat in a slaughterhouse. The shot of the blood spiralling out of the bathtub drain reinforces the impression of an animal having its throat cut, before being served at the dinner table.

There are too many connections between killing, cooking and eating in Hitchcock for them to be anything other than a controlled sensual impulse: the dead body hidden under the canapés in *Rope*; the unappetizing chicken found on Joan Fontaine's plate as she hears about the death of Cary Grant's friend in *Suspicion*; the police officer in *Torn Curtain* who dies from having his head "cooked" in a oven; the disgusting quails prepared by the wife of the inspector conducting the investigation in *Frenzy*; and, in that same film, the body lying among the sacks of potatoes. As we advance through Hitchcock's oeuvre, the criminal experimentation of his English period, the psychological torture found in his American films and the metaphysical terror of his second Hollywood period are gradually replaced by an image of "dead meat," by the notion of corpses as foodstuff. It is almost as though the return to England settled some sort of score with his native country, via the hands of modern-day Jack the Rippers sorting through cadaverous entrails. Alfred Kubin's stroller with the threatening hands, whose inexorable progress calls De Feure's suitor (and Norman Bates) to mind, Karl Hubbuch's dead body, fearfully abandoned, Karel Teige's photomontage of body parts ready to be ingested – all these point unmistakably to many images found in Hitchcock's work.

All the more terrifying is the inescapable presentiment of the characters' cadaverous destiny, as frighteningly exemplified by Anthony Perkins' final metamorphosis into his dead mother in *Psycho*. In this exhibition, we have Léon Frederic's interpretation of the corpse-like double. The French critic Serge Daney wrote, about the famous kiss in *North by Northwest*: "Notice Cary Grant's depraved, Brechtian appearance, his long hairy hands searching for a neck to strangle, his controlled sensuality and calculating euphoria. And Eva Saint Marie's skeletal hands, her bare forehead, her exaggerated ecstasy. There is obviously a lot more to this kissing scene than meets the eye."

Alberto Martini,
Self-Portrait
(detail), 1929

Bulging eyes are traditionally used to denote terror. The eye is like light-sensitive paper on which, it is said, the murderer's image remains imprinted for several seconds after the crime. This is exactly what is suggested by the glasses in *Strangers on a Train,* which reflect the murder of Farley Granger's wife in the fairground; or Janet Leigh's fixed and glassy stare in *Psycho,* from which the camera spirals backward, imitating the movement of the blood as it drains into the motel's sewer pipes. Tony Oursler's video "eye" admirably conveys the dual function of recording and communicating fear, and is equivalent to the terrifying voyeurism of Perkins, who is both monstrous, infantile executioner and pathetic victim of maternal over-protectiveness. Alberto Martini's self-portrait condenses all these fears into a single image.

In 1982, Robert Boyle, Hitchcock's favourite production designer, said of his work on *The Birds*: "I really didn't see it as being a melodrama. […] I just started doing a few drawings and I have to admit that what came out was basically *The Scream,* the painting by Edvard Munch, which I felt represented the kind of terror a lot of people feel about birds." Upon discovering the dead farmer with his pecked-out eyes, Jessica Tandy screams silently, mouth gaping, eyes dilated. In fact, the entire setting of *The Birds* is reminiscent of that famous painting: the distant lake, the bridge leading away from the viewer, the figure in the foreground who has come face to face with the horror.

In Hitchcock's work, the scream's dramatic and representative functions were carried over from silent films. The famous cut in *The Thirty-nine Steps,* from the close-up of a woman screaming to the train emerging from the tunnel, remains the most surprising application of Eisenstein's montage theory in all of cinema history.

D.P.

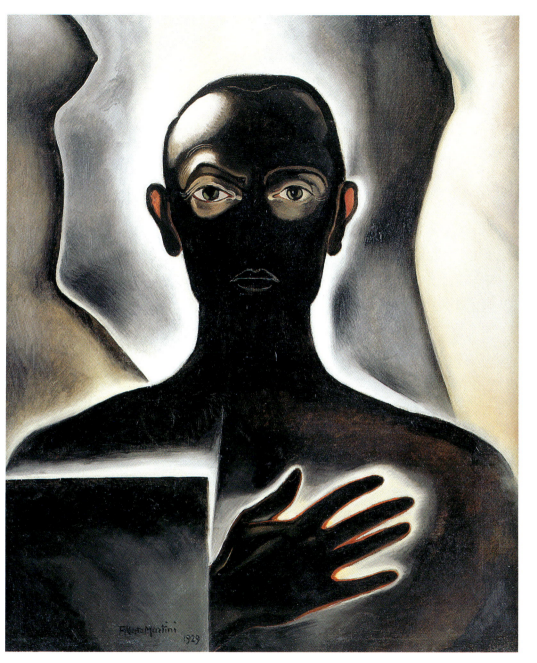

Alberto Martini, *Self-Portrait,* 1929

Alfred Kubin, *A Child's Soul,* about 1905

Edvard Munch, *The Scream,* 1895

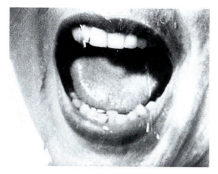

Janet Leigh in Psycho, 1960

The Thirty-nine Steps, 1935

Jessica Tandy in The Birds, 1963

To Catch a Thief, 1955

The first victim (The Lodger: A Story of the London Fog), 1927

John Stuart in Number Seventeen, 1932

Judith Anderson and Joan Fontaine in Rebecca, 1940

James Stewart in The Man Who Knew Too Much, 1956

Barbara Leigh-Hunt in Frenzy, 1972

Karel Teige, *Untitled,* about 1930

Philippe Halsman, *Alfred Hitchcock and Tippi Hedren for* The Birds, 1963

Sylvia Sidney's hands and the kitchen knife (Sabotage), 1936

Romolo Romani, *Scream,* 1904–1905

Odilon Redon, *"I continued to gaze on the chair, and fancied I saw on it a pale blue misty outline of a human figure,"* 1896

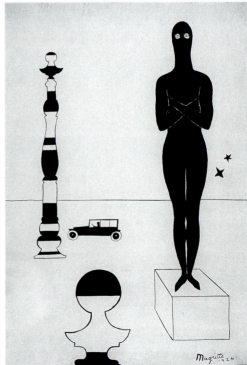

René Magritte, *Fantomas,* 1926

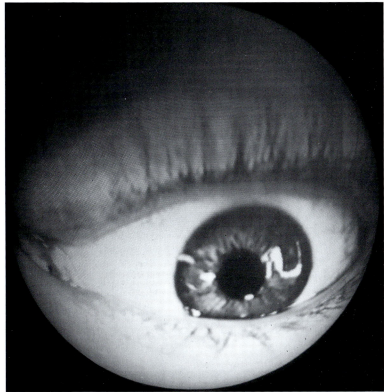

Tony Oursler, *Seed,* 1996

Georges De Feure, *The Suitor,* 1896

Alberto Martini, *The Man of the Crowd,* 1906

Tom Morgan, *Jack the Ripper,* date unknown

Alfred Kubin, *The Intruder,* about 1936

Alfred Kubin, *The Hour of Death,* 1903

Tom Morahan, *Jamaica Inn,* 1939

Alfred Kubin, *A Walk on the Seashore,* about 1900

Anthony Perkins for Psycho, 1960

Léon Spilliaert, *The Couple,* about 1902

Ingrid Bergman and Gregory Peck in Spellbound, 1945

Murder!, 1930

The farmer and his wife in The Thirty-nine Steps, 1935

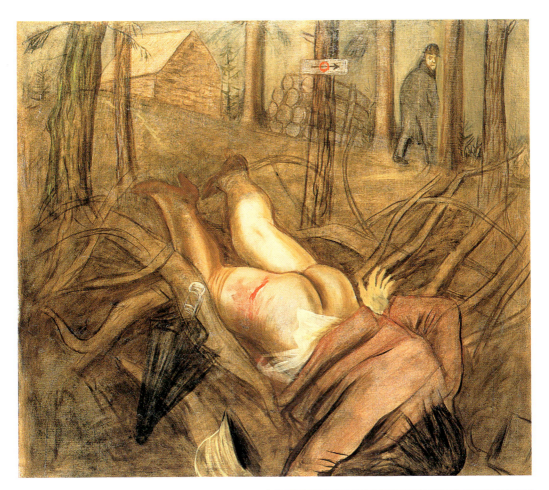

Karl Hubbuch, *Murder,* 1930

Anna Massey's body (Frenzy), 1972

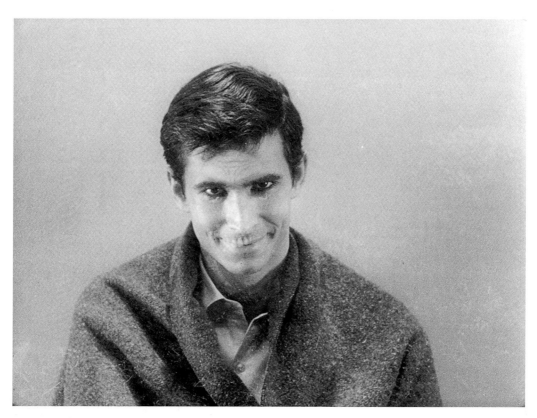

Anthony Perkins in Psycho, 1960

Alberto Martini, *Folly*, 1914–1915

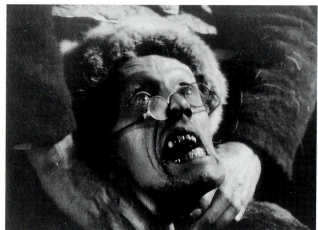

Head of Mrs. Bates from Psycho, 1960

The Mountain Eagle, 1927

The shrunken head (Under Capricorn),
1949

Anthony Perkins and John Gavin in Psycho,
1960

Léon Frédéric, *Studio Interior,* 1882

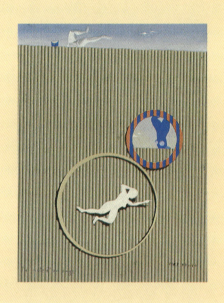

Forms and Rhythms

Jean-Luc Godard, in his colossal work *Histoire(s) du cinéma,* called Hitchcock *THE ARTIST.* And in 1959, Éric Rohmer had the following to say about *Vertigo*: "*[Strangers on a Train]* owed much, not just in terms of rigour, but also in terms of lyricism, to the haunting presence of a twin geometric pattern, that of the line and the circle. Here, the figure – drawn for us in Saul Bass's title sequence – is that of a spiral, or, more precisely, a helix: line and circle conjoined via a third dimension, that of depth. There are, strictly speaking, only two such spirals materially represented in the film: that of the lock of hair spilling onto Madeleine's neck, a copy of the neck of Carlotta Valdés (remember, it is she who sparks the detective's desire); and that of the staircase in the bell tower. The rest of the time, the helix is idealized, suggested by its cylinder of rotation – represented in Stewart's field of view as he follows Novak by car, in the vault of trees above the road, in the trunks of the sequoias, in the corridor that Madeleine mentions and that Scottie encounters in a dream (a dream, I must say, whose tawdry design clashes with the solemn grace of the real landscapes), and in a myriad of other patterns that only become apparent upon repeated viewings of the film. The polished stump of the thousand-year-old redwood and the circular dolly-shot around the kiss (in fact, it is the subjects who are rotating) are other allusions. [...] Poetry and geometry, far from being divorced, are here united. Here, we progress through space in the same manner as we do through time; in the same way our and the characters' thoughts progress. [...] The motion is always circular, but the circle is never complete; each rotation leads us a little deeper into memory. [...] The motion is all the more disquieting in that it manifests unresolved continuity, and simultaneously embodies the circle's softness and the straight line's cutting edge" (*Cahiers du cinéma,* No. 93, March 1959).

Rohmer's observations constitute the first *abstract* interpretation of Hitchcock's oeuvre. In other words, in addition to the commentaries learnedly apportioning anxiety, oneiricism and terror in due measure, the French film critics uncovered the constructivism manifest in the filmmaker's vision and style, to which the work of American painter Ralston Crawford bears a troubling resemblance. *Overseas Highway* is strongly reminiscent of the setting for Bodega Bay, the marina under attack in *The Birds.*

Also, the work of Saul Bass admirably reflects the director's architectural and radically geometrical tendencies: the credits for *North by Northwest, Psycho* and *Vertigo* explicitly conjoin the "circle's softness and the

Max Ernst, *The Fall of an Angel,* 1922

379

straight line's cutting edge," with which artists such as Bridget Riley continue to experiment.

At an early stage, the man who directed *The Ring* had already been influenced by the representational ideas of the avant-gardists: the boxer's coma is represented by a mélange of shapes and abstract gleams of light akin to the contemporaneous visual symphonies of Hans Richter. In *Sabotage,* the destruction of the city, as "imagined" by the terrorist, calls to mind the anamorphoses of Dziga Vertov's *The Man with a Movie Camera.* Similarly, there is an irresistible connection between the machine room in *Secret Agent* and the modernism of the many *ballets mécaniques* of the 1920s. Together with Lang's, Hitchcock's films provided the best examples of the alternation between representation and narration in film, of which German Expressionism was the most obvious aesthetic movement, as well as being the last to emphasize that kind of tension. Éric Rohmer, Murnau's faithful admirer and exegete, doubtless intended the title of his text *L'hélice et l'idée* ("The helix and the idea") to reflect that concept.

Hitchcock's all-encompassing vision, imposed by means of a restrictive geometry, gave rise to the invention of an unlimited number of shapes and forms. It is as though the world's chaos could be reorganized and structured by a rigid, abstract framework. Thus, the mise en scène in *Marnie*'s famous night-time theft sequence prefigures the heroine's psychological imprisonment and the risk of her incarceration.

The vertiginous, labyrinthine perspectives already envisioned by Gustave Caillebotte at the end of the 19th century recur consistently throughout Hitchcock's work, revealing a core of strength in his films that originates in a representational worldview borrowed from the previous century's masters.

The plunge down the stairs in *Blackmail* or the almost Godlike high-angle shot of Cary Grant running out of the UN building in *North by Northwest* are just some of a number of optical chasms, testaments to a crushing, agoraphobic perspective. James Stewart in *Vertigo* repeatedly suffers from this very malaise. The Belgian painter De Boeks unwittingly provided an apt image and the title for the film.

The architectural perspective, from an elevated vantage point, was definitely in vogue in the Modernist 1930s (see the works of Bernard Boutel de Monvel, Martin Lewis, Umbo and André Kertesz); in many of Hitchcock's films *(Spellbound, Rear Window, To Catch a Thief, Vertigo)* it gives rise to feelings of vertigo and falls, both imagined and real. There are many dream-like sequences in which women are rescued, *in extremis,* from the brink of yawning chasms *(Young and Innocent, North by Northwest).* The eponymous protagonist of *Saboteur,* though, cannot avoid plunging from the top of the gigantic and symbolic Statue of Liberty. Most of Hitchcock's fleeing couples must negotiate labyrinths in addition to overcoming heights, as illustrated in the drawing entitled *Rock Temple* by Paul Klee – the same artist who had created a very "architecturalized" and unusually "metaphysical" painting that was part of Hitchcock's collection. This drawing is strangely reminiscent of the legendary Mount Rushmore, with its monumental presidential faces, that Cary Grant and Eva Marie Saint must climb.

The juxtaposition of large and small is an important element in Hitchcock's particular brand of suspense. Light also contributes to the impression of monumental proportions as when, for example, a glass of milk in *Suspicion* is bathed in an intrinsic luminescence reminiscent of Spilliaert's and Edward Burra's "close-ups" of domestic objects. Today, Michael Snow pursues the same trend toward "monumentalization" by expertly using fake close-ups and trick perspectives to instill doubt in the viewer. Yet another variation on the tension created between what is nearby and what is far off, famously epitomized by the close-up of the hand with the gun in *Spellbound.*

The labyrinthine passages and streaked surfaces reflect Hitchcock's avant-garde tendency to lacerate the onscreen image, the iconography drawing attention away from a hidden sadism.

Has anyone fully grasped the significance of the fact that Hitchcock was a contemporary of Marcel Duchamp? After all, the latter's work contains more Symbolist elements – and is also more conceptual – than that of any other 20th century artist. The films created by the "master of suspense" are, first and foremost, traps that gradually draw the viewer's gaze into descending spirals, thus undermining our concept of reality. Could Hollywood have borrowed this notion from the *Rotos-relief* works exhibited at the Lépine competition, which were also inspired by the conjunction of a helix and an idea?

D.P.

Ray Milland in Dial M for Murder, 1954

Daniel Gélin in The Man Who Knew Too Much, 1956

The Thirty-nine Steps, 1935

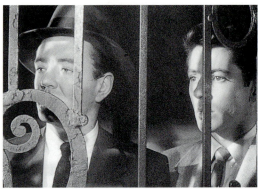

Robert Walker and Farley Granger in Strangers on a Train, 1951

Gustave Caillebotte, *The Balcony,* 1880

Paul Klee, *Captive (Figure of This World/Next World),* 1940

Carl Brisson in The Ring, 1927

Norah Baring in Murder!, 1930

Robin Irvine and Annette Benson in Downhill, 1927

Janet Leigh and John Gavin in Psycho, 1960

Marnie, 1964

Sabotage, 1936

Ivor Novello in Downhill, 1927

Blackmail, 1929

Alida Valli for The Paradine Case, 1947

Gregory Peck in Alida Valli's room (The Paradine Case), 1947

Gregory Peck and lawyer in The Paradine Case, 1947

Paul Klee, *Rock Temple,* 1925

Cary Grant and Eva Marie Saint on Mount Rushmore set (North by Northwest), 1959

Charles Borup, *Rails,* late 1920s   *Joseph Cotten in* Shadow of a Doubt, 1943

Alfred Junge, *Young and Innocent,* 1938   *Strangers on a Train,* 1951

Ralston Crawford, *Lights in an Aircraft Plant,* 1945

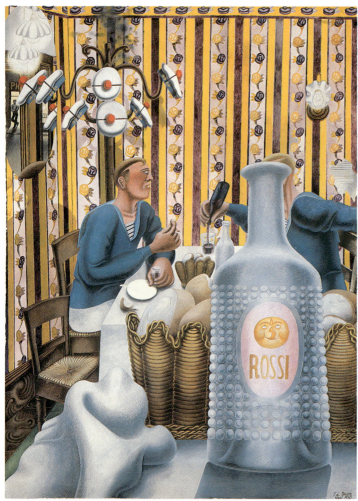

Edward Burra, *Rossi,* 1930

Ivor Novello and Isabel Jeans in Downhill, 1927

Ingrid Bergman for Notorious, 1946

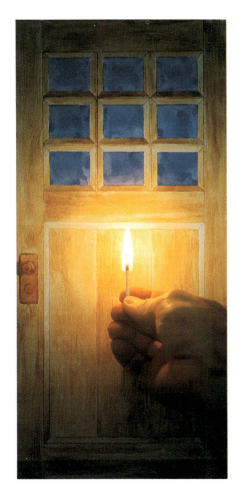

Michael Snow, *Door,* 1979

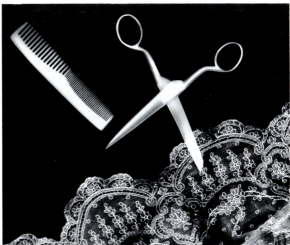

Georgi Zimin, *Still Life with Comb and Scissors,* 1928–1930

Ingrid Bergman in Spellbound, 1945

Léon Spilliaert, *Carafe,* about 1917

André Kertész, *Tokyo,* 1968

André Kertész, *Shadows, Paris,* 1931

Paul Sylbert, *The Wrong Man,* 1956

The assassination (Foreign Correspondent), 1940

Alfred Junge, set design for *Young and Innocent*, 1938

Umbo (pseudonym of Otto Umbehr), *Mystery of the Street*, 1928

Young and Innocent, 1938

Bernard Boutet De Monvel, *New York Rooftops,* about 1930

Martin Lewis, *East Side Night, Williamsburg Bridge (New York)*, 1928

Shadow of a Doubt, 1943

James Stewart for Vertigo, 1958

Cary Grant in To Catch a Thief, 1955

North by Northwest, 1959

The Thirty-nine Steps, 1935

Norman Lloyd in Saboteur, 1942

To Catch a Thief, 1955

Murder!, 1930

Hans Schmithals, *Combatants,* 1902–1905

Félix De Boeck, *Vertigo*, 1920

Leon M. Lion and John Stuart in Number Seventeen, 1932

Sabotage, 1936

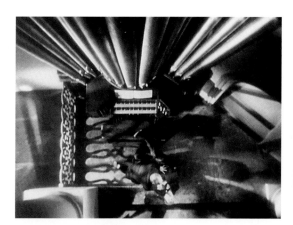

The organist's death (Secret Agent), 1936

Blackmail, 1929

James Stewart in Vertigo, 1958

Anny Ondra in Blackmail, 1929

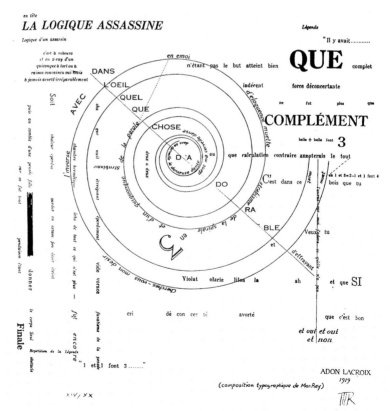

Man Ray, *Murderous Logic,* [1919]–1975

403

Saul Bass, *preliminary studies for opening credits,* Vertigo, 1958

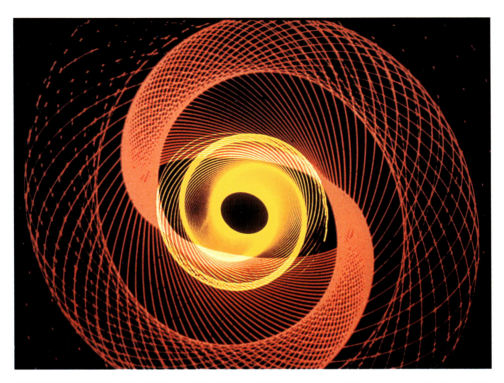

Opening credits, Vertigo, 1958

August Sander, *Spiral of Light Bulbs,* about 1930

Corolles [obverse]

Œuf à la coque [reverse]

Lanterne chinoise [obverse]

Lampe [reverse]

Poisson japonais [obverse]

Escargot [reverse]

Verre de Bohême [obverse]

Cerceaux [reverse]

Cage [reverse]

Marcel Duchamp, *Rotoreliefs* (Optical Disks) 1935

Saul Bass, *poster design,* Vertigo, 1958

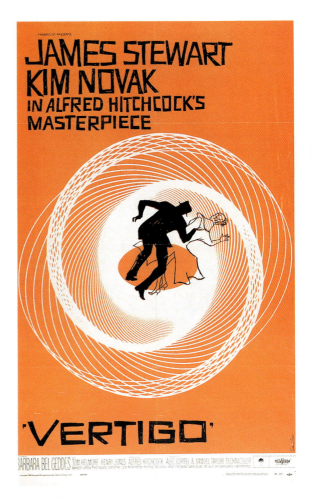

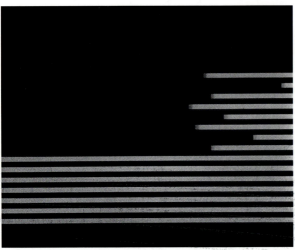

Saul Bass, *Opening credits,* Vertigo, 1958

Bridget Riley, *Blaze 4,* 1964

Hitchcock and Dalí: The Lost Dreams of *Spellbound*

Spellbound, as we know it today, reveals only part of the collaboration between Salvador Dalí and Alfred Hitchcock for the film's famous dream sequence: several scenes, though shot, were not included in the final cut. Here is a reconstruction of the whole dream in words and pictures, using the original script (from the Selznick Archives, Harry Ransom Humanities Research Center, University of Texas at Austin), production stills, and the storyboards drawn by William Cameron Menzies.

Dr. Constance Petersen (Ingrid Bergman), a psychiatrist in an asylum, falls in love with "Dr. Edwardes" (Gregory Peck), its newly hired director. She soon learns that he is actually a mental patient with a pathological fear of parallel lines and the colour white, and may also be an amnesiac imposter, "John Ballantine," accused of having killed the real Dr. Edwardes. Constance is convinced of the young man's innocence and, with the help of her former professor, Dr. Brulov (Michael Chekhov), analyses his strange dreams. Together they uncover the repressed trauma at the root of "J.B."'s condition, and identify Dr. Edwardes' true killer.

• • •

John Ballantine and Brulov. J.B. begins to talk.

J.B.
I can't make out just what sort of a place it was – although it was supposed to be a gambling house. There weren't any walls – just a lot of curtains hanging. With eyes painted on them. They were sitting at tables playing cards. But the cards were blank. And there was one man who came in holding a large pair of scissors. He started walking around the room cutting the drapes in half. And then a girl with hardly anything on slid down a long chute that led into the gambling room and started walking around kissing everybody.

Brulov
Did you recognize this kissing bug?

J.B.
She looked a little like Constance.

Brulov
Aha! This is plain, ordinary wishful dreaming. Go on.

J.B.
I was sitting in a corner playing cards with – with a man who had a beard. I was dealing him cards, turning them up one at a time. And he said, "I'll take another." I dealt another – the seven of clubs. Then he said, "That makes twenty-one. I win." Just as soon as he said this the proprietor came in – sliding down the chute – and accused him of cheating. The proprietor yelled, "I won't allow you to play here. This is my place. And if you try any more cheating, I'll fix you."

Brulov is sipping his coffee. Constance writes in a notebook.

J.B. (to Constance)
I'm sorry about that kissing bug.

Constance
I'm glad you didn't dream of me as an eggbeater – as one of my patients did.

J.B.
Why – what would that mean?

Constance
Never mind.

• • •

J.B.
Does it make sense to you, what I dreamed?

Constance
Not yet. You were trying to tell yourself something. What it is, we'll figure out later.

J.B.
There was a lot more to it.

Brulov
Go on – and try to recall the details – the more cockeyed the better for the scientific side.

J.B.
I was standing on a high place – a sloping roof on top of a high building. The wind was blowing a gale. And he was there. The man with the beard. He was standing on the edge of the roof leaning over into space as if he were going to plunge over any minute. I was frightened stiff. I couldn't move. I yelled at him to watch out. But the wind swept the words away. He stood there leaning over more and more. I knew he was going to fall but I couldn't do anything. Then he went over slowly – his feet in the air. I saw a man hiding behind a tall chimney. He had a mask on. And he laughed. He was holding a small wheel in his hand. I watched the wheel drop on the roof and – I tried to yell at him. But he laughed and disappeared.

Constance
Do you remember now who the man in the mask was?

J.B.
It – it was the proprietor from the gambling house. I remember now.

Constance (eagerly)
Why do you remember that now?

J.B.
Because of what he said. I remember him yelling at me, before he disappeared, that everything was now fixed.

Brulov
We will ask questions later, Constance. We are mixed up enough now.
(to J.B.)
Did something happen after the man fell off the roof?

J.B.
Yes – it got more and more confused.

The three figures begin receding as he continues.

● ● ●

J.B.
I don't remember how I got there, but I was in a ballroom. The dancers were dressed in white suits – and pretending to dance, but not moving. An orchestra was in the corner – dressed in white fur hats. And Dr. Brulov was leading it. They were playing "The Snow Maiden," by Rimsky-Korsakov. I was talking to Constance, and asking her to dance. She had a dance card and asked me to write my name in it. I refused, and grabbed her and started dancing – rather wildly. We danced out of the ballroom and I kissed her.

Brulov
And while you were kissing her she held up the dance card again and asked you to put your name in it?

J.B. (surprised)
How do you know?

Brulov
When you have been an analyst for thirty-five years, you can see upside down, inside out. The only time I am confused is when something makes sense. Go on. You started running away.

J.B.
That's right. The dance card kept getting bigger – it was full of names and addresses. And Constance seemed to turn into a statue. I started running, and the statue started chasing me. I ran down a huge slope. And I

heard something beating over my head. It was wings. The statue had wings. I couldn't see them – but a shadow kept hitting me. The statue was flying after me and holding a big book out in its hands. It was almost ready to grab me when I came to the bottom of the hill and started running up another hill.

• • •

The three again.

J.B.
I must have escaped – I don't remember now. That's all there was. I woke up and saw Dr. Brulov.

N.B.-P.

Salvador Dalí for Spellbound, 1945

William Cameron Menzies, *Spellbound,* 1945

Spellbound, 1945

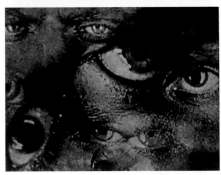

Fritz Lang, *Metropolis,* 1926–1927

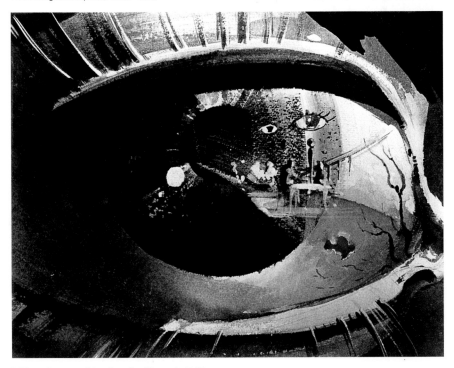

William Cameron Menzies, *Spellbound,* 1945

Salvador Dalí, *Study for the dream sequence in* Spellbound, 1944

Salvador Dalí (under the supervision of), *Set design for* Spellbound, 1945

Salvador Dalí tracing chalk outline of path of giant scissors on scenic "Eye" backdrop for Spellbound, 1945

Salvador Dalí, *The Eye,* 1944

Salvador Dalí (for Alfred Hitchcock), *Spellbound*, 1945

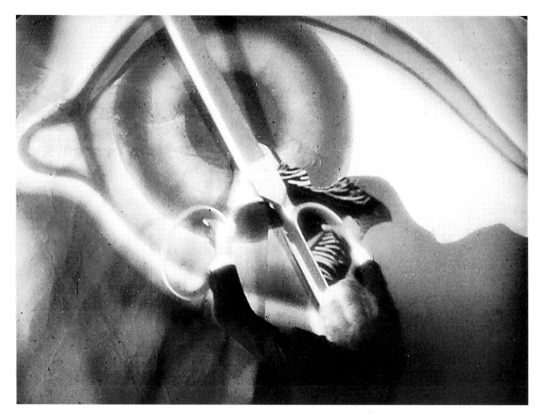

The dream sequence (Spellbound), 1945

Luis Buñuel, *Frame enlargement from the prologue to* Un chien andalou, 1929

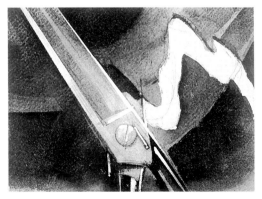

William Cameron Menzies, *Spellbound,* 1945

Spellbound, 1945

*Rhonda Fleming on gaming house set
during shooting of the dream sequence
(Spellbound),* 1945

Kurt Seligmann, *Ultrameuble,* 1938

Salvador Dalí, *Drawing for* Spellbound,
1944

Man Ray, *Object of Destruction,*
[1923]–1966

Spellbound, 1945

Spellbound, 1945

The dream sequence (Spellbound), 1945

Spellbound, 1945

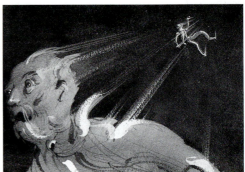

Max Ernst, *Two Children Are Threatened by a Nightingale,*
1924

Ingrid Bergman for Spellbound, 1945

The ballroom from the dream sequence (Spellbound), 1945

Salvador Dalí, *Untitled, Study for the ballroom from the dream sequence in* Spellbound, 1944

William Cameron Menzies, *Spellbound,* 1945

Gregory Peck and Ingrid Bergman during the ballroom scene (Spellbound), 1945

Alfred Hitchcock directing Ingrid Bergman and Gregory Peck (Spellbound), 1945

Ingrid Bergman transformed into a statue (Spellbound), 1945

Salvador Dalí, *Study for the dream sequence in* Spellbound, 1944

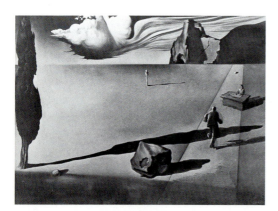

William Cameron Menzies, *Spellbound,* 1945

Ingrid Bergman transformed into a statue (Spellbound), 1945

Ingrid Bergman transformed into a statue (Spellbound), 1945

Ingrid Bergman transformed into a statue (Spellbound), 1945

Statue modelled on Ingrid Bergman's body (Spellbound), 1945

Salvador Dalí, *Untitled, Drawing for statue sequences*, 1944

Salvador Dalí, *Study for the dream sequence in* Spellbound, 1944

Spellbound, 1945

Spellbound, 1945

Spellbound, 1945

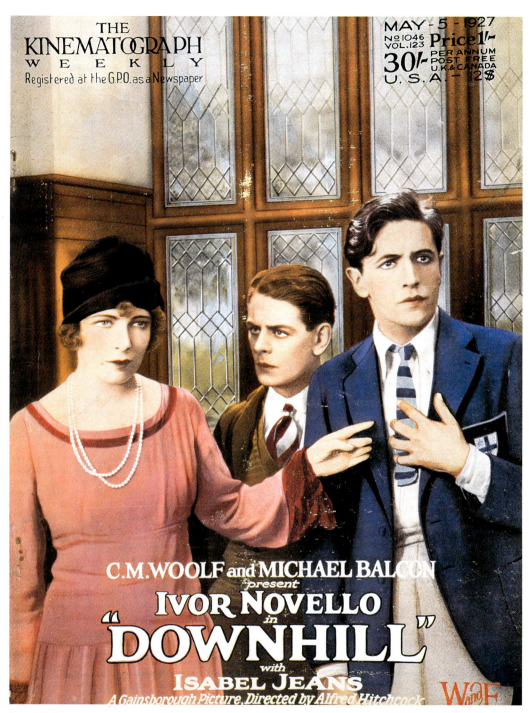

Downhill, *Cover page advertisement,* Kinematograph Weekly, 1927 (5 May)

Unsigned, *Les cheveux d'or (The Lodger: A Story of the London Fog),* 1927

Unsigned, *Le rideau déchiré (Torn Curtain),* 1966

Unsigned, *Frenzy,* 1972

Eryk Lipinski, *Akt oskarżenia (The Paradine Case),* 1947

Guy Jouineau and Guy Bourduge, *Sabotage,* 1936

Unsigned, *I prigionièri dell'ocèano (Lifeboat),* 1944

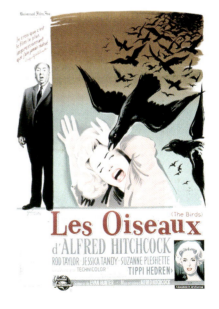

Boris Grinsson, *Les oiseaux (The Birds),* 1963

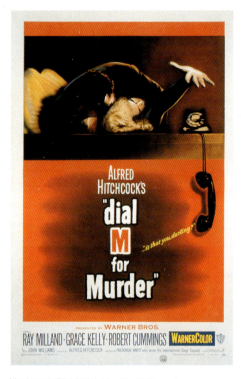

Unsigned, *Dial M for Murder,* 1954

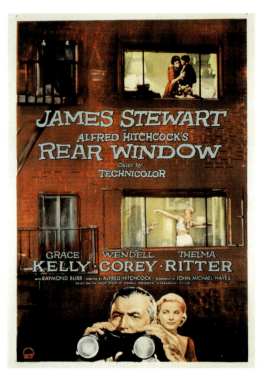

Unsigned, *Rear Window,* 1954

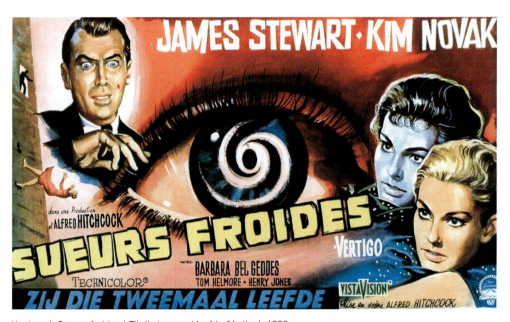

Unsigned, *Sueurs froides / Zij die tweemal leefde (Vertigo),* 1958

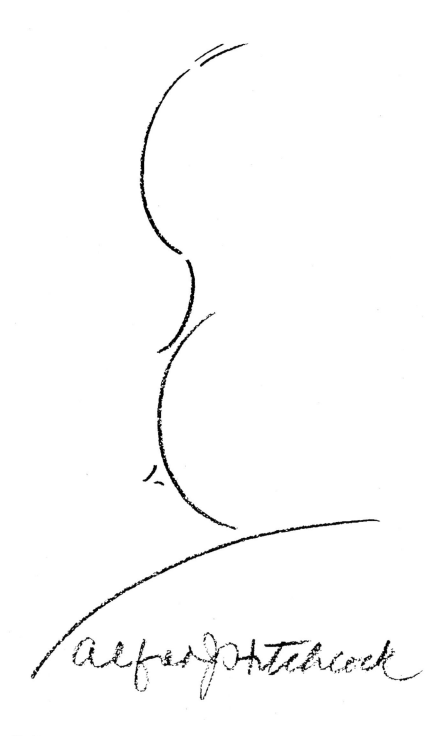

Alfred Hitchcock, *Self-Portrait*

Chronology

Alfred Hitchcock was born in London in 1899. He was the son of a wholesale grocer and the youngest of three children. He attended a Jesuit school.

When his father died in 1914, he left the Jesuits and entered the School of Engineering and Navigation. At the age of nineteen, he took an office job with a company that manufactured electrical cable and telegraph wire. During the same period, he attended drawing classes at the University of London, which enabled him to transfer to the company's advertising department. Soon after, he secured a position as graphic artist in the editorial department of the American film company Famous Players–Lasky.

From 1920 to 1922, Hitchcock made drawings and sets, then directed *Number Thirteen,* which remained unfinished for lack of funds. At this time, he met film editor and script girl Alma Reville, whom he later married and whose name appeared in the credits of Hitchcock movies for many years. Only death separated this apparently happily married couple.

In 1924, German producer Erich Pommer invited Hitchcock to Berlin, where he met F.W. Murnau. This meeting was of capital importance to his development, for Murnau, a major figure in the German silent movie tradition, unquestionably contributed to the Symbolist, metaphysical and dream dimension of Hitchcock's work.

In 1925, he directed his first movie, *The Pleasure Garden* (released 1927). But it was *The Lodger: A Story of the London Fog* (1927), a variation on the Jack the Ripper story, that foreshadowed the greatness to come.

The visual narrative technique and attention to lighting he inherited from German cinema were confirmed in *Blackmail* (1929) and *Murder!* (1930). But it was Hitchcock's next two movies that clearly demonstrated his mastery: *The Thirty-nine Steps* (1935) and *The Lady Vanishes* (1938). Combining humour and suspense, both of these films were box-office successes that opened Hollywood's doors to the British director.

His American period began auspiciously with *Rebecca* (1940), made at the instigation of David O. Selznick. Hitchcock then settled in Hollywood. *Rebecca* was followed by spy movies (*Notorious,* 1946), crime thrillers (*Rope,* 1948; *Strangers on a Train,* 1951) and black comedies (*The Trouble with Harry,* 1955).

Then came the visual – and philosophical – sophistication of the mature masterpieces, as Hitchcock the creator assumed the full power of his artistry. At the same time, his conception of the hero became clouded for lack of guidelines in the postwar years. The mature work is contemporary with that of Robert Bresson, Michelangelo Antonioni, Roberto Rossellini, Ingmar Bergman and even Jean-Luc Godard (whose first movie, *À bout de souffle,* was made in 1959). Hitchcock made in succession *Dial M for Murder* (1954), *Rear Window* (1954), *The Man Who Knew Too Much* (remake, 1956), *Vertigo* (1958), *North by Northwest* (1959), *Psycho* (1960), *The Birds* (1963) and *Marnie* (1964).

At the age of seventy-six, Alfred Hitchcock made his last movie, a comedy entitled *Family Plot* (released 1976).

He died in Hollywood in 1980.

Police station, Leytonstone, 1911

William Hitchcock with son Alfred in front of the family business, about 1906

Alfred Hitchcock and Alma Reville, mid 1920s

Alfred Hitchcock with actors. Left to right: Standing: Jameson Thomas, Gibb McLaughlin, Alfred Hitchcock, Ian Hunter and Carl Brisson; Seated: Dorothy Boyd, Lilian Hall-Davies, Estelle Brodig and Eve Gray

Madeleine Carroll with Alma and Alfred Hitchcock, 1935

Alfred Hitchcock and Alma (centre) at work

Ada, Jack and Alfred Hitchcock at Shoreham, 1923

Alfred Hitchcock and Alma, about 1926

Alfred, Alma and Pat Hitchcock aboard the Queen Mary *at Southampton en route for America,* 1939

Alfred Hitchcock during the making of Rebecca, 1940

Philippe Halsman, *Alma Reville,* 1962

Alfred Hitchcock, Ingrid Bergman and Edith Head during pre-production on Notorious, 1946

Cary Grant and Alfred Hitchcock during shooting of Suspicion, 1941

Philippe Halsman, *Alfred Hitchcock and François Truffaut,* 1962

Elliott Erwitt, *Alfred Hitchcock and Vera Miles during the making of* The Wrong Man, 1956

Alfred Hitchcock showing Ingrid Bergman around an English town during shooting of Under Capricorn, 1949

Marlene Dietrich and Alfred Hitchcock during shooting of Stage Fright, 1950

Alfred Hitchcock preparing for his cameo
appearance in Marnie, 1964

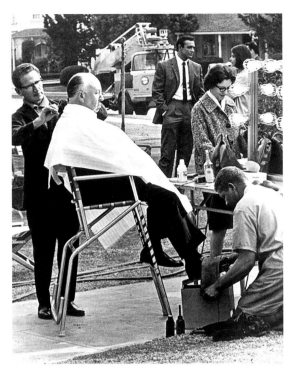

Alfred Hitchcock in Paris

Portrait of Alfred Hitchcock, publicity still for his television show Alfred Hitchcock Presents *or* The Alfred Hitchcock Hour, *1960s*

Alfred Hitchcock receiving an honorary degree from Columbia University, New York, 1972

Filmography

Great Britain

The Pleasure Garden (prod. 1925/rel. 1927)
The Mountain Eagle (prod. 1925/rel. 1927)
The Lodger: A Story of the London Fog (prod. 1926/ rel. 1927)
Downhill (prod./rel. 1927)
Easy Virtue (prod./rel. 1927)
The Ring (prod./rel. 1927)
The Farmer's Wife (prod. 1927/rel. 1928)
Champagne (prod./rel. 1928)
The Manxman (prod. 1928/rel. 1929)
Blackmail (prod./rel. 1929)
Juno and the Paycock (prod./rel. 1930)
Murder! (prod./rel. 1930)
The Skin Game (prod. 1930–1931/rel. 1931)
Number Seventeen (prod. 1931/rel. 1932)
Rich and Strange (prod./rel. 1932)
Waltzes from Vienna (prod./rel. 1933)
The Man Who Knew Too Much [original version] (prod./rel. 1934)
The Thirty-nine Steps (prod./rel. 1935)
Secret Agent (prod. 1935/rel. 1936)
Sabotage (prod./rel. 1936)
Young and Innocent (prod. 1937/rel. 1938)
The Lady Vanishes (prod. 1937/rel. 1938)
Jamaica Inn (prod. 1938/rel. 1939)
Aventure malgache (1944)
Bon voyage (1944)
Under Capricorn (prod. 1948/rel. 1949)
Stage Fright (prod. 1949/rel. 1950)
Frenzy (prod. 1971/rel. 1972)

The United States

Rebecca (prod. 1939/rel. 1940)
Foreign Correspondent (prod./rel. 1940)
Mr. and Mrs. Smith (prod. 1940/rel. 1941)
Suspicion (prod./rel. 1941)
Saboteur (prod./rel. 1942)
Shadow of a Doubt (prod. 1942/rel. 1943)
Lifeboat (prod. 1943/rel. 1944)
Spellbound (prod. 1944/rel. 1945)
Notorious (prod. 1945–1946/rel. 1946)
The Paradine Case (prod. 1946–1947/rel. 1947)
Rope (prod./rel. 1948)
Strangers on a Train (prod. 1950/rel. 1951)
I Confess (prod. 1952/rel. 1953)
Dial M for Murder (prod. 1953/rel. 1954)
Rear Window (prod. 1953/rel. 1954)
To Catch a Thief (prod. 1954/rel. 1955)
The Trouble with Harry (prod. 1954/rel. 1955)
The Man Who Knew Too Much [remake] (prod. 1955/ rel. 1956)
The Wrong Man (prod./rel. 1956)
Vertigo (prod. 1957/rel. 1958)
North by Northwest (prod. 1958/rel. 1959)
Psycho (prod. 1959–1960/rel. 1960)
The Birds (prod. 1962/rel. 1963)
Marnie (prod. 1963–1964/rel. 1964)
Torn Curtain (prod. 1965–1966/rel. 1966)
Topaz (prod. 1968–1969/rel. 1969)
Family Plot (prod. 1975/rel. 1976)

Select Bibliography

ON ALFRED HITCHCOCK

Books

AUILER, Dan. *Hitchcock's Notebooks: An Authorized and Illustrated Look inside the Creative Mind of Alfred Hitchcock.* New York: Spike, 1999.

AUILER, Dan. *Vertigo: The Making of a Hitchcock Classic,* foreword by Martin Scorsese. New York: St. Martin's Press, 1998.

AUZEL, Dominique. *Alfred Hitchcock.* Toulouse: Milan, 1988.

BARR, Charles. *English Hitchcock.* Moffat, Scotland: Cameron & Hollis, 1999.

BAZIN, André. *Le cinéma de la cruauté. Eric von Stroheim, Carl Th. Dreyer, Preston Sturges, Luis Buñuel, Alfred Hitchcock, Akira Kurosawa.* Paris: Flammarion, 1975.

BOGDANOVICH, Peter. *Who the Devil Made It: Conversations with Legendary Film Directors.* New York: Ballantine Books, 1998.

BOUZEREAU, Laurent. *The Alfred Hitchcock Quote Book.* New York: Carol Publishing Group, 1993.

BRAUDY, Leo. "Hitchcock, Truffaut, and the Irresponsible Audience," *Focus on Hitchcock,* Albert J. La Valley (ed.). Englewood Cliffs, N.J.: Prentice-Hall, 1972.

BRILL, Lesley. *The Hitchcock Romance: Love and Irony in Hitchcock's Films.* Princeton, N.J.: Princeton University Press, 1988.

CHABROL, Claude and Éric ROHMER. *Hitchcock,* pref. Dominique Rabourdin. Paris: Éditions Universitaires, 1957, repr. 1993.

CONDON, Paul and Jim SANGSTER. *The Complete Hitchcock.* London: Virgin, 1999.

HITCHCOCK, Alfred. "Direction," *Footnotes to the Film,* Charles Davy (ed.). New York: Arno Press and The New York Times, 1970.

DEUTELBAUM, Marshall and Leland POAGUE. *A Hitchcock Reader.* Ames: Iowa State University Press, 1986.

DOUCHET, Jean. *Alfred Hitchcock.* Paris: L'Herne, 1967.

DOUCHET, Jean. *Hitchcock.* Paris: L'Herne, 1985.

DOUCHET, Jean. *Hitchcock.* Paris: Cahiers du cinéma, 1999.

DURGNAT, Raymond. *The Strange Case of Alfred Hitchcock: Or, The Plain Man's Hitchcock.* London: Faber & Faber, 1974.

FALLACI, Oriana. *Limelighters,* trans. Pamela Swinglehurst. London: Michael Joseph, 1963.

FINLER, Joel W. *Alfred Hitchcock: The Hollywood Years.* London: B.T. Batsford, 1992.

FREEDMAN, Jonathan and Richard H. MILLINGTON. *Hitchcock's America.* New York: Oxford University Press, 1999.

FREEMAN, David. *The Last Days of Alfred Hitchcock: A Memoir Featuring the Screenplay of "Alfred Hitchcock's The Short Night."* Woodstock, N.Y: The Overlook Press, 1984.

GORDON, Douglas. *A Feature Film.* London: Artangel Afterlives, Book Works and Galerie du Jour–Agnès B. London: 1999.

GOTTLIEB, Sidney. *Hitchcock on Hitchcock: Selected Writings and Interviews.* Berkeley: University of California Press, 1995.

HARRIS, Robert A. and Michael S. LASKY. *The Complete Films of Alfred Hitchcock.* Secaucus, N.J.: Citadel Press, 1976.

KAGANSKY, Serge. *Alfred Hitchcock.* Paris: Hazan, 1997.

KAPS, Emmanuelle. *Alfred Hitchcock (1899-1980), Symboles et symbolisme.* Master's thesis under the dir. of Jean-Philippe Chimot, Université de Paris-I, 1996.

KAPSIS, Robert E. *Hitchcock: The Making of a Reputation.* Chicago: University of Chicago Press, 1992.

KROHN, Bill. *Hitchcock at Work.* London: Phaidon Press, 2000.

Le siècle d'Hitchcock. Paris: L'Étoile, 1999.

LEFEBVRE, Martin. Psycho, *de la figure au musée imaginaire, Théorie et pratique de l'acte de spectature.* Montréal: Harmattan, 1997.

LEFF, Leonard J. *Hitchcock and Selznick: The Rich and Strange Collaboration of Alfred Hitchcock and David O. Selznick in Hollywood.* Berkeley: University of California Press, 1987, repr. 1999.

LEITCH, Thomas M. *Find the Director and Other Hitchcock Games.* Athens: University of Georgia Press, 1991.

MODELSKI, Tania. *The Women Who Knew Too Much: Hitchcock and Feminist Theory.* New York: Methuen, 1988.

NARBONI, Jean, ed. *Alfred Hitchcock.* Paris: L'Étoile, 1982.

NOURMAND, Tony and Mark H. WOLFF. *Hitchcock Poster Art from the Mark H. Wolff Collection,* graphic design by Graham Marsh and text by Mark H. Wolff. London: Aurum Press, 1999.

PAGLIA, Camille. *The Birds.* London: British Film Institute, 1998.

REBELLO, Stephen. *Alfred Hitchcock and the Making of* Psycho. London: Marion Boyars, 1998.

ROTHMAN, William. *Hitchcock: The Murderous Gaze.* Cambridge, Mass.: Harvard University Press, 1982.

RYALL, Tom. *Alfred Hitchcock and the British Cinema.* Urbana: University of Illinois Press, 1986.

RYALL, Tom. *Blackmail.* London: British Film Institute, 1993.

SAMUELS, Charles Thomas. *Encountering Directors.* New York: G.P. Putnam's Sons, 1972.

SARRIS, Andrew. "Alfred Hitchcock," *The American Cinema: Directors and Directions, 1929–1968.* New York: Dutton, 1968.

SLOAN, Jane. *Alfred Hitchcock: A Filmography and Bibliography.* Berkeley: University of California Press, 1995.

SPOTO, Donald. *The Art of Alfred Hitchcock: Fifty Years of His Motion Pictures.* New York: Hopkinson and Blake, 1976.

SPOTO, Donald. *The Art of Alfred Hitchcock: Fifty Years of His Motion Pictures,* 2d ed., completely rev. and updated. New York: Doubleday, 1992.

SPOTO, Donald. *The Dark Side of Genius: The Life of Alfred Hitchcock.* New York: Ballantine Books, 1983, repr. 1994.

STERRITT, David. *The Films of Alfred Hitchcock.* Cambridge, England: Cambridge University Press, 1993.

TAYLOR, John Russell. *Hitch: The Life and Times of Alfred Hitchcock.* Boston: Faber & Faber, 1978, repr. New York: Da Capo Press, 1996.

TRUFFAUT, François, with the collaboration of Helen G. SCOTT. *Hitchcock,* rev. ed. New York: Simon & Schuster, 1984.

TRUFFAUT, François. *Le cinéma selon Hitchcock.* Paris: Laffont, 1966.

TRUFFAUT, François. *Les films de ma vie.* Paris: Flammarion, 1975.

VANOYE, F. "Histoires de couteaux ou Comment détailler les femmes (Dostoievski, Conrad, Hitchcock)," *Cinéma et Littérature, Cahiers du RITM.* Paris: Université de Paris-X, 1999.

VILLIEN, Bruno. *Hitchcock.* Paris: Colona, 1982, repr. Paris: Rivages, 1985.

WOOD, Robin. *Hitchcock's Films Revisited.* New York: Columbia University Press, 1989, repr. London: Faber & Faber, 1991.

YACOWAR, Maurice. *Hitchcock's British Films.* Hamden, Conn.: Archon Books, 1977.

ZIZEK, Slavoj (ed.). *Everything You Always Wanted to Know About Lacan (But Were Afraid to Ask Hitchcock).* London and New York: Verso, 1992.

Articles

ALBERA, François. "La position du voyageur couché: Hitchcock avec Klossowski." *Cinémathèque,* No. 15, Spring 1999.

ARNAUD, Philippe. "L'engendrement des images: *Vertigo* d'Alfred Hitchcock." *Cinémathèque,* No. 13, Fall 1995.

DELVAUX, Claudine. "Propositions pour un système des objets (en gros plan) chez Alfred Hitchcock." *Revue belge du cinéma,* No. 10, Winter 1984–1985.

DEMONSABLON, Philippe. "Lexique mythologique pour l'œuvre de Hitchcock." *Cahiers du Cinéma,* No. 62, Aug.–Sept. 1966.

"Directed by Alfred Hitchcock." *Revue belge du cinéma,* No. 9, Fall 1984.

GARRETT, Greg. "Hitchcock's Women on Hitchcock: A Panel Discussion with Janet Leigh, Tippi Hedren, Karen Black, Suzanne Pleshette and Eva Marie Saint." *Literature/Film Quarterly,* Vol. 27, No. 2, 1999.

McGILLIGAN, Patrick. "Alfred Hitchcock: Before the Flickers." *Film Comment,* Vol. 35, No. 4, July–Aug. 1999.

MATHER, Philippe. "Les raccords cachés dans *La corde* d'Alfred Hitchcock." *Cinémathèque,* No. 3, Spring 1993.

SALT, Barry. "From Caligari to Who?" *Sight and Sound,* Vol. 48, No. 2, 1979.

SIMOND, Clotilde. "Du Mac Guffin dans les images: *Zabriskie Point,* Michelangelo Antonioni, *North by Northwest.*" *Cinémathèque,* No. 15, Spring 1999.

VAN WERT, William F. "Compositional Psychoanalysis: Circles and Straight Lines in *Spellbound.*" *Film Criticism,* Vol. 3, Spring 1979.

WOOD, Robin. "Normes et variations: *Les trente-neuf marches* et *Jeune et innocent.*" *Tausend Augen,* No. 16, Spring 1995.

Special issue, *Cahiers du cinéma,* No. 537, July–Aug. 1999.

Special issue, *Les inrockuptibles,* No. 216, 13–19 Oct. 1999.

ON CINEMA

Books

AUMONT, Jacques. *L'œil interminable: cinéma et peinture.* Paris: Séguier, 1995.

AUMONT, Jacques, ed. *La couleur en cinéma.* Paris: Cinémathèque française, 1995.

BONITZER, Pascal. *Peinture et cinéma, Décadrages.* Paris: Cahiers du cinéma/L'Étoile, 1987.

DANTO, Arthur. *After the End of the Art: Contemporary Art and the Pale of History.* Princeton: Princeton University Press, 1997.

EBERWEIN, Robert T. *Film & the Dream Screen: A Sleep and a Forgetting.* Princeton: Princeton University Press, 1984.

GOULD, Michael. *Surrealism and the Cinema (Open Eye Screening).* Cranbury, N.J.: A.S. Barnes and Company, 1976.

KUENZLI, Rudolf E. *Dada and Surrealist Film.* Cambridge: Mass. and London: The MIT Press, 1996.

KYROU, Ado. *Le surréalisme au cinéma.* Paris: Arcanes, 1953.

KYROU, Ado. *Le surréalisme au cinéma.* Paris: Ramsay and Le Terrain vague, 1985.

MacCABE, Colin. *Godard: Images, Sounds, Politics.* London: British Film Institute, 1980.

PAÏNI, Dominique. *Le cinéma, un art moderne,* foreword by Hubert Damisch. Paris: Cahiers du cinéma, 1997.

SCHMIED, Wieland. *Neue Sachlichkeit und magischer Realismus in Deutschland, 1918-1933.* Hannover: Fackelträger Verlag, 1969.

DALLE VACCHE, Angela. *Cinema and Painting: How Art Is Used in Film.* Austin: University of Texas Press, 1996.
VIRMAUX, Alain and Odette. *Les surréalistes et le cinéma, Anthologie.* Paris: Seghers, 1976.

Articles
BIGWOOD, James. "Salvador Dalí, Reluctant Film Maker. A Portrait of the Artist Portraying Himself." *American Film,* Vol. 5, No. 2, Nov. 1979.
URRUTIA, Antonio. "Dalí and the Cinema, Homage to Salvador Dalí." *XXe siècle Review,* Special Issue, New York, 1980.

Exhibition Catalogues
Art and Film since 1945: Hall of Mirrors. Los Angeles: Museum of Contemporary Art, 1996.
Cinéma Cinéma. Contemporary Art and the Cinema Experience. Eindhoven: Stedelijk Van Abbe Museum, 1999.
David Reed Paintings Motion Pictures. San Diego: Museum of Contemporary Art, 1998.
Douglas Gordon. Hannover: Kunstverein Hannover, 1998.
Figures du moderne, 1905-1919, L'expressionnisme en Allemagne. Paris: Musée d'art moderne, 1992.

L'effet cinéma. Montréal: Musée d'art contemporain de Montréal, 1996.
Lost Paradise: Symbolist Europe. Montréal: The Montreal Museum of Fine Arts, 1995.
Notorious: Alfred Hitchcock and Contemporary Art. Oxford: Museum of Modern Art Oxford, 1999.
Peinture cinéma peinture, Direction des musées de Marseille. Paris: Hazan, 1989.
Robert Natkin. Recent Paintings from Hitchcock Series. New York: Gimpel & Weitzenhoffer, 1985.
Salvador Dalí: The Early Years. London: Southbank Centre, 1994.
Salvador Dalí. Rétrospective. Paris: Centre Georges-Pompidou, Musée national d'art moderne, 1979.
Spellbound: Art and Film. London: British Film Institute and Hayward Gallery, 1996.
Stan Douglas. Monodrama and Loops. Vancouver: UBC Fine Arts Gallery, 1992.
The Director's Eye: Drawings and Photographs by European Film Makers. Oxford: Museum of Modern Art Oxford, 1996.
Surrealistas, surrealismo y cinema. Barcelona: Cultural Centre of the La Caixa Foundation, 1991.
Vertigo. Paris: Thaddaus Ropac, 1991.

List of Works Illustrated

"Yet each man kills the thing he loves"
(Oscar Wilde)

Alberto Martini
Italian, 1876–1954
The Oval Portrait
Illustration for the story by Edgar Allan Poe (1842)
1905–1907
India ink on cardboard
25 x 18 cm
Milan, private collection

F. Fizzi
Jack the Ripper
"John Saunders Reeves, dock labourer,
finds the body of Martha Tabram on the landing
at 37 George Yard Buildings – the first certain victim
(possibly No. 3)"
Frontispiece of *Famous Crimes*, Vol. II, No. 15
1888
Photographic document
London, Mary Evans Picture Library
10011758/09

R. Taylor
Jack the Ripper
"Self-appointed 'vigilantes' in the East End
of London look suspiciously at a dubious-looking
passer-by"
Illustrated London News
1888
Photographic document
London, Mary Evans Picture Library
10011756/0

Dr. Crippen is hanged at Pentonville prison,
London
Le petit journal
1910 (23 November)
Photographic document
London, Mary Evans Picture Library
10027010/06

Anonymous
Dr. Hawley Harvey Crippen (1862–1910) and his
mistress Ethel Le Neve in the witness box
1910
Photographic document
London, Mary Evans Picture Library
10046436/03

Albert Goodwin
British, 1845–1932
Saint Paul's from the South
1898
Oil on canvas
95.3 x 143.5 cm
The Montreal Museum of Fine Arts
1908.60

George Earle
British, 1824–1908
Going North, King's Cross Station
About 1890
Oil on canvas
97 x 176 cm
York, National Railway Museum
1995-7843

Dante Gabriele Rossetti
British, 1828–1882
Salutatio Beatricis (The Salutation of Beatrice)
1859
Oil on panel (frame designed by the artist)
75.9 x 80.9 cm (each of two panels)
Ottawa, National Gallery of Canada
NGC 6750

Anonymous
British
Three Eyes
Early 19th century
Watercolour on ivory, watercolour on vellum,
watercolour on vellum
1 cm (diam.), 1.8 cm (diam.),
1 cm (diam. of ring without frame)
The Cleveland Museum of Art,
gift of Mr. and Mrs. John W. Starr
1961.327, 1961.328, 1961.330

Edward Burne-Jones
British, 1833–1898
Fides
1872
Tempera and gouache on panel
178.1 x 63.2 cm
Vancouver Art Gallery, Founders Fund
VAG 34.16

Ingrid Bergman in Under Capricorn
Prod.: 1948 / Rel.: 1949
Frame enlargement
Paris, Cinémathèque française collection
© Transatlantic Pictures

Ingrid Bergman and Joseph Cotten in Under Capricorn
Prod.: 1948 / Rel.: 1949
Frame enlargement
Paris, Cinémathèque française collection
© Transatlantic Pictures

Dante Gabriele Rossetti
British, 1828–1882
Bocca Baciata (Lips That Have Been Kissed)
1859
Oil on panel
32.2 x 27.1 cm
Museum of Fine Arts, Boston,
gift of James Lawrence
1980.261

Julia Margaret Cameron
British, born in India, 1815–1879
The Three Sisters (Love, Peace and Faith)
1868
Albumen silver print
32.6 x 23.7 cm
Bath, The Royal Photographic Society Collection
RPS 2192/1

Julia Margaret Cameron
British, born in India, 1815–1879
The Angel at the Tomb
1869
Albumen silver print
58.4 x 45.9 cm
Bath, The Royal Photographic Society Collection
RPS 2289/2

Walter Bird
Ingrid Bergman in Under Capricorn
Prod.: 1948 / Rel.: 1949
Gelatin silver print
Bath, The Royal Photographic Society Collection
© Transatlantic Pictures

Julia Margaret Cameron
British, born in India, 1815–1879
Alethea
1872
Albumen silver print
51 x 41 cm
Bath, The Royal Photographic Society Collection
RPS 2287/3

Roger Furse
British, 1903–1972
Under Capricorn
Prod.: 1948 / Rel.: 1949
Costume design for Ingrid Bergman
Watercolour and pencil on paper
57 x 39.5 cm
Paris, BIFI (Bibliothèque du film)
© Transatlantic Pictures

Roger Furse
British, 1903–1972
Under Capricorn
Prod.: 1948 / Rel.: 1949
Costume design for Ingrid Bergman
Watercolour and pencil on paper
56 x 38 cm
Paris, BIFI (Bibliothèque du film)
© Transatlantic Pictures

Roger Furse
British, 1903–1972
Under Capricorn
Prod.: 1948 / Rel.: 1949
Hairstyle concept for Ingrid Bergman
Pencil on paper
37 x 29 cm
Paris, BIFI (Bibliothèque du film)
© Transatlantic Pictures

Walter Bird
Ingrid Bergman in Under Capricorn
Prod.: 1948 / Rel.: 1949
Gelatin silver print
Bath, The Royal Photographic Society Collection
© Transatlantic Pictures

Ingrid Bergman in Under Capricorn
Prod.: 1948 / Rel.: 1949
Frame enlargement
Paris, Cinémathèque française collection
© Transatlantic Pictures

Ingrid Bergman in Under Capricorn
Prod.: 1948 / Rel.: 1949
Frame enlargement
Paris, Cinémathèque française collection
© Transatlantic Pictures

Dante Gabriele Rossetti
British, 1828–1882
Proserpine
1877
Coloured chalk on paper
119.5 x 56 cm
Private collection, courtesy of Peter Nahum,
The Leicester Galleries

***Kim Novak for* Vertigo**
Prod.: 1957 / Rel.: 1958
Promotional still
Courtesy of the Academy of Motion Picture Arts
and Sciences
© 1958 Universal City Studios, Inc.
All rights reserved
Courtesy of Universal Studios Licensing, Inc.

George Frederic Watts
British, 1817–1904
Love and Death
About 1874–1877
Oil on canvas
248.9 x 116.8 cm
University of Manchester, The Whitworth Art Gallery

William Blake Richmond
British, 1842–1921
***Sleep and Death Carrying the Body of Sarpedon
into Lycia***
About 1875–1876
Oil on canvas
233.7 x 88.9 cm
Vancouver Museum
PA 104

Alberto Martini
Italian, 1876–1954
The Raven
Illustration for the poem by Edgar Allan Poe (1845)
1906
India ink on cardboard
18.5 cm (diam.)
Milan, private collection

Aubrey Beardsley
British, 1872–1898
The Black Cat
The Fall of the House of Usher
Illustrations for the stories by Edgar Allan Poe
(1843 and 1839)
From *The Uncollected Work of Aubrey Beardsley*
(London: John Lane, The Bodley Head Ltd.;
New York: Dodd, Mead and Company, 1925)
29.3 x 23.5 cm (each)
The Montreal Museum of Fine Arts

Arthur Rackham
British, 1867–1939
William Wilson
Unused illustration for the story
by Edgar Allan Poe (1839)
1933
Ink and watercolour on paper
23.5 x 17.8 cm
The University of Texas at Austin, Harry Ransom
Humanities Research Center, Art Collection
66.39.29.45
Reproduced with the kind permission
of the Arthur Rackham family

"Scoundrel! impostor! accursed villain! you shall
not – you shall not dog me unto death!"

Arthur Rackham
British, 1867–1939
The Pit and the Pendulum
Illustration for the story by Edgar Allan Poe (1843)
1935
Pen, ink and watercolour on paper
27.4 x 19 cm
The University of Texas at Austin, Harry Ransom
Humanities Research Center, Art Collection
66.39.27.36
Reproduced with the kind permission
of the Arthur Rackham family

"I now noticed the floor, too, which was of stone.
In the centre yawned the circular pit from whose
jaws I had escaped; but it was the only one in
the dungeon."

Alberto Martini
Italian, 1876–1954
The Colloquy of Monos and Una
Illustration for the story by Edgar Allan Poe (1841)
1907
India ink on cardboard
26 x 19 cm
Tischer collection
675/17

Alberto Martini
Italian, 1876–1954
William Wilson
Illustration for the story by Edgar Allan Poe (1839)
1936
India ink on cardboard
27 x 20 cm
Collection Tischer
692/34

Alberto Martini
Italian, 1876–1954
The Raven
Illustration for the poem by Edgar Allan Poe (1845)
About 1907
India ink on paper
36 x 25 cm
Milan, courtesy of Galleria Milano
7061

Alberto Martini
Italian, 1876–1954
The Oval Portrait
Illustration for the story by Edgar Allan Poe (1842)
1908
India ink on cardboard
28.6 x 20.5 cm
Milan, private collection

Alberto Martini
Italian, 1876–1954
The Conversation of Eiros and Charmion
Illustration for the story by Edgar Allan Poe (1839)
1906
India ink on cardboard
28 x 20 cm
Milan, private collection
Photo: Saporetti

Alberto Martini
Italian, 1876–1954
The Gold Bug
Illustration for the story by Edgar Allan Poe (1843)
1909–1910
India ink on cardboard
27 x 19 cm
Milan, private collection

Alberto Martini
Italian, 1876–1954
The Tell-Tale Heart
Illustration for the story by Edgar Allan Poe (1843)
1908
India ink on cardboard
28 x 20 cm
Tischer Collection
673/15

Kim Novak and James Stewart in Vertigo
Prod.: 1957 / Rel.: 1958
Frame enlargement
Paris, Cinémathèque française collection
© 1958 Universal City Studios Inc.
All rights reserved
Courtesy of Universal Studios Licensing, Inc.

Philippe Halsman
Latvian-born American, 1906–1979
Tippi Hedren for The Birds
Prod.: 1962 / Rel.: 1963
Promotional still
Paris, Magnum Photos
© P. Halsman/Magnum Photos
© 1963 Alfred J. Hitchcock Productions, Inc.
All rights reserved
Courtesy of Universal Studios

Odilon Redon
French, 1840–1916
"To Edgar Allan Poe"
Album of six lithographs
1882
Amsterdam, Rijksmuseum
Plate 1: *The Eye, like a Strange Ball that directs itself towards infinity*
26 x 19.6 cm
RP-P-1954-155

Plate 2: *Before the black sun of Melancholy, Lenore appears*
16.8 x 12.7 cm
RP-P-1954-156

Plate 3: *A Mask Sounding the Death Knell*
25.9 x 19.1 cm
RP-P-1954-157

Plate 4: *On the horizon the angel of Certitude, and in the somber heaven a questioning eye*
27.2 x 20.7 cm
RP-P-1954-158

Plate 5: *The breath which leads living creatures is also in the Spheres*
27.1 x 20.7 cm
RP-P-1954-159

Plate 6: *Madness*
14.5 x 20.7 cm
RP-P-1954-160

Anthony Perkins in Psycho
Prod.: 1959–1960 / Rel.: 1960
Frame enlargement
Paris, Cinémathèque française collection
© 1960 Shamley Productions, Inc.
All rights reserved
Courtesy of Universal Studios Licensing, Inc.

Janet Leigh's eye (Psycho)
Prod.: 1959–1960 / Rel.: 1960
Frame enlargement
Paris, Cinémathèque française collection
© 1960 Shamley Productions, Inc.
All rights reserved
Courtesy of Universal Studios Licensing, Inc.

James Guthrie
British, 1874–1952
To the River
The Haunted Palace
Illustrations from *Some Poems of Edgar Poe*
(Shorne, England: Pear Tree Press, 1901-[1908])
27.2 x 21.5 cm; 26.9 x 21.3 cm
Montreal, McGill University, Rare Books
and Special Collections Division
R007240

Gaetano Previati
Italian, 1852–1920
A Descent into the Maelström
Illustration for the story by Edgar Allan Poe (1839)
1890
Charcoal on paper, 44.5 x 38.0 cm
Milan, private collection

Kim Novak in Vertigo
Prod.: 1957 / Rel.: 1958
Frame enlargement
Paris, Cinémathèque française collection
© 1958 Universal City Studios, Inc.
Courtesy of Universal Studios Licensing, Inc.

Anne Grey and John Stuart in Number Seventeen
Prod.: 1931 / Rel.: 1932
Frame enlargement
Paris, Cinémathèque française collection
© Canal + Image International

Nita Naldi in The Pleasure Garden
Prod.: 1925 / Rel.: 1927
Frame enlargement
Paris, Cinémathèque française collection
Courtesy of Carlton International

Fernand Khnopff
Belgian, 1858–1921
Iris
Illustration for the album of poems by Pol de Mont
(Antwerp: J. E. - Buschmann Rijnpoortvest, 1894)
28 x 18 x 6 cm
Paris, Galerie Elstir

Fernand Khnopff
Belgian, 1858–1921
Bruges-la-Morte
About 1892
Chalk and coloured pencil on paper
8.5 x 12.3 cm
Private collection

Victor Burgin
British, b. 1941
The Bridge (detail)
1984
Gelatin silver print, 1/6, 35 x 34 cm

New York, John Weber Gallery
© Victor Burgin
(Not exhibited)

Sir John Everett Millais
British, 1829–1896
Study for Ophelia
1852
Ink on paper
15.2 x 27.9 cm (arched top)
Plymouth City Art Gallery, Alfred A. de Pass
collection, United Kingdom
Plymg. 1926.12.23

Odilon Redon
French, 1840–1916
Ophelia
About 1905
Oil on paper
60 x 44 cm
New York, The Woodner family collection

Willy Schlobach
Belgian, 1864–1951
The Dead Woman
1890
Pastel on paper
62 x 183 cm
Brussels, Bibliothèque Royale de Belgique

Kim Novak pretends to drown herself beneath
the Golden Gate Bridge (Vertigo)
Prod.: 1957 / Rel.: 1958
Production still
Paris, BIFI (Bibliothèque du film)
© 1958 Universal City Studios, Inc.
Courtesy of Universal Studios Licensing, Inc.

Joan Fontaine and Judith Anderson in Rebecca
Prod.: 1939 / Rel.: 1940
Production still
London, The Cinema Museum
© Marie Claire Patin
© Buena Vista International Inc.

Joan Fontaine in Rebecca
Prod.: 1939 / Rel.: 1940
Production still
Courtesy of the Academy of Motion Picture Arts
and Sciences
© Buena Vista International Inc.

Judith Anderson and Joan Fontaine in Rebecca
Prod.: 1939 / Rel.: 1940
Production still
London, The Cinema Museum
© Guy Edmonds
© Buena Vista International Inc.

William Holman Hunt
British, 1827–1910
My Beautiful Lady and *Of My Lady in Death*
Illustrations for poems by Thomas Woolner (1850),
from the frontispiece of the first issue of
*The Germ: Thoughts towards Nature in Poetry,
Literature and Art*
1850 (January)
Etching on chine collé
43.8 x 29.8 cm
Toronto, Art Gallery of Ontario
78/101

Kim Novak in **Vertigo**
Prod.: 1957 / Rel.: 1958
Production still
London, The Cinema Museum
Richard Hamilton
© 1958 Universal City Studios, Inc.
All rights reserved
Courtesy of Universal Studios Licensing, Inc.

**"I don't think I can be labelled
a Catholic artist . . . "**

Georges Rouault
French, 1871–1958
Christ Crucified
About 1939
Oil on canvas
76.9 x 59.5 cm
The Montreal Museum of Fine Arts
1953.1088
© Estate of Georges Rouault/ADAGP (Paris)/
SODRAC (Montreal) 2000

Edvard Munch
Norwegian, 1863–1944
Into the Forest
1915
Lithograph
43.5 x 47 cm
Toronto, Art Gallery of Ontario, gift of Vivian
and David Campbell, 1991
91/61
© The Munch Museum/The Munch-Ellingsen
Group/SODART (Canada) 2000

*Cary Grant and Eva Marie Saint
in* **North by Northwest**
Prod. 1958 / Rel.: 1959
Production still
Courtesy of the Academy of Motion Picture Arts
and Sciences
© Warner Bros.

Maurice Denis
French, 1870–1943
The Solitude of Christ
1918
Oil on canvas
88 x 136 cm
Private collection
© Estate of Maurice Denis/ADAGP (Paris)/
SODRAC (Montreal) 2000

The Manxman
Prod.: 1928 / Rel.: 1929
Production still: Malcolm Keen
London, British Film Institute Collections
© 1929 Canal + Image UK Ltd.

Montgomery Clift in **I Confess**
Prod.: 1952 / Rel.: 1953
Frame enlargement
Paris, Cinémathèque française collection
© Warner Bros.

Stanley Spencer
British, 1891–1959
Christ Carrying the Cross
1920
Oil on canvas
153 x 142.9 cm
London, Tate Gallery
4117
(Not exhibited)

*Ivor Novello, June Tripp and Malcolm Keen
in* **The Lodger: A Story of the London Fog**
Prod.: 1926 / Rel.: 1927
Frame enlargement
Paris, Cinémathèque française collection
Courtesy of Carlton International

Ivor Novello facing the mob **(The Lodger: A Story
of the London Fog)**
Prod.: 1926 / Rel.: 1927
Frame enlargement
Paris, Cinémathèque française collection
Courtesy of Carlton International

Topaz
Prod.: 1968–1969 / Rel.: 1969
Frame enlargement
Paris, Cinémathèque française collection
© 1969 Universal Pictures
All rights reserved
Courtesy of Universal Studios Licensing, Inc.

Montgomery Clift in **I Confess**
Prod.: 1952 / Rel.: 1953
Frame enlargement
Paris, Cinémathèque française collection
© Warner Bros.

Henri De Groux
Belgian, 1867–1930
Study for The Mocking of Christ
About 1925
Etching, heightened with watercolour, gouache,
and gold and silver paint (1/1)
64 x 80 cm
Private collection

All the world's a stage . . .

Félix Vallotton
Swiss, 1865–1925
The Patriotic Ditty (detail)
1893
Woodcut, 24.5 x 36.8 cm
Geneva, Cabinet des estampes du Musée d'Art
et d'Histoire
E 67/163

Walter Richard Sickert
German-born British, 1860–1942
The Old Bedford: Cupid in the Gallery
About 1890
Oil on canvas
126.5 x 77.5 cm
Ottawa, National Gallery of Canada, gift of the
Massey Collection of English Painting, 1946
NGC 4810
© Walter Richard Sickert, DACS
(Great Britain)/SODART (Canada) 2000

The Thirty-nine Steps
Prod. / Rel.: 1935
Production still
London, British Film Institute Collections
Courtesy of Carlton International

Walter Richard Sickert
German-born British, 1860–1942
In the Cabaret at the End of the Pier
About 1920
Oil on canvas, 61 x 50.8 cm
The Montreal Museum of Fine Arts,
gift of Dr. John Parkinson
1946.963
© Walter Richard Sickert, DACS
(Great Britain)/SODART (Canada) 2000

Walter Richard Sickert
German-born British, 1860–1942
Noctes Ambrosianae
Date unknown
Etching and aquatint, 15/50
30 x 34.3 cm
Toronto, Art Gallery of Ontario, gift of Touche Ross,
1980
80/55
© Walter Richard Sickert, DACS
(Great Britain)/SODART (Canada) 2000

Édouard Vuillard
French, 1868–1940
Loge (Downstage at the Théâtre Antoine)
About 1895
Oil on panel
31.5 x 49.5 cm
Private collection
© Estate of Édouard Vuillard/ADAGP (Paris)/
SODRAC (Montreal) 2000

Félix Vallotton
Swiss, 1865–1925
The Patriotic Ditty
1893
Woodcut
24.5 x 36.8 cm
Geneva, Cabinet des estampes du Musée d'Art
et d'Histoire
E 67/163

The Pleasure Garden
Prod.: 1925 / Rel.: 1927
Frame enlargement
Paris, Cinémathèque française collection
Courtesy of Carlton International

Guy Pène Du Bois
American, 1884–1958
In the Wings
1921
Oil on panel
50.8 x 38.1 cm
Oberlin, Ohio, Allen Memorial Art Museum, Oberlin
College, gift of Mrs. Malcolm L. McBride, 1948
AMAM 1948.44

Murder!
Prod. / Rel.: 1930
Frame enlargement
Paris, Cinémathèque française collection
© 1931 Canal + Image UK Ltd.

The Thirty-nine Steps
Prod. / Rel.: 1935
Production still
Brussels, Cinémathèque Royale de Belgique
Courtesy of Carlton International

O.E. Hasse in I Confess
Prod.: 1952 / Rel.: 1953
Frame enlargement
Paris, Cinémathèque française collection
© Warner Bros.

The Man Who Knew Too Much
Prod.: 1955 / Rel.: 1956
Frame enlargement
Paris, Cinémathèque française collection
© 1955 Filwite Productions, Inc.
All rights reserved
Courtesy of Universal Studios Licensing, Inc.

Georges Rouault
French, 1871–1958
The Circus
1936
Oil on canvas
69.9 x 108 cm
The Montreal Museum of Fine Arts, Millennium Gift
of Sara Lee Corporation
2000.10
© Estate of Georges Rouault/ADAGP (Paris)/
SODRAC (Montreal) 2000

Murder!
Prod. / Rel.: 1930
Frame enlargement
Paris, Cinémathèque française collection
© 1931 Canal + Image UK Ltd.

Antonio Donghi
Italian, 1897–1963
Equestrian Circus
1927
Oil on canvas
150 x 100 cm
Private collection
(Not exhibited)

Wylie Watson in **The Thirty-nine Steps**
Prod. / Rel.: 1935
Frame enlargement
Paris, Cinémathèque française collection
Courtesy of Carlton International

Antonio Donghi
Italian, 1897–1963
The Cabaret Singer
1925
Oil on canvas
148 x 100 cm
Private collection
(Not exhibited)

Anny Ondra and Cyril Ritchard in **Blackmail**
Prod. / Rel.: 1929
Frame enlargement
Paris, Cinémathèque française collection
© 1929 Canal + Image UK Ltd.

Anny Ondra in **Blackmail**
Prod. / Rel.: 1929
Frame enlargement
Paris, Cinémathèque française collection
© 1929 Canal + Image UK Ltd.

Esme Percy in **Murder!**
Prod. / Rel.: 1930
Frame enlargement
Paris, Cinémathèque française collection
© 1931 Canal + Image UK Ltd.

Walter Richard Sickert
German-born British, 1860–1942
Sir Thomas Beecham Conducting
About 1935
Oil on burlap
98.5 x 104.5 cm
New York, The Museum of Modern Art, Bertram F.
and Susie Brummer Foundation Fund, 1955
© Walter Richard Sickert, DACS (Great
Britain)/SODART (Canada) 2000

Bernard Herrmann in
The Man Who Knew Too Much
Prod.: 1955 / Rel.: 1956
Frame enlargement
Paris, Cinémathèque française collection
© 1955 Filwite Productions
All rights reserved
Courtesy of Universal Studios Licensing, Inc.

Auguste Chabaud
French, 1882–1955
Hôtel-Hôtel
1907–1908
Oil on paper, mounted on cradled panel
38.5 x 53.5 cm
Saint-Tropez, Musée de l'Annonciade
1985 1.1

Mr. and Mrs. Smith
Prod.: 1940 / Rel.: 1941
Frame enlargement
Paris, Cinémathèque française collection
© Warner Bros.

Paul B. Haviland
French, 1880–1950
Entrance to Luna Park
1909
Platinum print
12.1 x 9.4 cm
Ottawa, National Gallery of Canada, purchased
from the Bernstein Development Foundation Fund
NGC 30500

Lighted advertisement **(Blackmail)**
Prod. / Rel.: 1929
Frame enlargement
Paris, Cinémathèque française collection
© 1929 Canal + Image UK Ltd.

Downhill
Prod. / Rel.: 1927
Frame enlargement
Paris, Cinémathèque française collection
Courtesy of Carlton International

Rich and Strange
Prod. / Rel.: 1932
Frame enlargement
Paris, Cinémathèque française collection
© 1932 Canal + Image UK Ltd.

The Bijou Theatre (Sabotage)
Prod. / Rel.: 1936
Frame enlargement
Paris, Cinémathèque française collection
Courtesy of Carlton International

André Kertész
Hungarian-born American, 1894–1985
Circus, May 19, 1920, Budapest
1920 (later print)
Gelatin silver print
25.3 x 20.4 cm
Toronto, Art Gallery of Ontario, gift of Sandra Ball
and Marcia Reid, 1987
87/329

The fairground (The Ring)
Prod. / Rel.: 1927
Frame enlargement
Paris, Cinémathèque française collection
© 1927 Canal + Image UK Ltd.

Herbert List
German, 1903–1975
Optician's Display
1936 (later print)
Gelatin silver print
30 x 40 cm
Hamburg, estate of Herbert List
S-FR-AUG-001A

John Gielgud in Secret Agent
Prod.: 1935 / Rel.: 1936
Frame enlargement
Paris, Cinémathèque française collection
Courtesy of Carlton International

Theo von Alten in Champagne
Prod. / Rel.: 1928
Frame enlargement
Paris, Cinémathèque française collection
© 1928 Canal + Image UK Ltd.

Joseph Sacco
French?
Eye of a Young Woman
1844
Tempera on ivory mounted on leather in glass
and gilt frame placed; velvet-lined shagreen case
Box: 12.1 x 8.9 x 2 cm (closed)
Painting: 3.2 x 3.8 cm
Houston, The Menil Collection
X3059

Ingrid Bergman in Notorious
Prod.: 1945 / Rel.: 1946
Frame enlargement
Paris, Cinémathèque française collection
© Buena Vista International, Inc.

Grace Kelly and James Stewart for Rear Window
Prod.: 1953 / Rel.: 1954
Production still
Courtesy of the Academy of Motion Picture Arts
and Sciences
© Universal Studios
All rights reserved
Courtesy of Universal Studios Licensing, Inc.
Presented by special agreement
with Mr. Sheldon Abend

Herbert Bayer
Austrian-born American, 1900–1985
Good Night, Marie
1932
Silver print, 23/40
34.4 x 26 cm
Toronto, Art Gallery of Ontario, gift of Sandra Ball
and Marcia Reid, 1987
87/320
© Estate of Herbert Bayer/VG Bild-Kunst
(Bonn)/SODRAC (Montreal) 2000

Herbert Bayer
Austrian-born American, 1900–1985
The Lonely Metropolitan
1932
Gelatin silver print
34 x 26.9 cm
Berlin, Bauhaus-Archiv / Museum für Gestaltung
© Estate of Herbert Bayer/VG Bild-Kunst
(Bonn)/SODRAC (Montreal) 2000

George Grosz
German, 1893–1959
People in the Street
1915–1916
Ink on paper, 27.6 x 21.7 cm
Private collection
(Not exhibited)

Sabotage
Prod. / Rel.: 1936
Frame enlargement
Paris, Cinémathèque française collection
Courtesy of Carlton International

George Grosz
German, 1893–1959
Kurfürstendam
1925
Oil on canvas
81.3 x 61.3 cm
Madrid, Museo Thyssen-Bornemisza

René Magritte
Belgian, 1898–1967
Edward James in front of **On the Threshold of Liberty**
1937
Gelatin silver print
10.8 x 16.7 cm
New York, The Metropolitan Museum of Art,
Ford Motor Company Collection, gift of Ford Motor
Company and John C. Waddell, 1987
1100.157
© Estate of René Magritte/ADAGP (Paris)/
SODRAC (Montreal) 2000

Alain Fleischer
French, b. 1944
Exhibition in the North of France
1992
Cibachrome print mounted on aluminum
60 x 90 cm
Collection of the artist

Merry Alpern
American, b. 1955
Untitled No. 28
From the "Window" series
1994
Gelatin silver print
50.8 x 40.6 cm
Collection of the artist, courtesy of the
Bonnie Benrubi Gallery, New York

Rear Window
Prod.: 1953 / Rel.: 1954
Production still
Courtesy of the Academy of Motion Picture Arts
and Sciences
© Universal Studios
Courtesy of Universal Studios Licensing, Inc.
Presented by special agreement
with Mr. Sheldon Abend

Bill Brandt
German-born British, 1904–1983
Portrait of a Young Girl, Eaton Place, London
1955
Gelatin silver print
23 x 19.6 cm
Cologne, Museum Ludwig
ML/F 1977/94

Rear Window
Prod.: 1953 / Rel.: 1954
Production still: the apartment buildings as seen
from James Stewart's window
Courtesy of the Academy of Motion Picture Arts
and Sciences
© Universal Studios
Courtesy of Universal Studios Licensing, Inc.
Presented by special agreement
with Mr. Sheldon Abend

Women

Grace Kelly for **Rear Window (detail)**
Prod.: 1953 / Rel.: 1954
Promotional still
Paris, BIFI (Bibliothèque du film)
© Universal Studios
Courtesy of Universal Studios Licensing, Inc.
Presented by special agreement with
Mr. Sheldon Abend

Fernand Khnopff
Belgian, 1858–1921
Red Lips
1897
Photograph heightened with pencil, coloured pencil
and pastel
28.2 x 20 cm
Private collection

The Lodger: A Story of the London Fog
Prod.: 1926 / Rel.: 1927
Frame enlargement
Paris, Cinémathèque française collection
Courtesy of Carlton International

Grace Kelly for **Rear Window**
Prod.: 1953 / Rel.: 1954
Promotional still
Paris, BIFI (Bibliothèque du film)
© Universal Studios
Courtesy of Universal Studios Licensing, Inc.
Presented by special agreement with
Mr. Sheldon Abend

Ingrid Bergman for **Notorious**
Prod.: 1945 / Rel.: 1946
Promotional still
Courtesy of the Academy of Motion Picture Arts
and Sciences
© Buena Vista International Inc.

Fernand Khnopff
Belgian, 1858–1921
On Animality
1885
Pencil, coloured chalk and watercolour on paper
28.3 x 25.4 cm
Private collection

Ernst Stöhr
Austrian, about 1860–1917
The Woman
1898
Pastel, 66.1 x 72.8 cm
Sankt Pölten, Stadtmuseum

Man Ray
American, 1890–1976
The Avignon Fort
From *Les mains libres,* a book of drawings illustrated
with poems by Paul Éluard (Paris: Éditions Jeanne
Bucher, 1937), 594/650
Book: 28.2 x 22.8 cm
Illustration: 19.3 x 26 cm
The Montreal Museum of Fine Arts Library Collection
© Man Ray Trust/ADAGP (Paris)/
SODRAC (Montreal) 2000

Franz Von Stuck
German, 1863–1928
Pygmalion
About 1926
Oil on canvas, 60.5 x 50 cm
Munich, Museum Villa Stuck, on permanent loan
from the Federal Republic of Germany
G-L 91 1-6

Auguste Rodin
French, 1840–1917
Eternal Idol
1889
Bronze
17 x 14 x 7 cm
Paris, Musée Rodin
S. 39

Édouard Vuillard
French, 1868–1940
The Nape of Misia's Neck
About 1897–1899
Oil on cardboard mounted on cradled panel
13.5 x 33 cm
Private collection
© Estate of Édouard Vuillard/ADAGP (Paris)/
SODRAC (Montreal) 2000

James Mason and Eva Marie Saint
in **North by Northwest**
Prod.: 1958 / Rel.: 1959
Frame enlargement
Paris, Cinémathèque française collection
© Warner Bros.

Domenico Gnoli
Italian, 1933–1970
Curly Red Hair
1969
Acrylic and sand on canvas
200 x 140 cm
Brussels, private collection

René Magritte
Belgian, 1898–1967
The Rape
1945
Oil on canvas, 65.3 x 50.4 cm
Paris, Musée National d'Art Moderne, Centre
Georges Pompidou, bequest of Georgette Magritte
AM 1987-1097
© Estate of René Magritte/ADAGP (Paris)/
SODRAC (Montreal) 2000

Max Ernst
German-born American and French, 1891–1976
. . . majestic
Illustration for *Rêve d'une petite fille qui voulut
entrer au Carmel*
1929–1930
Collage of cut engravings mounted on paper
and touched with ink
15.9 x 10.5 cm
Houston, The Menil Collection
81-045 DJ D
© Estate of Max Ernst/ADAGP (Paris)/
SODRAC (Montreal) 2000

René Magritte
Belgian, 1898–1967
Untitled
Drawing for Paul Éluard's poem "Moralité du
Sommeil" (Antwerp: L'Aiguille Aimantée, April 1941)
1941
India ink on paper, 17.8 x 12.9 cm
Brussels, Musées royaux des Beaux-Arts de
Belgique
11729
© Estate of René Magritte/ADAGP (Paris)/
SODRAC (Montreal) 2000

Kim Novak in **Vertigo**
Prod.: 1957 / Rel.: 1958
Frame enlargement
Paris, Cinémathèque française collection
© 1958 Universal City Studios, Inc.
All rights reserved
Courtesy of Universal Studios Licensing, Inc.

Cindy Sherman
American, b. 1954
Untitled (Film Still #81)
1979
Gelatin silver print
25.4 x 20.3 cm
Private collection

Kim Novak in Vertigo
Prod.: 1957 / Rel.: 1958
Frame enlargement
Paris, Cinémathèque française collection
© 1958 Universal City Studios, Inc.
All rights reserved
Courtesy of Universal Studios Licensing, Inc.

Grace Kelly in To Catch a Thief
Prod.: 1954 / Rel.: 1955
Frame enlargement
Paris, Cinémathèque française collection
© Paramount Pictures

Eva Marie Saint in North by Northwest
Prod.: 1958 / Rel.: 1959
Frame enlargement
Paris, Cinémathèque française collection
© Warner Bros.

Giorgio De Chirico
Greek-born Italian, 1888–1978
Antique Woman
Design for Vogue (New York)
1937 (March 15)
31.2 x 23.2 cm
New York, Fashion Institute of Technology,
Gladys Marcus Library
FITLP.V337
© Estate of Giorgio De Chirico/SIAE (Rome)/
SODRAC (Montreal) 2000

Edith Head
American, 1897–1982
To Catch a Thief
Prod.: 1954 / Rel.: 1955
Costume design for Grace Kelly
Ink, watercolour and pencil on paper, 45 x 30 cm
London, British Film Institute Collections
© Paramount Pictures

Ingrid Bergman for Notorious
Prod.: 1945 / Rel.: 1946
Promotional still
Courtesy of the Academy of Motion Picture Arts
and Sciences
© Buena Vista International Inc.

Ingrid Bergman for Notorious
Prod.: 1945 / Rel.: 1946
Promotional still
Courtesy of the Academy of Motion Picture Arts
and Sciences
© Buena Vista International Inc.

Joan Fontaine for Rebecca
Prod.: 1939 / Rel.: 1940
Promotional still
Courtesy of the Academy of Motion Picture Arts
and Sciences
© Buena Vista International Inc.

Meredith Frampton
British, 1894–1984
Portrait of a Young Woman
1935
Oil on canvas
205.7 x 107.9 cm
London, Tate Gallery
4820

Cecil Beaton
British, 1904–1980
Marlene Dietrich
About 1935
Gelatin silver print
25.4 x 20.3 cm
Ottawa, National Gallery of Canada, gift of Rodney
and Cozette de Charmoy Grey, Geneva, 1978
NGC 20804

Cassandre (pseudonym of Adolphe Mouron)
Ukrainian-born French, 1901–1968
Covers for Harper's Bazaar (New York)
1938 (15 March and October)
31.2 x 23.2 (each)
New York, Fashion Institute of Technology,
Gladys Marcus library
FITLP.HB 138 and 938

Herbert List
German, 1903–1975
Slave I
1936
Gelatin silver print
30 x 40 cm
Hamburg, estate of Herbert List
S-GB-SKL-001A

Man Ray
American, 1890–1976
Restored Venus
[1936]–1971
Plaster and rope
71 x 40 x 40 cm
Milan, Galleria Gio' Marconi
© Man Ray Trust/ADAGP (Paris)/
SODRAC (Montreal) 2000

Janet Leigh in Psycho
Prod.: 1959–1960 / Rel. 1960
Production still
Courtesy of the Academy of Motion Picture Arts
and Sciences
© 1960 Shamley Productions, Inc.
All rights reserved
Courtesy of Universal Studios Licensing, Inc.

Gus MacNaughton, Jerry Verno and Robert Donat
in The Thirty-nine Steps
Prod. / Rel.: 1935
Production still
London, The Cinema Museum
Richard Hamilton

Marnie
Prod.: 1963–1964 / Rel.: 1964
Frame enlargement
Paris, Cinémathèque française collection

Wilhelm Leibl
German, 1844–1900
The Corset (fragment)
About 1880–1881
Oil on panel
27 x 21.5 cm
Cologne, Wallraf-Richartz-Museum
WRM 1177

Catherine Lacy's feet (The Lady Vanishes)
Prod.: 1937 / Rel.: 1938
Frame enlargement
Paris, Cinémathèque française collection
Courtesy of Carlton International

Alfred Stieglitz
American, 1864–1946
Dorothy True
1919
Gelatin silver print
24.3 x 19.3 cm
New York, The Metropolitan Museum of Art,
gift of Paul Rosenfeld, 1928
28.126

Betty Balfour in talent agent's office
(Champagne)
Prod. / Rel.: 1928
Production still
London, The Cinema Museum
Marie Claire Patin

Alfred Hitchcock and Tippi Hedren on the set
of Marnie
Prod.: 1963–1964 / Rel.: 1964
Production still
Courtesy of the Academy of Motion Picture Arts
and Sciences

Margaret Lockwood in The Lady Vanishes
Prod.: 1937 / Rel.: 1938
Frame enlargement
Paris, Cinémathèque française collection
Courtesy of Carlton International

Clarence John Laughlin
American, 1905–1985
The Masks Grow to Us
1947
Gelatin silver print
33.7 x 26.0 cm
The Historic New Orleans Collection
1981.247.1.799
Clarence John Laughlin/© The Historic New Orleans
Collection
Artist's note: "In our society, most of us wear
protective masks of various kinds. Very often,
the end result is that the masks grow to us –
displacing our original characters, with our *assumed*
characters. Visually, this is what is happening here –
the disturbing thing being that the mask is like the
girl *herself* – grown harder, and more superficial."

Tippi Hedren in The Birds
Prod.: 1962 / Rel.: 1963
Production still
Paris, BIFI (Bibliothèque du film)

Joel McCrea and Laraine Day
in Foreign Correspondent
Prod. / Rel.: 1940
Frame enlargement
Paris, Cinémathèque française collection

Teresa Wright and Henry Travers
in Shadow of a Doubt
Prod.: 1950 / Rel.: 1951
Frame enlargement
Paris, Cinémathèque française collection

Cary Grant and Eva Marie Saint
in North by Northwest
Prod.: 1958 / Rel.: 1959
Production still
By kind permission of Éditions Hazan

Fernand Khnopff
Belgian, 1858–1921
The Cigarette
About 1912
Pastel and charcoal on paper
15.8 cm (diam.)
Private collection, courtesy of the Galerie Bern'Art,
Brussels

Edvard Munch
Norwegian, 1863–1944
Woman (The Sphinx)
1899
Lithograph retouched with brush and black ink,
crayon and scraper on wove paper, laid down
on cardboard
53.2 x 69.8 cm
Ottawa, National Gallery of Canada
NGC 26569
© The Munch Museum/The Munch-Ellingsen
Group/SODART (Canada) 2000

Odilon Redon
French, 1840–1916
Haunting
1894
Lithograph
24.1 x 20.2 cm
Amsterdam, Rijksmuseum
RP-P-1949-227

Desire and Double Trouble

Robert Delaunay
French, 1885–1941
Paris Lovers: The Kiss
1929
Oil on plywood, 37.4 x 55.1 cm
Cologne, courtesy of Galerie Gmurzynska
(Not exhibited)

Francis Picabia
French, 1879–1953
Aello
About 1930
Oil on canvas, 169 x 169 cm
Private collection
© Estate of Francis Picabia/ADAGP (Paris)/
SODRAC (Montreal) 2000

Ingrid Bergman and Cary Grant for **Notorious**
Prod.: 1945 / Rel.: 1946
Promotional still
Courtesy of the Academy of Motion Picture Arts
and Sciences
© Buena Vista International Inc.

Ivor Novello and June Tripp in **The Lodger:
A Story of the London Fog**
Prod.: 1926 / Rel.: 1927
Frame enlargement
Paris, Cinémathèque française collection
Courtesy of Carlton International

Lillian Hall Davis and Ian Hunter in **The Ring**
Prod. / Rel.: 1927
Frame enlargement
Paris, Cinémathèque française collection
© 1927 Canal + Image UK Ltd.

Lillian Hall Davis and Carl Brisson in **The Ring**
Prod. / Rel.: 1927
Frame enlargement
Paris, Cinémathèque française collection
© 1927 Canal + Image UK Ltd.

Gregory Peck and Ingrid Bergman for **Spellbound**
Prod.: 1944 / Rel.: 1945
Promotional still
Brussels, Cinémathèque Royale de Belgique
© Buena Vista International Inc.

Gregory Peck and Ingrid Bergman for **Spellbound**
Prod.: 1944 / Rel.: 1945
Promotional still
Paris, BIFI (Bibliothèque du film)
© Buena Vista International Inc.

James Stewart and Grace Kelly in **Rear Window**
Prod.: 1953 / Rel.: 1954
Frame enlargement
Paris, Cinémathèque française collection
© Universal Studios
All rights reserved
Courtesy of Universal Studios Licensing, Inc.
Presented by special agreement
with Mr. Sheldon Abend.

Montgomery Clift and Anne Baxter in **I Confess**
Prod.: 1952 / Rel.: 1953
Frame enlargement
Paris, Cinémathèque française collection
© Warner Bros.

Grace Kelly and Cary Grant in **To Catch a Thief**
Prod.: 1954 / Rel.: 1955
Frame enlargement
Paris, Cinémathèque française collection
© Paramount Pictures

Auguste Rodin
French, 1840–1917
Fugit amor (Fleeting Love)
1881
Bronze
35.7 x 44.2 x 28.7 cm
Paris, Musée Rodin
S. 491

Auguste Rodin
French, 1840–1917
Large Clenched Hand with Imploring Figure
Date unknown (posthumous cast)
Bronze
42 x 32.9 x 27.2 cm
Paris, Musée Rodin
S. 791

Auguste Rodin
French, 1840–1917
The Kiss
About 1916
Bronze
69.9 x 38.7 x 43.2 cm
MacKenzie Art Gallery, University of Regina
Collection, gift of Mr. Norman MacKenzie
1916-5

Julia Margaret Cameron
British, born in India, 1815–1879
The Parting of Lancelot and Guinevere
1874
Albumen silver print
34.9 x 29 cm
Munich, Münchner Stadtmuseum

Emil Rudolf Weiss
German, 1875–1942
The Kiss
1899
Woodcut
36.1 x 43.2 cm
Vienna, Graphische Sammlung Albertina
5769

René Magritte
Belgian, 1898–1967
Duo
1928
Ink on paper
49.1 x 59.5 cm
Berkeley, University of California,
Berkeley Art Museum
1970.5
© Estate of René Magritte/ADAGP (Paris)/
SODRAC (Montreal) 2000

Giorgio De Chirico
Greek-born Italian, 1888–1978
Hector and Andromache
1916
Oil on canvas, 90 x 60 cm
Private collection
© Estate of Giorgio De Chirico/SIAE (Rome)/
SODRAC (Montreal) 2000

Nova Pilbeam and Derrick de Marney
in **Young and Innocent**
Prod.: 1937 / Rel.: 1938
Production still
London, British Film Institute Collections
Courtesy of Carlton International

Cary Grant and Ingrid Bergman in **Notorious**
Prod.: 1945 / Rel.: 1946
Production still
Courtesy of the Academy of Motion Picture Arts
and Sciences
© Buena Vista International Inc.

Fernand Khnopff
Belgian, 1858–1921
With Grégoire Le Roy: My Heart Longs
for Other Times
1889
Pencil, chalk and coloured pencil on paper
25.5 x 14.5 cm
The Hearn Family Trust

James Stewart and Kim Novak (Madeleine/Judy)
for **Vertigo**
Prod.: 1957 / Rel.: 1958
Promotional still
Courtesy of the Academy of Motion Picture Arts
and Sciences
© 1958 Universal City Studios, Inc.
All rights reserved
Courtesy of Universal Studios Licensing, Inc.

James Stewart and Kim Novak: Scottie between
Madeleine and Judy for **Vertigo**
Prod.: 1957 / Rel.: 1958
Promotional still
Paris, BIFI (Bibliothèque du film)
© 1958 Universal City Studios, Inc.
All rights reserved
Courtesy of Universal Studios Licensing, Inc.

Herbert Bayer
Austrian-born American, 1900–1985
College Fashions
Cover for *Harper's Bazaar* (New York)
1940 (August)
31.3 x 23.2 cm
New York, Fashion Institute of Technology,
Gladys Marcus Library
FITLP.HB540
© Estate of Herbert Bayer/VG Bild-Kunst
(Bonn)/SODRAC (Montreal) 2000

James Stewart and Kim Novak for **Vertigo**
Prod.: 1957 / Rel.: 1958
Promotional still
Brussels, Cinémathèque Royale de Belgique
© 1958 Universal City Studios, Inc.
All rights reserved
Courtesy of Universal Studios Licensing, Inc.

Dante Gabriele Rossetti
British, 1828–1882
Rosa Triplex
1874
Chalk on paper, 51 x 73.5 cm
The Hearn Family Trust

Grace Kelly and Anthony Dawson
for **Dial M for Murder**
Prod.: 1953 / Rel.: 1954
Production still
Paris, BIFI (Bibliothèque du film)
© Warner Bros.

Madeleine Carroll and Robert Donat for
The Thirty-nine Steps
Prod. / Rel.: 1935
Promotional still
London, British Film Institute Collections
Courtesy of Carlton International

Unsigned
Blackmail
Anny Ondra and Cyril Ritchard
1929
Lobby card for U.S. release, 28 x 36 cm
Courtesy of the Mark H. Wolff collection
© 1929 Canal + Image UK Ltd.

Kim Novak and James Stewart for Vertigo
Prod.: 1957 / Rel.: 1958
Promotional still
Courtesy of the Academy of Motion Picture Arts
and Sciences
© 1958 Universal City Studios, Inc.
All rights reserved
Courtesy of Universal Studios Licensing, Inc.

Oscar Homolka and Sylvia Sidney for Sabotage
Prod. / Rel.: 1936
Promotional still
London, British Film Institute Collections
Courtesy of Carlton International

Teresa Wright threatened by Joseph Cotten
for Shadow of a Doubt
Prod.: 1942 / Rel.: 1943
Production still
Paris, BIFI (Bibliothèque du film)
© 1942 Universal Pictures Company, Inc.
All rights reserved
Courtesy of Universal Studios Licensing, Inc.

Robert Walker in *Strangers on a Train*
Prod.: 1950 / Rel.: 1951
Production still: the strangulation scene seen
through the broken window
Courtesy of the Academy of Motion Picture Arts
and Sciences
© Warner Bros.

Cary Grant and Eva Marie Saint
in North by Northwest
Prod.: 1958 / Rel.: 1959
Frame enlargement
Paris, Cinémathèque française collection
© Warner Bros.

Vera Miles and Alfred Hitchcock during shooting
of The Wrong Man
Prod. / Rel.: 1956
Production still
Courtesy of the Academy of Motion Picture Arts
and Sciences
© Warner Bros.

Alfred Hitchcock and Mary Scott during shooting
of the television episode Mr. Blanchard's Secret
1956
Production still
Paris, BIFI (Bibliothèque du film)

Alfred Hitchcock and Ingrid Bergman during
the making of Spellbound
Prod.: 1944 / Rel.: 1945
Production still
The University of Texas at Austin, Harry Ransom
Humanities Research Center, Art Collection
© Buena Vista International Inc.

Félix Vallotton
Swiss, 1865–1925
From the series "Intimités I"
The Fine Pin, 1898, 25 x 32.3 cm
The Lie, 1897, 25 x 32.3 cm
Murder, 1898, 25 x 32.8 cm
Print Pulled from the Destroyed Blocks,
Date unknown
Woodcut
Geneva, Cabinet des estampes du Musée d'Art
et d'Histoire
E79/533, E79/531, E79/485, E79/530

Unsigned
Spellbound
1945
Poster for U.S. release
Offset print mounted on canvas
108.6 x 73.7 cm
Courtesy of the Academy of Motion Pictures Arts
and Sciences
© Buena Vista International Inc.
(Not exhibited)

Max Klinger
German, 1857–1920
"Paraphrase on the Discovery of a Glove,"
or "The Glove"
1878–1881
Engraving and aquatint
Place, 1/10, 22.8 x 32.8 cm
The Act, 2/10, 25 x 19 cm
Desires, 3/10, 28.3 x 10.7 cm
The Rescue, 4/10, 14.4 x 10.5 cm
Triumph, 5/10, 11 x 24 cm
Homage, 6/10, 12.3 x 29.5 cm
Fears, 7/10, 11 x 24 cm
Tranquillity, 8/10, 11.1 x 23.5 cm
The Abduction, 9/10, 9 x 22 cm
Cupid, 10/10, 11 x 24 cm
Milan, Fondazione Antonio Mazzotta

Edvard Munch
Norwegian, 1863–1944
Vampire
1895–1902
Colour woodblock and lithograph
49.8 x 65.8 cm
Toronto, Art Gallery of Ontario, gift of Vivian
and David Campbell, 1991
91/60
© The Munch Museum/The Munch-Ellingsen
Group/SODART (Canada) 2000

Edvard Munch
Norwegian, 1863–1944
The Kiss of Death
1899
Lithograph
45.2 x 62.4 cm
Ottawa, National Gallery of Canada
NGC 17331
© The Munch Museum/The Munch-Ellingsen
Group/SODART (Canada) 2000

Disquiet

Léon Spilliaert
Belgian, 1881–1946
Vertigo (detail)
1908
India ink wash, watercolour and chalk on paper
64 x 48 cm
Ostend, Museum voor Schone Kunsten
1975/696
© Estate of Léon Spilliaert/SABAM (Brussels)/
SODRAC (Montreal) 2000

Arnold Böcklin
Swiss, 1827–1901
Ruin by the Sea
1881
Oil on fabric
111 x 82 cm
The Cleveland Museum of Art,
Mr. and Mrs. William H. Marlatt Fund
1979.57

I Confess
Prod.: 1952 / Rel.: 1953
Frame enlargement
Paris, Cinémathèque française collection
© Warner Bros.

The Hillcrist home (The Skin Game)
Prod.: 1930–1931 / Rel.: 1931
Frame enlargement
Paris, Cinémathèque française collection
© 1931 Canal + Image UK Ltd.

The ashes of Manderley (Rebecca)
Prod.: 1939 / Rel.: 1940
Frame enlargement
Paris, Cinémathèque française collection
© Buena Vista International, Inc.

Joseph Mallord William Turner
British, 1775–1851
Dolbadern Castle, North Wales
1800
Oil on canvas, 119.5 x 90 cm
London, Royal Academy of Arts

James Basevi
Rebecca
Prod.: 1939 / Rel.: 1940
Set design for Manderley estate
London, British Film Institute Collections
© Buena Vista International Inc.

The Manxman
Prod.: 1928 / Rel.: 1929
Production still
London, British Film Institute Collections
Courtesy of Carlton International
© 1929 Canal + Image UK Ltd.

The Man Who Knew Too Much
Prod.: 1955 / Rel.: 1956
Frame enlargement
Paris, Cinémathèque française collection
© 1955 Filwite Productions, Inc.
All rights reserved
Courtesy of Universal Studios Licensing, Inc.

Murder!
Prod. / Rel.: 1930
Frame enlargement
Paris, Cinémathèque française collection
© 1931 Canal + Image UK Ltd.

Alfred Junge
German, 1886–1964
The Man Who Knew Too Much
Prod.: 1955 / Rel.: 1956
Set design: "Exterior, shoe-mender's"
Charcoal and ink wash on paper
56 x 78 cm
Paris, BIFI (Bibliothèque du film)
© Alfred Junge
© 1955 Filwite Productions, Inc.
All rights reserved
Courtesy of Universal Studios Licensing, Inc.

Joseph Cundall (Cundall and Fleming)
British, 1818–1895
Elz Castle
About 1867
Albumen print
28.4 x 22.6 cm
Munich, Dietmar Siegert collection

Fernand Khnopff
Belgian, 1858–1921
Le lac d'amour, Bruges
About 1904–1905
Pencil and pastel on paper
47 x 101 cm
The Hearn Family Trust

Charles Lacoste
French, 1870–1959
London Docks, Sunday Dawning
Date unknown
Oil on board
40 x 50 cm
Paris, Galerie Elstir

Algernon Newton
British, 1880–1968
The Deserted Factory
1941
Oil on canvas
56 x 76.3 cm
Ottawa, National Gallery of Canada, gift of the
Massey Collection of English Painting, 1946
NGC 4801

Stage Fright
Prod.: 1949 / Rel.: 1950
Frame enlargement
Paris, Cinémathèque française collection
© Warner Bros.

Carel Willink
Dutch, 1900–1983
The Letter
1932
Oil on canvas
61.5 x 92.5 cm
Amsterdam, Stedelijk Museum
A741

Edward Hopper
American, 1882–1967
North Truro Station
1930
Watercolour and pencil on paper
35.6 x 50.8 cm
Buffalo, Albright-Knox Art Gallery, gift of
Mrs. Howell H. Howard, 1963
RCA 1963:4

Alfred Junge
German, 1886–1964
Young and Innocent
Prod.: 1937 / Rel.: 1938
Set design: "The mill"
Charcoal and ink wash on paper
56 x 78 cm
Paris, BIFI (Bibliothèque du film)
© Alfred Junge

Derrick de Marney in **Young and Innocent**
Prod.: 1937 / Rel.: 1938
Frame enlargement
Paris, Cinémathèque française collection
Courtesy of Carlton International

Edward Hopper
American, 1882–1967
Lighthouse Hill
1927
Oil on canvas
71.8 x 100.3 cm
Dallas Museum of Art, gift of
Mr. and Mrs. Maurice Purnell

Alvin Langdon Coburn
American, 1882–1966
The Haunted House
1904
Platinum print
18.6 x 23.1 cm
Bath, The Royal Photographic Society Collection
RPS 506

Anthony Perkins in **Psycho**
Prod.: 1959–1960 / Rel.: 1960
Frame enlargement
Paris, Cinémathèque française collection
© 1960 Shamley Productions, Inc.
All rights reserved
Courtesy of Universal Studios Licensing, Inc.

Anthony Perkins in **Psycho**
Prod.: 1959–1960 / Rel.: 1960
Production still
London, The Cinema Museum
Marie Claire Patin
© 1960 Shamley Productions, Inc.
All rights reserved
Courtesy of Universal Studios Licensing, Inc.

Holly King
Canadian, b. 1957
Place of Desire
1989
Gelatin silver print
157.5 x 121.9 cm
Collection of the artist

The house at night (Under Capricorn)
Prod.: 1948 / Rel.: 1949
Frame enlargement
Paris, Cinémathèque française collection
© Transatlantic Pictures

The house at daybreak (Under Capricorn)
Prod.: 1948 / Rel.: 1949
Frame enlargement
Paris, Cinémathèque française collection
© Transatlantic Pictures

Harland Fraser
Shadow of a Doubt
Prod.: 1942 / Rel.: 1943
Storyboard drawing
Courtesy of the Academy of Motion Picture Arts
and Sciences
© 1942 Universal Pictures Company, Inc.
Courtesy of Universal Studios Licensing, Inc.

Dorothea Holt
Shadow of a Doubt
Prod.: 1942 / Rel.: 1943
Drawing: mixed media on paper
Courtesy of the Academy of Motion Picture Arts
and Sciences
© 1942 Universal Pictures Company, Inc.
Courtesy of Universal Studios Licensing, Inc.

Alfred Junge
German, 1886–1964
The Man Who Knew Too Much
Prod.: 1955 / Rel.: 1956
Set design: "Stairwell at the dentist's"
Charcoal and ink wash on paper
55 x 77 cm
Paris, BIFI (Bibliothèque du film)
© Alfred Junge
© 1955 Filwite Productions
Courtesy of Universal Studios Licensing, Inc.

Robert Boyle
American, b. 1910
Shadow of a Doubt
Prod.: 1942 / Rel.: 1943
Storyboard drawing
Courtesy of the Academy of Motion Picture Arts
and Sciences
© 1942 Universal Pictures Company, Inc.
Courtesy of Universal Studios Licensing, Inc.

Blackmail
Prod. / Rel.: 1929
Frame enlargement
Paris, Cinémathèque française collection
© 1929 Canal + Image UK Ltd.

Downhill
Prod. / Rel.: 1927
Frame enlargement
Paris, Cinémathèque française collection
Courtesy of Carlton International

Downhill
Prod. / Rel.: 1927
Frame enlargement
Paris, Cinémathèque française collection
Courtesy of Carlton International

Anny Ondra in Blackmail
Prod. / Rel.: 1929
Frame enlargement
Paris, Cinémathèque française collection
© 1929 Canal + Image UK Ltd.

Number Seventeen
Prod.: 1931 / Rel.: 1932
Frame enlargement
Paris, Cinémathèque française collection
© Canal + Image International

John Stuart in Number Seventeen
Prod.: 1931 / Rel.: 1932
Frame enlargement
Paris, Cinémathèque française collection
© Canal + Image International

Leon M. Lion in Number Seventeen
Prod.: 1931 / Rel.: 1932
Frame enlargement
Paris, Cinémathèque française collection
© Canal + Image International

Cindy Sherman
American, b. 1954
Untitled (Film Still #51)
1979
Gelatin silver print
20.3 x 25.4 cm
Courtesy of the artist and Metro Pictures
MP #51

Odilon Redon
French, 1840–1916
We both saw a large pale light
Plate 2 from six illustrations for the French
translation of Edward Bulwer-Lytton's story
The Haunted and the Haunters
1896
Lithograph
45.1 x 31.8 cm
Ottawa, National Gallery of Canada
NGC 15708.2

Spellbound
Prod.: 1944 / Rel.: 1945
Frame enlargement
Paris, Cinémathèque française collection
© Buena Vista International Inc.

Wilhelm Hammershøi
Danish, 1864–1916
Interior, Strandgade 25
1915
Oil on canvas
73.5 x 66.5 cm
Marin Karmitz collection

Sylvia Sidney in Sabotage
Prod. / Rel.: 1936
Frame enlargement
Paris, Cinémathèque française collection
Courtesy of Carlton International

Sabotage
Prod. / Rel.: 1936
Frame enlargement
Paris, Cinémathèque française collection
Courtesy of Carlton International

Édouard Vuillard
French, 1868–1940
The Two Doors
About 1891
Oil on panel, 31.5 x 14.5 cm
Private collection
© Estate of Édouard Vuillard/ADAGP
(Paris)/SODRAC (Montreal) 2000

Édouard Vuillard
French, 1868–1940
Woman by an Open Door
1893
Oil on panel, 28.2 x 23.5 cm
Private collection
© Estate of Édouard Vuillard/ADAGP
(Paris)/SODRAC (Montreal) 2000

Anny Ondra in Blackmail
Prod. / Rel.: 1929
Frame enlargement
Paris, Cinémathèque française collection
© 1929 Canal + Image UK Ltd.

Alida Valli for The Paradine Case
Prod.: 1946–1947 / Rel.: 1947
Production still
The University of Texas at Austin, Harry Ransom
Humanities Research Center, Art Collection
© Buena Vista International Inc.

Alvin Langdon Coburn
American, 1882–1966
Weirs Close
1904
Platinum print, 27.4 x 22 cm
Bath, The Royal Photographic Society
RPS 505

Édouard Vuillard
French, 1868–1940
Perfect Harmony (Madame Gillou at Home)
1931
Oil on canvas, 72 x 92 cm
Private collection
© Estate of Édouard Vuillard/ADAGP
(Paris)/SODRAC (Montreal) 2000

The cast of Rope
Prod. / Rel.: 1948
Production still
Paris, BIFI (Bibliothèque du film)
© 1948 Transatlantic Pictures Corp.
All rights reserved
Courtesy of Universal Studios Licensing, Inc.

*Leopoldine Konstantin and Claude Rains
in* Notorious
Prod.: 1945 / Rel.: 1946
Frame enlargement
Paris, Cinémathèque française collection
© Buena Vista International Inc.

Judith Anderson in Rebecca
Prod.: 1939 / Rel.: 1940
Frame enlargement
Paris, Cinémathèque française collection
© Buena Vista International Inc.

Léon Spilliaert
Belgian, 1881–1946
Wind
About 1902
India ink wash and ink on paper
38.4 x 30.9 cm
Brussels, Musées royaux des Beaux-Arts de
Belgique
7853
© Estate of Léon Spilliaert/SABAM
(Brussels)/SODRAC (Montreal) 2000

Judith Anderson in Rebecca
Prod.: 1939 / Rel.: 1940
Production still
Courtesy of the Academy of Motion Picture Arts
and Sciences
© Buena Vista International Inc.

The Thirty-nine Steps
Prod. / Rel.: 1935
Frame enlargement
Paris, Cinémathèque française collection
Courtesy of Carlton International

William Degouve De Nuncques
French-born Belgian, 1867–1935
Leprous Forest
1898
Oil on canvas
66.5 x 127 cm
Private collection

Headlights in the woods (Young and Innocent)
Prod.: 1937 / Rel.: 1938
Frame enlargement
Paris, Cinémathèque française collection
Courtesy of Carlton International

Kim Novak in Vertigo
Prod.: 1957 / Rel.: 1958
Frame enlargement
Paris, Cinémathèque française collection

Max Ernst
German-born American and French, 1891–1976
**Vision Induced by the Nocturnal Aspect
of Porte Saint-Denis**
1927
Oil on canvas
64.5 x 81 cm
Private collection

Saboteur
Prod. / Rel.: 1942
Frame enlargement
Paris, Cinémathèque française collection

Willie Doherty
Irish, b. 1959
Unapproved Road
1992
Black-and-white photograph on aluminum,
edition of 3
122 x 183 cm
Courtesy of the Alexander and Bonin Gallery,
New York

Psycho
Prod.: 1959–1960 / Rel.: 1960
Frame enlargement
Paris, Cinémathèque française collection

Janet Leigh in Psycho
Prod.: 1959–1960 / Rel.: 1960
Frame enlargement
Paris, Cinémathèque française collection

Georges De Feure
French, 1868–1943
Windmill by Moonlight
Date unknown
Oil on cardboard
57.5 x 45.5 cm
Stephane Heuer collection

Foreign Correspondent
Prod. / Rel.: 1940
Frame enlargement
Paris, Cinémathèque française collection

Raphaël Delorme
French, 1890–1962
Untitled (Woman and Steamship)
1928
Oil on panel
61 x 46 cm
Paris, Galerie Alain Blondel

The Wrong Man
Prod. / Rel.: 1956
Frame enlargement
Paris, Cinémathèque française collection

Marnie
Prod.: 1963–1964 / Rel.: 1964
Frame enlargement
Paris, Cinémathèque française collection

**Donald Calthrop chased through the
British Museum (Blackmail)**
Prod. / Rel.: 1929
Frame enlargement
Paris, Cinémathèque française collection

Donald Calthrop caught (Blackmail)
Prod. / Rel.: 1929
Frame enlargement
Paris, Cinémathèque française collection

John Rogers Cox
American, 1915–1990
Grey and Gold
1942
Oil on canvas
91.5 x 151.8 cm
The Cleveland Museum of Art, Artists for Victory Inc.,
collection, Mr. and Mrs. William H. Marlatt Fund
1943.60
(Not exhibited)

North by Northwest
Prod.: 1958 / Rel.: 1959
Frame enlargement
Paris, Cinémathèque française collection

Robert Cummings and Norman Lloyd in Saboteur
Prod. / Rel.: 1942
Frame enlargement
Paris, Cinémathèque française collection

North by Northwest
Prod.: 1958 / Rel.: 1959
Frame enlargement
Paris, Cinémathèque française collection

Léon Spilliaert
Belgian, 1881–1946
Pursuit
1910
India ink wash and pastel on paper, 50 x 65 cm
Private collection

Shadow of a Doubt
Prod.: 1942 / Rel.: 1943
Frame enlargement
Paris, Cinémathèque française collection

Cindy Bernard
American, b. 1959
Ask the Dust: Vertigo
1990
Colour photograph, 5/21
31.8 x 59.7 cm
John Baldessari collection

Ralston Crawford
Canadian-born American, 1906–1978
Whitestone Bridge
1939
Oil on canvas, 102.2 x 81.3 cm
Rochester, New York, University of Rochester,
Memorial Art Gallery, Marion Stratton Gould Fund
51.2

Léon Spilliaert
Belgian, 1881–1946
Night
1908
India ink wash and pastel on paper, 48 x 63 cm
Brussels, Musée d'Ixelles, collection of the Belgian
government, on loan from the Ministère de la
Communauté française de Belgique
7594
(Not exhibited)

Ralston Crawford
Canadian-born American, 1906–1978
Overseas Highway
1939
Oil on canvas
45.7 x 76.2 cm
Lugano-Castagnola,
Fondazione Thyssen-Bornemisza Collection
1978.60

Donald Calthrop in Blackmail
Prod. / Rel.: 1929
Frame enlargement
Paris, Cinémathèque française collection

Ingrid Bergman in Notorious
Prod.: 1945 / Rel.: 1946
Production still
Courtesy of the Academy of Motion Picture Arts
and Sciences

John Vernon and Karin Dor in Topaz
Prod.: 1968–1969 / Rel.: 1969
Frame enlargement
Paris, Cinémathèque française collection

The Man Who Knew Too Much
Prod.: 1955 / Rel.: 1956
Photograph of matte painting
Paris, Cinémathèque française collection

Vertigo
Prod.: 1957 / Rel.: 1958
Frame enlargement
Paris, Cinémathèque française collection

Giorgio De Chirico
Greek-born Italian, 1888–1978
Piazza d'Italia (Autumn Melancholy)
1914
Oil on canvas
51 x 64 cm
Private collection

Giorgio De Chirico
Greek-born Italian, 1888–1978
Piazza d'Italia
Before 1935
Oil on canvas
25 x 35.2 cm
Toronto, Art Gallery of Ontario
71/87
© Estate of Giorgio De Chirico/SIAE (Rome)/
SODRAC (Montreal) 2000

The Lodger: A Story of the London Fog
Prod.: 1926 / Rel.: 1927
Frame enlargement
Paris, Cinémathèque française collection
Courtesy of Carlton International

Robert Walker in Strangers on a Train
Prod.: 1950 / Rel.: 1951
Frame enlargement
Paris, Cinémathèque française collection
© Warner Bros.

Léon Spilliaert
Belgian, 1881–1946
Vertigo
1908
India ink wash, watercolour and chalk on paper
64 x 48 cm
Ostend, Museum voor Schone Kunsten
1975/696
© Estate of Léon Spilliaert/SABAM (Brussels)/
SODRAC (Montreal) 2000

Claude Rains in Notorious
Prod.: 1945 / Rel.: 1946
Frame enlargement
Paris, Cinémathèque française collection
© Buena Vista International Inc.

Léon Spilliaert
Belgian, 1881–1946
Staircase
1909
India ink wash, watercolour and pastel on paper
49 x 71 cm
Brussels, private collection
© Estate of Léon Spilliaert/SABAM
(Brussels)/SODRAC (Montreal) 2000

Léon Spilliaert
Belgian, 1881–1946
The Liner or *The Strand*
1909
Watercolour and pastel on paper
70 x 60 cm
Private collection
055
© Estate of Léon Spilliaert/SABAM
(Brussels)/SODRAC (Montreal) 2000

Anthony Perkins for Psycho
Prod.: 1959–1960 / Rel.: 1960
Promotional still
Courtesy of the Academy of Motion Picture Arts
and Sciences
© 1960 Shamley Productions, Inc.
Courtesy of Universal Studios Licensing, Inc.

Philippe Halsman
Latvian-born American, 1906–1979
Tippi Hedren for The Birds
Prod.: 1962 / Rel.: 1963
Promotional still
Paris, Magnum Photos
© P. Halsman/Magnum Photos
© 1963 Alfred J. Hitchcock Productions, Inc.
Courtesy of Universal Studios

Philippe Halsman
Latvian-born American, 1906–1979
Tippi Hedren for The Birds
Prod.: 1962 / Rel.: 1963
Production still
Paris, Magnum Photos
© P. Halsman/Magnum Photos
© 1963 Alfred J. Hitchcock Productions, Inc.
Courtesy of Universal Studios Licensing, Inc.

Arthur Rackham
British, 1867–1939
The Seven Ravens
Illustration for the fairy tale by the Brothers Grimm
1900
Pen and watercolour on paper, 24 x 19.5 cm
Free Library of Philadelphia Rare Book Department
Reproduced with the kind permission
of the Arthur Rackham family
"Who has been eating off my plate?"

Tippi Hedren in The Birds
Prod.: 1962 / Rel.: 1963
Production still
Brussels, Cinémathèque Royale de Belgique
© 1963 Alfred J. Hitchcock Productions, Inc.
Courtesy of Universal Studios Licensing, Inc.

Robert Boyle
American, b. 1910
The Birds
Prod.: 1962 / Rel.: 1963
Original pre-production sketches, 53.3 x 69.9 cm
Courtesy of the Academy of Motion Picture Arts
and Sciences
© 1963 Alfred J. Hitchcock Productions, Inc.
Courtesy of Universal Studios Licensing, Inc.

Harold Michelson
American, b. 1920
The Birds
Prod.: 1962 / Rel.: 1963
Storyboards (3): Melanie and the children take cover in the convertible
Original drawings: 17 drawings on 6 pages
31.5 x 66 cm
Courtesy of the Academy of Motion Picture Arts and Sciences
© 1963 Alfred J. Hitchcock Productions, Inc.
All rights reserved
Courtesy of Universal Studios Licensing, Inc.

Harold Michelson
American, b. 1920
The Birds
Prod.: 1962 / Rel.: 1963
Original drawings (24 on 8 pages): storyboard for the schoolyard sequence, images 129–511
31.8 x 66 cm
Courtesy of the Academy of Motion Picture Arts and Sciences
© 1963 Alfred J. Hitchcock Productions, Inc.
All rights reserved
Courtesy of Universal Studios Licensing, Inc.

Max Ernst
German-born American and French, 1891–1976
Forest Bird
1927–1928
Oil on paper, mounted on cardboard
31 x 22.2 cm
Paris, Musée Picasso
M.P. 3595
© Estate of Max Ernst/ADAGP (Paris)/
SODRAC (Montreal) 2000

Alfred Kubin
Czech, 1877–1959
The Bat (Cemetery Wall)
1900–1903
India ink and wash on paper
24.8 x 18.2 cm
Linz, Oberösterreichisches Landesmuseum
© Estate of Alfred Kubin/VG Bild-Kunst (Bonn)/
SODRAC (Montreal) 2000

Léon Spilliaert
Belgian, 1881–1946
Bird of Prey
1904
India ink wash, ink and pencil on paper
43 x 57 cm
Brussels, Bibliothèque Royale de Belgique
S.V 81455
© Estate of Léon Spilliaert/SABAM (Brussels)/
SODRAC (Montreal) 2000

Georges Braque
French, 1882–1963
The Black Birds
1956–1957
Oil on canvas
181 x 229 cm
Paris, Paule and Adrien Maeght collection
© Estate of Georges Braque/ADAGP (Paris)/
SODRAC (Montreal) 2000

Nikolai Roerich
Russian, 1874–1947
Ominous
1901
Oil on canvas
103 x 230 cm
Saint Petersburg, The State Russian Museum

The Birds
Prod.: 1962 / Rel.: 1963
Frame enlargement: final shot
Paris, Cinémathèque française collection
© 1963 Alfred J. Hitchcock Productions, Inc.
All rights reserved
Courtesy of Universal Studios Licensing, Inc.

Eldon Garnet
Canadian, b. 1946
NO
1997
Chromogenic prints (3/4, 2/4)
124 x 124 cm (each)
Eldon Garnet collection

Gregory Crewdson
American, b. 1962
Untitled (Birds around Home)
1997
Chromogenic print
101.6 x 127 cm
Courtesy of Luhring Augustine Gallery, New York, and the artist

Philippe Halsman
Latvian-born American, 1906–1979
Tippi Hedren for The Birds
Prod.: 1962 / Rel.: 1963
Promotional still
Paris, Magnum Photos
© P. Halsman/Magnum Photos
© 1963 Alfred J. Hitchcock Productions, Inc.
All rights reserved
Courtesy of Universal Studios Licensing, Inc.

René Magritte
Belgian, 1898–1967
Deep Waters
1941
Oil on canvas
65 x 50 cm
Private collection
© Estate of René Magritte/ADAGP (Paris)/
SODRAC (Montreal) 2000

Sheer Terror

Alberto Martini
Italian, 1876–1954
Self-portrait
1929
Oil on canvas
64 x 83 cm
The Montreal Museum of Fine Arts

Alfred Kubin
Czech, 1877–1959
A Child's Soul
About 1905
Tempera on cardboard
21.7 x 29.9 cm
Linz, Oberösterreichisches Landesmuseum
© Estate of Alfred Kubin/VG Bild-Kunst (Bonn)/
SODRAC (Montreal) 2000

Edvard Munch
Norwegian, 1863–1944
The Scream
1895
Pencil and lithographic ink
35.4 x 25 cm
© The Munch Museum/The Munch-Ellingsen
Group/SODART (Canada) 2000

Janet Leigh in Psycho
Prod.: 1959–1960 / Rel.: 1960
Production still
Paris, BIFI (Bibliothèque du film)
© 1960 Shamley Productions, Inc.
Courtesy of Universal Studios Licensing, Inc.

The Thirty-nine Steps
Prod. / Rel.: 1935
Frame enlargements
Paris, BIFI (Bibliothèque du film)
Courtesy of Carlton International

Jessica Tandy in The Birds
Prod.: 1962 / Rel.: 1963
Frame enlargement
Paris, Cinémathèque française collection
© 1963 Alfred J. Hitchcock Productions, Inc.
Courtesy of Universal Studios Licensing, Inc.

To Catch a Thief
Prod.: 1954 / Rel.: 1955
Frame enlargement
Paris, Cinémathèque française collection
© Paramount Pictures

The first victim (The Lodger: A Story
of the London Fog)
Prod.: 1926 / Rel.: 1927
Frame enlargement
Paris, Cinémathèque française collection
Courtesy of Carlton International

John Stuart in Number Seventeen
Prod.: 1931 / Rel.: 1932
Frame enlargement
Paris, Cinémathèque française collection
© Canal + Image International

Judith Anderson and Joan Fontaine in Rebecca
Prod.: 1939 / Rel.: 1940
Production still
London, British Film Institute Collections
Courtesy of Buena Vista International Inc.

James Stewart in The Man Who Knew Too Much
Prod.: 1955 / Rel.: 1956
Frame enlargement
Paris, Cinémathèque française collection
© 1955 Filwite Productions
Courtesy of Universal Studios Licensing Inc.

Barbara Leigh-Hunt in *Frenzy*
Prod.: 1971 / Rel.: 1972
Production still
London, The Cinema Museum
Guy Edmonds
© 1972 Universal Pictures Limited
Courtesy of Universal Studios Licensing, Inc.

Karel Teige
Czech, 1900–1951
Untitled
About 1930
Photocollage
15.7 x 21.5 cm
June and Robert Leibowits collection

Philippe Halsman
Latvian-born American, 1906–1979
Alfred Hitchcock and Tippi Hedren for The Birds
Prod.: 1962 / Rel.: 1963
Promotional still
Paris, Magnum Photos
© P. Halsman/Magnum Photos
© 1963 Alfred J. Hitchcock Productions, Inc.
Courtesy of Universal Studios Licensing Inc.

Sylvia Sidney's hands and the kitchen knife (Sabotage)
Prod. / Rel.: 1936
Frame enlargement
Paris, Cinémathèque française collection
Courtesy of Carlton International

Romolo Romani
Italian, 1884–1916
Scream
1904–1905
Pencil on cardboard
48 x 32 cm
Cologne, Museum Ludwig
ML/DEP. 7217

Odilon Redon
French, 1840–1916
I continued to gaze on the chair,
and fancied I saw on it a pale blue misty outline
of a human figure
Plate 1 from six illustrations for the French
translation of Edward Bulwer-Lytton's story
The Haunted and the Haunters
1896
Lithograph
45.1 x 31.8 cm
Ottawa, National Gallery of Canada
NGC 15708.1

René Magritte
Belgian, 1898–1967
Fantomas
1926
India ink on paper
45 x 27 cm
Milan, Fondazione Antonio Mazzotta
© Estate of René Magritte/ADAGP (Paris)/
SODRAC (Montreal) 2000

Raymond Burr in Rear Window
Prod.: 1953 / Rel.: 1954
Frame enlargement
Paris, Cinémathèque française collection
© Universal Studios
All rights reserved
Courtesy of Universal Studios Licensing, Inc.
Presented by special agreement
with Mr. Sheldon Abend

Tony Oursler
American, b. 1957
Seed
1996
Video installation
45.5 x 45.5 x 262 cm
Toronto, Thomas H. Bjarnason collection
Courtesy of the artist and Metro Pictures

Georges De Feure
French, 1868–1943
The Suitor
1896
Oil on canvas, 81 x 65 cm
Private collection

Alberto Martini
Italian, 1876–1954
The Man of the Crowd
Illustration for the story by Edgar Allan Poe (1840)
1906
India ink on cardboard, 27.4 x 20 cm
Milan, private collection

Tom Morgan
Jack the Ripper
Date unknown
Photographic document
London, Mary Evans Picture Library
10010405/07

Alfred Kubin
Czech, 1877–1959
The Intruder
About 1936
India ink, watercolour and spatter on paper
42.8 x 33.5 cm
Linz, Oberösterreichisches Landesmuseum
© Estate of Alfred Kubin/VG Bild-Kunst (Bonn)/
SODRAC (Montreal) 2000

Alfred Kubin
Czech, 1877–1959
The Hour of Death
1903
Engraving, 32 x 23 cm
Milan, Fondazione Antonio Mazzotta
© Estate of Alfred Kubin/VG Bild-Kunst (Bonn)/
SODRAC (Montreal) 2000

Tom Morahan
Jamaica Inn
Prod.: 1938 / Rel.: 1939
Set design
Charcoal and monochrome wash
50 x 35 cm
London, British Film Institute Collections
Courtesy of Carlton International

Alfred Kubin
Czech, 1877–1959
A Walk on the Seashore
About 1900
India ink, wash and spraying on paper
32 x 39.7 cm
Vienna, Graphische Sammlung Albertina
33.468
© Estate of Alfred Kubin/VG Bild-Kunst (Bonn)/
SODRAC (Montreal) 2000

Anthony Perkins for Psycho
Prod.: 1959–1960 / Rel. 1960
Production still
London, British Film Institute Collections
© 1960 Shamley Productions, Inc.

Léon Spilliaert
Belgian, 1881–1946
The Couple
About 1902
India ink wash on paper
29.1 x 37.4 cm
Brussels, Musées royaux des Beaux-Arts
de Belgique
7851
© Estate of Léon Spilliaert/SABAM (Brussels)/
SODRAC (Montreal) 2000

***Ingrid Bergman and Gregory Peck in* Spellbound**
Prod.: 1944 / Rel.: 1945
Production still
The University of Texas at Austin, Harry Ransom
Humanities Research Center, Art Collection
© Buena Vista International Inc.

Murder!
Prod. / Rel.: 1930
Production still
London, British Film Institute Collections
© 1931 Canal + Image UK Ltd.

***The farmer and his wife in* The Thirty-nine Steps**
Prod. / Rel.: 1935
Production still
London, British Film Institute Collections
Courtesy of Carlton International

Karl Hubbuch
German, 1891–1979
Murder
1930
Oil on canvas, 69 x 78 cm
Wiesbaden, Frank Brabant collection

***Anna Massey's body* (Frenzy)**
Prod.: 1971 / Rel.: 1972
Frame enlargement
Paris, Cinémathèque française collection
© 1972 Universal Pictures Limited

***Anthony Perkins in* Psycho**
Prod.: 1959–1960 / Rel.: 1960
Frame enlargement
Paris, Cinémathèque française collection
© 1960 Shamley Productions, Inc.

Alberto Martini
Italian, 1876–1954
Folly
From the album *Misteri*
(Milan: Bottega di Poesia, 1923)
1914–1915
Lithograph, 34/50
35 x 25 cm
Paris, Galerie Elstir

***Head of Mrs. Bates* (Psycho)**
Prod.: 1959–1960 / Rel.: 1960
Wax, teeth and hair
32 x 27 x 23 cm
Paris, Cinémathèque française collection
© 1960 Shamley Productions, Inc.

The Mountain Eagle
Prod.: 1925 / Rel.: 1927
Production still
London, British Film Institute Collections

***The shrunken head* (Under Capricorn)**
Prod.: 1948 / Rel.: 1949
Frame enlargement
Paris, Cinémathèque française collection
© Transatlantic Pictures

***Anthony Perkins and John Gavin in* Psycho**
Prod.: 1959–1960 / Rel.: 1960
Frame enlargement
Paris, Cinémathèque française collection
© 1960 Shamley Productions, Inc.

Léon Frédéric
Belgian, 1856–1940
Studio Interior
1882
Oil on canvas, mounted on panel
158 x 117 cm
Brussels, Musée d'Ixelles
C.C.202

Forms and Rhythms

Max Ernst
German-born American and French, 1891–1976
The Fall of an Angel
1922
Collage and oil on paper
44 x 34 cm
Private collection
© Estate of Max Ernst/ADAGP (Paris)/
SODRAC (Montreal) 2000
(Not exhibited)

Ray Milland in Dial M for Murder
Prod.: 1953 / Rel.: 1954
Production still
Paris, BIFI (Bibliothèque du Film)
© Warner Bros.

Daniel Gélin in The Man Who Knew Too Much
Prod.: 1955 / Rel.: 1956
Frame enlargement
Paris, Cinémathèque française collection
© 1955 Filwite Productions, Inc.
All rights reserved
Courtesy of Universal Studios Licensing Inc.

The Thirty-nine Steps
Prod. / Rel.: 1935
Frame enlargement
Paris, Cinémathèque française collection
Courtesy of Carlton International

Robert Walker and Farley Granger in Strangers on a Train
Prod.: 1950 / Rel.: 1951
Frame enlargement
Paris, Cinémathèque française collection
© Warner Bros.

Gustave Caillebotte
French, 1848–1894
The Balcony
1880
Oil on canvas
65.4 x 54 cm
Private collection

Paul Klee
Swiss, 1879–1940
Captive (Figure of This World/Next World)
1940
Oil and distemper on glue sizing, on burlap
55 x 50 cm
Riehen/Basel, Fondation Beyeler
73.3
© Estate of Paul Klee/VG Bild-Kunst
(Bonn)/SODRAC (Montreal) 2000

Carl Brisson in The Ring
Prod. / Rel.: 1927
Frame enlargement
Paris, Cinémathèque française collection
© 1927 Canal + Image UK Ltd.

Norah Baring in Murder!
Prod. / Rel.: 1930
Frame enlargement
Paris, Cinémathèque française collection
© 1931 Canal + Image UK Ltd.

Robin Irvine and Annette Benson in Downhill
Prod. / Rel.: 1927
Frame enlargement
Paris, Cinémathèque française collection
Courtesy of Carlton International

Janet Leigh and John Gavin in Psycho
Prod.: 1959–1960 / Rel.: 1960
Promotional still
Courtesy of the Academy of Motion Picture Arts
and Sciences
© 1960 Shamley Productions, Inc.
All rights reserved
Courtesy of Universal Studios Licensing Inc.

Marnie
Prod.: 1963–1964 / Rel.: 1964
Production still
Courtesy of the Academy of Motion Picture Arts
and Sciences
© 1964 Geoffrey Stanley, Inc.
All rights reserved
Courtesy of Universal Studios Licensing Inc.

Sabotage
Prod. / Rel.: 1936
Frame enlargement
Paris, Cinémathèque française collection
Courtesy of Carlton International

Ivor Novello in Downhill
Prod. / Rel.: 1927
Frame enlargement
Paris, Cinémathèque française collection
Courtesy of Carlton International

Alida Valli for The Paradine Case
Prod.: 1946–1947 / Rel.: 1947
Promotional still
The University of Texas at Austin, Harry Ransom
Humanities Research Center, Art Collection
© Buena Vista International Inc.

Blackmail
Prod. / Rel.: 1929
Frame enlargement
Paris, Cinémathèque française collection
© 1929 Canal + Image UK Ltd.

**Gregory Peck in Alida Valli's room
(The Paradine Case)**
Prod.: 1946–1947 / Rel.: 1947
Production still
The University of Texas at Austin, Harry Ransom
Humanities Research Center, Art Collection
© Buena Vista International Inc.

Gregory Peck and lawyer in **The Paradine Case**
Prod.: 1946–1947 / Rel.: 1947
Production still
The University of Texas at Austin, Harry Ransom
Humanities Research Center, Art Collection
© Buena Vista International Inc.

Paul Klee
Swiss, 1879–1940
Rock Temple
1925
India ink on paper, mounted on cardboard
16.5 x 27 cm
Milan, Fondazione Antonio Mazzotta
© Estate of Paul Klee/VG Bild-Kunst (Bonn)/
SODRAC (Montreal) 2000

Cary Grant and Eva Marie Saint
on Mount Rushmore set **(North by Northwest)**
Prod.: 1958 / Rel.: 1959
Production still
Courtesy of the Academy of Motion Picture Arts
and Sciences
© Warner Bros.

Charles Borup
d. 1949
Rails
Late 1920s
Gelatin silver print
29.1 x 24.4 cm
Bath, The Royal Photographic Society Collection
RPS 9440

Joseph Cotten in **Shadow of a Doubt**
Prod.: 1942 / Rel.: 1943
Frame enlargement
Paris, Cinémathèque française collection
© 1942 Universal Pictures Company, Inc.
All rights reserved
Courtesy of Universal Studios Licensing Inc.

Alfred Junge
German, 1886–1964
Young and Innocent
Prod.: 1937 / Rel.: 1938
Set design: "Wooden model"
Charcoal and ink wash on paper
56 x 78 cm
Paris, BIFI (Bibliothèque du film)
© Alfred Junge

Strangers on a Train
Prod.: 1950 / Rel.: 1951
Frame enlargement
Paris, Cinémathèque française collection
© Warner Bros.

Ralston Crawford
Canadian-born American, 1906–1978
Lights in an Aircraft Plant
1945
Oil on canvas
77.1 x 102.2 cm
Washington, National Gallery of Art, gift of
Mr. and Mrs. Burton Tremaine
1971.87.1

Edward Burra
British, 1905–1976
Rossi
1930
Gouache over graphite heightened with gum arabic
on paper
65.3 x 48.5 cm
Ottawa, National Gallery of Canada
NGC 6493
© Alex Reid and Lefevre Ltd., London

Ivor Novello and Isabel Jeans in **Downhill**
Prod. / Rel.: 1927
Frame enlargement
Paris, Cinémathèque française collection
Courtesy of Carlton International

Ingrid Bergman for **Notorious**
Prod.: 1945 / Rel.: 1946
Promotional still
Courtesy of the Academy of Motion Picture Arts
and Sciences
© Buena Vista International Inc.

Michael Snow
Canadian, b. 1929
Door
1979
Photomontage, 2/2
208.6 x 99.9 cm
The Montreal Museum of Fine Arts, purchase,
Canada Council matching grant
1979.32

Georgi Zimin
Russian, 1900–1985
Still Life with Comb and Scissors
1928–1930
Gelatin silver print
23.7 x 29.5 cm
Cologne, Museum Ludwig
ML/F 1992/104

Ingrid Bergman in **Spellbound**
Prod.: 1944 / Rel.: 1945
Frame enlargement
Paris, Cinémathèque française collection
© Buena Vista International Inc.

Léon Spilliaert
Belgian, 1881–1946
Carafe
About 1917
Wash on paper, 29 x 22 cm
Ostend, Deforche-Tricot Collection
© Estate of Léon Spilliaert/SABAM
(Brussels)/SODRAC (Montreal) 2000

André Kertész
Hungarian-born American, 1894–1985
Tokyo
1968
Gelatin silver print, 35.4 x 28 cm
Toronto, Art Gallery of Ontario, gift of
Ann and Harry Malcolmson, 1997
97/2078

André Kertész
Hungarian-born American, 1894–1985
Shadows, Paris
1931
Gelatin silver print, 25.2 x 20.3 cm
Ottawa, National Gallery of Canada, gift of the
American Friends of Canada Committee Inc.
NGC 37887

Production designer: Paul Sylbert
The Wrong Man
Prod. / Rel.: 1956
Storyboard drawing for post-credits scene
(Hitchcock's cameo)
Courtesy of the Academy of Motion Picture Arts
and Sciences
© Warner Bros.

The assassination **(Foreign Correspondent)**
Prod. / Rel.: 1940
Frame enlargement
Paris, Cinémathèque française collection
© Canal + Image International

Alfred Junge
German, 1886–1964
Young and Innocent
Prod.: 1937 / Rel.: 1938
Set design: "Courthouse corridor"
Charcoal and ink wash on paper
56 x 78 cm
Paris, BIFI (Bibliothèque du film)
© Alfred Junge

Umbo (pseudonym of Otto Umbehr)
German, 1902–1980
Mystery of the Street
1928 (later print)
Gelatin silver print, 23.5 x 17.9 cm
Paris, Musée National d'Art Moderne/Centre de
création industrielle, Centre Georges Pompidou
AM 1980-205

Young and Innocent
Prod.: 1937 / Rel.: 1938
Production still
Brussels, Cinémathèque Royale de Belgique
Courtesy of Carlton International

Bernard Boutet De Monvel
French, 1881–1949
New York Rooftops
About 1930
Oil on canvas
70 x 76 cm
Musée des Beaux-Arts d'Orléans
76.1.1

Martin Lewis
Australian-born American, 1881–1962
East Side Night, Williamsburg Bridge (New York)
1928
Etching
33.2 x 38.9 cm
The Montreal Museum of Fine Arts,
gift of Patricia Lewis in memory of Martin Lewis
Gr.1995.3

Shadow of a Doubt
Prod.: 1942 / Rel.: 1943
Frame enlargement
Paris, Cinémathèque française collection
© 1942 Universal Pictures Company, Inc.
All rights reserved
Courtesy of Universal Studios Licensing Inc.

James Stewart for **Vertigo**
Prod.: 1957 / Rel.: 1958
Production still
London, The Cinema Museum
Richard Hamilton
© 1958 Universal City Studios, Inc.
All rights reserved
Courtesy of Universal Studios Licensing, Inc.

Cary Grant in **To Catch a Thief**
Prod.: 1954 / Rel.: 1955
Production still
Paris, BIFI (Bibliothèque du film)
© Paramount Pictures

North by Northwest
Prod.: 1958 / Rel.: 1959
Frame enlargement
Paris, Cinémathèque française collection
© Warner Bros.

The Thirty-nine Steps
Prod. / Rel.: 1935
Frame enlargement
Paris, Cinémathèque française collection
Courtesy of Carlton International

Norman Lloyd in Saboteur
Prod. / Rel.: 1942
Frame enlargement
Paris, Cinémathèque française collection

To Catch a Thief
Prod.: 1954 / Rel.: 1955
Frame enlargement
Paris, Cinémathèque française collection

Murder!
Prod. / Rel.: 1930
Frame enlargement
Paris, Cinémathèque française collection

Hans Schmithals
German, 1878–1964
Combatants
1902–1905
Pastel on paper, 105 x 67 cm
Paris, Galerie Elstir
(Not exhibited)

Félix De Boeck
Belgian, 1898–1995
Vertigo
1920
Oil on canvas, 68 x 59 cm
Private collection
059

Leon M. Lion and John Stuart in Number Seventeen
Prod.: 1931 / Rel.: 1932
Frame enlargement
Paris, Cinémathèque française collection

Sabotage
Prod. / Rel.: 1936
Frame enlargement
Paris, Cinémathèque française collection

The organist's death (Secret Agent)
Prod.: 1935 / Rel.: 1936
Frame enlargement
Paris, Cinémathèque française collection

Blackmail
Prod. / Rel.: 1929
Frame enlargement
Paris, Cinémathèque française collection

James Stewart in Vertigo
Prod.: 1957 / Rel.: 1958
Production still
Courtesy of the Academy of Motion Picture Arts and Sciences

Anny Ondra in Blackmail
Prod. / Rel.: 1929
Frame enlargement
Paris, Cinémathèque française collection

Man Ray
American, 1890–1976
Murderous Logic
[1919]–1975
Typographic composition printed on paper
73.5 x 53.5 cm
Milan, Galleria Gio' Marconi

Saul Bass
American, 1920–1996
Opening credits, Vertigo
Prod.: 1957 / Rel.: 1958
Preliminary studies
Courtesy of the Academy of Motion Picture Arts and Sciences

Opening credits, Vertigo
Prod.: 1957 / Rel.: 1958
Frame enlargement
Paris, Collection Cinémathèque française

Opening credits, Vertigo
Prod.: 1957 / Rel.: 1958
Frame enlargement
Paris, Collection Cinémathèque française

August Sander
German, 1876–1964
Spiral of Light Bulbs
Advertisement for the Osram Company
About 1930
Gelatin silver print
29.5 x 22.9 cm

New York, The Metropolitan Museum of Art,
Ford Motor Company Collection, gift
of Ford Motor Company and John C. Waddell, 1987
1987.1100.45

Marcel Duchamp
French, 1887–1968
Rotoreliefs
Optical Disks
Registered Patterns
Corolles [obverse]
Œuf à la coque [reverse]
Lanterne chinoise [obverse]
Lampe [reverse]
Poisson japonais [obverse]
Escargot [reverse]
Verre de Bohême [obverse]
Cerceaux [reverse]
Cage [reverse]
1935
Six rotating disks (33 1/3 rpm)
Colour offset lithographs mounted on cardboard
20 cm (diam. each)
Paris, Cinémathèque Française collection
P.0038–P.0043
© Estate of Marcel Duchamp/ADAGP
(Paris)/SODRAC (Montréal) 2000

Saul Bass
American, 1920–1996
Vertigo
Prod.: 1957 / Rel.: 1958
Poster for U.S. release
Offset print
104.1 x 68.6 cm
Beverly Hills, courtesy of the Academy of Motion
Picture Arts and Sciences
© 1958 Saul Bass
© 1958 Universal City Studios, Inc.
All rights reserved
Courtesy of Universal Studios Licensing Inc.

Opening credits, Psycho
Prod.: 1959–1960 / Rel.: 1960
Frame enlargement
Paris, Cinémathèque française collection
© 1960 Shamley Productions, Inc.
All rights reserved
Courtesy of Universal Studios Licensing Inc.

Bridget Riley
British, b. 1931
Blaze 4
1964
Emulsion on hardboard
94.6 x 94.6 cm
Collection of the artist

Hitchcock and Dalí

*James Basevi, Alfred Hitchcock and Salvador Dalí
for* Spellbound
Prod.: 1944 / Rel.: 1945
Production still
The University of Texas at Austin, Harry Ransom
Humanities Research Center, Art Collection
© Buena Vista International Inc.
© Salvador Dalí, VEGAP (Spain)/
SODART (Canada) 2000

Salvador Dalí for Spellbound
Prod.: 1944 / Rel.: 1945
Promotional still
The University of Texas at Austin, Harry Ransom
Humanities Research Center, Art Collection
© Buena Vista International Inc.
© Salvador Dalí, VEGAP (Spain)/
SODART (Canada) 2000

William Cameron Menzies
American, 1896–1957
Spellbound
Prod.: 1944 / Rel.: 1945
Storyboard No. 2
Photograph with black and red pencil marks
18.1 x 22.9 cm
The University of Texas at Austin, David O. Selznick
Collection, Harry Ransom Humanities Research
Center, Art Collection
© Buena Vista International Inc.

Spellbound
Prod.: 1944 / Rel.: 1945
Frame enlargement
Paris, Cinémathèque française collection
© Buena Vista International Inc.
© Salvador Dalí, VEGAP (Spain)/
SODART (Canada) 2000

Fritz Lang
Austrian, naturalized American, 1890–1976
Metropolis
1926–1927
Frame enlargement: Freder's nightmare
(Not exhibited)

William Cameron Menzies
Spellbound
Prod.: 1944 / Rel.: 1945
Storyboard No. 8
Black and white photograph
17.8 x 23.5 cm
The University of Texas at Austin, David O. Selznick
Collection, Harry Ransom Humanities Research
Center, Art Collection
© Buena Vista International Inc.

Salvador Dalí
Spanish, 1904–1989
Study for the dream sequence in **Spellbound**
1944
Oil on panel
89 x 113.8 cm
Gala–Salvador Dalí Foundation
0329, 0330, 0331
© Kingdom of Spain, Universal Heir of Salvador
Dalí/SODART (Canada) 2000
© Gala–Salvador Dalí Foundation, by appointment
of the Kingdom of Spain/SODART (Canada) 2000

Salvador Dalí (under the supervision of)
Spanish, 1904–1989
Set design for **Spellbound**
1945
Oil on canvas
518.8 x 1158.2 cm
Private collection
Courtesy of James Bigwood
(Not exhibited)

*Salvador Dalí tracing chalk outline of path
of giant scissors on scenic "Eye" backdrop
for* **Spellbound**
Prod.: 1944 / Rel.: 1945
Production still
The University of Texas at Austin, Harry Ransom
Humanities Research Center, Art Collection
© Buena Vista International Inc.
© Salvador Dalí, VEGAP (Spain)/
SODART (Canada) 2000

Salvador Dalí
Spanish, 1904–1989
The Eye
1944
Study for the dream sequence in *Spellbound*
Oil on panel
58.7 x 84 cm
Private collection
838
© Kingdom of Spain, Universal Heir of Salvador
Dalí/SODART (Canada) 2000
© Gala–Salvador Dalí Foundation, by appointment
of the Kingdom of Spain/SODART (Canada) 2000

Salvador Dalí (for Alfred Hitchcock)
Spanish, 1904–1989
*Rhonda Fleming, Gregory Peck and Edward
Fielding in the dream sequence* (Spellbound)
Prod.: 1944 / Rel.: 1945
Frame enlargement
New York, Museum of Modern Art
© Salvador Dalí, VEGAP (Spain)/
SODART (Canada) 2000
Courtesy of James Bigwood
(Not exhibited)

The dream sequence (Spellbound)
Prod.: 1944 / Rel.: 1945
Frame enlargement
Paris, Cinémathèque française collection
© Buena Vista International Inc.
© Salvador Dalí, VEGAP (Spain)/
SODART (Canada) 2000

Luis Buñuel
Spanish, 1900–1983
Frame enlargement from the prologue to
Un chien andalou
1929
(Not exhibited)

William Cameron Menzies
American, 1896–1957
Spellbound
Prod.: 1944 / Rel.: 1945
Storyboard No. 7
Pencil on paper, mounted on cardboard
38.1 x 39.4 cm
The University of Texas at Austin, David O. Selznick
Collection, Harry Ransom Humanities Research
Center, Art Collection
© Buena Vista International Inc.

The gaming house from the dream sequence
(Spellbound)
Prod.: 1944 / Rel.: 1945
Production still
The University of Texas at Austin, Harry Ransom
Humanities Research Center, Art Collection
© Buena Vista International Inc.
© Salvador Dalí, VEGAP (Spain)/
SODART (Canada) 2000

*Rhonda Fleming on gaming house set during
shooting of the dream sequence* (Spellbound)
Prod.: 1944 / Rel.: 1945
Production still
The University of Texas at Austin, Harry Ransom
Humanities Research Center, Art Collection
© Buena Vista International Inc.
© Salvador Dalí, VEGAP (Spain)/
SODART (Canada) 2000

Kurt Seligmann
Swiss-born American, 1900–1962
Ultrameuble
1938
Mixed media
Whereabouts unknown (perhaps destroyed)
(Not exhibited)

Salvador Dalí
Spanish, 1904–1989
***Drawing for* Spellbound**
1944
India ink and pencil on paper, 15.8 x 20 cm
Private collection
© Salvador Dalí, VEGAP (Spain)/
SODART (Canada) 2000
Courtesy of James Bigwood
(Not exhibited)

Man Ray
American, 1890–1976
Object of Destruction
[1923]–1966
Metronome and photograph
23.5 x 10.8 x 10.8 cm
Private collection
© Man Ray Trust/ADAGP (Paris)/
SODRAC (Montreal) 2000

Spellbound
Prod.: 1944 / Rel.: 1945
Sheet from original storyboard No. 14
1944
Mixed media on paper
15.8 x 20 cm
Private collection
© Prudence Cuming Associates Limited
© Salvador Dalí, VEGAP (Spain)/
SODART (Canada) 2000

Spellbound
Prod.: 1944 / Rel.: 1945
Frame enlargement
Paris, Cinémathèque française collection
© Buena Vista International Inc.
© Salvador Dalí, VEGAP (Spain)/
SODART (Canada) 2000

Spellbound
Prod.: 1944 / Rel.: 1945
Sheet from original storyboard No. 15
1944
Mixed media on paper, 15.8 x 20 cm
Private collection
© Prudence Cuming Associates Limited
© Salvador Dalí, VEGAP (Spain)/
SODART (Canada) 2000

Spellbound
Prod.: 1944 / Rel.: 1945
Sheet from original storyboard No. 24
1944
Mixed media on paper, 15.8 x 20 cm
Private collection
© Prudence Cuming Associates Limited
© Salvador Dalí, VEGAP (Spain)/
SODART (Canada) 2000

Spellbound
Prod.: 1944 / Rel.: 1945
Frame enlargement
Paris, Cinémathèque française collection
© Buena Vista International Inc.

***The dream sequence* (Spellbound)**
Prod.: 1944 / Rel.: 1945
Frame enlargement
Paris, Cinémathèque française collection
© Buena Vista International Inc.
© Salvador Dalí, VEGAP (Spain)/
SODART (Canada) 2000

Spellbound
Prod.: 1944 / Rel.: 1945
Sheet from original storyboard No. 25
1944
Mixed media on paper
15.8 x 20 cm
Private collection
© Prudence Cuming Associates Limited
© Salvador Dalí, VEGAP (Spain)/
SODART (Canada) 2000

Max Ernst
German-born American and French, 1891–1976
Two Children Are Threatened by a Nightingale
1924
Oil on panel, wood structure
69.8 x 57.1 x 11.4 cm
New York, The Museum of Modern Art, purchase,
1937
© 2000 The Museum of Modern Art, New York
© Estate of Max Ernst/ADAGP (Paris)/
SODRAC (Montreal) 2000
(Not exhibited)

***Ingrid Bergman in* Spellbound**
Prod.: 1944 / Rel.: 1945
Promotional still
The University of Texas at Austin, Harry Ransom
Humanities Research Center, Art Collection
© Buena Vista International Inc.

The ballroom from the dream sequence
(Spellbound)
Prod.: 1944 / Rel.: 1945
Production still
The University of Texas at Austin, Harry Ransom
Humanities Research Center, Art Collection
© Buena Vista International Inc.
© Salvador Dalí, VEGAP (Spain)/
SODART (Canada) 2000

Salvador Dalí
Spanish, 1904–1989
Untitled (Study for the ballroom from the dream sequence in Spellbound)
1944
Oil on canvas, 50.5 x 60.5 cm
Private collection
© Salvador Dalí, VEGAP (Spain)/
SODART (Canada) 2000
(Not exhibited)

Spellbound
Prod.: 1944 / Rel.: 1945
Sheet from original storyboard No. 13
1944
Mixed media on paper, 15.8 x 20 cm
Private collection
© Prudence Cuming Associates Limited
© Salvador Dalí, VEGAP (Spain)/
SODART (Canada) 2000

Spellbound
Prod.: 1944 / Rel.: 1945
Sheet from original storyboard No. 32
1944
Mixed media on paper, 15.8 x 20 cm
Private collection
© Prudence Cuming Associates Limited
© Salvador Dalí, VEGAP (Spain)/
SODART (Canada) 2000 *

Gregory Peck and Ingrid Bergman during the ballroom scene (Spellbound)
Prod.: 1944 / Rel.: 1945
Production still
The University of Texas at Austin, Harry Ransom Humanities Research Center, Art Collection
© Buena Vista International Inc.

Alfred Hitchcock directing Ingrid Bergman and Gregory Peck (Spellbound)
Prod.: 1944 / Rel.: 1945
Production still
The University of Texas at Austin, Harry Ransom Humanities Research Center, Art Collection
© Buena Vista International Inc.

Ingrid Bergman transformed into a statue (Spellbound)
Prod.: 1944 / Rel.: 1945
Production still
The University of Texas at Austin, Harry Ransom Humanities Research Center, Art Collection
© Buena Vista International Inc.

Salvador Dalí
Spanish, 1904–1989
Study for the dream sequence in Spellbound
1944

Oil on panel, 89 x 113.8 cm
Gala–Salvador Dalí Foundation
0329, 0330, 0331
© Kingdom of Spain, Universal Heir of Salvador Dalí/SODART (Canada) 2000
© Gala–Salvador Dalí Foundation, by appointment of the Kingdom of Spain/SODART (Canada) 2000

William Cameron Menzies
American, 1896–1957
Spellbound
Prod.: 1944 / Rel.: 1945
Storyboard No. 25
Photograph with paint
17.8 x 23.5 cm
The University of Texas at Austin, David O. Selznick Collection, Harry Ransom Humanities Research Center, Art Collection
© Buena Vista International Inc.

Ingrid Bergman transformed into a statue (Spellbound)
Prod.: 1944 / Rel.: 1945
Production still
The University of Texas at Austin, Harry Ransom Humanities Research Center, Art Collection
© Buena Vista International Inc.
© Salvador Dalí, VEGAP (Spain)/
SODART (Canada) 2000

Ingrid Bergman transformed into a statue (Spellbound)
Prod.: 1944 / Rel.: 1945
Production still
The University of Texas at Austin, Harry Ransom Humanities Research Center, Art Collection
© Buena Vista International Inc.
© Salvador Dalí, VEGAP (Spain)/
SODART (Canada) 2000

Ingrid Bergman transformed into a statue (Spellbound)
Prod.: 1944 / Rel.: 1945
Production still
The University of Texas at Austin, Harry Ransom Humanities Research Center, Art Collection
© Buena Vista International Inc.
© Salvador Dalí, VEGAP (Spain)/
SODART (Canada) 2000

Statue modelled on Ingrid Bergman's body (Spellbound)
Prod.: 1944 / Rel.: 1945
Production still
The University of Texas at Austin, Harry Ransom Humanities Research Center, Art Collection
© Buena Vista International Inc.
© Salvador Dalí, VEGAP (Spain)/
SODART (Canada) 2000

Salvador Dalí
Spanish, 1904–1989
Untitled. Drawing for statue sequences
1944
Ink, ink wash and pencil on board
57.5 x 38.8 cm
Private collection
© Salvador Dalí, VEGAP (Spain)/
SODART (Canada) 2000
Courtesy of James Bigwood
(Not exhibited)

Salvador Dalí
Spanish, 1904–1989
Study for the dream sequence in Spellbound
1944
Oil on panel
89 x 113.8 cm
Gala–Salvador Dalí Foundation
0329, 0330, 0331
© Kingdom of Spain, Universal Heir of Salvador
Dalí/SODART (Canada) 2000
© Gala–Salvador Dalí Foundation, by appointment
of the Kingdom of Spain/
SODART (Canada) 2000

Salvador Dalí
Spanish, 1904–1989
Spellbound
Prod.: 1944 / Rel.: 1945
Sheet from original storyboard No. 32
1944
Mixed media on paper
15.8 x 20 cm
Private collection
© Prudence Cuming Associates Limited
© Salvador Dalí, VEGAP (Spain)/
SODART (Canada) 2000

Spellbound
Prod.: 1944 / Rel.: 1945
Frame enlargement
Paris, Cinémathèque française collection
© Buena Vista International Inc.
© Salvador Dalí, VEGAP (Spain)/
SODART (Canada) 2000

Spellbound
Prod.: 1944 / Rel.: 1945
Sheet from original storyboard No. 38
1944
Mixed media on paper
15.8 x 20 cm
Private collection
© Prudence Cuming Associates Limited
© Salvador Dalí, VEGAP (Spain)/
SODART (Canada) 2000

Spellbound
Prod.: 1944 / Rel.: 1945
Sheet from original storyboard No. 39
1944
Mixed media on paper
15.8 x 20 cm
Private collection
© Prudence Cuming Associates Limited
© Salvador Dalí, VEGAP (Spain)/
SODART (Canada) 2000

Downhill
Prod. / Rel.: 1927
Cover page advertisement,
Kinematograph Weekly
1927 (5 May)
Lithograph
22 x 30 cm
London, The Cinema Museum
Guy Edmonds

Unsigned
**Les cheveux d'or (The Lodger: A Story
of the London Fog)**
Prod.: 1926 / Rel.: 1927
Poster for French release
Offset print mounted on canvas
152.5 x 113 cm
Private collection
Philippe Le Jeune
© Mappemonde

Unsigned
Le rideau déchiré (Torn Curtain)
Prod.: 1965–1966 / Rel.: 1966
Poster for French release
Offset print mounted on canvas
120 x 160 cm
Private collection
© Universal Pictures
All rights reserved
Courtesy of Universal Studios Licensing, Inc.

Unsigned
Frenzy
Prod.: 1971 / Rel.: 1972
Poster for French release
Offset print mounted on canvas
163 x 125 cm
Paris, BIFI (Bibliothèque du film)
© 1972 Universal Pictures Limited
All rights reserved
Courtesy of Universal Studios Licensing, Inc.

Eryk Lipinski
Polish, 1908–1991
Akt oskarżenia (The Paradine Case)
Prod.: 1946–1947 / Rel.: 1947
Poster for Polish release
Offset print mounted on canvas
91 x 64 cm
Paris, BIFI (Bibliothèque du film)
Eryk Lipinski
© Buena Vista International Inc.

Guy Jouineau and Guy Bourduge
Sabotage
Prod. / Rel.: 1936
Poster for French re-release
Offset print mounted on canvas
159 x 121 cm
Paris, BIFI (Bibliothèque du film)
© Jouineau Bourduge

Unsigned
I prigionièri dell'ocèano (Lifeboat)
Prod.: 1943 / Rel.: 1944
Poster for Italian release
Offset print
205.7 x 104.1 cm
Beverly Hills, courtesy of the Academy of Motion
Picture Arts and Sciences
© 20th Century Fox

Boris Grinsson
Les oiseaux (The Birds)
Poster for French release
Offset print mounted on canvas
120 x 160 cm
Private collection
© 1963 Alfred J. Hitchcock Productions, Inc.
All rights reserved
Courtesy of Universal Studios Licensing, Inc.
© Estate of Boris Grinsson/ADAGP (Paris)/
SODRAC (Montreal) 2000
(Not exhibited)

Unsigned
Dial M for Murder
Prod.: 1953 / Rel.: 1954
Poster for U.S. release
Offset print mounted on canvas
109 x 72 cm
Paris, BIFI (Bibliothèque du film)
© Warner Bros.

Unsigned
Rear Window
Prod.: 1953 / Rel.: 1954
Poster for U.S. release
Offset print mounted on canvas
108 x 72 cm
Paris, BIFI (Bibliothèque du film)
© Universal Studios
All rights reserved
Courtesy of Universal Studios Licensing, Inc.
Presented by special agreement
with Mr. Sheldon Abend

Unsigned
Sueurs froides / Zij die tweemal leefde (Vertigo)
Prod.: 1957 / Rel.: 1958
Poster for Belgian release
Offset print mounted on canvas
40 x 58 cm
Paris, BIFI (Bibliothèque du film)
© Universal Studios

List of Figures

Oscar Homolka in Sabotage
Prod. / Rel.: 1936
Frame enlargement
Paris, Cinémathèque française collection
Courtesy of Carlton International

Fritz Lang
German-born American, 1890–1976
Spies
1928
Production still

Judith Anderson in Rebecca
Prod.: 1939 / Rel.: 1940
Frame enlargement
Paris, Cinémathèque française collection
© Buena Vista International Inc.

Philip Hermogenes Calderon
British, 1833–1898
Whither?
1867
Oil on canvas
86.5 x 111.5 cm
Royal Academy of Arts, London

Notorious
Prod.: 1945 / Rel.: 1946
Frame enlargement
Paris, Cinémathèque française collection
© Buena Vista International Inc.

Notorious
Prod.: 1945 / Rel.: 1946
Production still
© Buena Vista International Inc.

George Grosz
German-born American, 1893–1959
John the Woman Slayer
1918
Oil on canvas
86.5 x 81 cm
Hamburg, Hamburger Kunsthalle
N. 5112
© Fotowerkstatt Elke Walford

Thomas Theodor Heine
German, 1867–1849
Jealousy
1894
Gouache on paper
31 x 52 cm
Munich, Private collection

Esme Percy in Murder!
Prod. / Rel.: 1930
Frame enlargement
Paris, Cinémathèque française collection
© 1931 Canal + Image UK Ltd.

Herbert Marshall in Murder!
Prod. / Rel.: 1930
Frame enlargement
Paris, Cinémathèque française collection
© 1931 Canal + Image UK Ltd.

Judith Anderson in Rebecca
Prod.: 1939 / Rel.: 1940
Frame enlargement
Paris, Cinémathèque française collection
© Buena Vista International Inc.

Judith Anderson in Rebecca
Prod.: 1939 / Rel.: 1940
Frame enlargement
Paris, Cinémathèque française collection
© Buena Vista International Inc.

**The estate of Manderley in flames
(Rebecca)**
Prod.: 1939 / Rel.: 1940
Frame enlargement
Paris, Cinémathèque française collection
© Buena Vista International Inc.

Franz von Stuck
German, 1863–1928
The Damnation of the Nibelungen
About 1920
Oil on canvas
98 x 41.2 cm
Private collection

Fritz Lang
German-born American, 1890–1976
Das Nibelungen (II)
1924
Production still: final scene

**Henri Langlois – The Man Who Never Feared
The Unknown**

Anonymous
*In the foyer of the Plaza-Athénée in Paris,
Alfred Hitchcock is decorated with the rank
of Chevalier de la Légion d'honneur
by Henri Langlois*
1971 (June)
Photograph
Private collection

Donald Spoto – Hitchcock and the World of Dream

Joseph Cotten's hands (Shadow of a Doubt)
Prod.: 1942 / Rel.: 1943
Frame enlargement
Paris, Cinémathèque française collection
© 1942 Universal Pictures Company, Inc.
Courtesy of Universal Studios Licensing, Inc.

James Stewart's nightmare (Vertigo)
Prod.: 1957 / Rel.: 1958
Production still
London, The Cinema Museum
© 1958 Universal City Studios, Inc.
Courtesy of Universal Studios Licensing, Inc.

Gregory Peck and Ingrid Bergman in Spellbound
Prod.: 1944 / Rel.: 1945
Frame enlargement
Paris, Cinémathèque française collection
© Buena Vista International Inc.

Anthony Perkins in Psycho
Prod.: 1959–1960 / Rel.: 1960
Frame enlargement
Paris, Cinémathèque française collection
© 1960 Shamley Productions, Inc.
Courtesy of Universal Studios Licensing, Inc.

The mummified Mrs. Bates (Psycho)
Prod.: 1959–1960 / Rel.: 1960
Frame enlargement
Paris, Cinémathèque française collection
© 1960 Shamley Productions, Inc.
Courtesy of Universal Studios Licensing, Inc.

Jessica Tandy in The Birds
Prod.: 1962 / Rel.: 1963
Frame enlargement
Paris, Cinémathèque française collection
© 1963 Alfred J. Hitchcock Productions, Inc.
Courtesy of Universal Studios Licensing, Inc.

Leopoldine Konstantin and Claude Rains in Notorious
Prod.: 1945 / Rel.: 1946
Frame enlargement
Paris, Cinémathèque française collection
© Buena Vista International Inc.

Dominique Païni – The Wandering Gaze: Hitchcock's Use of *Transparencies*

Marcel Duchamp
French, 1887–1968
Draft Piston
1914
Positive print on celluloid
29.9 x 23.7 cm
Private collection
© Estate of Marcel Duchamp / ADAGP (Paris) / SODRAC (Montreal) 2000

Marlene Dietrich
1942
Photograph

Rear projection technology
"The New Mitchell Background Projector"
Ink on paper

La science au théâtre: The Ride of the Valkyries as staged in Paris
La nature, No. 1047, 1893 (24 June)

Phantasmagorical effects: theatrical performance as part of a show entitled La nonne sanglante
Mid 19th century

Albrecht Dürer
German, 1471–about 1528
Draftsman Drawing a Reclining Nude
Illustration for the treatise *Underweysung der Messung mit dem Zirckel und Richtscheyt (A Course in the Art of Measurement with Compass and Ruler)*
1575
7.5 x 21.5 cm
Berlin, Staatliche Museen Preußischer Kulturbesitz
© Staatliche Museen Preußischer Kulturbesitz, Berlin
Jörg P. Anders

The Lady Vanishes
Prod.: 1937 / Rel.: 1938
Frame enlargement
Paris, Cinémathèque française collection
Courtesy of Carlton International

Herbert Marshall in Murder!
Prod. / Rel.: 1930
Frame enlargement
Paris, Cinémathèque française collection
© 1931 Canal + Image UK Ltd.

The Skin Game
Prod.: 1930–1931 / Rel.: 1931
Frame enlargement
Paris, Cinémathèque française collection
© 1931 Canal + Image UK Ltd.

Nova Pilbeam, Derrick de Marney and Edward Rigby in **Young and Innocent**
Prod.: 1937 / Rel.: 1938
Production still
London, British Film Institute Collections
Courtesy of Carlton International

On the set of **Young and Innocent**
Prod.: 1937 / Rel.: 1938
Production still
London, British Film Institute Collections
Courtesy of Carlton International

Shot from the movie theatre scene (Saboteur)
Prod. / Rel.: 1942
Frame enlargement
Paris, Cinémathèque française collection
© 1942 Universal Pictures Company, Inc.
All rights reserved
Courtesy of Universal Studios Licensing, Inc.

Shot from the movie theatre scene (Saboteur)
Prod. / Rel.: 1942
Frame enlargement
Paris, Cinémathèque française collection
© 1942 Universal Pictures Company, Inc.
All rights reserved
Courtesy of Universal Studios Licensing, Inc.

May Whitty and Margaret Lockwood in **The Lady Vanishes**
Prod.: 1937 / Rel.: 1938
Production still
Paris, BIFI (Bibliothèque du film)
Courtesy of Carlton International

May Whitty and Margaret Lockwood in **The Lady Vanishes**
Prod.: 1937 / Rel.: 1938
Frame enlargement
Paris, Cinémathèque française collection
Courtesy of Carlton International

Gregory Peck and Ingrid Bergman in **Spellbound**
Prod.: 1944 / Rel.: 1945
Frame enlargement
Paris, Cinémathèque française collection
© Buena Vista International Inc.

Gregory Peck and Ingrid Bergman in **Spellbound**
Prod.: 1944 / Rel.: 1945
Frame enlargement
Paris, Cinémathèque française collection
© Buena Vista International Inc.

Caspar David Friedrich
German, 1774–1840
Landscape in the Riesengebirge
About 1823
Oil on canvas
35 x 48.8 cm
1052
Hamburg, Hamburger Kunsthalle
© 1991 Maurice Guillaud

The final scene of **Marnie**
Prod.: 1963–1964 / Rel.: 1964
Frame enlargement
Paris, Cinémathèque française collection
© 1964 Geoffrey Stanley, Inc.
All rights reserved
Courtesy of Universal Studios Licensing, Inc.

Ray Milland in **Dial M for Murder**
Prod.: 1953 / Rel.: 1954
Frame enlargement
Paris, Cinémathèque française collection
© Warner Bros.

Jane Wyman and Richard Todd in **Stage Fright**
Prod.: 1949 / Rel.: 1950
Frame enlargement
Paris, Cinémathèque française collection
© Warner Bros.

North by Northwest
Prod.: 1958 / Rel.: 1959
Frame enlargement
Paris, Cinémathèque française collection
© Warner Bros.

Jacques Aumont – Paradoxical and Innocent

Leon M. Lion and John Stuart in **Number Seventeen**
Prod.: 1931 / Rel.: 1932
Frame enlargement
Paris, Cinémathèque française collection
© 1932 Canal + Image UK Ltd.

Detectives Hodgson and Benson in **Suspicion**
Prod. / Rel.: 1941
Frame enlargement
Paris, Cinémathèque française collection
© Warner Bros.

Henry Fonda and "the right man" in **The Wrong Man**
Prod. / Rel.: 1956
Frame enlargement
Paris, Cinémathèque française collection
© Warner Bros.

Psycho
Prod.: 1959–1960 / Rel.: 1960
Frame enlargement
Paris, Cinémathèque française collection
Courtesy of Universal Studios Licensing, Inc.

**Ivor Novello in The Lodger: A Story
of the London Fog**
Prod.: 1926 / Rel.: 1927
Frame enlargement
Paris, Cinémathèque française collection
Courtesy of Carlton International

James Stewart and Kim Novak in Vertigo
Prod.: 1957 / Rel.: 1958
Frame enlargement
Paris, Cinémathèque française collection
Courtesy of Universal Studios Licensing, Inc.

**Robert Donat and Madeleine Carroll
in The Thirty-nine Steps**
Prod. / Rel.: 1935
Frame enlargement
Paris, Cinémathèque française collection
Courtesy of Carlton International

Anne Grey in Number Seventeen
Prod.: 1931 / Rel.: 1932
Frame enlargement
Paris, Cinémathèque française collection
© 1932 Canal + Image UK Ltd.

Young and Innocent
Prod.: 1937 / Rel.: 1938
Frame enlargement
Paris, Cinémathèque française collection
Courtesy of Carlton International

The Thirty-nine Steps
Prod. / Rel.: 1935
Frame enlargement
Paris, Cinémathèque française collection
Courtesy of Carlton International

Robert Donat in The Thirty-nine Steps
Prod. / Rel.: 1935
Frame enlargement
Paris, Cinémathèque française collection
Courtesy of Carlton International

Michael Chekhov in Spellbound
Prod.: 1944 / Rel.: 1945
Frame enlargement
Paris, Cinémathèque française collection
© Buena Vista International Inc.

The Thirty-nine Steps
Prod. / Rel.: 1935
Frame enlargement
Paris, Cinémathèque française collection
Courtesy of Carlton International

Jean Louis Schefer – Hitchcock's Female Portraits

Ingrid Bergman's reflection (Under Capricorn)
Prod.: 1948 / Rel.: 1949
Frame enlargement
Paris, Cinémathèque française collection
© Transatlantic Pictures

Kim Novak in Vertigo
Prod.: 1957 / Rel.: 1958
Frame enlargement
Paris, Cinémathèque française collection
Courtesy of Universal Studios Licensing, Inc.

Grace Kelly in Rear Window
Prod.: 1953 / Rel.: 1954
Frame enlargement
Paris, Cinémathèque française collection
Courtesy of Universal Studios Licensing, Inc.
Presented by special arrangement
with Sheldon Abend

**Ingrid Bergman and Michael Wilding
in Under Capricorn**
Prod.: 1948 / Rel.: 1949
Frame enlargement
Paris, Cinémathèque française collection
© Transatlantic Pictures

Alain Bergala – Alfred, Adam and Eve

Henry Kendall and Joan Barry in Rich and Strange
Prod. / Rel.: 1932
Frame enlargement
Paris, Cinémathèque française collection
© 1932 Canal + Image UK Ltd.

Joan Barry in Rich and Strange
Prod. / Rel.: 1932
Frame enlargement
Paris, Cinémathèque française collection
© 1932 Canal + Image UK Ltd.

Joan Barry and Henry Kendall in Rich and Strange
Prod. / Rel.: 1932
Frame enlargement
Paris, Cinémathèque française collection
© 1932 Canal + Image UK Ltd.

Tommaso di ser Giovanni Cassai Masaccio
Italian, 1401–1428
Adam and Eve Expelled from Paradise
1424–1428
Fresco
214 x 90 cm
Florence, Church of Santa Maria del Carmine,
Brancacci Chapel
© Scala, Florence

Cary Grant and Ingrid Bergman in Notorious
Prod.: 1945 / Rel.: 1946
Frame enlargement
Paris, Cinémathèque française collection
© Buena Vista International Inc.

Cary Grant and Joan Fontaine in Suspicion
Prod. / Rel.: 1941
Production still
Courtesy of the Academy of Motion Picture Arts
and Sciences
© Warner Bros.

Gérard Genette – Hitchcock the Metaphysician

Martin Balsam in Psycho
Prod.: 1959-1960 / Rel.: 1960
Frame enlargement

**Pierre Gras – Hitchcock: Eating
and Destruction**

Vivien Merchant and Alex McCowen in Frenzy
Prod.: 1971 / Rel.: 1972
Frame enlargement
Paris, Cinémathèque française collection
© 1972 Universal Pictures Limited
All rights reserved
Courtesy of Universal Studios Licensing, Inc.

Frenzy
Prod.: 1971 / Rel.: 1972
Frame enlargement
Paris, Cinémathèque française collection
© 1972 Universal Pictures Limited
All rights reserved
Courtesy of Universal Studios Licensing, Inc.

Anny Ondra's murderous hand (Blackmail)
Prod. / Rel.: 1929
Frame enlargement
Paris, Cinémathèque française collection
© 1929 Canal + Image UK Ltd.

Edith Evanson and James Stewart in Rope
Prod. / Rel.: 1948
Frame enlargement
Paris, Cinémathèque française collection
© 1948 Transatlantic Pictures
All rights reserved
Courtesy of Universal Studios Licensing, Inc.

Frenzy
Prod.: 1971 / Rel.: 1972
Frame enlargement
Paris, Cinémathèque française collection
© 1972 Universal Pictures Limited
All rights reserved
Courtesy of Universal Studios Licensing, Inc.

**Sally Shafto – Hitchcock's Objects,
or the World Made Solid**

Sabotage
Prod. / Rel.: 1936
Frame enlargement
Paris, Cinémathèque française collection
Courtesy of Carlton International

The Ring
Prod. / Rel.: 1927
Frame enlargement
Paris, Cinémathèque française collection
© 1927 Canal + Image UK Ltd.

Christian Schad
German, 1894–1982
Nude Bust
1929
Oil on canvas
55.5 x 53.5 cm
Wuppertal, Von der Heydt-Museum
© Estate of Christian Schad / VG Bild-Kunst (Bonn) /
SODRAC (Montreal) 2000

Under Capricorn
Prod.: 1948 / Rel.: 1949
Frame enlargement
Paris, Cinémathèque française collection
© Transatlantic Pictures

**Julia Tanski – The Symbolist Woman
in Alfred Hitchcock's Films**

Eva Marie Saint in North by Northwest
Prod.: 1958 / Rel.: 1959
Frame enlargement
Paris, Cinémathèque française collection
© Warner Bros

The Lodger: A Story of the London Fog
Prod.: 1926 / Rel.: 1927
Frame enlargement
Paris, Cinémathèque française collection
Courtesy of Carlton International

The Lodger: A Story of the London Fog
Prod.: 1926 / Rel.: 1927
Frame enlargement
Paris, Cinémathèque française collection
Courtesy of Carlton International

Alida Valli in The Paradine Case
Prod.: 1946–1947 / Rel.: 1947
Frame enlargement
Paris, Cinémathèque française collection
© Buena Vista International Inc.

Tippi Hedren in The Birds
Prod.: 1962 / Rel.: 1963
Frame enlargement
Paris, Cinémathèque française collection
© 1963 Alfred J. Hitchcock Productions, Inc.
All rights reserved
Courtesy of Universal Studios Licensing, Inc.

Fernand Khnopff
Belgian, 1858–1921
Who Shall Deliver Me?
1891
Coloured pencils on paper, 22 x 13 cm
Private collection
© Bulloz, Paris

Ingrid Bergman on the set of Notorious
Prod.: 1945 / Rel.: 1946
Production still
Courtesy of the Academy of Motion Picture Arts
and Sciences
© Buena Vista International Inc.

Edward Burne-Jones
British, 1833–1898
The Hand Refrains
From the series "Pygmalion and the Image"
About 1868
Oil on canvas, 99 x 76.3 cm
Birmingham Museum and Art Gallery
© A.C.L. Brussels

**Nathalie Bondil-Poupard – Such Stuff
As Dreams Are Made On: Hitchcock
and Dalí, Surrealism and Oneiricism**

Jean-Jacques Grandville
French, 1803–1847
First Dream: Crimes and Atonements
Engraving published in Le Magasin pittoresque,
1847 (July)
© Paris, Bibliothèque Nationale

Spellbound
Prod.: 1944 / Rel.: 1945
Unused poster design
The University of Texas at Austin, Harry Ransom
Humanities Research Center, Art Collection
© Buena Vista International Inc.

Critic's Dream Sequence
Caricature published in News Chronicle,
1946 (18 May)
Archival document
Selznick Archives, Harry Ransom Humanities
Research Center, University of Texas at Austin

**Stéphane Aquin – Hitchcock
and Contemporary Art**

Saul Bass
American, 1920–1996
Opening credits of North by Northwest
Prod.: 1958 / Rel.: 1959
Frame enlargement
Paris, Cinémathèque française collection
© Warner Bros.

Saul Bass
American, 1920–1996
Opening credits of North by Northwest
Prod.: 1958 / Rel.: 1959
Frame enlargement
Paris, Cinémathèque française collection
© Warner Bros.

Gregory Crewdson
American, b. 1962
Untitled
From the series "Natural Wonder"
1992–1997
Colour print
102 x 127.5 cm
© Ediciones Universidad de Salamanca, 1999
Courtesy of Luhring Augustine Gallery and the artist

Sarah Morris
American, b. 1967
Midtown-SOLO (9W57)
1999
Gloss household paint on canvas
213.4 x 213.4 cm
New York, Friedrich Petzel Gallery SM 99/010

**Nathalie Bondil-Poupard –
Alfred Hitchcock: An Artist in Spite of Himself**

Alfred Hitchcock and a watercolour by Rodin
Archival photograph
Courtesy of the Academy of Motion Picture Arts
and Sciences
© Alfred J. Hitchcock Trust

Fidelio Ponce De Léon
Cuban, 1895–1949
Five Women
1941
Oil on canvas
84.2 x 112 cm
Private collection

Chaim Soutine
French, 1893–1943
The Tree
About 1939
Oil on canvas
63.5 x 71.1 cm
Private collection
© Cologne, Benedikt Taschen Verlag GmbH, 1993
© Estate of Chaim Soutine / ADAGP (Paris) /
SODRAC (Montreal) 2000

Alfred Hitchcock with Strange Hunt *by Paul Klee*
Archival photograph
Courtesy of the Academy of Motion Picture Arts
and Sciences
© Alfred J. Hitchcock Trust
© Estate of Paul Klee / VG Bild-Kunst (Bonn) /
SODRAC (Montreal) 2000

Paul Klee
Swiss, 1879–1940
Strange Hunt
1937
Watercolour on linen and burlap
82 x 54 cm
New York, Private collection
© Estate of Paul Klee / VG Bild-Kunst (Bonn) /
SODRAC (Montreal) 2000

Paul Klee
Swiss, 1879–1940
Odyssey
1924
Oil sketch watercolour and spatter on paper sized
with chalk and glue, mounted on cardboard
32.5 x 50.2 cm
Location unknown
© ARS, New York
© Estate of Paul Klee / VG Bild-Kunst (Bonn) /
SODRAC (Montreal) 2000

*Alfred Hitchcock sketching a camera setup during
the making of* Spellbound
Prod.: 1944 / Rel.: 1945
Production still
The University of Texas at Austin, Harry Ransom
Humanities Research Center, Art Collection
© Buena Vista International Inc.

Dominique Païni – Hitchcock in Quebec

*Alfred Hitchcock and crew members during
shooting of* I Confess
Prod.: 1952 / Rel.: 1953
Gelatin silver print
40 x 50 cm
Montreal, private collection
© Archives de la Ville de Québec

Robert Daudelin – *Marnie*: Early Testament?

Tippi Hedren in Marnie
Prod.: 1963–1964 / Rel.: 1964
Frame enlargement
Paris, Cinémathèque française collection
© 1963 Alfred J. Hitchcock Productions, Inc.
All rights reserved
Courtesy of Universal Studios Licensing, Inc.

Tippi Hedren in Marnie
Prod.: 1963–1964 / Rel.: 1964
Frame enlargement
Paris, Cinémathèque française collection
© 1963 Alfred J. Hitchcock Productions, Inc.
All rights reserved
Courtesy of Universal Studios Licensing, Inc.

**Simon Beaudry – Hitchcock in Quebec:
Code of Silence**

*Alfred Hitchcock with Anne Baxter, Renée Hudon
and Lucien-Hubert Borne during shooting of*
I Confess
Prod.: 1952 / Rel.: 1953
Gelatin silver print
40 x 50 cm
Montreal, Private collection
© Archives de la Ville de Québec

(recto)
*Alfred Hitchcock with Father Paul Lacouline,
technical advisor, on the set of* I Confess

(verso)
*Self-portrait (caricature), dedicated "To 'Père'"
by Alfred Hitchcock during shooting of* I Confess
Prod.: 1952 / Rel.: 1953
Gelatin silver print and ballpoint pen
10 x 12.5 cm
Montreal, private collection

Chronology

Alfred Hitchcock
British, 1899–1980
Self-Portrait
Caricature
Paris, BIFI (Bibliothèque du film)
© Alfred J. Hitchcock Trust

Police station, Leytonstone
1911
Archival photograph
The young Alfred Hitchcock was sent here by his
father after he misbehaved. The chief of police
locked him in a cell and said: "This is what we do to
naughty boys." The episode is doubtless the source
of the filmmaker's fear of unjustified incarceration –
a theme that would recur time and again in his films.
London, Vestry House Museum
© Vestry House Museum
(London Borough of Waltham Forest)

*William Hitchcock with son Alfred
in front of the family business*
About 1906
Archival photograph
London, British Film Institute Collections

Alfred Hitchcock and Alma Reville
Mid 1920s
Archival photograph
London, British Film Institute Collections

Alfred Hitchcock with actors
Left to right:
Standing: Jameson Thomas, Gibb McLaughlin,
Alfred Hitchcock, Ian Hunter and Carl Brisson;
Seated: Dorothy Boyd, Lilian Hall-Davies,
Estelle Brodig and Eve Gray
Archival photograph
London, British Film Institute Collections

Madeleine Carroll with Alma and Alfred Hitchcock
1935
Archival photograph
London, British Film Institute Collections

Alfred Hitchcock and Alma (centre) at work
Archival photograph
London, British Film Institute Collections

Ada, Jack and Alfred Hitchcock at Shoreham
1923 (October)
Archival photograph
London, Vestry House Museum
© Vestry House Museum
(London Borough of Waltham Forest)

Alfred Hitchcock and Alma
About 1926
Archival photograph
London, Vestry House Museum
© Vestry House Museum
(London Borough of Waltham Forest)

*Alfred, Alma and Pat Hitchcock aboard
the* Queen Mary *at Southampton en route
for America*
1939 (March)
Archival photograph
London, British Film Institute Collections

Philippe Halsman
Latvian-born American, 1906–1979
Alma Reville
1962
Promotional still
Paris, Magnum Photos
© P. Halsman / Magnum Photos

Alfred Hitchcock during the making of Rebecca
Prod.: 1939 / Rel.: 1940
Archival photograph
Paris, BIFI (Bibliothèque du film)
© Buena Vista International Inc.

*Alfred Hitchcock, Ingrid Bergman and Edith Head
during pre-production on* Notorious
Prod.: 1945–1946 / Rel.: 1946
Photograph
Courtesy of the Academy of Motion Picture Arts
and Sciences
© Buena Vista International Inc.

*Cary Grant and Alfred Hitchcock
during shooting of* Suspicion
Prod. / Rel.: 1941
Production still
Courtesy of the Academy of Motion Picture Arts
and Sciences
© Warner Bros.

Philippe Halsman
Latvian-born American, 1906–1979
Alfred Hitchcock and François Truffaut
1962
Promotional still
Paris, Magnum Photos
© P. Halsman / Magnum Photos

*Alfred Hitchcock showing Ingrid Bergman
around an English town during shooting
of* Under Capricorn
Prod.: 1948 / Rel.: 1949
Archival photograph
London, The Cinema Museum
Guy Edmonds
© Transatlantic Pictures

Elliott Erwitt
French-born American, b. 1928
Alfred Hitchcock and Vera Miles
during the making of **The Wrong Man**
Prod. / Rel.: 1956
Archival photograph
© Warner Bros.
© E Erwitt / Magnum Photos

Marlene Dietrich and Alfred Hitchcock
during shooting of **Stage Fright**
Prod.: 1949 / Rel.: 1950
Production still
Paris, BIFI (Bibliothèque du film)
© Warner Bros.

Alfred Hitchcock in Paris
Archival photograph
Paris, BIFI (Bibliothèque du film)
Jean Lattes
© GAMMA

Alfred Hitchcock preparing for his cameo
appearance in **Marnie**
Prod.: 1963–1964 / Rel.: 1964
Production still
Courtesy of the Academy of Motion Picture Arts
and Sciences
© 1964 George Stanley, Inc.
All rights reserved
Courtesy of Universal Studios Licensing, Inc.

Portrait of Alfred Hitchcock
Publicity still for his television show *Alfred Hitchcock*
Presents or *The Alfred Hitchcock Hour*
Early 1960s
18 x 23 cm
Promotional still
London, The Cinema Museum
Photo by Richard Hamilton
© Alfred J. Hitchcock Trust

Alfred Hitchcock receiving an honorary degree
from Columbia University, New York
1972
Archival photograph
London, British Film Institute Collections

Finito di stampare nell'ottobre 2000
presso le Arti Grafiche Salea di Milano
per conto delle Edizioni Gabriele Mazzotta